ESSENTIAL BACKGROUND FOR
ENGLISH LEARNERS

你不可不知道的
英语学习背景知识

对语言的不解与误解，往往源自背景文化知识的欠缺
【英汉对照】

美国历史
重大事件及著名人物

Major Events and Famous People in the
History of the United States

郝澎◎编著

U0748435

图书在版编目（CIP）数据

美国历史重大事件及著名人物／郝澎编著.—海口：南海出版公司，2007.2（2019.7重印）
（你不可不知道的英语学习背景知识）
ISBN 978-7-5442-3591-4

Ⅰ.美... Ⅱ.郝... Ⅲ.美国－历史－大事记－汉、英②名人－生平事迹－美国－汉、英
Ⅳ.K712.05②K837.12

中国版本图书馆 CIP 数据核字(2006)第 138855 号

MEIGUO LISHI ZHONGDA SHIJIAN JI ZHUMING RENWU

美国历史重大事件及著名人物

编　　著	郝　澎
责任编辑	张建军
装帧设计	动力图文
出版发行	南海出版公司　　　　　　　　电话(0898)66568511
社　　址	海南省海口市海秀中路 51 号星华大厦五楼　　邮编 570206
电子信箱	nhpublishing@163.com
经　　销	新华书店
印　　刷	秦皇岛市佳泽文化传播有限公司
开　　本	787 × 1092 毫米　1/16
印　　张	20.25
字　　数	330 千字
版　　次	2007 年 2 月第 1 版　　2019 年 7 月第 7 次印刷
书　　号	ISBN 978-7-5442-3591-4
定　　价	46.00 元

Contents
目录

Chapter Four

The Revolutionary War 美国革命战争 (独立战争)

Preface
前言

前言
PREFACE

    在某些人看来,语言仅仅是工具,学习英语,就是掌握其语音、语法和词汇。这些东西掌握了,英语也就学好了。这是对于学习外语的一种颇为流行的错误看法。学者们早已指出,语言不仅是交流的工具,而且是文化的载体。语言从整体上反映一个民族的文化,而该民族的文化又无时无刻地对语言的发展变化起着制约作用。语言与文化二者的关系是你中有我,我中有你,相互渗透、互为因果、互相制约、互相推动。其实,即使是英语的一个单词、一个短语,更不必说一条成语,都可能负载着有关讲英语民族的大量的文化信息。读书时只把单词按字面意义串起来,不考察其文化背景,往往会发生误解。许多人学习英语多年,一接触稍有难度的文章,即使并无词汇或语法方面的障碍,理解往往流于肤浅,不能体味其言外之意或微言大义。其原因无非是背景知识的欠缺。甚至那些貌似武断的语法规则,也可能与文化相关,因为它们往往反映了讲英语民族的独特思维方式。与文化联系更密切的是语用。使用英语时最重要、难度最大的不是正确,而是得体。在特定的时间、特定的地点、对特定的人讲特定的话,这就是得体。得体的背后,有一套文化规则在起作用。人们在进行跨文化交流时产生的隔阂、障碍、误解乃至交流的失败,其根源多在文化差异。所以在学习英语时,有必要系统学习英美民族的历史沿革、政治制度、宗教信仰、价值体系、思维方式、神话寓言、文学艺术、风俗习惯等文化知识。

　　为了使英语学习者在较短时间内全面了解英美文化，我们编写了这套"你不可不知道的英语学习背景知识"丛书。目前该丛书已经出版了五本。《英美民间故事与民俗》介绍脍炙人口的英美民间故事、传说、迷信、动物和植物的象征、社交礼节、身体语言、婚俗及节假日等常识。《古希腊罗马神话与西方民间传说》重点介绍古希腊罗马神话。古希腊罗马神话是西方人文精神的摇篮，现代西方文明的根基之一，西方文学、艺术和音乐的题材宝库，也是英语成语的重要来源之一。现代西方文明的另一根基是基督教。基督教早已渗透到西方文化的各个方面，是西方文学、艺术和音乐的另一重大题材库。不了解基督教，了解英美文化就无从谈起。而《圣经》又是基督教的经典，基督教文化的支柱，英语成语的最大来源。《基督教与圣经》提供了这方面的基本知识。任何一个民族的文化现状，都是其历史发展的结果。英美人目前的政治制度、思想观念、价值体系乃至民族特性，无不可从其历史中找出答案。《英国历史重大事件及著名人物》和《美国历史重大事件及著名人物》是两国历史的概述。

　　编写英文部分时，我们的原则是力求语言简明平实，通俗易懂，词汇量限制在3000常用词范围内，使高中生中英语较佳者、普通大学生和广大英语爱好者不必借助字典就可以读懂大部分内容；英语教师在教授英美文化时，只需将书中文字略加改动，便可直接用于教学。为便于学习，尤其是为了使读者了解专有名词所对应的中文，我们还提供了译文。此外，为使丛书更加活泼有趣，我们插入了不少"题外话"，介绍更多相关的语言和文化知识，开阔读者的视野，启发进一步的思考。

　　由于丛书涉及领域较广，编者水平有限，疏漏在所难免，望专家和广大读者不吝赐教。

编　者

2007 年 1 月

目录
CONTENTS

Chapter One

The Discovery and Exploration of America　美洲的发现与考察

Chapter Two

Colonial America　十三个殖民地

Chapter Three

Background and Causes of the Revolutionary War 美国革命战争的背景及原因

Contents

目 录

Chapter Five

Forming a New Government 新政府的建立

Chapter Six

Expansion and Progress 扩张与进步

Contents
目录

Contents

目　录

Chapter Nine

Industrialization and Reform　工业化与改革

Chapter Ten

Overseas Expansion　海外扩张

Chapter Eleven

World War I　第一次世界大战

Contents
目 录

Chapter Twelve

The Twenties　二十年代

Chapter Thirteen

Depression and the New Deal　大萧条与新政

Chapter Fourteen

World War II　第二次世界大战

Chapter Fifteen

The Cold War　冷战

Chapter Sixteen

Postwar American Society　战后美国社会

Contents
目　录

Chapter Seventeen

The United States in the 1960s　20 世纪 60 年代的美国

Chapter Eighteen

The United States in the 1970s　20 世纪 70 年代的美国

Chapter Nineteen

Since 1980　20 世纪 80 年代以来

CHAPTER ONE
The Discovery and Exploration of America
美洲的发现与考察

1. The First Americans

最早的美洲人

The history of the United States is usually called "American history", because it goes back to a period long before the United States was officially formed.

The first people known to have lived in the Western Hemisphere were American Indians. Most scientists believe these people wandered into North America from Asia at least 15,000 years ago. At the time, ice covered much of the northern half of the earth and sea level was very low. As a result, a piece of underwater land was exposed to form a kind of bridge linking Siberia and Alaska. Some Asian hunters, following the animals that they hunted, must have wandered across what is now the Bering Strait to America. By the time the first Europeans reached North America there were already Indians living nearly all parts of North and South America where human being could live.

About 20 million Indians lived in North

美利坚合众国的历史在英文里通常称作 "American history (阿美利加史)",因为这段历史的开端要追溯到美国正式建国之前很久。

生活在西半球已知的最早的人类是美洲印第安人。大多数科学家认为这些人是在至少 15000 年前从亚洲漫游到北美的。当时冰雪覆盖着北半球的大部分地区,海平面很低。结果,一片海床露出海面,形成连接西伯利亚和阿拉斯加的陆桥。一些亚洲的猎人在追逐猎物时,一定不知不觉跨过了白令海峡,到了美洲。首批欧洲人到达美洲时,印第安人已居住在南北美洲所有宜于居住的地方。

哥伦布到达新大陆时,北美洲大约有两千万人。他们分属于数百个部落,语言不同,生活方式各

America when Columbus reached the New World. They belonged to hundreds of tribes, spoke different languages and had different ways of life. Most of them lived in small villages. Men hunted, fished, and made war, and women took care of the crops, mostly maize (corn), beans, potatoes, and pumpkins, or gathered food in the woods. They had no cattle, sheep, goats, or pigs, because there were many wild animals for food. They had no horses or oxen used to plow fields and carry heavy loads. They never developed vehicles with wheels, because they had no horses or oxen to pull them. Some tribes wandered about hunting and gathering food and never established permanent homes. These North American Indians all lived in family groups, but were loyal to large tribes of relatives. Some tribes formed alliances for the purposes of keeping peace among neighbours and making war on enemies.

Some Indian tribes of North America were friendly to the early European settlers and helped them survive in the wilderness of the New World. But as more and more Europeans arrived and took more and more land to make new homes, they became a threat to the Indian way of life, and Indians and whites became enemies. The Indians suffered a lot because they had been isolated from the Old World for thousands of years. People of the Old World had learned to use iron and raise domestic animals. Europeans had acquired gunpowder, paper, and the compass from the Chinese. The Indians of North America, on the other hand, had none of these. In their fighting against European conquerors with horses and guns, they were doomed to defeat.

异。他们大多数人聚居在小村落里。男人打猎、捕鱼、作战，妇女照料庄稼或在树林里采集食物。农作物主要有玉米、豆类、马铃薯和南瓜。印第安人没有牛、羊、猪一类的家畜，因为有足够的野兽供他们猎取为食。他们也没有用来耕种和挽重的牛马。他们从未能够制造出装有轮子的车辆，因为他们没有牛马来牵引车辆。有些部落只是四处游荡，打猎、采集食物，从不定居下来。这些北美印第安人以家族为单位聚居，但也效忠更大的亲族部落。一些部落结成部落联盟以维护邻近部落之间的和睦，并与共同的敌人作战。

有些北美的印第安部落对早期欧洲殖民者很友好，帮助他们在新大陆的蛮荒之地存活下来。但随着越来越多的欧洲人抵达美洲，占据越来越多的土地建立新家园，他们对印第安人的生活方式构成了威胁。印第安人和白人变成了对头。苦难降临在印第安人头上，因为他们与旧大陆脱离接触已长达数千年。旧大陆的人早已学会使用铁器和饲养家畜。欧洲人还从中国人那里学会制造火药、纸张和指南针。但北美印第安人却一样也没有。在与配备了马匹和枪支的欧洲征服者的对抗中，他们注定要失败。

题外话

大多数科学家认为北美印第安人是在最近的一次冰河期通过白令海峡的陆桥迁移到北美的。即使陆桥被海水淹没，人们也可以在冬季通过海峡的冰面到北美。印第安人的肤色、头发和面部特征都与亚洲人类似。

在哥伦布心目中，地球要比实际上小得多。他到美洲后，自以为到了印度，故称当地土著为印第安人。印第安人曾有高度的文明。中美洲的阿兹特克人和马雅人、秘鲁的印加人都曾有巨大的都市、宏伟的建筑，发达的农业、畜牧业和手工业。他们似乎懂得轮子的用途，只是没有将轮子用于生活和生产而已。马雅人还有丰富的天文学知识，有自己的历法和文字。相对而言，北美北部的印第安人的文化则显得落后。

2. The Discovery of America

It is probable that the first Europeans who landed on North America were the Vikings. The Vikings lived in Scandinavia, a region of Europe that includes what are now Denmark, Norway, and Sweden. These people were bold and loved adventures. Some of them sailed across the North Atlantic to settle on the islands of Iceland and Greenland. From there, a few daring people are believed to have sailed to what is now Newfoundland, Canada about 1,000 years ago. They explored the place and established a settlement, but the settlement lasted only a few years and their voyages were soon forgotten.

In 1453 the Ottoman Turks captured Constantinople (now Istanbul, Turkey), an important center for trade between Europe and Asia. The Turks closed the overland trade routes to Asia as well as the sea route through the Persian Gulf. European merchants had to find a new sea route to the Far East, a place of spices, silk, china and other

美洲的发现

最早在北美登陆的欧洲人可能是维金人。维金人生活在欧洲的斯堪的纳维亚，即包括现在丹麦、挪威和瑞典所在的那片地区。这些人生性勇猛而爱好冒险。他们当中的某些人渡过大西洋，在冰岛和格陵兰定居下来。据信几个胆子更大的人在一千年前航行到了现在的加拿大的纽芬兰。他们考察了该地，并建立了一个居民点，但居民点仅仅维持了几年，他们的航行不久就被忘却了。

1453 年奥斯曼帝国的土耳其人攻占了欧亚之间的贸易中心君士坦丁堡（现在的土耳其的伊斯坦布尔）。土耳其人既阻断了与亚洲贸易的陆上通道，也切断了穿过波斯湾的海上通道。欧洲商人不得不寻找新海路到达远东，从那里运回香料、丝绸、瓷器和其他贵重货物。1492 年，克里斯托弗·哥伦布从西

valuable goods. In 1492, Christopher Columbus set sail from Spain, trying to reach Asia by sailing west across the Atlantic Ocean.

Columbus was a sailor from Genoa, Italy. The Spanish king and queen provided him with money so that he could make his voyage. Like most educated people of his day, he knew that the world is round, but he thought it was small, and Europe, Africa and Asia made up the whole earth. He knew little about the Atlantic Ocean, and nothing about the American continent or the Pacific Ocean. When Columbus reached land in October 1492, he believed he had arrived in the Far East, a part of Asia known as the Indies. So he gave the natives a name "Indians". Actually, he landed on San Salvador, one of the islands just east of the North American mainland. Within the next 50 years, explorers, soldiers, and settlers from several European countries had flocked to America.

Columbus may never have realized that he reached a New World. Another Italian explorer, Amerigo Vespucci, however, claimed to have explored what is now the American mainland in 1497 and believed he had reached a "New World". Since he was the first person to refer to the lands he had visited as a "New World", a German geographer suggested in 1507 that the land be named America. Soon, this name was used throughout Europe. But most people now still honored Columbus as the discoverer of America.

班牙起航，试图跨过大西洋到达亚洲。

哥伦布是个意大利热那亚的水手，西班牙国王和王后资助了他的航行。与当时受过教育的人一样，他知道地球是圆的，但他认为地球不大，欧洲、非洲和亚洲构成了整个地球。他对大西洋知之甚少，对美洲大陆和太平洋更是一无所知。哥伦布于 1492 年 10 月登上陆地，自以为到达了远东，一个被称为印度的地方。于是他称当地土著为"印第安人"。其实，他登陆的地方是圣萨尔瓦多，北美大陆以东的一个岛屿。此后的 50 年间，探险家、军人和定居者从几个欧洲国家的出发，蜂拥来到美洲。

哥伦布可能至死也没意识到自己抵达的是新大陆。然而，另一个意大利探险家阿美利哥·韦斯普奇宣称他于 1497 年考察了美洲大陆，并相信自己到达了新大陆。由于他是将自己到过的这片陆地称为"新大陆"的头一个人，一位德国地理学家于 1507 年建议将这块土地定名为"阿美利加"。这个名字不久便在欧洲通用起来。但是大多数人仍然崇敬哥伦布，将他视为发现美洲的第一人。

题外话

阿美利哥·韦斯普奇本人声称于 1497 年发现美洲大陆，故新大陆以他的名字命名为阿美利加。但很多学者对他的说法表示怀疑，因为很难找到足够证据支持他的说法。

在 15 世纪，就支持远洋航行的财力而言，欧洲人远远不如中国人和阿拉伯人。早在 1405~1433 年间，郑和就率领庞大的中国船队七次下西洋，航程远达东非。当时中国的航海技术也堪称一流。但为什么偏偏是欧洲人，而不是中国人或阿拉伯人发现了美洲？原因在于欧洲人自古就是航海的民族。"大海邀请人类从事征服，从事掠夺，……鼓励人们追求利润，从事商业。"（黑格尔语）与当时的中国船相比，哥伦布的船要小得多，也寒碜得多。但欧洲人具有其他民族罕有的探索欲和冒险精神，正是这种特点使他们发现、占据并开发了所有新的陆地。

3. Early European Exploration in North America

欧洲人在北美的早期探险考察

News travelled slowly in the 16th century. People received news of the discovery of Columbus only through letters and by word of mouth. So the Spanish and Portuguese were the first to explore the newly discovered land. They explored the southern part of the New World in search of gold and other riches. The Spaniards quickly conquered the Inca of Peru, the Maya of Central America, and the Aztec of Mexico. The Portuguese took control of what is now Brazil. By 1600, Spain and Portugal controlled most of the hemisphere from Mexico southward.

Also during the 16th century, Spaniards explored much territory that became part of the United States. In 1513, Juan Ponce de Leon sailed from Puerto Rico and landed on the coast of what is now Florida. He explored much of Florida, trying to find a spring called the Fountain of Youth. This spring was said to have the magic power to make old people young again if they bathed in or drank its waters. Of course Ponce de Leon could never find such a fountain, but he claimed this part of

在 16 世纪，信息传播十分缓慢，人们只是通过信件和口口相传获悉哥伦布发现新大陆的消息的。所以西班牙和葡萄牙人最先考察了新发现陆地。他们考察了新大陆的南部，搜寻黄金和其他财富。西班牙人很快就征服了秘鲁的印加人、中美洲的玛雅人和墨西哥的阿兹特克人。葡萄牙人则控制了现在的巴西地区。到 1600 年，西班牙和葡萄牙已控制了西半球墨西哥以南的大部分地区。

在 16 世纪，西班牙人还考察了日后成为美国领土的很多地区。1513 年，胡安·庞塞·德莱昂从波多黎各起航，在现在的佛罗里达海岸登陆。他考察了佛罗里达的大部分地区，试图找到被称为"青春泉"的泉水。据说在青春泉中沐浴或饮了泉水会返老还童。当然庞塞·德莱昂不可能找到这样一眼泉水，但他宣布北美洲大陆的这一部分归西

the North American mainland for Spain. He then sailed around the southern tip of Florida and into the Gulf of Mexico. He next explored the southwest coast of Florida before returning to Puerto Rico. That same year, another Spanish explorer Vasco Núñez de Balboa travelled across the narrow piece of land between North and South America and became the first of the European explorers of America to see the Pacific Ocean.

In 1539, Hernando de Soto, a Spanish explorer, sailed from Cuba and landed on the west coast of Florida with about 600 followers. They marched north along the coast of the Gulf of Mexico, trying to find gold. For four years, de Soto and his soldiers travelled through and explored a very large area in what is now the southeastern United States, including Georgia, Alabama, Mississippi, and Arkansas. The explorers found no gold, but they became the first Europeans to see the Mississippi River.

In 1540, Francisco Vasquez de Coronado, another Spanish explorer, set out from the west coast of Mexico with about 300 Spanish soldiers and a large number of Indian troops and marched north, trying to find the "Seven Cities of Cibola". Indians and earlier Spanish explorers had reported these cities to be rich in gold. Coronado traveled through what are now Arizona, New Mexico, Texas, Oklahoma, and Kansas. He did not discover any important cities, but his exploration, as well as that of de Soto, gave Europeans a good idea of the vastness of North America.

In the first half of the 16th century England and France sent out some explorers and fur traders to the New World, but their discoveries

班牙所有。此后他绕过佛罗里达的南端，驶入墨西哥湾。他接着考察了佛罗里达的西南岸之后才返回波多黎各。同年，另一个西班牙探险家巴斯科·努涅斯·德·巴尔沃亚跨过连接南北美洲的地峡，成为在美洲探险的欧洲人中头一个看到太平洋的人。

1539年，一个名叫埃尔南多·德·索托的西班牙探险家率领600人，从古巴出发，在佛罗里达西岸登陆。他们沿墨西哥湾海岸北上，试图找到黄金。德·索托和他的随从们穿越并考察了美国西南部的大片区域，包括现在的佐治亚、亚拉巴马、密西西比、阿肯色等州。探险者们没有找到黄金，但他们成为看到密西西比河的头一批欧洲人。

1540年，另一个西班牙探险家弗朗西斯科·巴斯奎兹·科罗纳多从墨西哥西海岸出发，率领300名西班牙士兵和众多印第安武士向北进发，试图发现"锡沃拉的七座黄金城"。印第安人和早期西班牙探险

埃尔南多·德·索托

were far less important than those of Portugal and Spain. John Cabot, an Italian navigator and explorer in the service of England, began to make plans for a more direct crossing to the East when news reached England that Christopher Columbus had reached "Asia" by sailing west. His plan gained the support of King Henry VII of England. In May 1497, with a crew of 18 men, Cabot sailed northwest from Bristol, and about a month later, he landed perhaps on present-day Cape Breton Island, which is now part of Nova Scotia. He then sailed along the Labrador, Newfoundland, and New England coasts. Believing that he had reached northeastern Asia, he formally claimed the region for Henry VII. In the following year, Cabot made his second voyage and may have sailed along the coast of North America to Chesapeake Bay. Cabot's voyages gave England a claim to the mainland of North America and led to the founding of the English colonies in America. The French navigator Jacques Cartier made several voyages to North America in 1534, 1535 and 1541. During his second voyage in 1534, Cartier sailed up Saint Lawrence River to the present sites of Montreal and Quebec. But neither France nor England established permanent settlements in North America until the 17th century.

题 外 话

据一则传说，庞塞·德莱昂将他发现的海岸命名为"佛罗里达"，是因为那里遍地开满鲜花。"佛罗里达"在西班牙语里意思是"多花的"。据另一传说，庞塞·德莱昂抵达那里时正值复活节，复活节在西班牙语里是"Pascua florida"，于是采用此名。

家曾描述过这些布满黄金的城市。科罗纳多穿越了现在的亚利桑那、得克萨斯、俄克拉何马和堪萨斯州。他未能发现任何重要的城市，但这次探险考察，跟德·索托的一样，使欧洲人充分认识到北美洲的辽阔。

16世纪前半期，英国和法国派出一些人到新大陆探险考察并做毛皮生意。但这些人的发现远远不及葡萄牙人和西班牙人的发现重要。当哥伦布向西航行到达"亚洲"的消息传到英国后，为英国效劳的意大利航海家和探险家约翰·卡博特开始计划找到一条通往东方的海上捷径。他的计划得到英格兰国王亨利七世的支持。1497 年 5 月，卡博特率领 18 名船员，从布里斯托尔出发向西北航行。大约一个月后，他可能在现在的新斯科舍的布雷顿角岛登陆。此后，他沿着拉布拉多、纽芬兰和新英格兰海岸航行。他相信自己已经抵达东北亚，就正式宣告这一地区归属亨利七世。第二年，卡博特再次远航，这一次有可能沿着北美海岸抵达了切萨皮克湾。卡博特的航行使英国得以主张北美大陆的所有权，使之后来能够在美洲建立殖民地。法国航海家雅克·卡蒂埃也于 1534、1535 和 1541年数次远航北美。在 1534 年的第二次航行中，卡蒂埃上溯圣劳伦斯河，直达现在蒙特利尔和魁北克的所在地。但是法国和英国直至 17世纪才在北美建立永久定居点。

CHAPTER TWO
Colonial America
十三个殖民地

1. Early European Settlement in North America

欧洲人在北美的早期定居点

The Spanish were the first Europeans to establish colonies in the Americas. They colonized Mexico, the West Indies, and South America early in the 16th century. They also founded St. Augustine in Florida, the oldest permanent settlement established by Europeans in what is now the United States, in 1565.

French, Dutch, and English colonists began arriving in the New World in the early 17th century. The French explorer Samuel de Champlain established a settlement at Acadia in Nova Scotia from 1604 to 1606, and in 1608 he traveled up the St. Lawrence River, and established a French settlement at Québec. Henry Hudson, an English explorer and sea captain, sailed to North America for the Dutch in 1609. He explored the river that now bears his name. The Dutch established a string of agricultural settlements between New Amsterdam (New York City) and Fort Orange (Albany, New York) after 1614. New Amsterdam grew as trade

西班牙人是在美洲建立殖民地的最早的欧洲人。他们在 16 世纪初就在墨西哥、西印度群岛和南美洲建立了殖民地。他们还于 1565 年在佛罗里达建立了圣奥古斯丁，这是欧洲人在现在的美国建立的最古老的永久定居点。

法国、荷兰和英国的殖民者于 17 世纪初开始抵达新大陆。法国探险家萨谬尔·德·尚伯兰于 1604~1606 年间在新斯科舍的阿卡迪亚建立了定居点，并于 1608 年上溯圣劳伦斯河，在魁北克建立了法国定居点。1609 年，英国探险家和船长亨利·哈得孙为荷兰人前往北美。他考察了现在以他的名字命名的河，即哈得孙河。1614 年后，荷兰人在新阿姆斯特丹 (纽约市) 和奥伦治要塞 (纽约州的奥尔巴尼) 之间建立了一连串的农业殖民点。随着与

with native Americans increased. By the time England took control of the Dutch colony in 1664, it had a European population of 6,000.

Among the European invaders of North America, only the English established permanent agricultural colonies. Most of the Spanish, French, and Dutch wanted to find gold in the Americas, to trade with native Americans, and to convert them to Christianity. Few Europeans settled permanently in their agricultural colonies in the Caribbean, Mexico, and South America. Most people worked there were African slaves and native peoples. In contrast, England sent more people to America than other European nations and most of these people wanted to settle down permanently as farmers.

The English came to settle in America for two main reasons. The first reason was religious. After King Henry VIII broke with the Catholic Church in the 1530s, the new Church of England became a Protestant church, but it kept much of Catholic beliefs and practices. Some church members, called Puritans, tried to "purify" the church by making more Protestant reforms. But when they were persecuted under the rule of James I and Charles I early in the 17th century, and lost their hope of reforming the church, Puritans became willing to settle in America, where they could worship as they pleased.

The second reason was economic. The population of England grew rapidly during the 16th and 17th centuries but the food supply did not. Many of England's largest landholders found they could make more money to raise sheep for wool than to grow crops, and made the peasants to leave their

印第安人贸易的增长，新阿姆斯特丹繁荣了起来。英国在 1664 年夺取这个荷兰殖民地时，该地已有 6000 欧洲居民。

在北美的欧洲入侵者中，只有英国人建立了永久性的农业殖民地。大多数西班牙人、法国人和荷兰人只想在美洲攫取黄金，与土著做交易，并使他们改信基督教。很少有欧洲人在加勒比地区、墨西哥和南美的农业殖民地永久定居下来。在那里干活的都是非洲奴隶和土著人。相形之下，英国派往美洲的人要多于其他欧洲国家，而且其中大多数人永久定居，从事农业。

英国人到美洲定居有两个主要原因。其一是宗教原因。英格兰国王亨利八世于 16 世纪 30 年代与天主教分裂，从此英格兰教会成为新教教会，但是它仍保留了大部分天主教的信仰和礼仪。有些教徒，称为清教徒，企图进行更多的新教改革，使教会更为"清洁"。但是，在 17 世纪初，清教徒在詹姆斯一世和查理一世统治时期受到迫害，觉得改革无望，此时就愿意到美洲定居，以享受信仰的自由。

第二个原因是经济原因。16 和 17 世纪里，英国人口增长迅速，但粮食产量却没有增加。许多英国的大地主发现，养羊获取的羊毛比种庄稼更有利可图，就迫使农民离开土地。结果，大批失业农民不得不前往新大陆谋生。

lands. As a result, large numbers of jobless peasants had to go to the New World to make a living.

The earliest colonists faced great hardship and danger in the wilderness of North America. Many of them died of hunger and disease, or in conflict with Indians. However, the colonists soon set up farms and plantations. They then built towns, roads, churches, and schools, and began many small industries. The colonists also developed political practices and social beliefs that have had a major influence on the history of the United States.

In the early 17th century, the British king began granting charters to companies and individuals for them to establish colonies in America. By the middle of the century, most of the settlements had developed into 13 British colonies. Each colony had a governor and its own lawmaking body, but the governor was appointed by the king or the British government and so had greater power. The 13 colonies stretched from what is now Maine in the north to Georgia in the south. They included the New England Colonies of Massachusetts, Connecticut, Rhode Island, and New Hampshire in the far north; the Middle Colonies of New York, New Jersey, Pennsylvania, and Delaware; Virginia and Maryland along Chesapeake Bay; and the Southern Colonies of North Carolina, South Carolina, and Georgia in the far south.

早期殖民者在北美的蛮荒之地面临巨大的困难和危险。许多人死于饥荒和疾病，或死于与印第安人的冲突。但是，殖民者仍建立起农场和庄园。此后，他们又兴建了城市、道路、教堂和学校，并开始从事小规模的制造业。同时，殖民者们还发展了自己的政治制度和社会观念，对日后的美国历史产生了重大影响。

17世纪初，英国国王开始向公司和个人颁发特许状，允许他们在美洲建立殖民地。到了17世纪中叶，大多数定居点逐渐发展起来，形成了13个殖民地。每个殖民地都有一个总督和自己的立法机构，但总督是由国王或英国政府任命的，具有较大的权利。这13个殖民地北起现在的缅因州，向南延伸到佐治亚州。其中包括最北面由马萨诸塞、康涅狄格、罗得岛和新罕布什尔组成的新英格兰殖民地；由纽约、新泽西、宾夕法尼亚和特拉华组成的中部殖民地；由最南方的北卡罗来纳、南卡罗来纳和佐治亚组成的南方殖民地。

英国探险家亨利·哈得孙

2. The New England Colonies

Virginia was the earliest permanent British colony in North America. New England was the second. In 1620, a group of Puritans sailed to the New World on the ship *Mayflower*. These Puritans came to be known as Pilgrims. They had separated from the Church of England and came to America for religious freedom. Before landing their leaders signed the *Mayflower Compact*. In this document, they agreed to make and obey just and equal laws for the common good. They landed at Plymouth in what is now Massachusetts and founded a colony there. The Pilgrims suffered greatly during the first winter. Shelters were poor, disease widespread, and food scarce. About half the members died. Fortunately, the Indians proved friendly. In the following year, the colonists worked hard in the fields and had a good harvest. So in early autumn of 1621, they set aside a day for celebrating peace and plenty, and invited the Indians to join them. That was the first Thanksgiving ever celebrated.

In 1629, Puritans founded the Massachusetts Bay Colony at what are now Salem and Boston. Plymouth became part of Massachusetts Colony in 1691. Between 1629 and 1640, about 20,000 more English colonists crossed the Atlantic Ocean to settle in New England. These Puritan settlers valued hard work and

新英格兰殖民地

弗吉尼亚是英国人在北美建立的最早的永久殖民地，新英格兰是第二个。1620年，一群清教徒乘"五月花号"船前往新大陆。这批清教徒史称"朝圣者"。他们脱离了英格兰教会，为了宗教自由而来到美洲。登陆前，这批人当中的首领签署了"五月花号公约"，约定为了共同的福祉制定并遵守公正而平等的法律。他们在现在的马萨诸塞州的普利茅斯登陆，就地建立起一个殖民地。头一个冬天里，朝圣者们的日子过得异常艰苦。他们房屋简陋，疾病蔓延，食物匮乏。近一半人未能存活下来。幸而印第安人对他们很友好。第二年的夏天，殖民者们在田间努力耕作，获得好收成。1621年秋天，他们留出一天的

朝圣者们于1620年登陆普利茅斯

commercial success, and they also believed in the importance of education. These puritanical values strongly influenced the culture of the American colonies and later of the United States. The Puritans also contributed to democracy in America. They held town meetings, where the adult males worked together to make laws.

Puritanism was the official religion of the Massachusetts Bay Colony. Everyone who lived there was forced to support the Puritan church. The clergy held great political power and kept watch over people's daily life to make sure that they lived according to puritan values.

As the population of Massachusetts grew, some settlers left to found other colonies in New England. Connecticut became a colony in 1636; Rhode Island, in 1647; New Hampshire, in 1680.

Because of its cold climate and rocky soils, New England was the poorest region. Unlike the

时间来庆祝和平与丰收，并邀请印第安人来作客。这是历史上头一个感恩节。

1629年，清教徒在现在的塞勒姆和波士顿成立了马萨诸塞海湾殖民地。普利茅斯于1691年成为马萨诸塞殖民地的一部分。在1629~1640年之间，又有大约两万名英国殖民者跨越大西洋到新英格兰定居。这些清教徒崇尚勤劳和经商致富，也很重视教育。这种清教徒的价值观对美洲殖民地以及日后的美国文化产生了重大影响。清教徒也对美洲的民主做出了贡献。他们举行市政会议，成年男子共同商议制定法律。

清教教派是马萨诸塞海湾殖民地的官方教派。当地的每个居民都必须支持它。牧师们在政治上权利

新英格兰英国移民的住宅

other regions of North America, its farms could not grow valuable export crops to ship to markets in Europe.

题外话

美国小说家霍桑在他的短篇小说《恩地科与红十字》里，揭露了马萨诸塞神权政治的危害。在塞勒姆，宗教的不宽容随处可见：一个天主教嫌犯戴着颈手枷；一个醉汉戴着足枷；一个福音传教士由于擅自讲解《圣经》而被挂牌示众；一个敢于出言顶撞教会长老的女人舌头被夹上劈开的木棍。还有一个少妇，与霍桑的长篇小说《红字》里的海丝特·白兰的一样，胸前必须佩带"A"字，以向公众昭示自己犯了通奸罪。

很大，他们监督人们的日常生活，以确保人们依照清教主义的价值观行事。

随着马萨诸塞人口的增长，一些居民离开这里到新英格兰的其他地区建立殖民地。康涅狄格于1636年，罗得岛于1647年，新罕布什尔于1680年先后建立殖民地。

由于气候寒冷，土壤贫瘠多石，新英格兰是最贫穷的地区。与北美的其他地区不同，新英格兰的农庄无法种植价值高的农产品出口欧洲。

第一个感恩节

3. The Middle Colonies

New York   While the British were founding their colonies in New England, the Dutch founded their town New Amsterdam on what is now Manhattan Island. In 1626, Peter Minuit, the Dutch governor bought Manhattan from the Indians for goods worth 60 Dutch guilders, or about $24. During the next few years, Dutch colonists started other settlements in neighbouring areas and then founded New Netherland, a colony that included what are now New York and northern New Jersey. In 1655, the Dutch extended their colony by taking from the Swedes what are now southern New Jersey and Delaware. However, the Dutch control of New Netherland ended when a conflict between the Dutch and English in Europe spread to the American colonies. King Charles II of England decided to take over New Netherland. He gave the territory to his brother James, the Duke of York. In 1664, an English fleet sailed to New Amsterdam and called for the surrender of New Netherland. Since his people refused to support him, the Dutch governor had to give up the colony without firing a shot. The English changed the name of the colony and its main town to New York, after the Duke of York, who later became King James II of England.

New Jersey   New Netherland had included the region between the Hudson and Delaware rivers. It had a few Dutch and Swedish settlers. After he took over New Netherland, the Duke of York divided the region between two of his

中部殖民地

纽约   正当英国人在新英格兰建立殖民地的时候，荷兰人在现在的曼哈顿岛建立了他们的城市新阿姆斯特丹。1626 年，荷兰总督彼得·米纽伊特以价值 60 个荷兰盾（约合 24 美圆）的货物从印第安人手中换得曼哈顿。在其后的几年里，荷兰殖民者在邻近的区域建立其他定居点，然后成立了新荷兰殖民地，包括现在的纽约州和新泽西州的北部。1665 年，荷兰人扩张了殖民地，从瑞典人手中夺得现在的新泽西州的南部和特拉华州。但后来荷兰与英国在欧洲的冲突波及到美洲殖民地，荷兰人对新荷兰的控制也随之告终。英国国王查理二世决定夺取新荷兰。他将这片领土赐予弟弟约克公爵詹姆斯。1664 年，一支英国舰队驶向新阿姆斯特丹，要求新荷兰投降。由于当地人不愿支持荷兰总督，他未开一枪便将这块殖民地拱手相让。英国人将这块殖民地与其首府的名字改为纽约，以向约克公爵表示敬意。约克公爵后来登基成为英国国王詹姆斯二世。

新泽西   新荷兰曾包括哈得孙河与特拉华河之间的一片区域。这里只有人数不多的荷兰和瑞典定居者。夺取新荷兰后，约克公爵将这片土地一分为二，分别赐予他的两

friends, Lord John Berkeley and Sir George Carteret. He named the area New Jersey in honor of Carteret, who had at one time been the governor of the island of Jersey off the coast of France. Berkeley and Carteret offered to sell the land to colonists at low prices. They also allowed settlers to have political and religious freedom. These policies attracted many settlers to New Jersey.

Delaware The other part of New Netherland was named Delaware after Lord De La Warr, who is said to have discovered Delaware Bay. The earliest colonists of this region were Swedes, who named it New Sweden. The Dutch took over the colony in 1655. When New Netherland fell to the English in 1664, the colony also became English property.

Pennsylvania In what is now Pennsylvania, Swedes established the first permanent settlement in 1643. In 1681, King Charles II of England gave the region to William Penn, in payment of a debt the king owed Penn's father. Penn called his land Sylvania, meaning a woodland. King Charles insisted that the land should be called Pennsylvania in memory of Penn's father. Penn was a Quaker (a member of the Society of Friends), and he hoped to make the colony in America a new home for English Quakers who had been persecuted in England for many years. He urged a

个朋友约翰·伯克利勋爵和乔治·卡特莱特爵士。卡特莱特一度是法国海岸附近的泽西岛的总督,于是约克公爵将赐给他的土地命名为新泽西。伯克利和卡特莱特将土地廉价出售给殖民者。他们也允许定居者们享有政治与宗教自由。这些政策吸引了许多人到新泽西定居。

特拉华 新荷兰的另一部分土地以德·拉·瓦尔勋爵的名字命名为特拉华,因为据说是德·拉·瓦尔发现了特拉华海湾。这一地区最早的殖民者是瑞典人,他们称之为新瑞典。荷兰人于 1655 年夺取这一殖民地。1664 年新荷兰落入英国人之手后,这一殖民地也就成了英国的领土。

宾夕法尼亚 在现在的宾夕法尼亚,瑞典人于 1643 年建立了第一个永久定居地。1681 年,英国国王查理二世将这一地区赐予威廉·佩恩,算是抵消了他欠给佩恩父亲的债务。佩恩将这一地区称为"夕尔法尼亚","林地"之意。查理二

威廉·佩恩

large number of Quakers and other settlers who wanted to have religious freedom to emigrate to Pennsylvania. Penn planned a city on the land and named it Philadelphia, which in Greek means "brotherly love". One of the first things Penn did in his colony was to buy land from the Indians and to sign a peace treaty with them. Both the Indians and the settlers kept the peace. While the Quakers governed the colony from 1682 to 1756, Pennsylvania had no army and only a small police force. Penn also built schools, and made the colony known for its religious freedom and democratic government. Under the government of Penn, Pennsylvania thrived and Philadelphia grew rapidly into the largest city in colonial America.

Virginia　Virginia was the earliest British colony. In 1607, the London Company sent about 100 British colonists to Virginia and founded Jamestown, the first permanent British settlement in North America. The town was named after James I, king of Britain at the time. Life was very hard at first, and the settlement would have failed entirely if it had not been for the leadership of Captain John Smith. Smith was a strong and practical man. He forced the settlers to stop searching for gold and silver and to start working for their survival, and made it a rule that "he who will not work shall not eat," so that everyone had to do his share. In about 1612, some Jamestown colonists began growing tobacco, which the London Company sold in Europe. They also succeeded in raising corn and pigs. Tobacco, corn, and pigs provided a solid basis for Jamestown's economy. In 1619, House of Burgesses, the first lawmaking body in the New

世主张称之为"宾夕法尼亚",以纪念佩恩的父亲。佩恩是个贵格会(公谊会)教徒。贵格会在英国多年受迫害,佩恩希望使这片美洲殖民地成为英国贵格会教徒的新家园。他劝说大批贵格会教徒和其他希望获得宗教自由的人移居宾夕法尼亚。佩恩在这片土地上规划了一座城市,将它命名为费拉德尔菲亚(费城),希腊语里意为"兄弟之爱"。佩恩为殖民地所做的头一件事是向印第安人购买土地,并与他们签订和约。印第安人和殖民者都恪守了和约。在1682~1756年贵格会执政期间,宾夕法尼亚没有军队,只有人数很少的警察。佩恩还建立了学校,并使他的殖民地获得了宗教自由和政治民主的美名。在佩恩执政时期,宾夕法尼亚繁荣起来,费城迅速成为美洲殖民地的最大城市。

弗吉尼亚　弗吉尼亚是最早的一个英国殖民地。1607年,伦敦公司派出大约100名殖民者到弗吉尼亚,建立了英国在北美的头一个定居地詹姆斯敦。这座城市以当时的英国国王詹姆斯一世的名字命名。起初生活异常艰苦,多亏有约翰·史密斯船长的领导,居民点才没有彻底垮掉。史密斯是个坚强而又讲求实际的人。他迫使殖民者停止寻找金银,开始为生存劳作。他定了一条制度,即"不劳动者不得食",使人人都必须各尽其职。1612年,詹姆斯敦的一些殖民者开始种植烟

World was established in Jamestown. This became a model for many of the lawmaking bodies in the United States. The same year that the burgesses met in Jamestown, Africans were sold in the colony as slaves. About 20 blacks arrived on a Dutch ship. Since there were not enough labourers in the colony, these Africans were bought by some of the richer landowners and were put to work in the fields. The slaves played an important role in the development of the colony in Virginia.

Maryland Maryland was founded by the Calverts, an English noble family of Catholics. In 1632, George Calvert, 1st Baron Baltimore, persuaded King Charles I of England to grant him the land north of the Potomac River. Calvert wanted to establish a colony where Catholics, who were persecuted in England, could enjoy religious freedom. He also wanted to make money by selling his land to rich English gentlemen. The same year his son Cecilius Calvert, 2nd Baron Baltimore became the owner of the Maryland area. Colonists, led by Leonard Calvert, Cecilius younger brother, established the first Maryland settlement in 1634 under a royal charter. The Maryland settlers also raised tobacco. As tobacco production increased, their colony grew and prospered. But the plan

草,由伦敦公司销往欧洲。他们种植玉米和养猪也获得成功。种植烟草玉米和养猪构成詹姆斯敦坚实的经济基础。1619年,詹姆斯敦成立了移民议会。这是新大陆的头一个立法机构,成为美国许多立法机构的样板。移民议会在詹姆斯敦开会的同一年,非洲人在殖民地被出卖为奴隶。大约20名黑人乘一艘荷兰船到达。由于殖民地缺少人手,这些非洲人被有钱的地主买走,派到农田里干活。奴隶们为弗吉尼亚殖民地的发展做出重要贡献。

马里兰 马里兰是由一个英国天主教贵族卡尔弗特家族建立的。1632年,乔治·卡尔弗特(巴尔的摩男爵第一)说服英国国王查理一世将波托马克河北岸的土地赐给了他。卡尔弗特想建立一个殖民地,使在英国受迫害的天主教徒可以享有宗教自由。他同时也想通过向有钱的英国绅士出售土地赚钱。当年,他的儿子塞西留斯·卡尔弗特(巴尔的摩男爵第二)获得马里兰地区的所有权。殖民者们在塞西留斯的弟弟莱奥纳德·

塞西留斯·卡尔弗特

for establishing a colony only for Catholics did not work. More Protestants than Catholics immigrated to Maryland. To prevent religious disputes and protect Catholics against discrimination, at the request of the Calverts, the Maryland assembly passed a law to give religious freedom to all Christians in 1649. It was an important step towards full religious liberty in America.

From the beginning of the 18th century, the Middle Colonies received tens of thousands of German, Scottish, Irish and French immigrants. Quite different from those in New England who were the same in culture and religion, many of these colonists were different from one another in language, culture and religion.

题 外 话

荷兰殖民者在美国文化中留下了一些明显的遗迹。比如，圣诞老人到各家各户赠送礼品的美国习俗，就源自荷兰殖民者。

4. The Southern Colonies

The Carolinas　In 1629, King Charles I of England gave his attorney general, Sir Robert Heath, a piece of land that included what are now the states of South Carolina and North Carolina. The land was named Carolina after King Charles I (*Carolus* in Latin). Heath, however, never developed the colony, so King Charles II gave the same land to eight of his favorite nobles in 1663, and made them ruling landlords of the colony. These

卡尔弗特的领导下，得到国王的特许，于 1634 年在马里兰建立了头一个定居点。马里兰的殖民者也种植烟草。随着烟草产量的增加，殖民地扩大并繁荣起来。但只为天主教徒建立殖民地的计划并没有实现。移居马里兰的新教徒比天主教徒还要多。为避免宗教纠纷，保护天主教徒使他们免受歧视，应卡尔弗特家族的要求，马里兰的议会于 1649 年通过一条法律，对所有的基督徒实行宗教信仰自由。这是美国朝着充分信仰自由迈出的重要的一步。

从 18 世纪初开始，中部殖民地接收了数十万来自于德国、苏格兰、爱尔兰和法国的移民。与文化单一、宗教单一的新英格兰地区不同，许多殖民者在语言、文化和宗教方面各具特色。

南 方 殖 民 地

南北卡罗莱纳　1629 年，英国国王查理一世赐予他的总检察长罗伯特·希思爵士一片土地，包括现在的南北卡罗莱纳两州，以查理（拉丁语里为"卡罗勒斯"）的名字命名为卡罗莱纳。但希思没有开发这片殖民地，于是查理二世又在 1663 年将同一块土地分给了 8 个他宠爱的贵族，使他们成为统治殖民

landlords finally divided the land into two colonies, North Carolina and South Carolina. In the north, the colonists raised tobacco and produced forest products. In the south, the settlers grew rice and indigo, a plant from which a deep blue dye is made. Since wealthy landlords were reluctant to give ordinary farmers a voice in the government, representative government developed slowly in the Carolinas.

Georgia Georgia was the last of the thirteen colonies to be settled. The first permanent settlement was not set up there until 1732, when King George II of England gave James Oglethorpe and others the right to start a separate colony between the settled part of Carolina and the Spanish colony in Florida, and this new colony was to be named Georgia after King George II. Oglethorpe planned to send to the colony people who were poor and in debt, and who wanted to make a new start. He also saw it as a place where Protestants from Europe could live and worship God as they pleased. People from many countries came to the colony. In 1739 a war broke out between Great Britain and Spain, and there were small battles on the southern frontier. Oglethorpe tried to capture Florida, but failed. In 1742 a Spanish force invaded Georgia but was defeated by Oglethorpe's troops. This ended Spanish attempts to capture Georgia.

北卡罗莱纳的印第安人

地的地主。这些地主们将土地分割成两个殖民地，北卡罗莱纳和南卡罗莱纳。在北卡罗莱纳，殖民者们种植烟草，生产木材。在南卡罗莱纳，殖民者们种植稻谷和木兰，一种用来生产靛蓝的植物。由于这些阔绰的地主们不愿让普通农民在政府中拥有发言权，代议制政府在南北卡罗莱纳发展缓慢。

佐治亚 佐治亚是 13 个殖民地中最后建立的一个。头一个永久定居点直到 1732 年才建立起来。当年英国国王乔治二世向詹姆斯·奥格尔索普和另外一些人授权，允许他们在卡罗莱纳和西班牙的佛罗里达殖民地之间另建殖民地。新建殖民地将以乔治二世的名字命名为佐治亚。奥格尔索普计划将穷人、欠债人和希望重过新生活的人送往殖民地。他也将这片殖民地视为欧洲新教徒的福地，他们可以在这里以自己愿意的方式生活、信仰上帝。人们从许多不同的国家来到佐治亚。1739 年，英国与西班牙之间爆发战争，佐治亚南部边界也发生小规模的战斗。奥格尔索普试图占领佛罗里达，但未能成功。1742 年，西班牙军队入侵佐治亚，但被奥格尔索普的部队击败。此后，西班牙再未尝试攻取佐治亚。

5. Life in Colonial America

殖民地时代美利坚人的生活

The people   As more and more people came to America from Britain and other countries of Western Europe to seek economic success and religious freedom, the population of the colonies grew steadily. Poor Europeans came to America often as indentured servants. An indentured servant agreed to serve his master for a certain number of years without pay. In return, the master paid the price charged to carry the servants to the New World, and provided the servant with food, clothing, and shelter. When this time had been served, the master was to give his servant a plot of land and the servant became a free man, and then could work for himself and take part in the government of the colony.

Many people came to America for religious reasons. In addition to Puritans, those who came to America for religious freedom included Roman Catholics, Quakers, Huguenots, Mennonites and even Jews.

Meanwhile more and more Africans were brought in and sold as slaves mostly in southern colonies. By the end of the colonial period, blacks made up about 20 per cent of the population. Different from the white indentured servants, Africans were made to work as slaves for life. This was the beginning of slavery in North America. Slavery was more common in the South than in the North, since the Southern tobacco and rice plantations

人民　随着越来越多的人从英国和其他欧洲国家来到美洲，殖民地的人口稳步增长。欧洲的穷人往往以契约仆的身份来到美洲。契约仆立约为主人无偿服役若干年，作为补偿，主人为他支付前往新大陆的旅资，提供在新大陆的所需的粮食、衣物和住房。服役期满后，主人向仆人提供一块土地，仆人从此成为自由人，可以为自己工作，并可以参加殖民地的管理。

很多人出于宗教原因来到美洲。除了清教徒，为宗教信仰自由来到美洲的还有天主教徒、贵格会教徒、胡格诺派、门诺派、乃至犹太教徒。

同时，越来越多的非洲人被运到美洲，主要在南方殖民地被出卖为奴隶。到了殖民时代末期，黑人已达到总人口的**20%**。与白人契约仆不同，非洲人终身为奴，被迫做工。这就是北美奴隶制的开端。奴隶制在南方比在北方更为盛行，因为南方种植烟草和水稻的庄园规模很大，需要众多劳力从事繁重的工作。庄园主们发现购买奴隶干活更便宜。奴隶们是从非洲西海岸运到美洲的。由于奴隶船上的生活条件恶劣，许多非洲人死在前往美洲的

were large and needed large numbers of laborers to do hard work. The plantation owners found it cheaper to buy slaves to do the work. The slaves were brought to America from the west coast of Africa. Because of harsh conditions on the slave ships, many of the Africans died on the way to America. Those who survived lost their freedom and much of their culture.

Economy When the colonists produced enough food to stay alive, they began to export products that they could not use up themselves. New England exported fish, whale oil, furs, lumber, ships and leather goods. The middle colonies sent wheat and other grain, flax and pig iron. The southern colonies exported tobacco, rice, indigo and lumber. The colonists traded chiefly with Britain and depended heavily on England for such goods as gunpowder, china, glass, wine, tea, linen, wool and silk.

Different from Europe, Colonial America provided many economic and social opportunities for poor lower-class people. Any colonists, except slaves, as long as they were willing to work hard, could become wealthy. They could easily obtain land, which was plentiful at the time. They could start new businesses, or follow the professions of lawyer, doctor, teacher, and clergyman.

Religion In the early days, many colonies set up an established religion—an official church supported by taxes. Anglicanism (the Episcopal Church) was the official religion of Virginia, Maryland, Georgia, the Carolinas, and New York. Puritanism (which came to be called Congregationalism) was established in Massachusetts, Connecticut, and New Hampshire. The power of estab-

途中。那些存活下来的则失去了自由，也失去了自己的大部分文化。

经济 当殖民者们能够生产足够的粮食供自己消费后，便开始出口那些他们自己消费不完的产品。新英格兰出口鱼、鲸油、毛皮、木材、船只和皮货。中部殖民地出口小麦、亚麻和生铁。南部殖民地出口烟草、稻米、靛蓝和木材。殖民者们主要与英国进行贸易，依赖英格兰来获得火药、瓷器、玻璃、酒、茶叶、亚麻布、呢绒和丝织品。

与欧洲不同，北美殖民地为贫穷的社会下层人民提供了许多改善经济和社会地位的机会。奴隶以外的任何殖民者，只要肯努力工作，都有致富的可能。他们很容易获得土地，因为当时尚有充足的土地可供开发。他们可以开办新的实业，或者从事律师、医生、教师和牧师的职业。

宗教 许多殖民地在成立初期就建立了由纳税支持的官方教会。安立甘宗（主教派教会）是弗吉尼亚、马里兰、佐治亚、南北卡罗莱纳和纽约的官方教会。清教教派（日后被称为公理宗）在马萨诸塞、康涅狄格和新罕布什尔是官方教派。官方教派的势力在塞勒姆巫术审判案中可见一斑。审判于1692年在马萨诸塞海湾殖民地的塞勒姆镇举行。有19名男女经审判被证明有罪，并以行巫术的罪名处以绞刑。另一个人因拒绝申明是否犯有行巫术罪而被巨石压死。另有大约

lished religion was made clear by Salem witchcraft trials. The trials were held in 1692 in Salem, a town in the Massachusetts Bay Colony. Nineteen people, both men and women, were proved guilty after a trial and hanged as witches. Another man was pressed to death with large stones for refusing to state whether he was innocent or guilty to the witchcraft charge. About 150 other people were imprisoned on the witchcraft charges.

Religious toleration, however, increased steadily during the colonial period, because people practiced many different forms of worship. In the 18th century, the strict rules of earlier times had been largely relaxed. But there were still many religious inequalities. Catholics did not have right to vote and to hold public religious services. Although some colonial governments allowed Jews to worship in public, they were barred from voting and holding public office in nearly all the colonies.

As time passed, religious enthusiasm became weak. Then a movement aiming at strengthening people's religious belief, known as the Great Awakening started in the American colonies during the 1730s and 1740s. The movement began in the Middle Colonies and spread to New England and to some areas of the South. The most famous leader of the movement was Jonathan Edwards. The Great Awakening had a strong influence

150人以行巫术的罪名被判入狱。

然而，在殖民时代，宗教宽容不断增长，因为人们持有各种不同形式的宗教信仰。到了18世纪，殖民地早期严格的规定大多不再坚持。但仍有许多宗教上的不平等。天主教徒没有选举权，也不可公开举行宗教仪式。某些殖民地虽然允许犹太人公开举行宗教仪式，但犹太人在几乎所有的殖民地都没有选举权或担任公职的权利。

随着时间的流逝，宗教热情逐渐衰退。接着，在18世纪30～40年代，北美殖民地兴起了一场旨在加强人们宗教信仰的运动，即大觉醒运动。这场运动兴起于中部殖民

审判女巫

on American religious life. It democratized Calvinist theology by promising that man could, by a voluntary act of faith, achieve salvation by his own efforts. On the one hand, the call for a return to complete faith was the opposite to Enlightenment thought, which called for a greater questioning of faith and a less important role for God in the daily affairs of man. But at the same time, Edwards drew on the thought of men like John Locke and Isaac Newton in an attempt to make religion rational. Perhaps most important, it helped make the religious doctrines of many sects — particularly those of the Baptists and the Methodists — more accessible to the poor and oppressed Americans.

Education　Even when they were struggling to make a living, the colonists did not forget to educate their children. In most colonies of New England primary and secondary schools were established for boys. Massachusetts even made a law to require every town to pay for a primary school. The first Puritan settlers believed that everyone should be able to read the Bible at an early age. Many churches in New England also established colleges to train ministers. For example, Puritans founded both Harvard College (now Harvard University) in Massachusetts in 1636 and Yale College (now Yale University) in Connecticut in 1701, though during the colonial period, only about 200 boys at most, and no women at all, attended each college. In the south, farms and plantations were so widely separated that it was impossible to set up schools. Some planters joined with their nearest neighbours and hired tutors for their children; others' children were sent to England for schooling. It was forbidden, however, to teach slave children to read or

地，波及新英格兰和南方部分地区。运动最著名的领导人是乔纳森·爱德华兹。大觉醒运动对美利坚人的宗教生活产生重大影响。它应许人们可以通过自觉的信仰、自身的努力获得拯救，从而使加尔文主义的神学民主化。但另一方面，它又号召完全彻底的信仰，这与启蒙运动的思想相抵触。启蒙运动号召对信仰持较强的怀疑态度，降低上帝在人们日常生活中的重要作用。但同时爱德华兹也从约翰·洛克和伊萨克·牛顿两人的思想里汲取养分，力图使宗教理性化。或许最重要的是，这场运动使许多教派的教义，特别是洗礼宗和循道宗的教义，传达到贫苦和受压迫的美利坚人当中。

教育　甚至在为生存而挣扎的同时，殖民者们没有忘记教育他们的儿童。在新英格兰的大多数殖民地都建立了供男孩子受教育的小学和中学。马萨诸塞甚至制定一条法律，要求每个城镇都要出资开办一所小学。最初的清教徒殖民者认为，每个人都应当从小就学会阅读《圣经》。新英格兰的许多教堂还成立了培训牧师的学院。例如，清教徒于1636年在马萨诸塞创立了哈佛学院(现在的哈佛大学)，于1701年在康涅狄格创立了耶鲁学院（现在的耶鲁大学），尽管在殖民时代，每所学院至多只有两百名男青年学习，妇女则一个也没有。在南方，农场和庄园过于分散，无法开办学

write. In the Middle Colonies, Pennsylvania attached greater importance to education. The first school in the colony was begun in 1683, and after that, every Quaker community provided elementary education for its children. There were also many private schools for boys of rich families and night schools for adults. Girls of rich families had private teachers. Among the nine colonial colleges established in the 17th and 18th centuries, only the college in Pennsylvania (which later became the University of Pennsylvania) was free from the control of churches.

Government   The structure of government in all the colonies was similar. Each had a governor, a council that served both as adviser to the governor and as the upper house of the legislature, and a representative assembly, or lower house. In self-governing colonies, qualified voters elected the governor and the members of both houses of the legislature. In other colonies, king or the owner of the colony appointed the governor, and the governor selected the council. Voters elected only members of the assembly. Like the House of Commons—the lower house of the English Parliament — the colonial assemblies had the sole right to decide what taxes should be placed on people and how public funds should be spent. This meant that the colonial lawmakers could control the officials by holding back their salaries, and protect the interests of the people they represented.

The democracy of the colonies, however, was not complete. Only white male property owners were given the right to vote. In some colonies, voters also had to meet certain religious qualifications. Blacks, both slave and free, were denied the right

校。有些庄园主与最近的邻居合雇家庭教师给孩子们上课；另外一些孩子则送往英国上学。但教奴隶的孩子们读书写字则被禁止。在中部殖民地，宾夕法尼亚最重视教育。这个殖民地的头一所学校开办于1683 年，从那以后，每个贵格会社区都要为儿童们提供初等教育。还有许多为有钱人家开办的私立学校和为成年人开办的夜校。有钱人家的女孩子由私人教师教授。在 17 和 18 两个世纪里在殖民地创立的九所学院里，只有宾夕法尼亚的学院 (日后成为宾夕法尼亚大学) 不受教会的控制。

政府   所有的殖民地的政府都有类似的结构。每个殖民地都有一个总督，一个参议会，参议会起到总督顾问和立法机构上院的作用，还有一个代表大会，相当于下院。在自治的殖民地里，有资格的选民选举出总督和立法机构的两院代表。在其余的殖民地，英国国王或殖民地的拥有者任命总督，总督挑选参议会成员。选举人只选出代表大会的议员。就像当时英国议会的下议院，殖民地的代表大会只有权决定该征收何种赋税，以及公共资金该如何使用。这意味着殖民地的立法者们可以通过拒绝发放薪金的办法来控制官员的行为，保护他们所代表的人民的利益。

然而，殖民地的民主并不完全。只有拥有财产的白人男性享有选举权。在某些殖民地，选举人还

1770年左右的哈佛学院

to vote. So were women. In spite of these restrictions, government, on the whole, was more democratic in the colonies than in England or other European countries.

For many years, the colonists were allowed to have almost complete control of their own affairs. They became used to governing themselves according to their own beliefs and ideals, and developed a sense of unity and independence. As a result, when the British government began to place the British colonies more firmly under its control during the mid-18th century, the colonies were determined to protect the liberties they had enjoyed against any attempt by the British government to take them away. Relations between the American Colonies and Great Britain began to break down, and a series of bitter quarrels led to the Revolutionary War in 1775.

须满足某些宗教信仰的条件。黑人，无论是奴隶还是自由人，一律没有选举权。妇女亦是如此。虽然有诸如此类的限制，总的来看，殖民地的政府要比英国的和其他欧洲国家的更为民主。

多年来，殖民地人民自己的事务几乎全由他们自己管理。殖民者们习惯按照自己的信念和理想管理自己，养成了一种团结和独立意识。结果，当英国政府在18世纪开始对殖民地实行较严厉的控制时，殖民地就决意要捍卫自己曾享有的自由，反对英国政府剥夺他们自由的任何企图。美利坚殖民地与英国的关系开始恶化，一连串的激烈争议导致1775年的革命战争(独立战争)。

题 外 话

在政治制度上，殖民地人民继承了几个世纪以来英国人民所争取到的政治权利。这些权利受到《大宪章》和《权利法案》和以司法裁决为基础的习惯法的保障。英国人民的权利包括：陪审团审判的权利；不受无理监禁的权利；向政府请愿以纠正其滥用权威的权利；就政治发表意见的权利。

塞勒姆巫师审判案是新英格兰清教主义历史上的一个污点。在 17 世纪的欧美，对巫术的迷信仍十分流行。依照当时的英国法律，行巫术者可处以死刑。1692 年，马萨诸塞州塞勒姆村的几个年轻女子被发现举止反常。她们钻到桌子下面，发出怪叫，说自己在忍受折磨。人们疑心她们中了巫术，便逮捕了一批嫌犯，并对之进行审讯。这一事件持续了大约一年，由于一些重要牧师出面制止而结束。那些被误判死刑者的家属得到了补偿。某些历史学家认为，此事件的主要原因是逐巫运动的领导者，一个名叫塞缪尔·帕里斯的牧师得到了塞勒姆村贫苦农民的支持。那些农民看到商人阶层的地位日益上升，将他们视为对自己生活方式的威胁。

美国人对天主教徒的歧视直到 20 世纪仍有所表现。直至 20 世纪中叶，所谓的 WASPs，即白种盎格鲁—撒克逊新教徒（White Anglo-Saxon Protestants）仍是统治阶层，尽管他们在美国总人口的比重已下降到不足 20%。肯尼迪在 1960 年竞选总统时，其天主教家庭背景被视为他的弱点之一。

CHAPTER THREE
Background and Causes of the Revolutionary War
美国革命战争的背景及原因

1. The French and Indian War

法国印第安人战争

Great Britain and France had struggled for control of eastern North America throughout the colonial period. As their settlements moved inland, both nations insisted that they owned the vast territory between the Appalachian Mountains and the Mississippi River. Their struggle led to the outbreak of the French and Indian War in 1754. In Europe the war was known as the Seven Years' War, for that was how long the war lasted.

The war was really fought mainly between the French and the British. Both sides fought with the support of Indian allies, who wanted to keep their lands. The war broke out over the control of the Ohio River Valley. The river valley was important to the trade and territorial expansion of both the French and the British.

In May 1754, 22-year-old lieutenant colonel George Washington led a small band of colonial troops to the disputed territory to force the French

在整个殖民时期，英法两国一直在争夺北美东部的控制权。随着殖民地向内陆扩展，两个国家都坚持声称自己拥有阿巴拉契亚山脉和密西西比河之间的广大领土。两国的争端导致 1754 年法国印第安人战争的爆发。这场战争在欧洲称为七年战争，因为它持续了 7 年。

这场战争的交战双方实际上主要是法国人和英国人。双方都有印第安人的支持，因为印第安人要保卫自己的土地。战争的起因是争夺俄亥俄河河谷地区的控制权。该河谷对于英法两国的贸易和领土扩张至关重要。

1754 年 5 月，当时只有 22 岁的乔治·华盛顿中校率领一小队殖民地军队前往有争议的地区，企图迫使法国人撤退。法国人在尼塞斯

to withdraw. The French defeated Washington at Fort Necessity, in the first battle of the French and Indian War. During the next two years, things went badly for the British. They suffered one defeat after another. In 1756, William Pitt became the political leader of Britain. He sent vigorous young officers and more regular troops to North America. Then the tide turned against the French. Their forts fell one by one. Britain's powerful navy cut off French supplies of men and ammunition, leaving the French colonial forces little hope. In 1759, the British led by General James Wolfe began attacking French forces near the city of Quebec. After nearly three months of fighting, Wolfe's army defeated the French and captured the city. About a year later Montreal surrendered to the British.

The peace treaty was signed in Paris in 1763. Under this treaty, Great Britain received from France Canada and all French territory east of the Mississippi River except New Orleans. From Spain, the ally of France, Britain received Florida. As a result, the British controlled all of North America from the Atlantic Ocean to the Mississippi River.

The French and Indian War was a turning point in American history. It helped bring about the American Revolution. Britain had spent so much money fighting the war that the people in Great Britain were taxed heavily and the nation was in debt. After the war, Britain had to find ways to strengthen its control over its enlarged American territory. Under the circumstances, it seemed only fair that the colonists should help to pay the expense of getting and protecting the new territory. George III, who had become king of Great Britain

提堡打败了华盛顿。这是法国印第安人战争中的头一场战斗。在接下来的两年里，局势越来越不利于英国人。他们连吃败仗。1756 年，威廉·皮特出任英国首相，将更有朝气的年轻军官和更正规的部队派往北美。此后局势发生转变，开始不利于法国。他们的要塞连连失守。英国的强大海军切断了法国兵员和弹药的补给线，使法国殖民地军队处于绝望境地。1759 年，由詹姆斯·沃尔夫将军率领的英军开始进攻魁北克城附近的法国军队。经过近 3 个月的战斗，沃尔夫的军队打败了法国人，夺取了魁北克。大约一年后，蒙特利尔投降了英国。

1763 年，和约在巴黎签署。根据和约，英国从法国手中获得加拿大以及除新奥尔良以外的密西西比河以东的全部领土。英国还从法国盟国西班牙手中得到佛罗里达。结果，英国控制了从大西洋到密西西比河之间所有的北美地区。

法国印第安人战争是美国历史上的一个转折点。它是引发美国革命的重要因素。英国为打赢这场战争投入大量资金，英国人须缴纳繁重赋税，国家也背上债务。战后，英国必须设法强化对扩大了的美洲领土的控制。在此情况下，殖民者为夺取和保卫新领土分担一些开支似乎顺理成章。1760 年即位的英国国王乔治三世吩咐议会通过立法控制殖民地的贸易，使之有利于母

in 1760, told the British Parliament to pass laws to control the trade of the colonists for the good of the mother country and make colonies pay their share of the increasing expenses of the British government.

国，同时迫使殖民地分担英国政府日益增加的开支。

沃尔夫将军阵亡

2. The Stamp Act

《印花税法》

In 1764, Parliament passed the *Sugar Act*. This act put a tax of three pence on each gallon of molasses imported into the colonies from ports outside the British Empire. Rum producers in Northern colonies were angry because their rum industries depended on imported molasses, and

1764 年，英国议会通过《糖税法》，向殖民地从英帝国以外港口进口的每加仑糖浆征收 3 便士的关税。北方殖民地的朗姆酒制造商感到愤慨，因为他们的朗姆酒制造业依赖进口的糖浆，如果他们上税，

they would make little profit on rum if they had to pay the tax. However, it was the *Stamp Act* of 1765 that made nearly every colonist angry. Under the act, stamps of different values must be bought and put on newspapers, legal documents, and other printed matter. The money collected from the stamp sales was to pay for the army of about ten thousand men that the government planned to send to protect the colonies. There were other laws passed that the colonists thought unfair. For example, officials were allowed to search the house of anyone who was thought to be hiding goods on which he had not paid the required tax. The colonists had to take English soldiers into their homes, and provide them with free food and place to stay.

The colonists bitterly opposed the *Stamp Act*. They said that the tax not only took money from the pockets, but also threatened to take away their freedom. They wanted to keep their right to tax themselves through their elected representatives. For more than a hundred years, they had voted their own taxes to pay for the management of their colonies. But they were not represented in Parliament. Therefore, they argued, Britain had no right to tax them. Their principle was "no taxation without representation".

To fight against the *Stamp Act*, patriots formed secret clubs called *Sons of Liberty*. These groups decided to destroy every stamp printed in the name of the *Stamp Act*. American merchants also threatened not to buy anything from Great Britain. The colonial boycott and resistance alarmed Britain's leaders. In 1766, Parliament abolished the *Stamp Act*.

就没有多少利润可赚。然而，使殖民地几乎人人感到愤慨的，是1765年的《印花税法》。依照这一法规，报纸、法律文件和其他印刷品上必须贴有不同面值的印花才能发行或生效。政府计划派遣大约一万人的军队保卫殖民地，销售印花的税款将用于维持这支部队的开支。议会通过的另外一些法规，殖民者们也认为不够公平。例如，如有任何人被怀疑私藏未按要求上税的货物，官员有权搜查他们的住所。殖民者必须在家中接纳英军士兵，并向他们提供食物和住宿。

殖民者们强烈反对《印花税法》。他们声称印花税不但掏走了他们的钱，而且对他们的自由构成威胁。他们希望有权选出自己的代表，通过他们的认可来课税。一百多年来，他们都是通过投票来决定课税支付殖民地的管理费用的。但是，他们在英国议会里没有代表。因此，他们认为，英国无权向他们课税。他们的原则是"没有代表不得课税"。

为对抗《印花税法》，爱国者们组织了秘密团体，称为"自由之子"。这些团体决定销毁以《印花税法》的名义印制的每一枚印花。美利坚商人也威胁不再采购任何英国货。殖民地的抵制和反抗使英国当局感到震惊。1766年，议会废除了《印花税法》。

3. The Townshend Acts

Peace did not last long, however. Parliament still believed it had the right to tax and control the colonies. In 1767, the government, determined to raise money in the colonies, passed a new set of tax laws known as the *Townshend Acts*. They put taxes on tea, glass, lead, paint and paper that colonies could receive only from Britain. Some of the money raised by these taxes was to be used to pay the salaries of the colonial governors and judges. This meant that the colonial lawmakers could no longer control the royal officials by holding back their salaries. It also meant that again there was taxation without representation. Another act set up a customs agency in Boston to collect taxes efficiently.

The *Townshend* Acts was met with strong protests in the American Colonies. The Massachusetts legislature, led by Samuel Adams, urged colonies to cooperate in resisting English taxation. Merchants agreed not to buy British goods, and the colonists began trying to do without British products. The boycott was so effective that the British merchants suffered more from the tax laws than the colonists. In 1770, Parliament had to remove all the Townshend taxes except the one on tea. This duty was kept to show that Parliament still had the right to tax the colonies.

《汤森法案》

然而，和平并没有维持多久。英国议会仍认为它有权向殖民地课税，有权控制殖民地。1767 年，政府决心要在殖民地筹集资金，于是通过了一套新的税法，称为《汤森法案》。《汤森法案》向茶叶、玻璃、铅、颜料和纸张等货物征税，而殖民地只能从英国进口这些货物。征集的税款将部分用于支付殖民地总督和法官的薪金。这意味着殖民地的立法者们不再能通过拒发薪金的办法控制国王派遣的官员们的行为。这也意味着没有代表但须纳税。另一项法案还授权在波士顿建立了海关署，以便更有效地征税。

《汤森法案》在美洲殖民地遭到强烈抗议。塞缪尔·亚当斯领导的马萨诸塞议会敦促诸殖民地合作以抵制英国的征税。商人们约定不再采购英国货物，殖民地人民也开始尽量不使用英国产品。抵制行动效果显著，英国商人遭受的损失比殖民地人民更严重。1770 年，议会被迫废除了所有的汤森税，只剩下茶税一项。这项税赋保留下来是为了显示议会仍有权向殖民地课税。

4. The Boston Massacre

波士顿惨案

The conflict between Britain and colonies turned into violence in 1770. In Boston, tensions between townspeople and British troops grew. On March 5, a crowd of Americans shouted insults and threw snowballs at some British soldiers. The frightened soldiers fired into the crowd, killing five people and wounding several others. This incident was called the Boston Massacre. After the incident, prominent Bostonians urged the British to remove their troops from the city. When the British did so, further violence was avoided. The captain and a group of soldiers involved in the shooting were tried for murder. Most of them, including the captain, were found not guilty. Only two were later found guilty of manslaughter. They were branded on their thumbs as punishment.

英国和殖民地的冲突于 1770 年发展成暴力对抗。在波士顿，市民与英军的关系日趋紧张。3 月 5 日，一群美利坚人高声叫骂，并向英军士兵投掷雪球。惊慌的士兵向人群开枪，打死 5 人，打伤数人。这一事件史称"波士顿惨案"。事件发生之后，波士顿的著名人士敦促英国政府将波士顿的驻军撤出。英国答应了，避免了暴力升级。在事件中开枪的上尉和数名士兵以谋杀罪受审。他们当中的大多数，包括上尉，被宣判无罪。只有两人被确认犯有杀人罪。作为惩罚，他们的拇指被打上烙印。

波士顿惨案

这场冲突中只有五人遇难，却被称为"the Boston Massacre"（确切些应译成"波士顿大屠杀"）。这在局外人看来，似乎有些夸张。若在别的国家，士兵开枪打死平民乃家常便饭，打死数百人也算不了什么。再说几名士兵面对四百名挑衅的暴民，很难保持情绪稳定，似乎也并非没有理由开枪。但美国人的祖先们却不依不饶。英国征税，是为了保障殖民地人民的安全，"取之于民，用之于民"，有何不妥？但美国人的祖先们就是不买账。他们所关心的不是安全，而是自由。他们要求享有英国人自从《大宪章》以来一直为之奋斗的全部权利，不达此目的决不罢休。美国历史上的很多类似事件表明，美国人是被自由与民主"宠坏了"的、心性高傲的孩子，受不得丝毫的委屈。懂得这一点，便可以理解他们的许多做法。

5. The Boston Tea Party and the "Intolerable Acts"

波士顿茶党案与"不可容忍的法令"

To avoid paying the Townshend tax on tea, the colonial merchants smuggled in their tea. Then in 1773, Britain's East India Company, which was losing money, asked Parliament for help. Parliament passed the *Tea Act*, which enabled the East India Company to sell its tea below the price of smuggled tea. This meant many colonial tea merchants would be put out of business, and Britain's East India Company would be able to gain complete control of the American tea trade. This also meant when the colonists bought the British tea, they would be paying the tax and admitting the right of Britain to tax them. Patriots decided to take further actions.

During the night of December 16, 1773, Sons of Liberty, dressed as Indians, went aboard East India Company ships in Boston Harbor, quickly broke open the chests, and threw all the tea into the

为了逃避缴纳汤森税中的茶税，殖民地商人开始走私茶叶。1773 年，蒙受亏损的英国东印度公司向议会求助。议会通过《茶法》，使东印度公司能够以低于走私茶的价格销售茶叶。这意味着殖民地的茶商将被挤出市场，英国东印度公司将垄断殖民地的茶叶贸易。这同时也意味着当殖民地人民购买英国茶叶时，他们将缴纳茶税，承认英国向他们课税的权利。爱国者们决定采取进一步行动。

1773 年 12 月 16 日夜，自由之子社的成员们装扮成印第安人的模样，登上停泊在波士顿港的东印度公司的船只，迅速打破箱子，将所

harbor. This action was called the Boston Tea Party.

The Boston Tea Party made the British government very angry. It passes a series of acts early in 1774 to punish the Bostonians. These laws, called the "Intolerable Acts" by the Americans, closed the port of Boston to trade until the colonists paid for the destroyed tea; changed the form of government of Massachusetts, taking away all the colonists' rights of self-government; and required the colonists to provide rooms and food for British soldiers. The British government had intended to use the laws to punish one colony, but they alarmed all the other colonies. If this could happen to Massachusetts, it could happen to all. Contrary to Britain's expectation, the Intolerable Acts became an important force in uniting Britain's 13 American Colonies. They led to the First Continental Congress, a gathering of representatives from 12 of the American Colonies and brought the colonists closer to movement for American independence.

有的茶叶统统倾倒在海里。这次行动称为"波士顿茶党案"。

波士顿茶党案激怒了英国政府。1774 年初，政府通过一系列的法令惩罚波士顿人。美利坚人称这些法令为 "不可容忍的法令"。这些法令关闭了波士顿港，直至殖民地人民赔偿所有被销毁的茶叶；改变了马萨诸塞政府的形式，剥夺殖民地人民的所有自治权；要求殖民地人民为英军士兵提供食宿。英国政府本打算利用法令惩罚一个殖民地，但却使其他所有殖民地都感到惊恐。这种事既然可能在马萨诸塞发生，在任何其他地方都可能发生。与英国的预料相反，不可容忍的法令却成为促进 13 个美利坚英国殖民地团结的有力因素。它们促使 12 个殖民地的代表召开第一届大陆会议，使殖民地人民向独立运动迈进。

题 外 话

抵制东印度公司的茶叶可以理解，而将三百多箱茶叶统统到在海里，似乎有些不近情理。但这正是不肯受委屈的美国人的做法。英国议会里的埃德蒙·伯克同情美洲人，为他们辩护说，"纳税而又心情愉快，正如热恋而又头脑清醒，人类无此天赋。"

所谓"不可容忍法令"也包括 "魁北克法案"。《独立宣言》里也将此法案当做英国的罪状之一。其实美国人误解了这一法案，将它视为对波士顿人的惩罚。这一法案的主要意图是安抚魁北克省的法国移民。法案将魁北克省的边界向南扩充到俄亥俄河，保障在该省实行法国的民法，保障法国加拿大人信奉天主教的权利，并允许魁北克的天主教会向教徒课税。

6. The First Continental Congress

第一届大陆会议

On September 5, 1774, delegates from all the colonies except Georgia met in the *First Continental Congress* in Philadelphia. These men met to protest the Intolerable Acts and decide how to protect their rights in united actions. The twelve colonies sent 56 distinguished men, including Samuel Adams and John Adams of Massachusetts and George Washington and Patrick Henry of Virginia. The delegates agreed that what they wanted was only fair treatment from Great Britain, rather than independence. The Congress declared that Parliament had no right to pass laws that affected America, and each colonial assembly alone had the right to regulate its own internal affairs. It demanded that the colonists should be given all the rights of Englishmen. The delegates voted to cut off all trade with Great Britain until Parliament abolished the Intolerable Acts. The Congress agreed to hold another Continental Congress the following May, if Britain did not change its policies before that time.

1774年9月5日，佐治亚以外的所有各殖民地代表聚集费城，召开第一届大陆会议。这些代表们聚会以抗议不可容忍法令，商议如何联合行动捍卫自己的权利。12个殖民地派出56位著名人士，包括马萨诸塞的塞缪尔·亚当斯和约翰·亚当斯、弗吉尼亚的乔治·华盛顿和帕特里克·亨利。代表们一致认为，他们希望得到的只是英国的公正对待，而不是独立。会议宣告英国议会无权通过涉及美利坚殖民地的法律，只有每个殖民地的议会才有权管理自己的内部事务。会议要求殖民地人民应当得到英国人的全部权利。代表们投票赞成断绝与英国的一切贸易往来，直至议会废除不可容忍法令。会议决定，如果英国在翌年5月前仍不改变其政策，届时将举行下一届大陆会议。

🎯 题外话

英国国王乔治三世的私生活无可指摘，办事严谨而有责任感，但不明智，完全缺乏想象力。据说他11岁时尚不能正常阅读，其智商恐怕不会太高。独立战争之所以爆发，并以英国失败告终，与乔治三世的刚愎自用、决策失误有关。实际上，当时殖民地的大多数人忠于国王，即使第一届大陆会议的代表们也表现温和，尽量避免谈论独立。当时的英国著名政治家、前首相威廉·皮特读过会议通过的文件后说："若论真正的贤明、非凡的稳健、完美的智慧、果敢的精神、崇高的感情和质朴的语言，……费城会议堪称光绝人寰。"可惜国王毫无让步之意。乔治在1774年11月里写道："新英格兰的那些政府现在处于叛乱状态，必须用战斗来决定它们是属于这个国家还是独立。"

CHAPTER FOUR

The Revolutionary War
美国革命战争（独立战争）

1. A War Became Inevitable

战争一触即发

At first, independence was not the colonists' goal. Not all of the colonists actively opposed British rules. Some of the colonists remained loyal to Britain. However, most colonists had a deep belief in government by the people and had learned to elect people to public office who would represent their views and challenge the power of the ruling class. They believed that British policies threatened their freedom. The colonists also shared an increasing sense of nationalism. By 1774, the colonists no longer thought of themselves as transplanted Europeans, but rather as Americans.

The disobedience of the American Colonies angered the British government. In late 1774, George III declared, "The die is now cast, the colonies must either submit or triumph." In 1775, Parliament declared Massachusetts, which took the lead in protest against Britain, to be in rebellion. The British government ordered its troops in Boston to take swift action against the rebels. The

起初，独立并非殖民地人民的意图。并非所有的殖民者都积极反对英国的统治。部分殖民者始终效忠英国。但大部分人都深信政府必须是民选的，而且他们已经习惯于选出代表他们意愿、敢于挑战统治阶级权力的人担任公职。他们认为英国的政策威胁了他们的自由。殖民地人民的民族意识也逐渐增强。到了 1774 年，殖民者们认为自己不再是欧洲移民，而是美利坚人。

美洲殖民地的抗命激怒了英国政府。1774 年末，乔治三世宣告说："骰子已经投下，殖民地要么必须服从，要么必须战胜我们。"1775 年，议会宣告带头抗议英国政策的马萨诸塞处于叛乱状态。英国政府命令波士顿驻军采取迅速行动打击叛乱者。此后不久便爆发了革

Revolutionary War, also called the American Revolution, broke out soon afterward. It lasted eight years from 1775 to 1783, and resulted in American independence.

命战争，亦称美国革命。这场战争从 1775 年到 1783 年持续了 8 年，结果是美国的独立。

题外话

威廉·皮特于 1775 年初在英国议会中提出一项动议，主张撤消美利坚人称为"不可容忍法令"的一系列法规，并撤退军队。他说："我告诉你们，那些法令必须撤消。……尊敬的议员阁下们，再也不能耽误时间了，每一分钟都充满了很多危险。不，就在我讲话的这个时刻，决定性的一击可能已经发生，结果将会使数百万人卷入其中。"但皮特的动议遭受重挫。相同的动议在下议院提出时，著名政治家和作家埃德蒙·伯克发表了他赞成同美利坚和解的演说，主张对美采取怀柔政策。但动议仍以 82 票对 197 票遭否决。倘若乔治和议员们多些政治智慧，这场战争并非不可避免。

2. Lexington and Concord

列克星敦与康科德

Expecting armed conflict, the men of Massachusetts began to organize into militia in the autumn of 1774. They called themselves Minutemen because they might get ready for military action at a minute notice. They drilled regularly and provided themselves with weapons and ammunition.

In February 1775, Parliament declared that Massachusetts was in open rebellion. In April, General Gage received secret orders from the British government to take military action against the Massachusetts troublemakers and arrest their leaders John Hancock and Samuel Adams. Boston patriots learned about the secret orders before Gage did. The leaders of the rebellion fled Boston to avoid arrest. Gage then sent about 700 British soldiers on the night of April 18 to seize arms and

看到战争迫在眉睫，马萨诸塞的人们开始在 1774 年秋组织民兵。他们自称"瞬息民兵"，因为他们能在一分钟内做好战斗准备。他们定时操练，并装备了武器和弹药。

1775 年 2 月，议会宣告马萨诸塞处于公开叛乱状态。4 月，盖奇将军接到英国政府的密令，要他采取军事行动打击马萨诸塞的捣乱分子，逮捕他们的首领约翰·汉考克和塞缪尔·亚当斯。波士顿的爱国者在盖奇收到密令之前就已获悉密令内容。叛乱首领逃离了波士顿。4 月 18 日夜，盖奇派遣 700 名英军士兵到波士顿附近的康科德镇搜索爱国者贮存的武器和弹药。得知盖

gunpowder stored by the patriots in the town of Concord, near Boston. Knowing Gage's plan, Paul Revere and another Patriot, William Dawes, jumped on their horses and rode through the countryside, spreading the news of the approaching redcoats. (The British soldiers were so nicknamed because they wore bright red jackets.)

When the redcoats reached the town of Lexington, on the way to Concord, on April 19, they were met by 70 minutemen. In an exchange of shots, 18 colonists were killed or wounded. The British continued on to Concord, where another fight took place. The British then turned back to Boston. Along the way, colonists fired at them from behind houses, trees and stone walls. About 1,600 British troops and 4,000 American militiamen took part in the action that day. British dead and wounded numbered about 250, and American losses came to about 90.

奇的计划后，保尔·瑞维尔和另一个爱国者威廉·道斯立即跃上马背，飞驰于乡间，将红衫军（英军士兵着鲜红上装，故得此绰号）即将来临的消息通知各家各户。

19 日，当红衫军在前往康科德途中抵达列克星敦镇时，他们遇到 70 名瞬息民兵。交火中，殖民者死伤 18 人。英军继续向康科德进发，在康科德再次与殖民者交战。在英军返回波士顿途中，殖民者们从房屋、树木和石墙后面向他们射击。大约有 1600 名英军与 4000 名瞬息民兵加入了战斗。英军死伤大约 250 人，美利坚人损失战士 90 名左右。

保尔·瑞维尔像

🖸 题 外 话

美国诗人朗费罗有一首著名诗，《保尔·瑞维尔星夜飞驰》，用生动的语言叙述了保尔·瑞维尔连夜传送消息的故事，使这一故事在美国家喻户晓。

约翰·汉考克，1776 年宣布独立时
任大陆会议主席

美国革命的鼓吹者、《独立宣言》的
签署人之一塞缪尔·亚当斯

保尔·瑞维尔星夜飞驰

3. The Second Continental Congress

第二届大陆会议

After the fighting at Lexington and Concord in April,   about 10,000 Minutemen throughout New England gathered around Boston.   As more and more men came to help them, the American forces decided to drive the British from the city.

On May 10, 1775, the *Second Continental Congress* met in Philadelphia. All the 13 colonies sent their delegates. Among noted delegates were Benjamin Franklin, Thomas Jefferson, and John Hancock. The Congress faced a choice of giving in to the home country or continuing to resist the unfair acts of British Parliament. They decided to resist, by force if necessary.

To defend the colonies, the Congress organized an army, which was mainly made up of the Minutemen in the Boston area. George Washington was appointed commander in chief. On July 8, 1775, the Congress issued a declaration setting forth the need to take up arms and the reasons for doing so, and called on the colonies to raise

列克星敦与康科德的战斗于 4 月打响后，全新英格兰的大约一万名瞬息民兵包围了波士顿。随着前来援助的人越来越多，美利坚军队决定将英军逐出波士顿。

1775 年 5 月 10 日，第二届大陆会议在费城召开。所有 13 个殖民地都派了代表。代表中的名人有本杰明·富兰克林、托马斯·杰斐逊和约翰·汉考克。会议面临一个抉择，即或者向母国妥协，或者继续反抗英国议会不公正的法令。代表们决定反抗，必要时使用武力。

为保卫殖民地，会议组建了一支军队，主要由波士顿地区的瞬息民兵构成。乔治·华盛顿被任命为总司令。1775 年 7 月 8 日，会议发布宣言，申明拿

华盛顿将军

troops and help pay for the war effort. At the same time, however, the delegates declared again that they were loyal to the crown. They asked King George III to prevent further hostile action by Great Britain, so that peaceful relation might be restored.

起武器的必要性及其理由，号召殖民地募集军队并协助筹款以应付战争开支。然而，与此同时，代表们重申他们忠于国王。他们恳请乔治三世制止英国进一步的敌对行动，以恢复两地之间的和平。

4. The Battle of Bunker Hill

邦克山战斗

In May 1775, as the Second Continental Congress was meeting, a small force led by Colonels Ethan Allen and Benedict Arnold attacked the British forts at Ticonderoga and Crown Point in northeastern New York. They took the forts, and seized badly needed cannons and ammunition, and sent these supplies to the Americans in the Boston area.

To gain an advantage over the British in Boston, the colonials seized a hill overlooking Boston in June and began to fortify it. The hill is now known as Bunker Hill. On June 17, the British attacked the Americans, and twice they were driven back with heavy losses. The third attempt succeeded, for the Americans had run out of ammunition, and they had to retreat. The fighting, usually called the Battle of Bunker Hill, was the bloodiest battle of the entire war. More than 1,000 British soldiers and about 400 Americans were killed or wounded.

Soon after the battle, Washington took command of the military camps near Boston on July 3, 1775. At the time the militiamen were poorly trained and not used to discipline. They lacked

1775 年 5 月，第二届大陆会议召开期间，伊森·艾伦和本尼狄克·阿诺德两位上校率领一支兵力不大的军队袭击了英国在纽约东北部的提康德罗加和王冠顶两个要塞。他们占领了要塞，夺取了急需的大炮和弹药，将这些物资运送给波士顿地区的美利坚人。

为占据有利地形以攻打波士顿城内的英军，殖民者们于 6 月攻占了一座俯瞰波士顿的小山，并开始在那里修筑工事。这座小山现在称为邦克山。6 月 17 日，英军向美利坚人发起进攻，但两次被击退，损失惨重。第三次进攻取得成功，因为当时美利坚人已用尽弹药，不得不撤退。这场战斗，通常称为邦克山战斗，是整个战争中最惨烈的一场。英军死伤 1000 余人，美利坚人死伤约 400 人。

这次战斗后不久，华盛顿于 7 月 3 日接管了波士顿附近的兵营。当时的瞬息民兵缺乏训练，而且不习惯于服从纪律。他们缺少武器和

weapons and ammunition. Most soldiers had joined the fighting to defend their families and farms. They expected to return home after a few months. Washington issued a series of orders immediately to establish order and discipline in the army.

The following spring, troops under Washington's command seized a high ground south of Boston overlooking Boston Harbour, and moved some heavy guns up on the high ground. The British realized that they could not hold Boston with American cannons pointed at them. They soon had to withdraw from Boston by sea and sailed to Canada. The Americans had freed Boston from British occupation.

弹药。大多数士兵参加战斗是为了保卫自己的家庭和农庄，他们本打算几个月后回家种田。华盛顿发布了一系列的军令维持秩序、整饬军纪。

次年春，华盛顿率领的军队夺取了波士顿以南的一个俯瞰波士顿港的高地，将几门大炮推上高地。英军意识到在美军的大炮瞄准他们的情况下，是不可能守住波士顿的。他们不久就从海上撤出波士顿，起航前往加拿大。美利坚人从英军手中解放了波士顿。

题外话

即使在邦克山战斗之后，大陆会议仍通过了致乔治三世的《橄榄枝请愿书》，用最恭顺的词句向国王陛下保证，"热切希望"恢复英国与殖民地之间的"旧有的和谐"并实现"愉快而恒久的和解"。直到 1776 年春，华盛顿和他的军官们每天晚餐时都要为英王的健康干杯。此时乔治三世若做出让步，还来得及。可惜他的愚蠢和顽固，使他失去了最后一个机会。

5. The Invasion of Canada

入侵加拿大

To prevent British forces from attacking New York from Canada, and at the same time to encourage the French in Canada to join the colonies in their rebellion against Great Britain, the Americans began an invasion of Canada. In the autumn of 1775, two American columns marched northward into Canada. One column, led by Richard Montgomery, captured Montreal and went on to the city of Quebec. Outside Quebec, it was joined by the

为防止英军从加拿大进攻纽约，同时为了鼓励加拿大的法国人参加殖民地反对英国的叛乱，美利坚人开始入侵加拿大。1775 年秋，两支美利坚人组成的纵队向北进军，侵入加拿大。一支由理查·蒙哥马利率领，在夺取了蒙特利尔后，继续向魁北克进发。在魁北克城外，这一纵队与本尼狄克·阿诺

other column under Benedict Arnold. Arnold's troops had made a difficult march across the interior of Maine. Disease and hunger had caused many of his men to turn back. But their joined attack failed to take the city. Montgomery died in the attack, Arnold was seriously wounded, and many Americans were taken prisoner. The Americans retreated to New York in the spring of the following year, after British reinforcements reached Canada.

德率领的另一纵队会师。阿诺德的部队经过艰苦跋涉，穿越缅因纵深地区才到达这里。疾病和饥饿使他手下很多人掉头而去。但两支队伍的合力进攻仍未能攻取魁北克。蒙哥马利阵亡，阿诺德受了重伤，许多美利坚人被俘。次年春，英国的增援部队抵达加拿大后，美利坚人撤回纽约。

6. Fighting in the South

南方的战斗

Americans enjoyed great success in the South at the start of the Revolutionary War. In urging his fellow Virginians to arm, Patrick Henry uttered the stirring words, "I know not what course others may take, but as for me, give me liberty or give me death."

In North Carolina, Governor Josiah Martin tried to crush the rebellious colonists by force. He raised an army of about 1,500 Loyalists and they marched toward the coast to join British troops arriving by sea. But on the way, the army was defeated by patriot militiamen in February 1776, in the Battle of Moore's Creek Bridge, near Wilmington. British troops under General Clinton had sailed southward from Boston. However, they failed to arrive in time to prevent the defeat at Moore's Creek Bridge. The British warships continued on to Charleston, South Carolina, the chief port in the South. In June, they tried to attack the city, but were driven off by American troops. The British warships had to leave to rejoin their forces in the North.

革命战争初期，美利坚人在南方取得重大胜利。帕特里克·亨利用激动人心的言辞鼓动弗吉尼亚人拿起武器。他说，"我不知他人做何种选择，但对我来说，不自由，毋宁死！"

在北卡罗莱纳，总督乔西阿·马丁试图用武力镇压反叛的殖民者。他募集了一支大约1500人的勤王军，向海边进发，打算与从海上抵达的英军会合。1776年2月，这支军队在途中与爱国的瞬息民兵相遇，在威尔明顿附近的摩尔溪桥战斗中被击败。克林顿将军率领的英军已经从波士顿乘船南下，但他们未能及时到达，以避免摩尔溪桥战斗的失利。英国军舰继续航行，前往南方的重要港口南卡罗莱纳的查尔斯顿。6月，英军试图攻占查尔斯顿，但被美军击退。英国军舰不得不离开，与北方的部队会合。

7. Moving Towards Independence

向 独 立 迈 进

When the Second Continental Congress opened in May 1775, few delegates wanted to break ties with the mother country. Even after fighting had grown bitter, many colonists still hoped for a peaceful settlement with Great Britain. But by the end of 1775 this possibility had faded. King George III had declared all the colonies to be in rebellion. He seemed to be determined to force them to give in. He also approved an act of Parliament closing all American ports to overseas trade. In addition, the king increased the British force by hiring 20,000 German troops to help crush the rebellious colonists. Since most of these hired soldiers were from Hesse-Kassel in central Germany, they were called Hessians. News of the king's use of foreigners shocked the colonists. The quarrel, they felt, was within the family. Why bring in outsiders, who were notorious for their savageness?

More and more Americans began to feel that the colonies had to break away form England. The desire of independence was inspired by a pamphlet called *Common Sense*, published in January 1776 by Thomas Paine, who had come from England a year earlier. Paine blamed the king for the colonies' troubles. He argued that it was foolish for the vast continent of America to be controlled by the tiny island of England 3000 miles away. This pamphlet demanded complete independence from Great Britain.

Meanwhile, the Second Continental Congress

1775 年 5 月第二届大陆会议召开时，很少代表愿意与母国决裂。即使在战斗已日趋激烈时，许多殖民者仍希望与英国达成和解。到了 1775 年年底，这一可能性已变得渺茫。国王乔治三世已经宣告所有 13 个殖民地已处于叛乱状态。他似乎决意要迫使它们屈服。他还批准了议会的一项法案，关闭了所有的美利坚港口，切断了海外贸易。此外，国王还雇用了 20000 名德国兵增援英军，镇压叛乱的殖民者。这些雇佣兵来自德国中部的黑森－卡塞尔地区，故被称为黑森人。国王雇用外国人的消息使殖民者们感到震惊。他们觉得，英国和殖民地之间的争端，毕竟是家庭内部的争端。为什么要让那些以残忍无情而恶名昭彰外国人参与？

越来越多的美利坚人感到殖民地不得不与英国决裂。一本名为《常识》的小册子激起人们独立的愿望。这本小册子发表于 1776 年 1 月，作者是一年前来自英国的托马斯·佩因。佩因指责国王是制造殖民地冲突的祸首。他试图说服人们，庞大的美洲大陆竟然让一个 3000 英里外的小小的岛屿统治，是一件荒谬的事。小册子力主完全脱离英国而独立。

与此同时，第二届大陆会议以

began to act as the central government of the 13 colonies, issuing and borrowing money, establishing a postal service, and creating a navy. The Congress also sent delegates abroad to seek foreign aid.

13 个殖民地的中央政府的名义行使权力，发行货币、举债、建立邮政系统、组建海军。大陆会议还向国外派出代表以寻求外国援助。

题 外 话

黑森人是欧洲出售雇佣兵制度的牺牲品。六个德国亲王参与这笔交易，将英国政府的大笔酬金装入自己的腰包。乔治三世缺少炮灰，德国亲王们则缺钱养家。据说其中一个亲王有 74 个孩子需要抚养。每个雇佣兵每日大约只可得 25 分钱报酬。黑森人对作战并无特殊兴趣，真正感兴趣的是战利品。但他们训练有素，战斗力很强，使美国军队不得不另眼相看。美国人在特伦顿打败黑森人后，自信心大增。很多黑森人受到美国土地的诱惑，开了小差，最终成了美国公民。

8. The Declaration of Independence

《独立宣言》

Support for American independence continued to build early in 1776. In June, Richard Henry Lee of Virginia introduced the resolution in the Continental Congress declaring that "these United Colonies are, and of right ought to be, free and independent States." The Congress appointed a committee to draw up a declaration of independence. The committee gave Thomas Jefferson the job of doing the writing. On July 2, the Congress approved Lee's resolution. Two days later, on July 4, the Congress adopted the *Declaration of Independence*. All ties with Great Britain were now cut, and a new nation, the United States of America was born.

The Declaration of Independence contains a new idea of government, which became model

1776年初，支持美利坚独立的呼声继续高涨。6 月，弗吉尼亚的理查·亨利·李在大陆会议提出一项决议案，宣布"联合起来的殖民地是，而且理应是，自由而独立的国家。"大陆会议任命了一个委员会起草一份独立宣言。委员会指定托马斯·杰斐逊执笔。7 月 2 日，大陆会议通过了李的决议案。两天后，会议通过了《独立宣言》。此时，与英国的一切联系全部断绝，一个新的国家，美利坚合众国诞生了。

《独立宣言》包含着关于政府的新观念，日后成为世界上所有国家和人民视为圭臬。这一新观念在《独立宣言》的开篇部分表述如下：

for countries and people all over the world. This new idea is explained at the beginning of the Declaration:

"We hold these truths to be self-evident, that all men are created equal, that they are endowed by their Creator with certain unalienable Rights, that among these are Life, Liberty, and the pursuit of Happiness. That to secure these rights, Governments are instituted among Men, deriving their just powers from the consent of the governed. That whenever any Form of Government becomes destructive of these ends, it is the Right of the People to alter or to abolish it, and to institute new Government, having its foundation on such principles and organizing its powers in such form, as to them shall seem most likely to effect their Safety and Happiness."

After the explanation of what kind of government the colonists believed in, the Declaration of Independence goes on to list all the complaints the colonists had against the British king, George III and say that the colonists have asked the king,

"我们认为下面这些真理是不言而喻的：人人生而平等，造物者赋予他们若干不可剥夺的权利，其中包括生命权、自由权和追求幸福的权利。为了保障这些权利，人类才在他们之间建立政府，而政府之正当权力，是经被治理者的同意而产生的。当任何形式的政府对这些目标具破坏作用时，人民便有权力改变或废除它，以建立一个新的政府；其赖以奠基的原则，其组织权力的方式，务使人民认为唯有这样才最可能获得他们的安全和幸福。"

在对殖民者们所企望的政府形式做出解释后，《独立宣言》进而列举了殖民地人民对英国国王乔治三世的种种不满，指出殖民地人民已再三恳请国王匡正这些不义之举，但国王拒绝了他们的请求。因而，宣言说，殖民地人民别无选择，只能宣布脱离英国，成为一个自由独立的国家。

《独立宣言》

over and over again, to change these unfair practices, but he has refused to do it. Therefore, the Declaration says, the colonists have no choice but to declare themselves a free country, independent of Great Britain.

题外话

用历史的眼光来检验,《独立宣言》有不少可以指摘之处。对乔治三世的种种指控有些似乎歪曲了事实,有些则近乎吹毛求疵。另外,《宣言》把英国议会的种种恶行转嫁到倒霉的国王头上去了。这样做似乎是为了打破美利坚人忠于国王的传统。最值得指摘是起草委员会提交的文本中本来包括对于英国国王鼓励奴隶贸易的谴责文字,但在某些代表的坚持下被大陆会议删除。不过,对杰斐逊也不能苛责。毕竟,他的使命不是撰写历史,而是影响历史进程。

9. The Campaign in New York

Soon after the British withdrew from Boston in March 1776, the war shifted from New England to the Middle Colonies. The British army, under the command of General William Howe, began to return from Canada to the American Colonies. Washington moved his army south to New York City, which he expected the British to attack. In July, Howe landed on Staten Island in New York Harbor. Howe was joined by General Clinton's men, following their defeat in South Carolina, and by Hessian troops from Europe. Washington was unable to defend the city because he had far fewer troops and those he had were poorly trained. During the next four months, the British took one position after another. Washington's skillful handling his army kept it from being completely destroyed by the more powerful enemy. The Americans finally managed to withdraw across the Hudson River to New Jersey, leaving New York City in the hands of the British.

纽约战役

英军于 1776 年 3 月从波士顿撤出后,战争从新英格兰转移到中部诸殖民地。英军在威廉·豪将军的指挥下开始从加拿大返回美利坚殖民地。华盛顿率军南下到纽约市,因为他预计英军将攻打该市。7 月,豪将军在纽约港的斯塔腾岛登陆。在南卡罗莱纳吃了败仗的克林顿将军的部队和从欧洲赶来的黑森部队与豪将军会师。华盛顿无法保卫这座城市,因为他的兵力过少,而且缺乏训练。在后来的 4 个月里,英军攻占了一个又一个的据点。华盛顿巧妙的指挥使他的军队在敌强我弱的情况下免于遭受覆灭之灾。美军终于设法渡过哈得孙河,进入新泽西,纽约市遂落入英军之手。

10. The Battle of Trenton and Princeton

特伦顿和普林斯顿战斗

The patriots' situation appeared dark at the end of 1776. To avoid being captured by the British, Washington's discouraged forces crossed the Delaware River into Pennsylvania in December, and camped across the river from Trenton, New Jersey. Howe believed he had broken the patriot rebellion. But he was quite mistaken. Although Washington had few troops, he decided to strike at Trenton. On Christmas night in 1776, during a storm, Washington and about 2,400 troops crossed the Delaware River. He surprised a force of Hessians at Trenton and took more than 900 prisoners.

Howe sent a force under Cornwallis to catch Washington. Cornwallis advanced toward Trenton on January 2, 1777 and planned to attack the Americans the next day. But during the night,

1776年末，爱国者们的处境困难，希望渺茫。为避免被英军俘获，华盛顿士气低落的部队在12月渡过特拉华河，进入宾夕法尼亚宿营，与新泽西的特伦顿隔河相望。豪将军认为他已经粉碎了爱国者们的叛乱，但他完全错了。虽然华盛顿兵力很少，却决定袭击特伦顿。1776年圣诞夜，华盛顿率领大约2400名士兵在暴风雪中渡过特拉华河。他偷袭了黑森军队，俘获900余人。

豪将军派遣康沃里斯率领一支部队追逐华盛顿。康沃里斯于1777年1月2日逼近特伦顿，计划次日进攻美军。但华盛顿的军队乘夜色

华盛顿渡过特拉华河

Washington's troops silently stole away and marched past Cornwallis' army. The following morning, Washington attacked at Princeton and defeated a smaller British force on its way to join Cornwallis. Washington then moved his troops northward to winter headquarters near Morristown, New Jersey. The victories at Trenton and Princeton, although minor, dramatically improved the morale of the American forces.

悄悄撤离，转移到康沃里斯的后方。次日清晨，华盛顿进攻普林斯顿，打败了正在前进与康沃里斯会合的一小支英军。华盛顿然后挥军北上，抵达新泽西的莫里斯敦附近的冬营地。特伦顿和普林斯顿战斗的胜利虽然不大，却大大提高了美军的士气。

11. The Philadelphia Campaign

费 城 战 役

In the summer of 1777, Howe's troops sailed from New York City to Chesapeake Bay. He then marched on to the American capital, Philadelphia. Washington positioned his troops between Howe's forces and Philadelphia to stop the British. The opposing armies clashed on September 11, 1777, at Brandywine Creek in southeastern Pennsylvania. One wing of the British army moved quickly around the Continental Army and attacked them from behind. The surprised Americans had to retreat. Howe's troops occupied Philadelphia later that month. The Continental Congress had fled to York, Pennsylvania, where it continued to direct American affairs.

On October 4, 1777, Washington struck back at British forces camping at Germantown, north of Philadelphia. But his complicated battle plan created confusion. In a heavy fog, American forces fired on one another. The Americans again had to retreat. Having easily occupied Philadelphia, Howe set up headquarters in the city.

1777 年夏，豪将军的部队从纽约市乘船南下切萨皮克湾，然后向美国首都费城进军。华盛顿将军队部署在豪将军的军队与费城之间，以阻击英军。两军于 9 月 11 日在宾夕法尼亚东南部的布兰迪万河交火。英军的一翼迅速包抄到大陆军的后方发起攻击。遭到偷袭的美军不得不撤退。豪将军的部队当月晚些时候占领了费城。大陆会议迁往宾夕法尼亚的约克城，继续主持美国政务。

1777 年 10 月 4 日，华盛顿向驻扎在费城北方日尔曼敦的英军发起反击。但由于作战计划过于复杂，军队调动出现混乱。在浓雾中，美军发生误会，相互射击。结果不得不再次撤退。豪将军轻取费城，在该城建立了司令部。

题外话

豪将军表面上打了胜仗,占领了费城,但他的行动使纽约州北部的伯戈因将军率领的英军陷于孤立,直接造成后来英军在萨拉托加的灾难。豪将军贪图享乐,在费城过上优哉游哉的生活。本杰明·富兰克林讽刺他说,豪将军未能占领费城,而是费城占领了豪将军。

12. Valley Forge

福吉谷

Washington withdrew his forces and set up winter quarters at nearby Valley Forge, 32 kilometers northwest of Philadelphia. About 11,000 soldiers spent a harsh and trying winter there. They suffered from a severe shortage of food, shelter and clothing. Perhaps more than 2,500 soldiers died from hunger, disease or exposure to the cold. Many soldiers deserted. Hard conditions reduced the army to about half its former size.

In February 1778, Baron Friedrich von Steuben, a German officer, arrived at Valley Forge. He volunteered his services to the American cause,

华盛顿将军队撤退到附近的福吉谷,建立越冬营地,位于费城西北 32 公里。大约 11000 名士兵在福吉谷度过了一个严酷的冬天。他们由于缺乏食物、营房和衣物而备受煎熬。死于饥饿、疾病和寒冷的士兵可能多达 2500 余人。许多士兵开了小差。艰苦的生活条件使兵员减少到原先的一半。

1778 年 2 月,德国军官弗里德里希·冯·施托伊本男爵来到福吉谷。他自愿为美国的独立服务,训

德国军官弗里德里希·冯·施托伊本男爵在福吉谷训练华盛顿的士兵

restored discipline and morale to the rebel forces by training and teaching many military tactics. By late spring, Steuben had made what remained of Washington's army into a well-trained and disciplined fighting force. With courage and steadiness, Washington managed to keep his army together during the very trying period.

练军队、教授战术，恢复了美军的纪律和士气。到春末时，施托伊本已将华盛顿军队的残部改变成一支训练有素、纪律严明的战斗力量。由于华盛顿的勇气与坚忍，他成功地将军队聚集在一起，度过了最艰难的时期。

13. Victory at Saratoga

萨拉托加大捷

While Howe won victories at Brandywine Creek and Germantown, another British force advanced southward from Canada under General John Burgoyne. Burgoyne wanted to gain control of the Lake Champlain and Hudson River, so as to isolate New England from the other colonies. In July 1777, he captured the Fort Ticonderoga in New York from the Americans without a struggle. But when he reached the upper Hudson River, he ran into trouble. His soldiers became exhausted, food and other supplies ran short, and militiamen fired on British soldiers from the woods. Burgoyne sent about 700 men to Bennington, in present-day Vermont, to search for horses and food. But a force of New England militia met and defeated them. Finally, Burgoyne and his men were surrounded near Saratoga, New

正当豪将军在布兰迪万河和日尔曼敦获胜之时，另一支英军由约翰·伯戈因将军率领从加拿大出发南下。伯戈因企图控制尚普兰湖与哈得孙河，以切断新英格兰与其余殖民地的联系。1777 年 7 月，他未遇抵抗就从美国人手中夺取了纽约的泰孔德罗加要塞。但当他抵达哈得孙河上游时，却遇到了麻烦。他的士兵已疲惫不堪，粮食和其他军需供应不足，民兵躲在树林里向英军士兵射击。伯戈因派出 700 人到现在的佛蒙特州的本宁顿去搜罗马匹与粮食。但一支新英格兰的民兵队伍与他们相遇，打败了他们。最后，伯戈因与他的部队被

约翰·伯戈因将军向霍雷肖·盖茨将军投降

York, by a Continental army under the command of General Horatio Gates. On October 17, Burgoyne surrendered to Gates. The Americans took nearly 6,000 prisoners and large supplies of arms. The victory at Saratoga was a turning point in the Revolutionary War. It stopped the British invasion from Canada, and saved the New England colonies. More important, it helped convince France that it could safely enter the war on the American side.

霍雷肖·盖茨将军率领的大陆军围困在纽约的萨拉托加附近。10 月 17 日，伯戈因向盖茨投降。美军接收了近 6000 名战俘和大批武器。萨拉托加大捷是革命战争的转折点。它阻止了英军从加拿大入侵美国，保住了新英格兰殖民地。更重要的是，它使法国确信，为支持美国而参战不会有风险。

14. Foreign Aid

外国援助

Before the Revolutionary War began, French leaders had hoped for a split between Great Britain, their long-time enemy, and the American Colonies. They believed that a colonists' victory would weaken the mighty British Empire. Ever since 1776, France had secretly given the Americans loans, gifts of money, and weapons. But France refused to ally itself openly with the Americans before they had proved themselves in battle. After the important victory the Americans won at Saratoga, France agreed to enter into an open alliance with the United States. Benjamin Franklin, who represented the Americans in France, played a key role in obtaining French support for the new country. Early in 1778, treaties of alliance were signed, and under their terms,

革命战争开始前，法国统治者一直希望他们的夙敌英国与它的殖民地分裂开来。他们相信，殖民地的胜利会削弱大英帝国的势力。自从 1776 年开始，法国就向美国秘密提供贷款、赠送资金和武器。但法国拒绝公开与美国结为盟友，因为美国人尚未证明自己有作战能力。美国人在萨拉托加取得重大胜利之后，法国同意与美国公开结盟。美国驻法国的代表本杰明·富兰克林为争得法国对这个新成立的国家的支持，起到了关键作用。1778 年初，

法国贵族拉斐特侯爵不但自愿到美军中服役，还用个人财产赞助美国革命 200000 美圆

France provided the Americans with the money, supplies, military equipment, troops and warships they badly needed to fight the war. France's entry into the Revolutionary War in 1778 forced Great Britain to defend the rest of its empire. The British expected to fight the French in the West Indies and elsewhere, and so they scattered their military resources. As a result, Britain no longer had a force strong enough to battle the Americans in the North.

In addition, the Americans benefited from the direct assistance of a number of foreign volunteers who served with the Continental army. Baron Friedrich von Steuben reorganized and trained the Continental army at Valley Forge; the Marquis de Lafayette, a wealthy French noble, gave valuable help as an aide to Washington.

15. The Articles of Confederation

During most of the Revolution War, the Continental Congress provided leadership for the 13 former British colonies. After the Declaration of Independence was adopted, each former colony called itself a state. The Congress drew up an agreement called the *Articles of Confederation* to unify the states under a central government. The Articles were adopted by Congress in 1777, and went into effect in 1781. They served as the new nation's constitution until the first government under the Constitution of the United States was formed in 1789.

双方签署了盟约。根据其中的条款，法国向美国提供他们作战急需的资金、物资、军事装备、军队及战舰。法国于 1778 年加入美国革命战争迫使英国保卫帝国的其他地区。英国要准备与法国在西印度群岛和其他地区作战，因而他们分散了军事资源。结果，英国不再有足够的力量在北方与美国人作战。

此外，美国人还得到几个在大陆军中服役的外国志愿者的直接帮助。弗里德里希·冯·施托伊本男爵在福吉谷重组并训练了大陆军；一个有钱的法国贵族拉斐特侯爵担任华盛顿的副官，是华盛顿的得力助手。

邦联条例

在革命战争的大部分时间里，大陆会议担任前英国的 13 个殖民地的领导工作。独立宣言通过后，殖民地改称为"州"。大陆会议起草了一份名为"邦联条例"的协议，将各州统一置于一个中央政府的统辖之下。邦联条例于 1777 年被大陆会议通过，并于 1781 年生效。邦联条例充当新国家的宪法，直至 1789 年依据美国宪法成立头一届政府。

The Articles attempted to balance the need for an effective national government with the traditional independence of each state. The document gave Congress only a limited number of powers for governing the nation. It allowed Congress to declare war and peace, manage foreign relations, establish and command an army and navy, and issue and borrow money. All the other powers and functions, however, were left to the separate states because many delegates distrusted a strong central government.

邦联条例试图既建立一个有效的全国政府,又保障各州的传统独立地位。这个文件赋予大陆会议仅仅有限的几项权力治理国家。它允许大陆会议宣战和议和,处理外交关系,组建并统帅陆军和海军,发行货币和贷款。然而所有其他各项权力和职能都留给了各州,因为许多代表对一个强有力的中央政府心存疑虑。

16. The War in the South

南方的战斗

After France entered the Revolutionary War, the British turned their attention to the South. British leaders believed that most Southerners supported the king. Although the British failed to find as much Loyalist support as they expected, they defeated the Americans in several important battles. In December 1778, a large British force that had sailed from New York City easily captured Savannah, a port city in the South. The Congress named Major General Benjamin Lincoln commander of the Southern Department of the Continental Army. In October 1779, Lincoln attempted to drive the British from Savannah, but failed, in spite of the assistance of French naval forces.

With most of Georgia firmly under its control, the British army shifted its attention to South Carolina. Early in 1780, British forces under General Clinton, who had replaced Howe as commander-in-chief of British forces, landed near Charleston.

法国加入革命战争后,英国将注意力转向南方。英国的统治者认为大多数南方人支持国王。虽然英国人实际上得到的保王党的支持不如预期的多,他们仍在几次重要战斗中打败了美军。1778 年 12 月,一支兵力强大的英军从纽约市乘船南下,轻取南方港口城市萨凡纳。大陆会议任命本杰明·林肯少将为大陆军南方军区司令。1779 年 10 月,林肯试图将英军逐出萨凡纳,虽有法国海军的支持,仍未能成功。

英军牢牢地控制了佐治亚大部分地区之后,将注意力转向南卡罗莱纳。1780 年初,克林顿将军接替豪将军为英军总司令,率领英军在查尔斯顿附近登陆。英军形成合围之势,缓慢向查尔斯顿推进,将守

They slowly closed in on the city, trapping its defenders. In May 1780 General Clinton's force took Charleston, capturing more than 5,000 American troops—almost the entire Southern army. Clinton placed General Cornwallis in charge of British forces in the South and returned to New York City.

With the help of local Loyalists, the British force gradually occupied most of South Carolina. In July 1780, the Continental Congress ordered General Gates, who had won a victory at Saratoga, to form a new Southern army to replace the one lost at Charleston. Gates hastily assembled a force made up largely of untrained militiamen and rushed to fight Cornwallis at a British base in Camden, South Carolina. At the Battle of Camden in August, the British commanded by Cornwallis drove the American army back. The British had defeated a second American army in the South.

Cornwallis' victory at Camden led him to act more boldly. In September, he invaded North Carolina. In October, the left wing of his army, which was made up of Loyalist troops, was surrounded and captured on Kings Mountain, just inside South Carolina. After the defeat at Kings Mountain, Cornwallis had to give up his attempt to occupy North Carolina and retreated to South Carolina.

In October 1780, Washington sent Nathanael Greene, one of his ablest generals, to replace Gates as commander of the Southern army. Greene tried to avoid battle with Cornwallis' far stronger force. Instead, he skillfully drew the British army under Cornwallis into the interior of North Carolina, far from British supply base on the coast. Though Greene lost nearly every battle, he so much weakened the British that they were forced to withdraw

卫者困在城中。1780年5月，克林顿将军攻陷查尔斯顿，俘获美军5000余人，几乎是南方军的总兵力。克林顿指派康沃里斯将军负责指挥南方英军，自己返回纽约市。

依靠当地保王党人的支援，英军逐渐占领了大部分南卡罗莱纳。1780年7月，大陆会议命令在萨拉托加获胜的盖茨将军组建一支新的南方军代替在查尔斯顿损失的部队。盖茨仓促拼凑了一支主要由未经训练的民兵组成的军队，赶往南卡罗莱纳卡姆登的英军基地，袭击康沃里斯。在8月份的卡姆登战斗中，康沃里斯率领的英军击溃了美军。至此，英军打败了第二支南方美军。

康沃里斯在卡姆登的胜利使他更为大胆地采取行动。9月，他攻入北卡罗莱纳。10月，他的左翼部队，主要由保王党人组成，在南卡罗莱纳边界上的金斯山被围困后缴械投降。在金斯山受挫后，康沃里斯不得不放弃攻占北卡罗莱纳的企图，撤回南卡罗莱纳。

1780年10月，华盛顿派遣自己最得力的将领之一纳撒内尔·格林替换盖茨为南方军司令。格林试图避免与兵力强大得多的英军正面作战。他巧妙地诱使康沃里斯的军队进入北卡罗莱纳的腹地，远离英军在海岸上的供应基地。格林虽然几乎没有打过胜仗，但他大大削弱了英军的实力，使英军不得不撤退到北卡罗莱纳的沿海城市威尔明

to the coastal city Wilmington, North Carolina. Greene then turned south and recaptured most of the inland positions held by the British in South Carolina and Georgia. By the summer of 1781, the British in the South occupied only the coastal cities of Savannah, Charleston, and Wilmington.

顿。格林然后挥军南下，重新占领了英军在南卡罗莱纳和佐治亚的大部分内陆据点。到 1781 年夏天，南方的英军占据的地盘只剩下沿海城市萨凡纳、查尔斯顿和威尔明顿。

17. Victory at Yorktown

约克敦大捷

Cornwallis moved his army from Wilmington into Virginia in the spring of 1781 and made it his new base in the campaign to conquer the South. Clinton ordered Cornwallis to adopt a defensive position along the Virginia coast and prepare to send his troops north. Cornwallis moved to Yorktown, near the mouth of Chesapeake Bay. Washington ordered Lafayette to block Cornwallis's possible escape from Yorktown by land. In the meantime Washington's 2,500 Continental troops in New York were joined by 4,000 French troops under the comte de Rochambeau. This allied force left an army facing Clinton's forces in New York while the main force marched rapidly southward to the head of Chesapeake Bay, where it linked up with a French fleet of 24 ships under the comte de Grasse. This fleet had arrived from the West Indies to block Chesapeake Bay and prevent

康沃里斯于 1781 年春命令军队从威尔明顿进入弗吉尼亚，将该地作为新的基地，以便发动攻势占领南方。克林顿命令康沃里斯在弗吉尼亚沿海地带采取守势，准备将他的部队派往北方。康沃里斯率军进入切萨皮克湾入口处附近的约克敦。华盛顿命令拉斐特切断康沃里斯可能从陆上逃离约克敦的退路，与此同时，华盛顿率领的 2500 名纽约的大陆军与罗尚博伯爵率领的 4000 名法军会合。联军留下一支部队与克林顿的军队对峙，其余的联军迅速南下前往切萨皮克湾的入口，与格拉斯伯爵指挥的由 24 艘军舰组成的法国舰队会师。这支舰队来自西

罗尚博伯爵

Cornwallis from escaping by sea. A British naval force sailed from New York City and battled de Grasse at the mouth of Chesapeake Bay in early September. But after several days, the British ships returned to New York for repairs. Cornwallis's army waited in vain for rescue or reinforcements from the British navy while de Grasse's fleet transported Washington's troops southward to Williamsburg, Virginia, where they went to join Lafayette's forces in the siege of Yorktown. A British rescue fleet, two-thirds the size of the French, set out for Virginia on October 17 with some 7,000 British troops, but it was too late. Throughout early October a combined French and American force of about 18,000 soldiers and sailors had slowly and steadily closed in on the trapped British troops. After several weeks of desperate fighting, Cornwallis realized that his position was hopeless. Unable to escape or to get help, Cornwallis surrendered his entire army on October 19. The total number of British prisoners taken was about 8,000, along with about 240 guns. The victory at Yorktown ended fighting in the Revolution and assured success to the American cause.

18. The Treaty of Paris

Britain's defeat at Yorktown ended the British attempt to crush the Revolution, but the fighting dragged on in some areas for two more years. However, British leaders feared they might lose other parts of Britain's empire if they continued the

印度群岛，目的是堵塞切萨皮克湾，以防止康沃里斯从海上逃跑。英国海军从纽约市出发，于9月初在切萨皮克湾入口处与格拉斯交战。但数日后，英舰返回纽约进行维修。康沃里斯的军队空等着英国海军的救助或增援，而同时格拉斯的军舰则将华盛顿的部队向南运送到弗吉尼亚的威廉斯堡，从那里出发与拉斐特的军队对约克敦形成合围之势。一支英军救援舰队，规模有法国舰队的三分之二，载着7000名英军士兵，于10月17日起航前往弗吉尼亚，但为时已晚。整个10月上旬，法美联军的大约18000名陆军和海军缓慢而稳步地向被围困的英军逼近，逐渐缩小包围圈。经过数周的殊死战斗，康沃里斯意识到英军处境已无望。在既无法逃脱又得不到救援的情况下，康沃里斯于10月19日率全军投降。英军战俘总数约8000，同时缴获240门大炮。约克敦大捷宣告革命战争结束，确保了美国独立事业的成功。

巴黎和约

英国在约克敦的失败结束了其扼杀革命的企图，但战争在某些局部地区仍持续了两年多。然而，英国的统治者担心，如果他们将美洲的战争继续下去，他们会失去英帝

war in America. The English people were tired of the war and wanted peace. Early in 1782, Parliament voted to end hostilities and begin peace talks. Finally, the Americans and the British signed the *Treaty of Paris* of 1783, officially ending the Revolutionary War.

In the Treaty of Paris, Britain recognized the independence of its former colonies and accepted the new nation's borders. The United States territory extended west to the Mississippi River, north to Canada, east to the Atlantic Ocean, and south to about Florida. Britain gave Florida to Spain. The treaty also granted the Americans fishing rights in the Newfoundland area. In addition, it instructed the Congress to recommend that the states restore property taken from Loyalists during the war.

The last British soldiers were withdrawn from New York City in November 1783.

国的其他地区。英国人民厌倦了战争，希望和平。1782 年初，英国议会投票赞成结束敌对状态，启动和谈。终于，美英双方签署了 1783 年的巴黎和约，正式结束了革命战争。

按照巴黎和约，英国承认其前殖民地的独立，并接受了新国家的边界。美国领土西抵密西西比河，北邻加拿大，东濒大西洋，南至佛罗里达一带。英国将佛罗里达割让给了西班牙。和约还给美国人以在纽芬兰海域的捕鱼权。此外，和约要求大陆会议建议各州归还在战争期间没收的保王党人的财产。

最后一批英国士兵于 1783 年 11 月撤出了纽约市。

题 外 话

从现代观点看，美国革命战争的规模很小。据史学家估计，美方在战斗中共死伤一万五千多人。战争中由于各种原因死亡的美方军事人员总数也不过二万五千余人。英方军事人员死亡总数约一万人。历次重要战斗中各方参战人数往往不过数千人。而 20 世纪的一场战役，动辄便有数万，乃至数十万人参战。但考虑到当时十三个殖民地的总人口不过二百五十万，这场战争的影响是相当大的。

另外，不应忽视，法国的参战对美国革命战争的胜利起到至关重要的作用。有人认为，没有法国的援助，美国人在 1778 年就不得不放弃独立。

19. Patrick Henry

帕 特 里 克·亨 利

Patrick Henry (1736-1799) was a famous statesman, lawyer, and orator at the time of the Revolutionary War in America. He is remem-

帕特里克·亨利 (1736-1799) 是独立战争期间著名政治家、律师和演说家。他的名言"不自由，毋宁

bered most for the words, "Give me liberty or give me death."

Henry was born in Hanover County, Virginia. He attended a local school for only a short time, but was taught by his father, who had a good education. As a young man, Henry wanted to become a businessman, but he did not do well in business. He then studied law and became a very successful lawyer.

1764, Henry was elected to the Virginia House of Burgesses. As one of the central figures of the American Revolution, Patrick Henry earned fame for his patriotic speeches. His speech against the Stamp Act in 1765 is one of his greatest public speeches. In it, he warned, "Caesar had his Brutus, Charles the First his Cromwell, and George the Third... may profit by their example." In answer to cries of treason from conservative members, Henry replied, "If this be treason, make the most of it."

Henry was a Virginia delegate to the First Continental Congress in Philadelphia in 1774, where he urged joined actions by the colonists. In his most famous speech at the Virginia Convention in Richmond in 1775, he tried to persuade Virginia to get ready for war against the British. His speech ended with the now historic words, "Is life so dear, or peace so sweet, as to be purchased at the price of chains and slavery? Forbid it, Almighty God! I know not what course others may take; but as for me, give me liberty, or give me death!" Henry was elected as the first governor of Virginia during the Revolutionary War.

After the war, the Constitution was written to establish a government for the United States.

死"使他永远留在人们的记忆中。

亨利出生于弗吉尼亚的汉诺威县。他在地方学校上学时间不长，但他父亲是个受过良好教育的人，担任了他的教师。亨利年轻时曾想经商，但在这方面没有什么成就。于是他开始学习法律，终于成为一名非常成功的律师。

1764年，亨利被选入弗吉尼亚议会。他成为美国革命中心人物之一，以其爱国主义演说闻名。他在1765年就《印花税法》发表的演说是他最伟大的演说之一。在演说中，他警告说，"恺撒有他的布鲁图斯，查理一世有他的克伦威尔，乔治三世……或许应从他们的先例中汲取教训。"说到这里，保守议员们大呼："叛国言论！叛国言论！"对此，亨利答道："如果这就是叛国言论，那就尽量从中获益吧。"

亨利作为弗吉尼亚代表于1774年出席费城举行的第一届大陆会议。会上，他敦促各殖民地联合行动。1775年，在里士满举行的弗吉尼亚州州议会上，他试图劝说弗吉

帕特里克·亨利

Henry did not completely approve of the Constitution. He thought it was too strong and endangered the rights of individuals and states. Henry was one of the men who fought to see that the first 10 amendments to the Constitution, known as the Bill of Rights, were added to the Constitution.

题 外 话

帕特里克·亨利是革命元勋,但由于长期担任公职,革命后已负债累累。为生活计,他辞去公职,重操律师旧业。此后联邦政府多次向他提供高级职位,又有六次被选为弗吉尼亚州州长,均被他谢绝,充分显示了民主革命家的本色。

尼亚为抗英战争做好准备。他的讲演以如下的不朽名句结束:"难道生命竟如此珍贵,和平竟如此美好,值得用枷锁和奴役来换取? 全能的上帝啊,制止此举! 我不知他人该做何选择,但对于我,不自由,毋宁死!"在革命战争期间,亨利被选举为首任弗吉尼亚州州长。

战后,为建立美国政府,制宪会议开始起草宪法。他对宪法不完全赞同。他认为宪法过于严苛,对个人和各州的权利构成威胁。由于亨利和其他人的共同努力,宪法的头 10 条修正案,即权利法案,写入了宪法。

20. Benjamin Franklin

本杰明·富兰克林

Benjamin Franklin (1706-1790) was the most famous American of the 18th century and one of the most famous and influential Americans who have ever lived. He was a printer, author, diplomat, philosopher, scientist, and a greatest statesman, and he did the most to make the United States a free and independent country. He was the only person who signed all four of the most important documents in American history: the Declaration of Independence, the Treaty of Alliance with France, the Treaty of Peace with Great Britain, and the Constitution of the United States. Franklin's services as a diplomat in France helped greatly in winning the Revolutionary War. Many historians consider him the ablest and most successful diplo-

本杰明·富兰克林 (1706-1790) 是 18 世纪最著名的美国人,也是有史以来最著名、影响最大的美国人之一。他是印刷工、作家、外交家、哲学家、科学家和伟大的政治家,在为美国成为独立、自由的国家的斗争中,他鞠躬尽瘁。美国历史上有四大重要文件:《独立宣言》、美法同盟条约、美英和约及美国宪法,富兰克林是签署了所有四个文件的唯一的美国人。他出使法国期间,为赢得革命战争的胜利做出了重要贡献。

富兰克林出生于波士顿,是一个有 17 个子女的大家庭中的第 15

mat that America has ever sent abroad.

Franklin was born in Boston, and was the 15th child in a family of 17 children. His father made candles and soap and did not earn very much. Franklin attended school in Boston for only two years. He proved himself excellent in reading and writing, but poor in arithmetic. At ten, Benjamin was taken into his father's business. Franklin did not care much for the trade of making candle. At 12, he began to learn from his brother James to be a printer. While working, Franklin devoted his spare time to reading. Through self-teaching, Franklin later made himself one of the best-educated persons of his time. After a while, he began to write articles for his brother's newspaper, and signed them "Mrs. Silence Dogood", and slipped them under the door of his brother's shop at night. James admired the articles, and printed several of them. But he refused to print any more when he discovered that Benjamin had written them. At 17, Benjamin left Boston and went to Philadelphia, which was then the largest city in the American Colonies. From 1723 to 1730, Franklin worked for various printers in Philadelphia and in London, England. When he was 24 he became an owner of a print shop. He began publishing *The Pennsylvania Gazette,* writing much of the material for this newspaper himself. His name gradually became known throughout the colonies, and *The Pennsylvania Gazette* developed into one of the most successful newspapers in the colonies.

But Franklin achieved even greater success with *Poor Richard's Almanac* than with his newspaper. He wrote the almanac under the name of Richard Saunders, an imaginary astronomer and

个孩子。他父亲制作蜡烛和肥皂，收入微薄。富兰克林只在波士顿上了两年学。他的学习成绩表明，他长于读书和写作，而拙于数学。10岁时，他开始帮父亲干活。富兰克林不大喜欢制作蜡烛的行业。12岁时，他开始跟哥哥詹姆斯学习印刷。在当印刷工期间，他的全部业余时间都用来读书。通过自学，富兰克林使自己成为当时最有学问的人之一。不久，他开始为哥哥印刷的报纸写文章，署名"悄然·行善夫人"，把写好的信在夜间通过门下的缝隙塞进哥哥的铺子里。詹姆斯赞赏这些文章，刊印了几篇。但当他发现文章是本杰明写的，就不再印了。17岁时，本杰明离开波士顿，去当时美洲殖民地最大的城市费城谋生。从1723年到1730年，富兰克林为费城和英国伦敦的印刷

本杰明·富兰克林

published it for every year from 1733 to 1758. Each issue was filled with wise and witty sayings of Poor Richard. Many of these sayings reflect Franklin's ideas on thrift, duty, hard work, and simplicity. "A penny saved is a penny earned." "Early to bed and early to rise, makes a man healthy, wealthy, and wise." "Up, Sluggard, and waste no

JOIN, or DIE.

1754 年春，法国与印第安战争爆发。富兰克林在自己的报纸上刊印"不联合即死亡"的漫画，用一条切成小段的蛇代表各殖民地，号召它们联合起来共同抗击法国与印第安人

life; in the grave will be sleeping enough." "God helps them that help themselves." "Little strokes fell great oaks." Other sayings reflect a shrewd understanding of human nature. "He's a fool that makes his doctor his heir." "He that falls in love with himself will have no rivals."

Franklin was interested in public affairs. In 1736, he became clerk of the Pennsylvania Assembly and the following year, he was appointed Philadelphia's postmaster. Then in 1753 he became

商做工。24 岁时，他自己开办了一家印刷所。他开始印行《宾夕法尼亚公报》，其中相当多的文章由自己亲笔撰写。他的名声逐渐传遍各殖民地，《宾夕法尼亚公报》也发展成殖民地最成功的报纸之一。

但富兰克林编写的《格言历书》（《穷理查历书》）则比他的报纸取得的成功更大。这部历书以一个虚构的天文学家理查·桑德斯的名义编写，从 1733 年到 1758 年每年出版一期。每期都刊登大量"穷理查"的格言和警句。许多格言警句反映了富兰克林本人关于节俭、责任、勤劳与朴素的见解。"省一分，挣一分。" "早睡觉、早起床，体健、财多、头清朗。" "懒虫快起床，莫误好时光，一日进坟墓，任你睡得香。" "自助者天助。" "小斧慢砍，巨树可断。"还有些格言警句反映了对人性的敏锐的观察，如"只有傻瓜才指定自己的医生为财产继承人。" "自恋者无情敌。"

富兰克林热心公共事业。1736 年，他开始担任宾夕法尼亚立法机关的秘书。次年，他出任费城邮政局长。1753 年升任殖民地邮政副总监。他恪尽职守，采取了多项急需

deputy postmaster general for all the colonies. He worked hard at this job, and introduced many needed reforms. Franklin engaged in many public projects to make Philadelphia a better city. In 1731 he founded what was probably the first public library in America. About this time, he organized the first fire company in that city and introduced methods for the improvement of street paving and lighting. He reformed the city police when he saw that criminals were getting away without punishment. He raised money to help build a city hospital, the Pennsylvania Hospital. Always interested in scientific studies, he founded the American Philosophical Society, an organization for the promotion of science, in 1743. The city had no school for higher education, so Franklin helped found the academy that grew into the University of Pennsylvania. As a result of projects such as these, Philadelphia became the most advanced city in the 13 colonies.

Franklin was one of the first persons in the world to experiment with electricity. He conducted his most famous electrical experiment at Philadelphia in 1752. He flew a homemade kite during a thunderstorm, and proved that lightning is electricity. Then he invented the lightning rod to save buildings from damage. He became the first scientist to study the movement of the Gulf Stream in the Atlantic Ocean. He spent much time charting its course and recording its temperature, speed, and depth. Franklin gave the world several other valuable inventions in addition to the lightning rod. He invented the most useful stove of his day, and bifocal eyeglasses, which allowed both reading and distant lenses to be set in a single frame. Franklin also showed Americans how to improve acid soil by us

的改革措施。富兰克林参与了多项旨在改善费城的公共建设工程。1731年，他创建了一座公共图书馆，这可能是当时美洲的头一座。大约在同时，他组建了费城的头一支消防队，并采用了先进的方法来改善街道的路面和照明。当他看到罪犯逍遥法外时，就着手改造城市的警察系统。他筹款协助建立了一家市立医院，即宾夕法尼亚医院。他毕生保持着对科学研究的兴趣，于1743年创建了美洲哲学会，一个旨在促进科学研究的组织。费城没有高等学府，于是富兰克林参与建立了一所学院，这所学院日后发展成为宾夕法尼亚大学。由于此类的工程建设，费城成为当时13个殖民地中最先进的城市。

富兰克林也是世界上最早对电进行实验的科学家之一。1752年，他在费城进行了最著名的电流实验。他在雷雨来临时放飞一只自制的风筝，证明天上的闪光即放电现象。然后他发明了避雷针，以保护建筑物，使之不致遭到雷击。他是研究大西洋湾流的头一位科学家。他花费大量的时间绘制湾流的路线，记录其温度、速度和深度。除避雷针外，富兰克林还为世人贡献了另外几项有价值的发明。他发明了当时热效最高的火炉和远近两用眼镜。他还教会美利坚人如何利用石灰来改良酸性土壤。富兰克林的科学研究为他获得多项最高荣誉。伦敦皇家学会选举他为会员，这对

ing lime. Franklin's scientific work won him many high honors. The Royal Society of London elected him to membership, a rare honor for a person living in the colonies.

In 1757, the Pennsylvania legislature sent Franklin to London to speak for the colony. Franklin remained in Great Britain during most of the next 15 years as a sort of unofficial ambassador and spokesman for the American point of view. Franklin also took part in the fight over the *Stamp Act*. In February 1766, Franklin appeared before the House of Commons to answer a series of 174 questions dealing with "taxation without representation". His knowledge of taxation problems impressed everyone, and his reputation grew throughout Europe.

About two weeks after the Revolutionary War began, the people of Philadelphia chose Franklin to serve in the Second Continental Congress. The Congress appointed him as postmaster general in 1775 because of his experience as a colonial postmaster.

Later, Franklin became one of the committee of five chosen to draft the Declaration of Independence. He was also one of the signers of that historic document. During the signing ceremonies, according to tradition, John Hancock warned his fellow delegates, "We must be unanimous; there must be no pulling different ways; we must all hang together." "Yes," Franklin replied, "we must indeed all hang together, or assuredly we shall all hang separately."

Soon after the colonies declared their independence in July 1776, Franklin was sent to France as the American envoy, and he remained there until

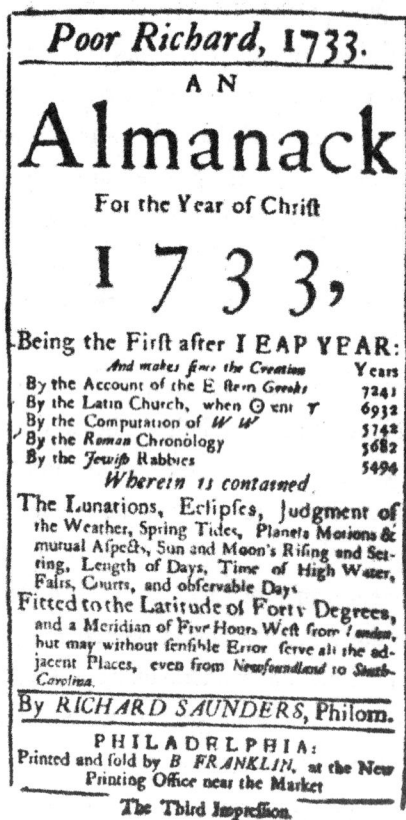

富兰克林的《格言历书》1733 年版封面

于殖民地居民来说是一项殊荣。

1757 年，宾夕法尼亚立法机构派遣富兰克林到伦敦为殖民地的利益申辩。在其后的 15 年中的大部分时间里，他以一种非正式大使和美利坚观点发言人的身份驻留英国。富兰克林也参加了反对《印花税法》的斗争。1766 年 2 月，富兰克林前往英国议会下院，回答有关"没有代表而课税"的 174 项质询。他在税务方面的知识给每个人都留下了深刻印象，他在全欧洲的名望

1785. He was very popular among the French people, who were charmed by his kindness, his simple dress and manner, his wise and witty sayings, and his tact and courtesy in greeting the nobility and common people alike. When the Americans won a victory at Saratoga, the French agreed to a treaty of alliance. Franklin then made arrangement for the French to send their fleet to America. He managed to keep loans and gifts of money flowing to the United States. Many historians believe that without this aid the Americans could not have won their independence. In 1778, Franklin was appointed minister to France. He helped draft the Treaty of Paris, which ended the Revolutionary War.

In 1787, Pennsylvania sent the 81-year-old Franklin to the Constitutional Convention. The delegates met in Independence Hall and drafted the Constitution of the United States. In the same year, he was elected president of the first antislavery society in America. His last public act was to sign

也随之增高。

革命战争开始后大约两周，费城的民众推选富兰克林出席第二届大陆会议。由于他具有担任殖民地邮政副总监的经验，会议于1775年任命他为邮政总监。

后来，富兰克林成为受命起草《独立宣言》的委员会的5个成员之一。他也是这一历史文件的签署人之一。据说在签名仪式上，约翰·汉考克向代表们发出警告说："我们必须达成一致，万万不可各行其是，我们必须摞在一起。""没错，"富兰克林答道，"我们的确必须紧紧摞起来，不然则会个个吊起来。"

殖民地于1776年7月宣告独立后，富兰克林作为特使被派往法国，在法国驻留到1785年。他在法国人中大受欢迎。他的宽厚的天性、简朴的服装、淳朴的举止、机智的应答、会见贵族和平民时表现的老练和周到，无不使法国人着迷。美利坚人在萨拉托加打了胜仗后，法国同意签署盟约。富兰克林然后做出安排，促使法国派遣舰队开赴美国。他还设法使贷款和赠款源源不绝地流向美国。许多历史学家认为，没有法国的援助，美国人不可能赢得独立。1778

富兰克林在制作远近两用眼镜

an appeal to Congress urging the abolition of slavery. Franklin died in Philadelphia in 1790, at the age of 84. He left $5,000 each to Boston and Philadelphia, to be used for public works.

题外话

富兰克林在巴黎时不戴假发，而戴美国农夫的皮帽。法国妇女对他的风度大加赞赏，模仿他那顶皮帽的式样把头发做得高高的，称之为"富兰克林发式"。此发式竟流行一时。

富兰克林是美国"国父"级的人物，美钞上和美国邮票上都有他的肖像。他在很多领域里都有建树。但他在遗嘱中却自称"印刷工"。

年，富兰克林被任命为驻法公使。他参与起草了巴黎和约，结束了革命战争。

1787 年，宾夕法尼亚派遣 81 岁的富兰克林参加制宪会议。代表们聚会在独立宫，起草了美国宪法。

同年，他当选美国头一个废奴协会的会长。他为公共事业所做的最后一件事是签署一份请愿书递交国会，敦促废除奴隶制。富兰克林于 1790 年逝世于费城，享年 84 岁。他为波士顿和费城各留下 5000 美圆，用于市政工程的建设。

21. Thomas Paine

托马斯·佩因

Thomas Paine (1737-1809) was a famous writer on politics, whose writings greatly influenced the American colonies to fight against Great Britain for their independence in the Revolutionary War. He was also a famous figure in Paris during the French Revolution.

Paine was born in England. His family was poor, and he received little schooling. He began working at the age of 13, and moved through various jobs, and finally became a tax collector. He was dismissed in 1772 for publishing an article calling for an increase in wages as a means of reducing corruption in government service. In 1774, when he was poor and alone, Paine met Benjamin Franklin, who was then serving as a representative of the American colonies in Great Britain. Franklin advised him to go to America.

托马斯·佩因 (1737-1809) 是著名政论家，在革命战争期间，他的文章极大地鼓舞了美洲殖民地反抗英国、争取独立的斗志。佩因也是法国革命期间的著名人物。

佩因出生于英格兰。由于家境贫困，他只读过几年书。他 13 岁开始做工，干过各种活儿，最终当上税务员。1772 年，他发表一篇文章呼吁用提高薪酬的办法消除政府官员的腐败，因此被解雇。1774 年，当他生活窘迫求告无门时，遇见了本杰明·富兰克林，富兰克林当时担任美洲殖民地驻英国的代表。富兰克林劝他到美洲谋生。

到达费城后不久，佩因担任《宾夕法尼亚杂志》的编辑工作，

Soon after he arrived in Philadelphia, Paine became an editor on the *Pennsylvania Magazine*, and began working for the cause of independence. In 1776, he published his most famous work, the 50-page pamphlet, *Common Sense*. In a dramatic, rhetorical style, the pamphlet demanded complete independence from Great Britain and the establishment of a strong federal union. Paine blamed the king for the colonies' troubles. He argued that it was foolish for the vast continent of America to be controlled by the tiny island of England 3000 miles away. George Washington, Thomas Jefferson, and other colonial leaders read *Common Sense* with approval, as did hundreds of thousands of ordinary Americans. The pamphlet became a best seller, and within a few months reached a total of 120,000 copies.

Paine served for a time in the American army. Paine wrote a series of pamphlets between 1776 and 1783 entitled *The American Crisis*. His words inspired the Americans who were fighting in the revolution. George Washington ordered the pamphlets read aloud to his troops. Paine's bold, clear words encouraged the Continental Army during the darkest days of the war.

In 1777 the Second Continental Congress appointed Paine secretary of the Committee of Foreign

托马斯·佩因

开始为独立事业而斗争。1776 年，他发表了自己最著名的作品，一本 50 页的小册子，名为《常识》。《常识》以激切而雄辩的言辞鼓吹完全脱离英国而独立，建立一个强大的联邦。佩因将殖民地的冲突归罪于国王。他试图说服人们，庞大的美洲大陆竟然让一个 3000 英里外的小小的岛屿统治，是一桩荒谬的事。乔治·华盛顿、托马斯·杰斐逊及其他殖民地领袖读过《常识》后，与千千万万的普通美利坚人一样，无不表示赞同。小册子成了畅销书，数月之内印数共达 120000 册。

佩因一度在美军中服役。他在 1776 年至 1783 年间写了一系列的小册子，冠名为《美国危机》。他的言论激发了美国人的斗志。乔治·华盛顿下令将这些小册子在军队里朗读。佩因的泼辣而明晰的词句鼓起了大陆军的士气，使他们度过了战争中最艰苦的岁月。

1777 年，第二届大陆会议任命佩因为外交事务委员会秘书。1779 年，他丢掉了这一职务，担任宾夕法尼亚立法机构的秘书。他关心美国军队的艰苦生活，建立基金来资助穷困的士兵，虽然他本人收入微薄。

1787 年佩因前往法国，继而到了英国。1791 和 1792 年旅居英国期间，他发表了《人的权利》。曾有不少人撰文驳斥英国政治

Affairs. In 1779, he lost the post and then became clerk of the Pennsylvania legislature. He was concerned for the difficult lives of American troops, and established a fund to support needy soldiers, though he himself had a meagre income.

Paine went to France in 1787 and then to England. While in England in 1791 and 1792, he published *Rights of Man*. It was most famous of all replies to the attack on the French Revolution by the British statesman Edmund Burke. A million and a half copies were sold in England alone before the book was banned by the British government. Paine was tried for treason and had to run away to France.

The National Assembly of France made Paine a French citizen. He became a member of the National Convention. But because he did not believe that the French king should be killed, he offended the leader of the radical revolutionists, and he was imprisoned for more than 10 months. While in prison, Paine worked on *Age of Reason*. The work stated his views on religion, and many people called it the "atheist's Bible". Although Paine believed in God, he disagreed with many accepted church teachings and objected to organized religion and saw the established churches of Europe as obstacles to social change. His views on religion made him one of the most hated men of his time.

In 1802 Paine returned to the United States with the help of President Thomas Jefferson. Paine found that the American people remembered him more for his opinions on religion than for his services to the Independence of Ameria. During his last years, Paine was poor, ill, and neglected by society. He died in New York City.

家埃德蒙·伯克对法国革命的攻击,《人的权利》是最著名的一篇。仅在英国,在被政府查禁之前,这本书已销售了150万册。佩因以叛国罪受审,不得不逃往法国。

法国国民议会授予佩因法国公民的身份,后来他当选了国民公会议员。但是他认为法国国王不应被处决,这一观点激怒了革命激进派的领袖,使他被囚禁长达10个月之久。佩恩在狱中写了《理性时代》,阐述自己的宗教观点。许多人称之为"无神论者的圣经"。虽然佩因相信上帝,但他对教会的许多正统教条持有异议,反对宗教组织,视欧洲的官方教会为社会变革的障碍。他的宗教观点使他成为当时人们最痛恨的人之一。

1802年,在托马斯·杰斐逊总统的斡旋下,佩因返回美国。他发现美国人已记不清他对美国独立的贡献,却念念不忘他的宗教观点。佩因晚年贫病交加,被社会遗忘。他死于纽约市。

🔘 题 外 话

佩因死后,美国报界评论说他"做过一些好事,也干了许多坏事。"当时美国的宗教势力很强,容不下一个哪怕对宗教表示怀疑的人。到了20世纪,人们开始对他重新评价,许多历史学家认为,佩恩是个只知奉献,不图回报的民主革命家;他对宗教的开明理性态度,使他可与法国的伏尔泰比肩。

CHAPTER FIVE
Forming a New Government
新政府的建立

1. Postwar Problems

战后问题

At the end of the Revolutionary War, the new United States was not a truly unified country. The Article of the Confederation gave to Congress only a limited number of powers for governing the nation. People generally felt a greater loyalty to their state than to the nation as a whole.

The new nation faced severe economic problems. To carry on the war, Congress had borrowed a large amount of money from Americans and foreign countries. But since the federal government could not collect taxes, it was unable to pay its debts. The government even had no means for raising money to defend the nation. Foreign countries refused to make trade agreements with the United States because the federal government had no power to enforce such agreements. The states had also to enforce law and order, deal with Indian tribes and negotiate with other governments. These and other problems the new nation faced demanded a strong federal government.

革命战争结束时，新的美国还不是一个真正统一的国家。邦联条例只赋予大陆会议以有限的权力治理国家。人们普遍更忠于自己所在的州，而不是整个国家。

新国家面临着严重的经济问题。为了进行战争，大陆会议曾向美国人和外国大量贷款。然而，由于联邦政府无权征税，因而无法还债。政府甚至无法筹集资金组织防务。外国拒绝与美国签署贸易协定，因为联邦政府无权保障协定的实施。美国还须实施法律、维持秩序，与印第安部落交涉，与外国政府谈判。新国家面对的诸如此类的问题都需要一个强有力的联邦政府。

2. The Constitutional Convention

制宪会议

Early in 1787, delegates from most of the states met in Philadelphia's Independence Hall to revise the Article of the Confederation. This conference later became known as the *Constitutional Convention*. George Washington was elected president of the convention, and other important members included James Madison of Virginia, Alexander Hamilton of New York, and Benjamin Franklin of Pennsylvania.

Although the original purpose of the meeting was to revise the Article of the Confederation, the delegates soon abandoned this idea. Instead, they agreed to write an entirely new Constitution.

Among the delegates, there were two different ideas of how the various states should be represented in the national legislature. Large states favoured the Virginia Plan, which proposed that the number of representatives of each state should be based on its population. Small states, on the other hand, supported the New Jersey Plan, which insisted that each state should have the same number of representatives. This problem was solved by a compromise, which set up a Congress consisting of two houses. In the upper house, the *Senate*, each state would have two senators. In the lower house, the *House of Representatives*, each state would be represented on the basis of population.

The Constitution became the basic law of the United States and united the country together into a solid political unit. The authors of the Con-

1787 年初，大多数州的代表聚会费城的独立厅，修改邦联条例。这次会议史称"制宪会议"。乔治·华盛顿当选会议主席，重要代表有弗吉尼亚州的詹姆斯·麦迪逊、纽约州的亚历山大·汉密尔顿、宾夕法尼亚州的本杰明·富兰克林等人。

会议最初的目的是修改邦联条例，但代表们很快放弃了这一想法。他们一致同意起草一部全新的宪法。

至于如何分配各州参加立法会议的名额，代表们持有两种不同的意见。人口较多的州赞成弗吉尼亚的提案，建议按人口数量的比例分配名额。人口较少的州，则赞同新泽西州的提案，坚持各州代表人数应相等。这一问题通过妥协解决了。按照妥协方案，建立包括两院的国会。在上院，即参议院，每州各有两名参议员。在下院，即众议院，代表名额按人口数量的比例分配。

宪法成为美国的基本法，它将国家团结起来，形成一个坚固的政治实体。宪法的制定者们，与建国

stitution, along with other early leaders such as Thomas Jefferson of Virginia, won lasting fame as the Founding Fathers of the United States.

初期的其他领袖人物，如弗吉尼亚的托马斯·杰斐逊等人，都以美国建国之父的美名流芳百世。

3. Basic Ideas of the Constitution

宪法的基本原则

The introduction to the *Constitution of the United States* begins with these words: "We the People of the United States..." This phrase makes it clear that the people are the most important part of the government. The government is to be run for and by the people. The purposes of the new government are "to form a more perfect union, establish justice, insure domestic tranquility, provide for the common defence, promote the general welfare, and secure the blessings of liberty."

Separation of powers The writers of the Constitution divided the government into three independent branches: the legislative, the executive, and the judicial. This division of the government into three branches is called the separation of powers.

The legislative branch is Congress, which represents the people and makes the laws. Congress has two houses. The upper one, the Senate, consists of two members from each state. The present membership is 100, since there are now 50 states. In the lower house, the House of Representatives, each state is represented according to population. The present membership is fixed by law at 435. The executive branch of the

美利坚合众国宪法的序言开篇就说："我们，合众国的人民……"这一词组表明，人民是政府的最重要部分。政府将为人民而建，并且由人民控制。建立新政府的目的是"组成一个更完善的联邦，树立正义，保障国内的安宁，建立共同的国防，增进全民福利并确保安享自由带来的幸福。"

三权分立　宪法的制定者将政府分成三个独立的机构：立法机构、行政机构和司法机构。这一制度称为"三权分立"。

立法机构是国会，它代表人民，制定法律。国会由两院组成。上议院，即参议院，由每州两名参议员组成。由于目前（21世纪）美国有50个州，参议员共有100人。在下议院，即众议院，各州众议员的人数由该州的人口决定。目前的法定众议员人数为435人。行政机构贯彻法律。这一机构的首长是总统，总统由一位副总统和数位行政助手协助执政。司法机构解释法律。它由联邦法院系统和法官构成。美国最高法院是联邦法庭的最

national government carries out the laws. The head of the branch is the President, who is helped by a vice president and many executive assistants. The judicial branch interprets the laws. It is made up of a system of federal courts and judges. The Supreme Court of the United States is the highest court in the nation. At present, the Supreme Court has nine justices, one of whom serves as chief justice.

Checks and balances Checks and balances are limitations on the power of any branch of government, with each branch having some control over the actions of the others. The United States system of government is based on a set of checks and balances, designed to prevent one official or branch of government from becoming too powerful. For example, the president can veto a bill passed by Congress. But the veto power is balanced by Congress's power to pass the bill again, if two-thirds of both the Senate and the House of Representatives vote for the bill. The president can check the courts by appointing federal judges, but such appointments must be approved by the Senate. The federal courts can check both the president and the Congress by declaring orders of the president and acts of Congress contrary to the Constitution. The House of Representatives has the power to draw up charges of impeachment against officials of the national government, even the president. If a majority of representatives thinks that the president or some other federal officials is guilty of a crime against the United States, Congress can remove him from office after the Senate sits as a court to hear the charges against the accused official.

高权力机构。最高法院目前有9名大法官，其中一名为首席大法官。

制约与平衡　制约与平衡是对某一政府分支机构权力的限制。每一机构都具有对其他分支机构形成制约的能力。美国政府系统就建立在一整套的制约与平衡的基础之上，旨在防止某一官员或某一政府分支机构权力过大。例如，总统有权否决国会通过的法案。但如果参议院和众议院各有三分之二的多数票再次通过该法案，总统的否决便被推翻。总统可以通过任命联邦大法官制约法院，但他的任命须通过参议院的批准。联邦法院可以制约总统和国会，手段是宣布总统的法令和国会的法案违反宪法。众议院有权提出对联邦政府官员乃至总统的弹劾。如果大多数众议员认为总统或其他联邦官员犯有危害美国的罪行，在参议院审理弹劾案之后，国会有权罢免该官员的公职。

制约与平衡也在国会两院之间发挥作用。一项法案必须在两院均通过之后才能成为法律。

联邦制　联邦制是一种中央政府和地方政府分权的体制。在美国，宪法规定权力分属于联邦政府和州政府。此外，州政府也与下属的行政区，如县、市和镇分享权力。

人权法案　1788年通过的美国宪法未能保障充分的个人权利。为限制中央政府、保障个人权利，10条宪法修正案，总称"人权法案"增添到宪法中，于1791年12月15

The system of checks and balances also works between the two houses of Congress. A bill must be passed by both houses before it becomes law.

Federalism Federalism is a system in which political power is shared by a central (national) government and smaller governmental units. In the United States, the Constitution divides powers between the national and state governments. In addition, the states share and divide powers with such local political subdivisions as counties, cities, and towns.

The Bill of Rights The United States Constitution, adopted in 1788, did not guarantee enough individual rights. To restrict the central government and assure individual rights, 10 amendments that became known as the *Bill of Rights* were added to the document and became law on December 15, 1791. The First Amendment guarantees a number of basic individual rights, including freedom of religion, speech, and the press. It also guarantees people the right to hold peaceful meetings and to ask the government to correct wrongs. Other amendments guarantees people to bear arms, prohibit the quartering of troops in private homes, protect people against unreasonable searches of their property, and guarantee the rights to trial by jury.

日正式成为宪法的一部分。第一条修正案保障几项基本人权，包括宗教信仰自由、言论和出版自由。它还保障人民和平集会的权利、要求政府纠正错误的权利。其他修正案保障人民有权携带武器、拒绝在私宅中驻兵、财产不受无理搜查、享有陪审团审判的权利等。

人权法案

题外话

对美国宪法的制定影响最大的政治理论家是英国政治哲学家洛克和法国政治哲学家孟德斯鸠。洛克在其发表于 1690 年的《政府论（下篇）》里，主张政权属于人民，而非统治者。他认为政府的出现来自人们订立的契约。人们同意给政府以权力是为了保障自己的生命、自由和财产不受侵犯。实际上，《独立宣言》就引用了洛克的文字："政府之正当权力，是经被统治者的同意而产生的。"洛克是最早主张三权分立的人之一。孟德斯鸠在其发表于 1748 年的《论法的精神》里，进一步发展了三权分立的学说。

民主政府不一定非有三权分立或制约与平衡的机制不可。比如在英国、加拿大和澳大利亚，行政权在首相或总理和内阁手中，而他们又是立法机构，即议会的成员。此外，在某些民主国家如英国和瑞士，法院无权宣布议会的立法无效。

其实，美国宪法不但包括立法、行政和司法机关三者之间的制衡，也包括针对人民的制衡，因为宪法制订者认为老百姓并非总能明智地推选官员。因此，宪法规定总统由选举团间接选举。法官们也是任命的，而非选举出来的。参议员也曾由各州议会选出，1913 年宪法第 17 条修正案通过之后才由各州选民直选。另外，宪法使老百姓不可能在一次选举中一举推翻现有政府，因为政府官员的任期长短不一。众议员任期两年，总统四年，参议员六年。

4. Setting Up the Government   建立政府

In 1789, George Washington was elected to serve as the first president. John Adams, with the second highest number of votes, became vice president. The government went into operation in 1789, with its temporary capital in New York City. The capital was moved to Philadelphia in 1790, and to Washington, D.C., in 1800.

To help the president carry out his duties, the first Congress created three executive departments: States, Treasury, and War. Washington chose Alexander Hamilton to be secretary of the treasury, the most important post at the time. He named Thomas Jefferson secretary of state, and Henry Knox, secretary of war.

The most serious problems facing the new government were financial. The federal treasury

1789年，华盛顿当选美国第一位总统。约翰·亚当斯得票数仅次于华盛顿，任副总统。政府当年开始施政，临时首都设在纽约市。后来，首都于 1790 年迁往费城，再于 1800 年迁往华盛顿特区。

为帮助总统履行职责，头一届国会创立了三个行政部门：国务院、财政部和陆军部。华盛顿遴选亚历山大·汉密尔顿为财政部长，这是当时最重要的职务。他提名托马斯·杰斐逊为国务卿，亨利·诺克斯为陆军部长。

新政府面对的最严重问题是财政问题。国库空虚，而政府运转急需资金。汉密尔顿提出一系列的建

was empty, and money was needed to run the government. Hamilton made a series of proposals to solve these problems and to place the nation on a solid financial basis. His proposals included establishing a government-supported national bank to control government finances, creating a new series of gold, silver, and copper coins, raising money by a tax on the manufacture of whiskey, and encouraging industry. In spite of the opposition of Jefferson and his followers, most of his proposals were approved in Congress.

5. The First Political Parties

Washington and many other early American leaders opposed political parties. But in the 1790s, a political division appeared between those who favored a strong federal government and those who opposed it. This division led to the establishment of two political parties in the United States. Hamilton and his followers, chiefly Northerners, formed the *Federalist Party*. The party favored a strong federal government and the interests of commerce and manufacturing over agriculture. Hamilton also wanted the new government to be on a sound financial basis. He proposed tax increases and the establishment of a national bank. And in the conflicts between France and Britain, the Federalist Party generally backed Britain. Jefferson and his followers, chiefly Southerners, established the *Democratic-Republican Party*. The party wanted a weak central government and generally sided with France. The Democratic-Repub-

议解决这些问题，为国家打下了牢固的财政基础。他的建议包括建立政府支持的国家银行以控制政府的财政；铸造一系列新的金、银、铜币；通过向威士忌酒制造业征税以筹集资金；鼓励工业。尽管杰斐逊和他的追随者们反对这些建议，其中的大多数仍在国会获得通过。

政党的出现

华盛顿和许多其他建国初期的领袖们都反对党派之争。但在 18 世纪 90 年代，赞成与反对建立一个强大联邦政府的人还是分成了两个政治派别。这一分歧导致美国出现了两个政党。汉密尔顿及其追随者，主要是北方人，形成了联邦党。联邦党赞成建立一个强大的联邦政府，将工商业的利益置于农业之上。汉密尔顿还希望新政府有牢靠的财政支持。他建议增加税收，成立中央银行。在法英冲突中，联邦党一般支持英国。杰斐逊和他的追随者，主要是南方人，建立了民主-共和党。民主-共和党希望建立一个权力较小的中央政府，在法英冲突中一般站在法国一边。民主-共和党后来演变成今日的民主党。（但当今的共和党在 1854 年才成

lican Party later developed into the present-day Democratic Party. (The Republican Party of today, however, was not founded until 1854.)

立。)

6. Foreign Affairs

外交事务

The new government also faced problems in foreign affairs. During the French Revolution, France went to war against Britain and Spain in 1793. France had helped the Americans in the Revolutionary War, and it now expected the United States to help it in return. Public opinion in the United States divided over which side to support. The Democratic-Republicans, believing in the French Revolution, generally backed France, while the Federalists usually sided with the British. President Washington was deeply worried about the dangers of a war to the weak, young United States. He did not want the new nation to become involved. He declared that the United States would remain neutral in the European war. He rejected French demands for support, and also sent diplomats to Britain and Spain to settle disputes with those countries by signing treaties.

新政府在外交事务中也遇到了问题。在法国革命中，法国于1793年向英国和西班牙宣战。法国曾在美国的革命战争中帮助过美国人，现在希望美国反过来帮助法国。美国的舆论对于支持何方意见不一。民主－共和党相信法国革命的正义性，一般支持法国，而联邦党则通常站在英国一边。华盛顿总统对于年轻弱小的美国政府所面临的战争危险深感忧虑。他不愿让这个新成立的国家卷入战争。他宣布美国在欧洲战争中保持中立。他拒绝提供法国要求的支持，派使节到英国和西班牙签订条约，解决与这两个国家的争端。

7. George Washington

乔治·华盛顿

George Washington (1732-1799) played so important a role in shaping the United States that he has been given the name of the "Father of the Country". He fully deserves the name because

乔治·华盛顿 (1732-1799) 在塑造美国的过程中发挥了巨大作用，因而被誉为"国父"。他无愧于这一美称，首先因为他是建国初期的大

first, he was the greatest hero in its earliest days, the commander of the Continental Army that won American independence in the Revolutionary War; second, he served as president of the convention that wrote the United States Constitution; and third, he was elected the first President of the United States.

Washington was a handsome man, tall, strong, and dignified. In his description of Washington's character, Thomas Jefferson wrote: "He was, indeed, in every sense of the words, a wise, a good and a great man. ... On the whole, his character was, in its mass, perfect... it may truly be said, that never did nature and fortune combine more perfectly to make a man great..."Many stories have been told about Washington. Most are probably not true. Probably he did not chop down his father's cherry tree, then confess by saying: "I cannot tell a lie, Pa."But this story shows that people were willing to believe almost anything about his honesty.

Washington was born on a plantation in Westmoreland County, Virginia, on February 22, 1732. He went to school at the age of seven and left school when he was 14 or 15. His best subject was arithmetic. George also studied enough history and geography to know something of the outside world. But he never learned as much about literature, foreign languages, and history as did Thomas Jefferson or James Madison. They had the advantage of much more formal education.

At 15, Washington began studying to be a surveyor. Two years later, he was appointed official surveyor for Culpeper County. His work was well paid. During the next three years, Washing-

英雄,大陆军的统帅,在革命战争中为美国赢得了独立。其次,他担任了制定美国宪法的制宪会议主席。再次,他当选了美国的第一位总统。

华盛顿身材高大,相貌英俊而威严。托马斯·杰斐逊这样描写华盛顿的性格:"他是一个不折不扣的既聪明又善良的伟人。……大体而论,他的性格是完美无缺的。……可以说,自然和运气两者从未能够如此完美地结合在一起来创造一个伟人……"人们讲了有关华盛顿的许多故事。其中大多数可能是杜撰的。很可能他并没有真的砍倒他父亲的樱桃树,然后承认说,"爸爸,我不能撒谎。"但这个故事说明人们愿意相信任何有关他诚实无欺的传闻。

华盛顿于1732年2月22日出生于弗吉尼亚威斯特摩兰县的一个农场里。他七岁上学,上到十四五岁。他学得最好的科目是算术。乔治也学到了不少历史和地理知识,因而对外面的世界有所了解。但他学到的文学、外语和历史知识从来就没有托马斯·杰斐逊或詹姆斯·麦迪逊那么多。杰斐逊和麦迪逊受过更多的正规教育,因而在学识方面具有优势。

15岁那年,华盛顿开始学习土地测量技术。两年后,他被指派担任库佩帕县测量员,工作报酬不错。此后的三年里,他为到那里定居的新来的人测量土地,接到的活

ton made more and more surveys for new settlers. He carefully saved his money and bought a lot of land.

George Washington's military career began when he was 21 years old, in 1753. Robert Dinwiddie, the governor of Virginia appointed him lieutenant colonel of militia, to serve in the French and Indian War. In May 1754, Washington led a small band of colonial troops to the disputed territory to force the French at Fort Duquesne to withdraw. After they defeated a small group of French troops, Washington's men built a fort south of Fort Duquesne and named it Fort Necessity. In July the French attacked Fort Necessity. About 30 of Washington's men were killed and 70 wounded. When Washington had few men, little food, and no gunpowder, he agreed to surrender Fort Necessity. The French let him march out of the fort and return to Virginia with his men and guns. Washington felt discouraged, but the colonists did not blame the young officer for losing the fort. They praised Washington and his men for their bravery.

In 1759, Washington married Mrs. Martha Dandridge Custis, a widow of a rich Virginia planter. The couple's combined property made them one of the richest families in Virginia. They

儿越来越多。他把自己挣到的钱积攒起来，购买了大片土地。

华盛顿的军事生涯开始于1753年，当时他21岁。弗吉尼亚总督丁维第任命他为民兵中校，参加法国印第安人战争。1754年5月，华盛顿率领一小队殖民地军队前往有争议的地区，企图迫使杜克斯内堡的法国人撤退。华盛顿的部队打败了一小股法国部队后，在杜克斯内堡南面建立了一个堡垒，称之为尼塞斯提堡。7月，法国军队攻打尼塞斯提堡，华盛顿手下有30人阵亡，70人负伤。当手下士兵所剩无几，且食物匮乏、弹药用尽时，华盛顿同意投降，放弃尼塞斯提堡。法国人允许他离开要塞，带着士兵和武器返回弗吉尼亚。华盛顿感到很沮丧，但殖民者们没有因为要塞失守而责怪这位年轻的军官。他们赞扬华盛顿和他的士兵们，钦佩他们的勇气。

1759年，华盛顿同一个弗吉尼亚富裕的农场主的寡妻玛莎·丹德里奇·卡斯提斯夫人结婚。夫妇两人的共有财

华盛顿像

settled down at Mount Vernon, where Washington worked again as a farmer.

Washington had been elected to the House of Burgesses in 1758, and during the next 15 years, he was reelected time and again to the legislature. His experience in a representative government gave him patience in later years when he had to deal with Congress during the Revolutionary War and as President.

Washington's peaceful life as a farmer ended when the American colonists began to protest against the taxes placed on them by Great Britain. He was on the side of the colonists. At first he was not in favour of demanding American independence, but merely wanted fair treatment of the colonists. Soon he realized that the colonies must fight for their freedom. In 1774, he was elected to the First Continental Congress. The next year, after the Battles of Lexington and Concord had began the Revolutionary war, the Second Continental Congress appointed him commander in chief of the Continental army.

Throughout the war, Washington had lots of difficulties. He seldom commanded more than 15,000 troops at any one time. He had to put up with many incompetent officers. His troops were poorly trained and lacked food, clothing, ammunition, and other supplies through out the war. His soldiers often went home without permission. His

产使他们成为弗吉尼亚最富裕的家庭之一。他们在沃农山庄定居下来，华盛顿重新开始务农。

华盛顿于1758年入选弗吉尼亚移民议会，在其后的15年里，他屡次当选这一立法机构的议员。他在代议制政府里积累的经验使他在后来的革命战争和他出任总统的年代里，当他不得不与大陆会议和国会打交道时，能够不急不躁，充满耐心。

当美利坚的殖民者们开始抗议英国向他们征税时，华盛顿的平静的务农生活结束了。他站在殖民者一边。起初，他不赞成美利坚独立的主张，只是希望殖民者们能够得到公正的对待。不久，他意识到殖民地必须用武力争取自由。1774年，他被选入第一届大陆会议。翌年，列克星敦与康科德的战斗打响，革命战争爆发。第二届大陆会议任命他为大陆军总司令。

在整个战争期间，华盛顿面对重重困难。他从来没有同时指挥过兵力超过15000人的军队。他不得

华盛顿夫人玛莎·华盛顿

army needed the help of the militia that was made up of storekeepers, farmers, and other private citizens. But militia was unreliable, and his army was defeated many times because the militia turned and ran when they saw British soldiers.

However, Washington knew from his experience in the French and Indian War that the British army had its weaknesses and could be beaten. His personal courage, his skillful use of Indian fighting methods, and his unwillingness to stop fighting in the face of defeats, eventually wore down the British strength and spirit.

When the Treaty of Paris had been signed and the war was over, Washington, now 51 years old, returned to Mount Vernon. For the next five years, he lived the peaceful and quiet life of a Virginia planter.

In 1786, some political leaders, including Washington, realized that Congress could not govern the new nation well under the weak Articles of Confederation. They agreed to call a meeting in 1787 to make changes in the Articles. Washington was elected to head the Virginia delegates. When the Constitutional Convention opened in May the delegates elected Washington president of the convention.

The delegates agreed to write an entirely new Constitution to replace the Articles. But they found it hard to agree on what kind of government they wanted. Debate went on throughout the summer. As president, Washington took little part in the debates, but helped hold the convention together. The convention finally reached agreement in September.

By the summer of 1788, enough states had

不容忍许多不称职的军官的作为。他的部队缺乏训练，始终没有足够的食物、衣服、弹药和其他装备。士兵们经常开小差。他的部队需要民兵的支持，而民兵则是由小商贩、农夫和其他老百姓拼凑而成，很不可靠。他的军队屡次战败，因为民兵一见到英军就临阵逃脱。

然而，华盛顿亲身经历过法国印第安战争，他知道英国军队有其弱点，是可以打败的。他个人的勇气、印第安式战术的熟练运用、面对失败百折不挠的毅力，最终消磨掉了英国人的兵力和士气。

在巴黎和约的签署结束战争后，51 岁的华盛顿返回沃农山庄。此后 5 年里，他过着一个弗吉尼亚农场主的平静的生活。

1786 年，一些政治领袖们，包括华盛顿本人，意识到国会无法通过软弱的《邦联条例》治理这个新成立的国家。他们一致赞同于 1787 年召开会议修改《邦联条例》。华盛顿被推选为弗吉尼亚代表团团长。制宪会议 5 月召开时，代表们推选华盛顿为制宪会议主席。

代表们同意起草一部全新的宪法替代《邦联条例》。但代表们在应建立一个什么样的政府这一问题上难以达成一致。辩论持续了一夏天。作为主席，华盛顿没有参加辩论，但由于他和其他人努力维系着代表们的团结，制宪会议才没有因分歧而破裂。制宪会议最终于 9 月达成共识。

approved the Constitution. Now a new government could be established. Throughout the country, people took it for granted that Washington would be chosen as the first President. In February 1789, Washington was elected President with a total of 69 votes from the 69 electors, without a single vote against him. John Adams was elected Vice President with 34 votes.

Washington believed in a strong government and in a united country. The new nation had many problems, and he dealt with each of them with courage and wisdom. He chose the members of his cabinet carefully, selecting the ablest, most respected men of the country. Among these cabinet members were Secretary of State Thomas Jefferson and Secretary of the Treasury Alexander Hamilton. Washington allowed his department heads to act independently. He did not try to prevent Hamilton, Jefferson, or the others from influencing Congress.

Washington was disturbed as he saw that Jefferson and Hamilton were disagreeing more and more with each other. Washington attempted to favor neither party. He tried to bring Hamilton and Jefferson into agreement and tried to discourage the growth of political parties.

In 1792, Washington began to make plans for retirement. But all political leaders asked him to continue as President. The following year, Washington again was elected President with the largest number of votes possible—132. Adams received 77 votes and was again the runner-up and Vice President.

During his second term, Washington was disappointed by the development of two parties

1788 年夏，足够多数的州通过了宪法。现在可以建立新政府了。全国人民都认为，华盛顿当选第一位总统是自然而然的事。1789 年 2 月，华盛顿以 69 位选举人的 69 票当选，无一人投反对票。约翰·亚当斯以 34 票当选副总统。

华盛顿相信政府应当强大，国家应当统一。新国家面临众多困难，他以自己的勇气和智慧将它们一一克服。他对内阁成员的遴选斟酌再三，精心选出国内能力最强、威望最高的人。内阁成员中有国务卿托马斯·杰斐逊和财政部长亚历山大·汉密尔顿。华盛顿允许他的部长们自主行事。他也无意阻止汉密尔顿、杰斐逊或其他人影响国会。

华盛顿看到杰斐逊和汉密尔顿之间的分歧日益尖锐，深感不安。他无意偏袒任何一方。他试图从中斡旋，使汉密尔顿和杰斐逊达成一致。他试图遏制党派的形成。

1792 年，华盛顿开始计划退休。但所有的政治领袖们都要求他留任总统。翌年，华盛顿再次以全部 132 票当选，亚当斯仅随其后，获得 77 票，再次当选副总统。

在第二任里，华盛顿由于两党的形成和它们之间不断的争论而感到失望。他也由于民主－共和党强烈批评他的外交政策而感到痛心。他觉得自己日渐衰老，政治使他身心疲惫，于是决定不再担任第三任总统。1796 年 9 月，他在费城的报

and their continuous disputes. He also felt hurt when the Democratic-Republicans strongly criticized his foreign policy. Feeling growing old and tired of politics, Washington decided that he would not serve a third term. He published his Farewell Address in Philadelphia newspapers in September 1796. In the address, he advises his fellow citizens to cherish the republic they had so recently formed, to respect the Constitution, and to obey the nation's laws. He warns against the dangers of placing party policies ahead of the welfare of the country and the government as a whole. Washington also advises the nation to avoid entanglement in the political struggles of other countries, particularly in Europe.

In the election that followed, Adams became

纸上发表了告别辞。在这篇文章里，他劝告同胞们珍惜他们刚刚建立的共和国，尊重宪法，遵守国家的法律。他警告说，将党派之见置于国家和政府的利益之上是危险的。华盛顿还提议美国应避免卷入外国的，特别是欧洲国家的政治斗争。

在接下来的选举中，亚当斯当选总统，杰斐逊当选副总统。华盛顿心情愉快地回到沃农山庄，时年65岁。他再次将时间用来管理农场。但是他只享受了不到三年的退休生活。1799年12月14日清晨，华盛顿醒来时喉部发炎，病情很快恶化，当天去世，享年67岁。

人民欢迎当选总统华盛顿

President and Jefferson Vice President. Washington happily went home to Mount Vernon. Now he was 65. Again he devoted his time to the management of his farms. But he enjoyed only less than three years of retirement. Early on the morning of December 14, 1799, Washington awoke with an inflamed throat. His condition became worse quickly. He died on the same day, at the age of 67.

题外话

现存最常见的华盛顿的画像是美国画家吉尔伯特·斯图亚特的作品。画像上的华盛顿双唇紧闭，吻部突出。据说华盛顿的长相并非如此，其突出的吻部是由于装了不合适的假牙造成的。

华盛顿的人格风范是一切政治家的楷模。当国家需要他时，他当仁不让，承当重任，将生死置之度外；完成了国家赋予他的使命后，他便归守田园，毫无恋栈之心。他曾三度回家务农。第一次是在法国印第安人战争结束后，他立即辞去上校军衔，解甲归田。第二次是在革命战争结束后。当时军官们对大陆会议感到不满，一位名叫路易斯·尼古拉的上校于1782年5月代表众军官上书华盛顿，称愿意拥戴他称帝。华盛顿斥责了尼古拉，要他放弃这个可怕的念头。他知道大陆会议没有钱遣散将士们，他就利用自己在8年戎马生涯中建立起的全部威望，向将士们说明国家的困难，要他们回家去，做个好公民。那些曾跟随他浴血奋战的人服从了他的最后一道命令。他自己再次返回沃农山庄，重新开始与牛马为伍的田园生活。此时农庄由于8年缺少照料而需重建，但却缺乏资金。在战争最艰苦的几年里，华盛顿拒绝接受薪金和补贴，反而将自己的几乎全部私产都用来购买大陆会议发行的战争债券。华盛顿最后一次回家，是在担任两届总统之后。在一个到处还是国王、君主、世袭制的世界上，华盛顿再次毫不犹豫地选择了放弃权利，做一个普通公民。华盛顿人格风范常使人想起古罗马的政治家和统帅辛辛纳图斯。当国家出现危难时，辛辛纳图斯立即抛下犁锄，拿起武器，统帅千军；打败强敌后，立即挂冠而去，重操耕作旧业。华盛顿因而被誉为"美国的辛辛纳图斯"。

纵观华盛顿的军事生涯，不难注意到，无论是在法国印第安人战争中，还是在革命战争中，华盛顿指挥的战斗胜少负多。之所以如此，客观原因很多，但不容否认，也有主观原因，即华盛顿的指挥才能实在并不高明。但华盛顿的价值不在于打了多少胜仗。他的价值在于屡败屡战，使美国人的士气不泄，直至拖垮英军。这种百折不挠的意志，是那些长胜将军们所不及的。

8. Adams as President

亚当斯担任总统

When Washington decided not to run for a third term as President in 1796, John Adams succeeded him in 1797. Relations with France grew worse after the United States signed treaties with Britain and Spain. French warships began to seize American merchant ships bound for Britain.

1796年，华盛顿决定不再竞选第三届总统，约翰·亚当斯于翌年当选继任。美国与英国和西班牙签订条约后，与法国的关系恶化。法国军舰开始羁押驶往英国的美国商船。与华盛顿一样，亚当斯希望用

Adams, like Washington, hoped to use diplomacy to solve foreign problems. He sent a delegation to France to try to settle the difficulties. But three agents of the French government insulted the diplomats with dishonorable proposals, including a demand for a bribe. This event made Americans feel very angry and shocked. Adams then asked Congress for money to prepare for war and gave American ships permission to fire on French ships. From 1798 to 1800, the United States and France fought a kind of undeclared war on the sea. Seeing that it could not win in a war with the United States, the French government agreed to receive another American delegation. This time, the two countries obtained a peace settlement.

During the years when the relationship between the United States and France became strained, the Federalist Party denounced the Democratic-Republicans for their support of France. In 1798, the Federalist Congress and President Adams, who was also a Federalist, approved the *Alien and Sedition Acts*. These laws made it a crime for anyone to publish "false, scandalous, and malicious writing" about the government and its officials, and gave the president power to deport any foreigners considered dangerous to the nation's

外交手段解决这一对外问题。他派遣一个代表团到法国，试图解决争端。但法国政府的三个代表提出向法国官员行贿等不光彩的要求来侮辱美国代表。这一事件使美国人感到愤怒与震惊。亚当斯要求国会拨款备战，允许美国船只向法国船只开火。从1798年到1800年，美法两国在海上实际上已是不宣而战。法国政府发现不可能打败美国，于是同意接受另一个美国代表团。这一次，两国达成和解。

在美法关系紧张的两年里，联邦党谴责民主－共和党支持法国。1798年，联邦党人控制的国会和身为联邦党人的亚当斯总统通过了《客籍法和镇压叛乱法》。这几项法律规定，任何人发表"虚假的、诽谤性的及恶意的作品"攻击政府及其官员，都要被视为犯罪。这几项法律还规定总统有权驱逐被认为对国家和平与安全构成威胁的任何外籍人士。这几项法律的真实目的在于使民主－共和党人缄口，遏制他们日益增长的力量。但他们的企图未能成功。《客籍法和镇压叛乱法》反而引起全国的抗议，使联邦

约翰·亚当斯

peace and safety. The real purpose of the acts was to silence the Democratic-Republicans and check their growing power. The plan failed, however. Instead the acts aroused a nationwide protest and gave the Federalists the reputation as a party of oppression. The Kentucky and Virginia state legislatures passed resolutions to declare the *Alien and Sedition Acts* against the Constitution.

The *Alien and Sedition Acts* made the Federalists very unpopular. They were defeated in the election of 1800, and since then they never won a presidential election again. They disappeared from the political scene some 15 years later.

党背上了压制不同政见的恶名。肯塔基和弗吉尼亚两州的立法机关通过决议，宣布《客籍法和镇压叛乱法》违反宪法。

《客籍法和镇压叛乱法》使联邦党声名狼藉。他们在 1800 年的选举中失利，从此一蹶不振，再未能赢得总统选举。大约 15 年后，联邦党从政治舞台上消失。

题 外 话

美国人历来珍视言论自由，对政府压制来自民间批评的任何企图心存戒惧。联邦党的倒台就是明证。

9. Alexander Hamilton

亚历山大·汉密尔顿

Alexander Hamilton (1755 or 1757-1804) was one of the most important statesmen and political leaders during the early years of the United States. He was one of the boldest American political thinkers of his time. He supported the establishment of a strong federal government and believed that the U.S. Constitution should be interpreted loosely to give the government greater powers. He served as the nation's first secretary of the treasury. He also was a leader of the Federalist Party.

Hamilton was born in the West Indies. He was sent to school in North America in 1772 and later studied at King's College, which later became Columbia University. In 1776, during the Revolu-

亚历山大·汉密尔顿 (1755 或 1757-1804) 是美国建国之初最重要的国务活动家和政治领袖，是当时美国最有胆识的政治思想家。他赞成建立一个强大的联邦政府，主张对美国宪法做宽泛的解释，以便赋予政府更大的权力。他出任美国的第一任财政部长。他也是联邦党的领袖之一。

汉密尔顿出生于西印度群岛。1772 年他被送到北美上学，后来就读于国王学院，即后来的哥伦比亚大学。1776 年，在革命战争中，汉密尔顿入伍任纽约炮兵连的上尉。从 1777 年至 1781 年，他担任乔

tionary War, Hamilton joined the army and was appointed captain of a New York artillery company. From 1777 to 1781, he served as a secretary and close assistant of General George Washington.

After the war, Hamilton became a lawyer, and built a good practice in New York City. In 1782, he became a delegate from New York to the Congress of the Confederation, which had been set up by the Articles of Confederation in 1781, but had little power. He was a member of the convention that drafted the U.S. Constitution, and he did more than almost anyone else to get it accepted by the states.

Hamilton was appointed secretary of the treasury by President Washington in 1789. He proposed that Congress establish a national bank to handle finances, raise taxes, and place duties on certain imports in order to protect domestic industry. This proposal was strongly opposed. Secretary of State Thomas Jefferson and many others were afraid of a bank with so much power. They did not like strong Federal control. They did not like Hamilton's idea of developing manufacturing, because they thought that it would hurt farmers' interests. The conflict of the two groups led to the development of the nation's first two political parties. Hamilton led the Federalist Party, which favored a strong federal government. The Democratic-Republican Party, headed by Jefferson and Madison, wanted a weak national government. Congress partly followed Hamilton's suggestions. Today, scholars agree that Hamilton's ideas have had lasting importance. Some of them even think Hamilton the greatest secretary of the treasury in the history of the United States.

治·华盛顿将军的秘书和副官。

战后，汉密尔顿操律师业，在纽约市开办事务所，生意兴隆。1782年，他以纽约州代表的身份出席国会。这个国会是根据邦联条例于1781年建立的，但权力甚微。汉密尔顿是美国宪法制宪会议成员，为使宪法在各州通过，他做出的贡献比几乎所有其他人都要大。

1789年，华盛顿总统任命汉密尔顿为财政部长。汉密尔顿建议国会建立国有银行以控制财政，增加赋税，对某些进口货物征收关税以保护本国的工业。这一建议遭到强烈反对。国务卿托马斯·杰斐逊和许多别的人担心国有银行的权力过大。他们不喜欢联邦政府控制过强。他们也不愿接受汉密尔顿发展制造业的计划，他们认为这一计划会伤害农民的利益。两派的对立促成美国头两个政党的形成。汉密尔顿领导的联邦党赞成建立一个强大的联邦政府。而以杰斐逊和麦迪逊为首的民主—共和党则希望建立一个权力较小的中央政府。国会部分采纳了汉密尔顿的建议。今天，学者们一致认为，汉密尔顿的思想具有持久的重要意义。他们当中有人甚至认为汉密尔顿是美国历史上最伟大的财政部长。

1796年，汉密尔顿由于个人财政困难和国会日益增强的反对力量而辞去财政部长的职务。1797年，约翰·亚当斯继任总统。亚当斯也是联邦党人，但他与汉密尔顿在外

In 1795, Hamilton resigned as treasury secretary because of personal financial problems and increased opposition in Congress. In 1797, John Adams became President. Adams was also a Federalist, but he and Hamilton disagreed about foreign policy and other issues. Their disputes caused a split among the Federalists. As a result, the Democratic-Republican candidates, Thomas Jefferson and Aaron Burr, won the election of 1800. Jefferson and Burr received an equal number of electoral votes. Although a Federalist, Hamilton declared in favour of Jefferson. He felt that Burr was dangerous and not to be trusted. Hamilton's support influenced the House to choose Jefferson. Burr became Vice President.

In 1804, Burr ran for governor of New York. Hamilton spoke against Burr, calling him unreliable. When Burr was defeated in the election, he blamed Hamilton and challenged Hamilton to a duel with pistols. The two men fought on July 11, 1804. Hamilton was shot and died the next day. He was only 47.

交政策和其他问题上意见不和。他们的争执导致联邦党的分裂。结果，民主-共和党候选人托马斯·杰斐逊和艾伦·伯尔在 1800 年的选举中获胜。杰斐逊和伯尔获得同样的票数。汉密尔顿虽然是联邦党人，他决定支持杰斐逊。他觉得伯尔为人阴险，很不可靠。汉密尔顿的支持影响了下议院，使他们选择了杰斐逊。伯尔成为副总统。

1804 年，伯尔竞选纽约州州长。汉密尔顿公开表示反对伯尔，称之为不可靠的人。伯尔竞选失利，将此归咎于汉密尔顿，提出与汉密尔顿用手枪决斗。决斗在 1804 年 7 月 11 日举行，汉密尔顿中弹，次日死去。时年仅 47 岁。

亚历山大·汉密尔顿

10. Jefferson as President

杰斐逊担任总统

Public reaction to the *Alien and Sedition Acts* helped Thomas Jefferson win election as president in 1800. The Democratic-Republicans'

公众对《客籍法和镇压叛乱法》的反感帮助托马斯·杰斐逊在 1800 年的总统选举中获胜。民主-

victory ended 12 years of Federalist control of the government. Now the political power had shifted from wealthy merchants and landowners to small farmers and property owners. Jefferson took steps to reduce government expenses and the national debt. Jefferson believed that government should play the smallest possible role in national life, but found that as president he could not avoid actions that expanded the role of government.

During his presidency Jefferson took a number of important actions. The most important was the purchase of Louisiana, which almost doubled the size of the United States. Soon after the purchase, Jefferson sent Meriwether Lewis and William Clark to explore the newly acquired territory. The two brave men went to the headwaters of the Missouri River, then across the Rockies to the Pacific. In foreign affairs, Jefferson defeated the Barbary pirates of North Africa. These pirates attacked American trading ships, demanding tribute and ransom. In 1801, Tripoli opened war on American shipping because it wanted more tribute money. Jefferson sent the little United States Navy to blockade Tripoli's ports, and finally forced Tripoli for peace.

共和党的胜利结束了长达 12 年的联邦党对政府的控制。现在，政权从富商和地主手中转移到小农和小业主手中。杰斐逊采取措施缩减政府开支和国债。杰斐逊认为，政府在国民生活中的作用越小越好。但他发现，他作为总统无法避免采取行动，而这些行动实际上扩大了政府的职能。

担任总统期间，杰斐逊采取了几项重大行动。最重要的是购买路易斯安那，这一购地举措使美国的国土增加了一倍。购地之后，杰斐逊派遣梅里韦瑟·刘易斯和威廉·克拉克考察新近获得的领土。这两个勇敢的人跋涉到密苏里河的源头，然后跨越落基山脉，抵达太平洋。在外交事务中，杰斐逊打败了北非的柏柏里海盗。这些海盗攻击美国商船，勒索贡物和赎金。1801 年，的黎波里为得到更多的贡款向美国船只开战。杰斐逊派遣弱小的美国海军封锁了的黎波里的港口，迫使的黎波里求和。

托马斯·杰斐逊

11. The Louisiana Purchase

路易斯安那购地

The Louisiana Purchase is one of Jefferson's greatest achievements. The Louisiana Territory was a vast area in the middle of the present United States, reaching from the Mississippi River westward to the Rocky Mountains. France had first claimed this territory, but gave it to Spain at the end of the French and Indian War. But when Napoleon rose to power, he wanted to restore the French empire in America. In 1800, he forced Spain to return Louisiana to France. Jefferson viewed French control of Louisiana as a danger to the United States. In 1803, Jefferson decided to buy New Orleans from the French. He sent James Monroe to Paris to help the American minister, Robert Livingston, negotiate with France.

At the time, Napoleon's situation had changed. The French ruler had given up his dream of an empire in America, because he was busy preparing for a war against England and needed money badly. In addition, he lacked troops to defend the large Louisiana Territory. Napoleon surprised Livingston and Monroe by offering to sell all of Louisiana (about 2.1 million square kilometers), including New Orleans, for $15 million. Seizing the chance to buy this vast territory at so low a price, the Americans accepted Napoleon's offer. This purchase almost doubled the size of the United States.

路易斯安那购地一举是杰斐逊取得的最大成就。路易斯安那是位于现在的美国的中部的一片广阔地区，东起密西西比河，西至落基山脉。法国最先主张这片领土的主权，但在法国印第安战争末期将它割让给了西班牙。拿破仑上台后，他试图恢复美洲的法帝国。1800年，拿破仑迫使西班牙将路易斯安那归还法国。杰斐逊认为，法国对路易斯安那的控制是对美国安全的威胁。1803年，杰斐逊决定从法国人手中购买新奥尔良。他派遣詹姆斯·门罗到巴黎协助美国公使罗伯特·利文斯顿与法国谈判。

当时，拿破仑的地位已发生变化。这个法国统治者已放弃了在美洲建立帝国的迷梦，因为他正在忙于准备与英国作战，急需资金。此外，他也缺少保卫庞大路易斯安那领土的军队。出乎门罗和利文斯顿的预料，拿破仑提出出售全部路易斯安那（大约210万平方公里），包括新奥尔良在内，售价1500万美圆。能够以如此的低价购得如此庞大的领土，实在是机会难得。美国人抓住了这一机会，接受了拿破仑的出价。这次购地使美国的国土增加了一倍。

🔘 题 外 话

路易斯安那是一片广阔肥沃的平原，面积比中国东北和华北的总和还要大。杰斐逊捡了个大便宜，自然喜出望外。但他是个主张严格依照宪法办事的人，而宪法在字面上并未赋予政府购买如此大片领土的权力，所以这笔交易似乎与他本人的一贯主张相抵触。他有些心虚。但他还是敦促参议院批准购买土地的条约，结果获得通过。杰斐逊事后承认，为了这笔交易，他将宪法"引申到了几乎将它撕裂的地步"。

12. Lewis and Clark Expedition

刘易斯和克拉克远征

When the United States bought the Louisiana Territory from France in 1803, few Americans knew anything about this vast region. In 1804, Jefferson sent Meriwether Lewis and William Clark to explore the northern part of the Louisiana Purchase. The explorers set out in May 1804 near St. Louis and travelled up the Missouri River. With the help of an Indian woman named Sacajawea, they crossed the Rocky Mountains into the area known as the Oregon Country, and then followed the Columbia and other rivers to the Pacific coast. They returned to St. Louis with information about the climate, geography, plants, animals, mineral resources, and the native peoples of the West. Lewis and Clark traveled a total of about 12,800 kilometers on the expedition.

The success of the expedition enabled the United States to claim

当美国在 1803 年购买路易斯安那领土时，很少美国人对这片广阔的地区有所了解。1804 年，杰斐逊派遣梅里韦瑟·刘易斯和威廉·克拉克考察路易斯安那购地的北部。两个探险家于 1804 年 5 月从圣路易斯附近出发，溯密苏里河而上。他们靠着一个名叫萨卡加维亚的印第安妇女的协助，翻越落基山，进入俄勒冈地区，然后沿哥伦比亚河和其他河流顺流而下，直到太平洋。两人返回圣路易斯时，带回来关于西部的气候、地理、动植物、矿产及土著人的资料。刘易斯和克拉克远征的总长度达 12800 公里。

这次远征的成功使美国能够宣称自己拥有俄勒冈地区的主权，这

刘易斯和克拉克远征

the Oregon region, which included what are now the states of Oregon, Washington, and Idaho. This claim opened the way for colonists to settle in the West in the mid-19th century.

13. The Unsuccessful Embargo

Jefferson was re-elected president in 1804. During his second term, he met with problems that arose from the war between Great Britain and France. Both nations began seizing American merchant ships. The British also seized American sailors and forced them into British service.

Jefferson found it necessary to use government powers to protect American shipping. He knew that the United States was not prepared for war. In any case, it would have been hard to decide whether to fight France or Britain. Jefferson believed that American goods were so important to Britain and France that cutting off the supply would force them to respect U. S. right. At his request, Congress passed the *Embargo Act of 1807*, which made it illegal for American goods to be exported to foreign countries.

But the embargo failed to bring about any change in British or French policy. Worse, it was a disaster for the American economy. Ships lay idle, sailors and shipbuilders lost their jobs, and exports piled up in warehouses. The embargo also hurt farmers, who normally sold tobacco, rice, and cotton to Great Britain. Many Americans turned to

片地区包括现在的俄勒冈、华盛顿和爱达荷三州。美国的这一领土主张为 19 世纪中期殖民者们在西部的拓殖打开了大门。

失败的禁运

杰斐逊于 1804 年再次当选总统。在他的第二任期内，遇到英法战争引起的问题。英法两国都开始扣押美国商船。英国还强迫美国水手在英国军队里服役。

杰斐逊发现必须运用政府的力量来保障美国的海运。他知道美国尚未做好战争的准备。即使有准备，也难以决定是对法国开战还是对英国开战。杰斐逊认为，美国的货物对英法两国至关重要，如果中断供应，会迫使两国尊重美国的权利。应他的要求，国会通过《1807年禁运法案》，法案规定出口美国货物为非法。

然而禁运却未能丝毫改变英法两国的政策。更糟的是，禁运变成了美国经济的灾难。船只被弃置不用，水手和造船工人失去了工作，出口商品大量积压。禁运对农民也造成了伤害，他们通常要将烟草、稻米和棉花出售给英国。许多美国人开始违法私运货物。迫于巨大的公众压力，国会通过了另一项法案，允许美国商船向英法两国以外

smuggling. Public opposition became so great that Congress passed another act, permitting American ships to trade with any countries but Great Britain and France. But this plan also failed.

的国家进行贸易。但这一计划也失败了。

14. Thomas Jefferson

托马斯·杰斐逊

Thomas Jefferson (1743-1826) is best remembered as the author of the Declaration of Independence and as one of the greatest presidents of the United States. He is also regarded as a great political thinker and diplomat, and a founder of the Democratic Party. During his two terms as President, the United States doubled its area when he bought territory west of the Mississippi called the Louisiana Purchase.

Jefferson was a handsome man, tall, straight, and well-built, with a kindly, gentle face. He was a man of many talents. He became one of the leading American architects of his time and designed the Virginia Capitol, the University of Virginia, and his own home, Monticello. He also enjoyed playing the violin in chamber music concerts. In addition, Jefferson served as president of the American Philosophical Society, an organization that encouraged a wide range of scientific and intellectual research. His collection of more than 6,400 books became a major part of the Library of Congress.

Jefferson was a truly democratic statesman. He disliked pomp and ceremony, the so-called "upper-class" snobbery. He believed that only virtue and talents made one man better than anoth-

托马斯·杰斐逊 (1743-1826) 是《独立宣言》的作者和美国最伟大的总统之一，为此他深受人们的怀念。他也是一个伟大的政治思想家和外交家，民主党的创始人。在他的两任期间，由于购买了被称为路易斯安那购地的密西西比河以西地区，美国的国土增加了一倍。

杰斐逊长相英俊，身材高大挺拔，体格健壮，相貌和善。他博学多才。作为美国当时最著名的建筑家之一，他设计了弗吉尼亚国会大厦、弗吉尼亚大学和他自己的住宅蒙蒂切洛。他喜欢在室内乐音乐会上演奏小提琴。此外，杰斐逊担任美国哲学学会会长，该组织旨在鼓励科学及思想领域里的广泛研究。他的 6400 余册藏书成为国会图书馆建立时的主要馆藏。

杰斐逊是个真正的民主政治家。他不喜欢讲排场，不喜欢所谓"上流社会"的摆架子。他认为只有德行和才干才能区分人的高下。金钱、头衔和出身不能给人以德行和才干。他相信大多数人可以自己

er; money, title or birth could not give a man virtue or talents. He believed that the majority of people could govern themselves and wanted to keep the government simple and frugal. Jefferson loved liberty in every form, and he worked for freedom of speech, press, religion, and other civil liberties. He hated "every form of tyranny over the mind of man". Jefferson strongly supported the addition of the Bill of Rights to the Constitution of the United States.

Thomas Jefferson was born on April 13, 1743, in Albemarle County, western Virginia. His father, Peter Jefferson, was a prosperous Virginia planter and had 162 hectares farmland. Peter Jefferson held several public offices in the county. He was a justice of the peace, a magistrate, commander of the county militia and member of the House of Burgesses. Thomas' mother, Jane Randolph Jefferson, came from one of the oldest families in Virginia.

Thomas began his studies under tutors. In 1760, when he was 16, he entered the College of William and Mary at Williamsburg. His favorite subjects were mathematics, music, and architecture. After his graduation from college in 1762, Jefferson began to study law and became a lawyer in 1767. He practiced law with great success.

In 1770, Jefferson's home burned to the ground. Fortunately, he had already started to build another house that he himself had designed. As quickly as possible, the new big house was completed. It was called *Monticello*, which is in Italian for "little mountain". This was where Jefferson lived the rest of life, except for the periods when he was away on official business, and the eight years

管理自己，希望政府机构从简，节约开支。杰斐逊热爱一切形式的自由，致力于争取言论、出版、宗教信仰等各项公民的自由权。他痛恨"任何形式的压制思想自由的暴政"。他极力主张在美国宪法中加入"人权法案"。

托马斯·杰斐逊1743年4月13日出生于西弗吉尼亚的奥尔伯马尔县。他的父亲彼得·杰斐逊是个富裕的弗吉尼亚农场主，拥有162公顷农田。彼得·杰斐逊在县城里担任几项公职。他是治安官、县长、县民兵指挥官和移民议会议员。托马斯的母亲简·兰道尔夫·杰斐逊出身弗吉尼亚的一个名门世家。

托马斯起初在家庭教师的指导下学习。1760年，他16岁时进入威廉斯堡的威廉和玛丽学院学习。他擅长的功课是数学、音乐和建筑。1762年毕业后，杰斐逊开始学习法律，于1767年取得律师资格。他从事律师业后大获成功。

1770年，杰斐逊的住宅在一场火灾中被夷为平地。幸而，当时他亲手设计的一所新宅已经开工。这所新建的大宅子在尽可能短的时间里竣工了。新宅命名为"蒙蒂切洛"，在意大利语里即"小山"之意。此后，除了几次因公出差和住在华盛顿的白宫里的8年外，他毕生都住在蒙蒂切洛。

1772年，杰斐逊娶了一个年轻的寡妇玛莎·维尔斯·斯克尔顿为妻。据传说，杰斐逊由于喜爱音乐

when he lived in the White House in Washington.

In 1772, Jefferson married a young widow Martha Wayles Skelton. According to legend, Jefferson's love of music helped him win his bride. Two rival suitors came to call one day but left without a word when they saw the couple playing a duet on the harpsichord and violin. The Jeffersons had six children, but only two daughters lived to grow up. Mrs. Jefferson herself died in 1782, after only 10 years of marriage. Jefferson brought up his two daughters. He never remarried.

Jefferson was elected to the Virginia House of Burgesses in 1769 and served there until 1775. He proved to have a talent for writing laws and resolutions in clear and simple English.

After the Revolutionary War began in 1775, Jefferson represented Virginia at the Second Continental Congress and took a leading part in it. The following year, Congress appointed a committee to draw up a declaration of independence. The committee asked Jefferson to prepare the draft and approved it with few changes. Congress adopted it on July 4. The Declaration of Independence remains Jefferson's best-known work. It is written so well

而在求婚者里占了上风。一天，另外两个求婚者来见玛莎，却看见玛莎和杰斐逊正在用拨弦古钢琴和小提琴表演二重奏。两人无话可说，快快离去。杰斐逊夫妇有6个子女，但只有两个女儿长大成人。1782年，两人结婚10年后，杰斐逊夫人去世。杰斐逊将两个女儿抚养大。他没有再婚。

杰斐逊于1769年被选入弗吉尼亚移民议会，担任议员直至1775年。他显示出具有用简明的英语起草法律和决议的才能。

革命战争于1775年开始后，杰斐逊代表弗吉尼亚出席第二届大陆会议，并在其中扮演了重要角色。第二年，大陆会议任命了一个委员会起草一个独立宣言。委员会指派杰斐逊执笔撰写草稿，然后对草稿略加更动，在委员会内部获得通过。7月4日又在大陆会议获得通过。《独立宣言》是杰斐逊最著名的作品。其出色的文笔使其中许多段落铭记在人们的心中，不断地被人们引用。

1776年秋，杰斐逊辞去大陆会议的职务，重返弗吉尼亚议会。他决定投身于社会改革。当时，少数豪门占据着弗吉尼亚的大部分土地，由于只有拥有土地的人才有选举权，这些豪门控制了政府。通过杰斐逊的努力，旧的法律得到更新，迫使大地产分

杰斐逊亲手设计的住宅蒙蒂切洛

that many parts of it has been remembered and quoted by Americans ever since.

In September 1776, Jefferson resigned from Congress and returned to the Virginia House of Delegates. He decided to devote himself to social reform. At the time, a few wealthy families owned most of the land in Virginia and, because only people who owned land could vote, these families controlled the government. By his efforts the old laws were changed to break up large estates so that more people could own land. This reform led to greater democracy in the state. Even more important were Jefferson's bills to establish religious freedom and to ensure the separation of church and state. His bills were adopted and Virginia ended the Anglican Church's position as a state church.

Jefferson had many slaves, but he believed slavery was morally wrong. He described it as a "great political and moral evil". He took no immediate actions against the evil system because he felt the people of his state were not ready for such a major step. He hoped the younger generation would end this system.

Jefferson was elected to Congress in 1783. In 1785, he succeeded Franklin as the U.S. diplomatic representative to France. During Jefferson's stay in France, American statesmen at home met in a convention in 1787 and drew up what became the Constitution of the United States. Jefferson's friend James Madison sent him a draft, and asked for his opinion on it. Based on Jefferson's suggestions, Madison proposed a Bill of Rights, consisting of the first ten amendments, which was added to the Constitution in 1791.

When Jefferson returned to the United States,

割开来，使更多的人能够拥有地产。这一改革使弗吉尼亚州享有更大的民主。更为重要的是杰斐逊制订了建立宗教自由和政教分离的法案。他的法案获得通过，圣公会在弗吉尼亚从此不再享有国教特权。

杰斐逊拥有不少奴隶，但他认为奴隶制是违背道德的。他将奴隶制说成是"政治和道德上的巨大罪恶"。他没有立即采取行动反对这一罪恶制度，因为他觉得对于这样的重大举措，弗吉尼亚的人民尚未做好准备。他希望年轻的一代人将结束奴隶制。

杰斐逊于1783年被选入国会。1785年，他接替富兰克林任美国驻法国使节。在他驻法期间，美国国内的政治家们于1787年召开会议，制订美国宪法。杰斐逊的朋友詹姆斯·麦迪逊送给他一份草稿，征求他的意见。根据杰斐逊的建议，麦迪逊提出了"人权法案"，共有10条修正案，于1791年加入宪法中。

杰斐逊返回美国后，华盛顿总统请求他出任国务卿。杰斐逊虽然渴望回到家乡过清静的生活，他还是在总统的劝说下接受了这个职务。但就任后不久便与财政部长亚历山大·汉密尔顿发生了冲突。汉密尔顿对民主持怀疑态度，主张建立一个强有力的政府，由受过教育的和有财产的人控制。杰斐逊则信任小农和劳工，不赞同汉密尔顿的主张。两人的政见分歧促使两个最早的政党逐步形成。联邦党接受汉

President Washington asked him to become secretary of state. Although Jefferson was eager to return to private life, he accepted the post at the president's urging. But he soon came into conflict with the secretary of the treasury, Alexander Hamilton. Hamilton distrusted democracy, and favoured a strong government in the hands of the educated and wealthy. Jefferson, with his faith in small farmers and labourers, disagreed with Hamilton. Their conflicting points of view led to the development of the first political parties. The Federalists adopted Hamilton's principles. Jefferson led the Democratic-Republicans.

In 1796, his Democratic-Republican supporters nominated Jefferson as a candidate for President to run against John Adams, the Federalist candidate. Adams won by a narrow margin over Jefferson. Jefferson became Vice President. Jefferson took no active part in the new Administration because he disagreed with Federalist policies. As leader of the opposition, he strengthened the organization of the Democratic-Republican Party. He found strong support among small farmers, frontier settlers, and Northern laborers.

The Democratic-Republicans again nominated Jefferson for President in 1800, and this time he won the election and became the third president of the United States. He was the first President to be inaugurated in Washington. Before him, new presidents had ridden in a luxurious coach, drawn by six horses, with footmen and guards to attend them. But Jefferson rode to the Capitol alone on horseback, wearing plain, simple clothing. He walked quietly into the Senate Chamber and read his inaugural address.

密尔顿的原则。杰斐逊则成为民主-共和党的领袖。

1796年，杰斐逊的民主-共和党的支持者提名他为总统候选人，与联邦党的候选人约翰·亚当斯竞选总统。亚当斯以微弱多数获胜，杰斐逊当选副总统。杰斐逊没有积极参与新政府的工作，因为他不赞成联邦党的政策。作为反对党领袖，他加强了民主-共和党的组织。他得到小农、边民和北方劳工的有力支持。

1800年，民主-共和党再次提名杰斐逊竞选总统。这一次他取得了胜利，当选第三位美国总统。他是在华盛顿宣誓就职的第一位总统。在他之前，新总统要乘坐六匹马拉的豪华马车，有仆人和卫兵随行。但是杰斐逊身着简朴的衣服，一个人骑马到了国会大厦。他一声不响地步入参院，宣读了他的就职演说。

在白宫，杰斐逊立下规矩，要客人与总统握手以代替鞠躬。他在与客人一同进餐时，要他们坐在圆桌周围，使大家感到无上下贵贱之分。

在第一任期内，杰斐逊安排购买了路易斯安那，使美国国土面积增加了近一倍。在外交上，他打败了北非的柏柏里海盗。

杰斐逊于1804年再次当选总统。在第二任期内，遇到英法战争引起的问题。杰斐逊要求国会通过一项法案，禁止美国人与英法进行贸易。但这个不得人心的法案结果演变成美国经济的一场灾难。

In the White House, Jefferson began the practice of having guests shake hands with the President instead of bowing. He also placed dinner guests at a round table so that everyone would feel equally important.

During his first term, Jefferson arranged the purchase of Louisiana, which almost doubled the size of the United States. In foreign affairs, Jefferson defeated the Barbary pirates of North Africa.

Jefferson was re-elected president in 1804. During his second term, he met with problems that arose from the war between Great Britain and France. Jefferson asked Congress to pass a law that forbade Americans to trade with either England or France. But this unpopular law turned out to be a disaster for the American economy.

At the end of his second term, Jefferson was offered the chance to run for a third time, but he refused. Like Washington, he did not think it wise for one person to remain in power for three terms.

Jefferson was 65 when he retired to Monticello. Now he could spend his leisure time reading and studying history, philosophy, science, religion and law he was interested in. In 1811, he was reconciled with John Adams, his former political enemy, and the two men renewed their old friendship. They wrote letters to each other for many years, discussing history, politics, philosophy, religion, and science until they died—both on the same day, July 4, 1826.

The most important work of

第二任期末，有人希望杰斐逊竞选第三任，但是他拒绝了。与华盛顿一样，他认为一个人连任三届总统并非明智之举。

杰斐逊65岁时退休到蒙蒂切洛家中。现在他可以利用闲暇来读书，研究自己感兴趣的历史、哲学、科学、宗教和法律。1811年，他与以前的政敌约翰·亚当斯和解，两人恢复了他们早年的友谊。两人多年保持书信往来，探讨历史、政治、哲学、宗教和科学问题，直至两人在同一天，即1826年7月4日逝世。

杰斐逊晚年所做的最重要的一件事，应当算是筹建弗吉尼亚大学。他亲自设计了的校舍、监督工程的进行、调整学校的课程、从国外聘任教师、并为图书馆挑选图书。1825年3月，杰斐逊有幸目睹

杰斐逊设计的弗吉尼亚大学图书馆

Jefferson's later years was probably the founding of the University of Virginia. He planned the buildings of the school, supervised their construction, and reorganized the curriculum, hired teachers from foreign countries, and selected the library books. In March 1825, Jefferson had the joy of seeing the University of Virginia open with 40 students.

Jefferson died on July 4, 1826, just 50 years after the adoption of the Declaration of Independence. The inscription that Jeffers wrote for his gravestone reads: "Here was buried Thomas Jefferson, Author of the Declaration of American Independence, of the Statute of Virginia for religious freedom, & Father of the University of Virginia." These were accomplishments that he ranked higher than being President of the United States.

了弗吉尼亚大学开学，首批 40 名学生入学。

杰斐逊于 1826 年 7 月 4 日逝世，正值《独立宣言》通过 50 周年。他为自己写的墓志是："这里埋葬着托马斯·杰斐逊，《独立宣言》、弗吉尼亚宗教自由法规的作者以及弗吉尼亚大学之父。"上述成就，在他看来，要高于他担任总统时取得的成就。

题外话

杰斐逊担任驻法大使期间，美国的马萨诸塞州爆发了谢司起义（Shays' Rebellion，1786-1787）。参加过革命战争的军人谢司率领 1200 人攻击了当地联邦军的火药库，但被击退。起义的原因是小农无法负担沉重土地税和高额的诉讼费，面临失去财产、因无法偿还债务而入狱的危险。杰斐逊得知此事，写信给大陆会议议员、未来的总统詹姆斯·麦迪逊，主张对起义者实行宽大处理。在信中他讨论了三种社会形式。第一种是无政府社会，如印第安人的社会。第二种是有政府社会，其中每一个公民都有使自己的意愿发挥影响的渠道。英国社会在较小程度上是如此；美国在更大程度上是如此。第三种是专制政府，是狼群治理羊群的政府。这种形式无疑邪恶的、不可取的。第一种社会形式是否最好，不能肯定，但对于人口众多的社会来说，是不适宜的。第二种社会形式则具有很多优势。它使社会中的大多数成员能够享受自由和幸福。但它也有其弊病，其中最大者是易于发生骚动。但与专制政府的统治下受到的压迫相比较，这一弊病则微不足道。杰斐逊说，如果要他选择，他宁可要动荡的自由，而不要安定的奴役。甚至这一弊病也会产生良好的后果。它可以预防政府的腐化变质，培养公众对政治的关注。杰斐逊认为，偶尔发生一些小规模的动乱，是一件好事，在政治生活中是必要的，正如暴风雨在自然界中是必要的一样。民众起义本身表明他们的权利受到了侵蚀；镇压起义，会使他们的权利受到进一步的侵蚀。动乱是使政府保持健康的一剂良药。正直的政府官员应对起义者宽大处理，不要采取高压政策。这封信充分表现出一个杰出政治家的高瞻远瞩和宽广的胸怀。

由于杰斐逊等人的影响，谢司起义的参加者后来都被赦免。谢司本人先被判处死刑，但一年后也被赦免。

杰斐逊对奴隶制口诛笔伐，自己却拥有奴隶。虽然当时废除奴隶制时机尚未成熟，但释放自家的奴隶似乎并非难事。即使像他那样的伟人，也难以摆脱历史的局限。

15. The War of 1812

James Madison succeeded Jefferson as president in 1809. For the next three years, he tried to protect American neutrality by using economic pressure against Britain, but without success. The British continued to interfere with U.S. ships, force American seamen into British service, and violate the nation's neutral rights and coastal waters. In addition, the British in Canada encouraged and supported Indians to attack Americans on the western frontier.

Attempts to reach an agreement with the British failed, and in 1812 Madison asked Congress to declare war against Britain. At the time, Congress was dominated by a group of young men known as "War Hawks". Most of the War Hawks came from Western and Southern states, where many of the people were in favor of going to war with Great Britain.

The war of 1812 began with an American invasion of the British territory of Canada. American forces attacked from Detroit, from Lake Champlain, and from the Niagara River. Each of the three attempts to invade Canada failed completely.

At sea, faced with the largest navy in the world, the tiny U.S. navy seemed to be hopeless to win. The government had to hire armed private ships to fight. Even so, the Americans won several victories against the British. The American warship *Constitution* defeated the British in two battles. Altogether, U.S. warships and armed pri-

1812 年战争

詹姆斯·麦迪逊于 1809 年继杰斐逊之后出任总统。此后 3 年里，他试图在经济上对英国施压，以维护美国的中立，但未能生效。英国继续干涉美国海上运输，迫使美国水手在英国军队里服役，无视美国的中立权，威胁沿岸水域的安全。此外，加拿大的英国人也鼓励支持印第安人在西部边境攻击美国人。

与英国达成协议的一切尝试均告失败后，1812 年麦迪逊要求国会向英国宣战。当时国会由一伙称为"鹰派"的年轻的好战分子所左右，鹰派中人大多来自西部和南部各州，那里有许多人主张与英国开战。

1812 年战争从美国入侵加拿大的英国领土开始。美国军队从底特律、尚普兰湖和尼亚加拉河发起进攻。但三次入侵加拿大的尝试均以彻底失败告终。

在海上，面对世界上最强大的海军，弱小的美国海军似乎毫无获胜希望。政府不得不雇用武装的私家船只作战。即使如此，美国竟然打了几次胜仗。美国战舰"宪法号"在两次海战中打败了英军。在这场战争中，美国的军舰和武装的私船总共俘获和摧毁英国商船 1500 艘。然而不久后，更强大的英国海军便肃清了海上的美国人，并于 1813

vate ships seized and destroyed about 1500 British merchant vessels during the war. In time, however, the much more powerful British navy drove the Americans from the sea and blockaded the United States coast in 1813. United States trade almost disappeared.

Early in the war, when the American invasion of Canada failed, the British seized Detroit and Fort Dearborn (Chicago), and took control of Lake Erie and the northern Northwest Territory. But in September 1813, a small fleet under the command of Oliver Hazard Perry, attacked the British and defeated them in the Battle of Erie. Perry's victory forced the British to pull out of Detroit and give up their control of the Northwest Territory. An American force under William Henry Harrison followed the retreating British into Canada and defeated them at the Battle of the Thames. The greatest Indian leader Tecumseh died while fighting. Another American force attacked York (now Toronto), the capital of Upper Canada, burned it and then withdrew. The following spring, American General Andrew Jackson defeated a Creek Indian force in Alabama. The Indians suffered heavy losses in these battles and their resistance east of the Mississippi River was finally broken.

After the defeat of Napoleon in Europe in 1814, Great Britain was then able to send over 15,000 troops to Canada. In September of the year, 11,000 British troops invaded New York. The American fleet met the British in the Battle of Lake Champlain, and defeated them. Without the support of their navy, the British army retreated to Canada and gave up its invasion of New York.

年封锁了美国海岸。美国的外贸近乎完全停滞。

战争初期，美军入侵加拿大失败后，英军夺取了底特律和迪尔伯恩堡(芝加哥)，控制了伊利湖和西北准州的北部。但在1813年9月，奥利佛·哈泽德·佩里率领的一支小舰队向英军发起攻击，在伊利湖战斗中打败了他们。佩里的胜利迫使英军撤出底特律，放弃对西北准州的控制。威廉·亨利·哈里森率领的美军尾随撤退的英军进入加拿大，在泰晤士河一役中打败英军。印第安人的最伟大首领特库姆塞阵亡。另一支美军袭击了上加拿大的首府约克(现在的多伦多)，将其付之一炬，然后撤回。第二年春，美国将军安德鲁·杰克逊在亚拉巴马打败一支克里克印第安人的部队。印第安人在几场战斗中损失惨重，他们在密西西比河以东的抵抗最终被粉碎了。

1814年，拿破仑在欧洲战败，英国得以派遣15000名官兵到加拿大。当年9月，11000名英军入侵纽约。美国舰队在尚普兰湖战斗中迎战英军，打败英军。失去海军力量的支持，英军撤回加拿大，放弃入侵纽约的计划。

与此同时，另一支英军进入切萨皮克湾，驱散了美国军队，向华盛顿特区进军。英军将包括议会大厦和白宫在内的政府建筑付之一炬，然后撤离。

英军然后乘船北上进攻巴尔的

Meanwhile, another British army entered Chesapeake Bay, scattered the U. S. troops and marched into Washington, D.C. After setting fire to government buildings, including the Capitol and the White House, the British withdrew from the city.

The British then sailed north to attack Baltimore but they met with tough resistance. British ships tried to destroy Fort McHenry, which protected the entrance of Baltimore's harbour. Although they bombarded the fort for a whole day and almost a whole night, the British failed to take it. One American who watched the attack was Francis Scott Key. When dawn came, he saw the American flag still flying over the walls of the fort. Key was so deeply moved that he started writing the words to "The Star-Spangled Banner".

Without success in their attacks at Lake Champlain and in Chesapeake Bay, the British sent an army of 7,500 men to capture New Orleans. In the battle fought in January 1815, the British suffered heavy losses. About 1,500 British soldiers were killed or wounded. The Americans lost few men in the battle. The victory at New Orleans restored the nation's pride and made a national hero of Andrew Jackson, the commander of U.S. troops.

Late in 1814, both sides were tired of war and eager for peace. Representatives from the United States and Great Britain signed a treaty of peace in Ghent, Belgium, in December 1814. The treaty ended the state of war and restored the boundaries as they had been before.

Neither side won the War of 1812 and little

摩，但遭到顽强抵抗。英国军舰试图摧毁保卫巴尔的摩港入口处的麦克亨利堡。他们对着这个要塞轰击了将近一天一夜，却未能占领它。一位名叫弗朗西斯·斯科特·基的美国人目睹了这次进攻。黎明时分，他看到美国国旗仍在要塞上空飘扬。基深受感动，立即动笔写下一首诗，这首诗后来成为"星条旗"的歌词。

在尚普兰湖和切萨皮克湾的进攻未能成功，英国派遣一支7500人的军队攻打新奥尔良。在1815年1月的战斗中，英军损失惨重，死伤大约1500人。而美军只有少数伤亡。新奥尔良的胜利恢复了美国人的民族自豪感，也使美军的指挥官安德鲁·杰克逊成为民族英雄。

1814年末，美英双方都厌倦了

詹姆斯·麦迪逊总统

was gained from the struggle, but the war did have important effects on the United States. First, it increased national patriotism and helped to unite the United States into one nation. Second, it practically ended Indian resistance in the Northwest and encouraged rapid settlement of the region.

战争，渴望恢复和平。当年 12 月，美英两国代表在比利时的根特签署和约，结束了战争状态，恢复了战前的边界。

1812 年的战争没有胜利者，双方均未能从中获得实际利益。但这场战争对于美国来说仍具有重要意义。首先，战争增强了爱国心，有助于将美国各州团结为一个国家。其次，战争几乎结束了印第安人在西北的反抗，促进了该地区的迅速移民开发。

题外话

1812 年战争在美国历史上似乎是一场莫名其妙的战争。某些历史学家称之为"沟通失误引起的战争"，是一场"不必要的战争"。在美国宣战之前两天，英国政府已经宣布将收回那些导致英美冲突的法令，以改善两国关系。如果当时有无线电通讯，这场战争本可避免。停战协议已签署 15 天后，消息仍未抵达战场，双方将士竟糊里糊涂地在新奥尔良打了这场战争中最残酷的一个战役。

16. Monroe as President

门罗担任总统

James Monroe succeeded Madison as president and served two terms from 1817 to 1825. The years of Monroe's presidency are generally known as The Era of Good Feeling because of its relative peace, unity, and optimism about the future. The Federalist Party gradually disappeared after the election of 1816, and there was now only one party, that of the Democratic-Republicans. The country prospered because industries grew fast and people began to settle in the West. In foreign relations, the United States acquired Florida from Spain.

In the early 19th century, Florida was the only part of southeastern North America that did not belong to the United States. One part of it,

詹姆斯·门罗继麦迪逊后出任总统，从 1817 年至 1825 年执政两任。门罗任总统期间史称"和睦时期"，因为当时美国比以前更加和平、更加团结，人们对未来充满乐观情绪。1816 年的选举后联邦党逐渐销声匿迹，只剩下一个政党，即民主–共和党。由于工业的迅速发展以及人们开始向西部移居，国民经济繁荣起来。在外交方面，美国从西班牙手中获得佛罗里达。

19 世纪初，佛罗里达是北美东南部唯一的一块不属于美国的领土。佛罗里达分为东西佛罗里达两

known as East Florida, was the long peninsula jutting into the Atlantic. The other part, called West Florida, was a narrow stretch of land extending west along the Gulf of Mexico to the Mississippi River, including parts of what are now Alabama, Mississippi, and Louisiana. Americans had long complained about Spanish control of East Florida. Indians used it as a base to attack American Southern settlements. Runaway slaves and prisoners fled there too. During the War of 1812, Spain let Britain use Pensacola as a naval base. In 1814, American troops led by General Andrew Jackson stormed into Florida and attacked Pensacola and drove the British out. In 1818, Monroe ordered Jackson to attack Florida Indians who had been harassing settlements in Alabama and Georgia partly because the Americans were not honoring their treaties with the Indians. Jackson chased the Indians into East Florida, defeated them and captured Pensacola. The American Secretary of State John Quincy Adams, who had been negotiating with Spain for the sale of Florida, knew he had an advantage over Spain. He told the Spanish ambassador that either Spain would

部分。东佛罗里达是伸入大西洋的狭长半岛。西佛罗里达是沿墨西哥湾向西延伸到密西西比河的狭长地带，包括现在的亚拉巴马、密西西比、路易斯安那三州的部分地区。美国人多年来一直对西班牙人控制东佛罗里达喷有烦言。印第安人利用它做基地，袭击美国南方居民点。逃亡奴隶和囚犯也将那里当做避难所。在 1812 年战争期间，西班牙允许英国使用彭萨科拉做海军基地。1814 年，美军在安德鲁·杰克逊将军的率领下突入佛罗里达，袭击了彭萨科拉，将英军逐出该地。1818 年，门罗命令杰克逊攻打佛罗里达的印第安人，因为印第安人一直在骚扰亚拉巴马和佐治亚的居民点。其实，印第安人之所以这样做，部分因为美国人未能遵守与印第安人签订的条约。杰克逊尾随印第安人进入东佛罗里达，击溃了他们，占领了彭萨科拉。美国国务卿约翰·昆西·亚当斯一直在与西班牙谈判出售佛罗里达事宜，这时意识到自己处于有利地位。他告知西

门罗总统

have to keep order in Florida, or she would have to sell the territory to the United States. Spain was troubled at that time by revolts in its South American colonies and could hardly afford to go to war with the United States. Finally, in 1819, Spain agreed to turn Florida over to the United States. The United States did not actually pay any money to Spain for Florida. However, it agreed to pay $5 million to U.S. citizens whose property had been damaged by Florida Indians.

The Era of Good Feeling, however, did not mean an end to all the country's disputes. Americans greatly divided about the issue of slavery. Many Northerners were demanding an end to slavery, while Southerners were defending it more and more. Jefferson accurately viewed the growing dispute as a warning of approaching disaster.

班牙大使，说西班牙必须在佛罗里达维持秩序，否则必须将这片领土出售给美国。西班牙当时正在被南美洲殖民地的起义搅得心神不宁，几乎无力与美国打一场战争。西班牙终于在 1819 年同意将佛罗里达出让给美国。美国得到了佛罗里达，但实际上却没有给西班牙任何经济补偿。只是美国同意拨出 500 万美圆，代替西班牙补偿印第安人对美国公民财产造成的损失。

然而，"和睦时期"并不意味着再无争议。在奴隶制问题上，美国人有巨大分歧。许多北方人要求结束奴隶制，而南方人则越来越顽固地捍卫它。杰斐逊将日益激化的争议视为灾难即将降临的先兆。

题外话

美国历史上的领土扩张大多是通过乘人之危，巧取豪夺得来的。吞并佛罗里达就是一个例子。不过话说回来，欧洲殖民国手中的领土都不是好来的，强盗抢强盗，不好说谁对谁错。倒霉的是印第安人，他们为保卫家园所做的努力，总被视为大逆不道的强盗行径。

17. The Monroe Doctrine   门罗主义

The Monroe Doctrine was a statement of United States policy on the activities and rights of European powers in the western hemisphere. It was set forth by President James Monroe in a message he delivered to the Congress of the United States on December 2, 1823, and eventually became one of the foundations of U.S. policy in

门罗主义是美国针对欧洲列强在西半球的活动及权利发布的政策声明。它是由美国总统詹姆斯·门罗于 1823 年 12 月 2 日在致国会的年度咨文中阐述的，最终成为美国对拉丁美洲政策的基础之一。

Latin America.

The Monroe Doctrine grew out of the changed situation in America. During and after the Napoleonic Wars, most of the Spanish colonies in America had taken advantage of unsettled conditions in Europe to break away from the mother country. As they won independence, most of these colonies formed themselves into republics with constitutions much like that of the United States. The United States quickly recognized the newly independent nations of Latin America. But it seemed that Spain, with the help of France, might try to recover its former colonies. Meanwhile, Russia, starting from its base in Alaska, began to expand southward. The United States did not like European nations' attempt to further colonize the western hemisphere. Monroe's statement was a strong warning to European powers to keep out. It made three major points:

1. European powers could no longer colonize the American continents.
2. Any attempt to interfere with the newly independent Spanish American republics would be considered an unfriendly act towards the United States.
3. The United States would not take any part in affairs of Europe or existing European colonies in the Western Hemisphere.

门罗主义是随着美洲局势的变化而形成的。在拿破仑战争中及战后，西班牙在美洲的大部分殖民地利用欧洲动荡不定的局势，纷纷脱离母国。在这些殖民地赢得独立时，大多数建立了共和制国家，采用了与美国相似的宪法。美国迅速承认了新独立的拉丁美洲国家。然而西班牙在法国的帮助下，似乎在跃跃欲试，企图恢复先前的殖民地。与此同时，俄国也从其在阿拉斯加的基地开始向南扩张。美国对欧洲国家进一步在西半球殖民的企图很反感。门罗的声明对于欧洲列强是一个严重警告，要它们不得染指西半球事务。门罗主义有如下三个基本论点：

1. 欧洲列强不得再在美洲大陆开拓殖民地。
2. 任何干涉新独立的西班牙美洲共和国的企图，将被视为对美国的敌对行为。
3. 美国将不干涉欧洲的内部事务，也不干涉欧洲国家在西半球现有的殖民地。

题外话

门罗主义宣布时，美国并无军事实力支持它，这项声明也并未引起重视。1870 年后，随着美国成为世界强国，门罗主义得到越来越多的阐释。美国利用它将西半球划入自己的势力范围，使欧洲列强不得染指。

CHAPTER SIX

Expansion and Progress
扩张与进步

1. The Westward Movement

西进运动

During the early 19th century, the United States changed a great deal. Its size doubled, and settlers by the thousands moved westward over the Appalachian Mountains into the new states and territories. Many of these pioneers even went beyond the country's western boundary and settled in Texas, California, and other western lands belonging to Mexico. "The West", with its open land, good farmland, and rich mineral and forest resources always attracted adventurers, poor Eastern farmers, unemployed workers, new immigrants—all brave, hardy people looking for a better life.

One of the most famous pioneers in United States history was Daniel Boone. He devoted his life to exploring and settling the frontiers of his growing nation. Boone found a pathway across the rugged wilderness of the Appalachian Mountains in 1769 and reached the unexplored area that became known as Kentucky. He cleared the Wilderness Road, which became a main route to the West

19世纪初，美国发生了重大变化。它的国土面积增加了一倍，成千上万的移民跨越阿巴拉契亚山脉涌入新成立的州和准州。这些拓荒者们当中有许多人甚至越过美国的西部边界，在得克萨斯、加利福尼亚和其他属于墨西哥的西部领土上定居下来。"西部"，以其开阔的土地、肥沃的农田、丰富的矿物和森林资源，总是吸引着冒险家、东部的贫农、失业工人和新移民前往。所有这些人都勤劳勇敢，向往着更幸福的生活。

在美国历史上最著名的拓荒者之一是丹尼尔·布恩。他用毕生的精力来勘探和开发他的年轻祖国的边疆地区。他于 1769 年发现了穿越阿巴拉契亚山脉崎岖荒野的一条通道，到达后来被称为肯塔基的未开发地区。他开辟了"荒野之路"，

for thousands of settlers.

After the Revolutionary War ended in 1783, the westward movement carried settlers onto two new frontiers. They were the Old Northwest and the Old Southwest. The Old Northwest extended from the Ohio River north to the Great Lakes and from Pennsylvania west to the Mississippi River. The Old Southwest at first consisted of Kentucky and Tennessee. It gradually expanded south to the Gulf of Mexico.

By 1820, American pioneers had established many frontier settlements as far west as the Mississippi River. By the 1830s, the Westward Movement had pushed the frontier across the Mississippi, into Iowa, Missouri, Arkansas, and eastern Texas. In the 1840s, large numbers of pioneers made the long journey across the Great Plains to the Far West. The pioneers included Easterners from both the North and South. Many other pio-

这条路后来成为成千上万移民西进的主要通道。

美国革命战争于 1783 年结束后，西进运动中的移民迁入两个新的边疆地区，即老西北和老西南地区。老西北南起俄亥俄河，北至大湖区，东邻宾夕法尼亚，西抵密西西比河。老西南起初包括肯塔基和田纳西，后来逐步向南扩张，直抵墨西哥湾。

到 1820 年，美国的拓荒者们已经建立了许多边疆居民点，这些居民点向西分布，直到密西西比河。到了 30 年代，西进运动已将边疆扩张到了密西西比河对岸，进入艾奥瓦、密苏里、阿肯色和得克萨斯东部。40 年代，大批拓荒者长

西进途中

neers came from Europe seeking a better life. Some people went west in search of religious freedom. The best known of these were the Mormons, who settled in Utah in 1847.

Most of the pioneers became farmers. But urban life also moved westward with the frontier. Busy towns and cities grew up in the West. Churches, banks, stores, hotels and schools were established in these urban centers.

As white people moved westward, native Americans east of the Mississippi River suffered a great deal. The white settlers destroyed their way of life and source of food by cutting down forests and killing off wild games. The federal government arranged treaties for the purchase of Indian land, setting up small areas for the Indians to live on. But few white people actually paid for the territories they took from the Indians. When the Indians resisted, government troops used force. Thousands of Indians chose to move west of the Mississippi, others were forced to move. During the 1830s, the Indian inhabitants of the Southeast — the Cherokees, Chickasaws, Choctaws, Creeks, and Seminoles, who were known as the "Five Civilized Tribes", were driven from their lands and marched to what is now Oklahoma. About 4,000 died from starvation, disease, and cold on the journey that their forced march became known as the "Trail of Tears".

题外话

白人移民与印第安人的冲突表明，两种截然不同的文化接触时必然会发生碰撞。而弱势文化若不能自我调节以适应新的环境，便难以逃脱被消灭的下场。

途跋涉越过大平原抵达最远的西部。拓荒者们当中有来自北方和南方的东部人。其他拓荒者许多来自欧洲，他们为追求更好的生活而来。有些人西进是为了宗教信仰自由。这些人当中最著名的要算是摩门教信徒，他们于1847年在犹他定居下来。

大多数拓荒者以务农为生。但随着边疆的西移，城市化的生活也在向西扩展。繁华的城镇在西部成长起来。在这些城镇里，教堂、银行、商店、旅店和学校纷纷建立起来。

随着白人的西进，密西西比河以东的印第安人开始了苦难的生活。白人移民砍伐森林、屠杀野兽，破坏了他们传统的生活方式和食物来源。联邦政府出面协商签订购买印第安人的土地的条约，划定小片地区供印第安人居住。但实际上很少有白人为他们占据的印第安人领土付款。当印第安人反抗时，政府便用武力镇压。成千上万的印第安人自愿迁移到密西西比河以西，其他人则被迫迁移。30年代，被称为"五大开化部落"的东南部印第安居民，包括切罗基人、奇卡索人、乔克托人、克里克人和塞米诺尔人，在胁迫下离开家园，成群结队迁徙到现在的俄克拉何马。由于大约4000人因饥饿、疾病和寒冷死于途中，这次被迫的大迁移被称为"泪水之旅"。

2. The Beginning of Industrialization

Industry developed slowly in America at first. Most manufactured goods were imported from Britain. But then, during the Napoleonic Wars and the War of 1812, U.S. trade with England almost stopped. To make up for the loss of imported products, Americans began to build factories and turned out manufactured goods for the American market.

In 1794, Eli Whitney, an American inventor, invented the cotton gin. This invention provided a fast, economical way to separate the cotton seeds from the fibers. Whitney's cotton gin made cotton growing profitable and quickly helped the United States become the world's leading cotton grower. In the early 19th century, several inventors, including Whitney, experimented with new methods for making guns. They produced standard, interchangeable parts for the guns they were making. Standard parts for weapons led to mass production. The system of interchangeable parts soon spread to the production of clocks and watches. Later, farm machinery, sewing machines, stoves, and other goods were also made this way. In time, this "American

工业化的开端

美国的工业发展起步缓慢，大多数工业品都要从英国进口。但是，在拿破仑战争和1812年战争期间，美英之间的贸易几乎陷于停顿。为弥补进口商品的短缺，美国人开始建立工厂，为美国的市场生产工业品。

1794年，美国发明家伊莱·惠特尼发明了轧花机。这项发明提供了一种将棉籽与棉纤维分离开来的高效而经济的方法。惠特尼的轧花机使种植棉花有利可图，从而使美国迅速成为世界棉花主要生产国。19世纪初，包括惠特尼在内的几位发明家实验用新的方法制造枪支。他们为这些枪支生产标准的、可互换的零件。枪支零件的标准化导致批量生产。可互换零件的概念不久引入钟表制造业。后来，农业机械、缝纫机、火炉及其他商品均

伊莱·惠特尼

system of manufacturing" was used in all industrial production.

As the United States increased in size, it needed improved networks of transportation. Industries wanted better and faster ways to get raw materials and to ship finished products to markets. Private companies constructed turnpikes, which linked the East with frontier settlements, helped farmers carry their produce to market. In 1811, the federal government began to build the National Road. This road led from Cumberland, Maryland, to Vandalia, Illinois. For many years, the National Road was the chief road for western migration and east-west trade.

Since water travel was cheaper, rivers and lakes were widely used wherever there were waterways. A major achievement was the building of the Erie Canal, started in 1817, and completed in 1825. It linked Buffalo on Lake Erie with Albany on the Hudson River, opening a route between the

按此法生产。这一"美式制造法"最终被运用于全部工业生产。

随着美国国土面积的扩大，需要改良交通网。工业需要更方便快捷的方式获取原材料，并将成品运往市场。私营公司修建了公路，将东部与边疆居民区联结起来，帮助将他们的农产品运往市场。1811 年，联邦政府开始修筑联邦公路。这条公路自马里兰州的坎伯兰通向伊利诺伊州的范代利亚，多年来是向西部移民和东西贸易的重要通道。

由于水运价格低廉，凡是能够通航的地方，河流和湖泊都得到广泛的利用。水上运输的一项重大成就是开凿伊利运河。工程于 1817 年开始，于 1825 年竣工。运河将伊利湖边的布法罗与哈得孙河边的奥尔巴尼联结起来，开辟了一条大西洋和大湖区之间的通道。通过这条路线，工业品和移民可以源源不断地运到西部，木材和农产品可以大批输往东方。运河大大降低了运输成本，使纽约市成为美国 19 世纪最大港口。与此同时，人们制造了更先进的船只。罗伯特·富尔顿设计制造了第一艘实用汽船"克莱蒙脱号"，于 1807 年从纽约市上溯到奥尔巴尼。"克莱蒙脱号"在

俄亥俄河上的汽船

Atlantic Ocean and the Great Lakes over which manufactured goods and settlers could flow into the West and timber and agricultural products could pour into the East. The canal greatly reduced freight costs and helped New York City become the nation's leading port during the 19th century. At the same time better ships were built. Robert Fulton designed and built the first commercially successful steamboat, the *Clermont*, which steamed up the Hudson River from New York to Albany in 1807. The *Clermont* opened a new era in the history of transportation.

The railroad soon began to compete with the steamboat in importance as a means of shipping. The first railroads in the United States were opened to traffic in the 1830s. By 1850, about 14,500 kilometers of railroad lines were in operation.

In 1840s, Samuel F. B. Morse developed the first successful telegraph in the United States. Morse also devised a code of dots and dashes to represent letters. The telegraph soon gave businesses the fastest means of communication yet known. An expanded postal system also helped speed communications.

Developments in printing spread information to more people than ever before. Faster printing presses reduced the cost of printing newspapers. After 1835, many newspaper publishers lowered the cost of their papers to a penny, a price even poor people could afford.

运输历史上开辟了一个新时代。

铁路不久便开始与汽船竞争最重要运输工具的地位。30年代，美国开通了首批铁路。到了1850年，正在运营的铁路已长达14500公里。

40年代，塞缪尔·莫尔斯研制出了美国的首台实用电报机。莫尔斯还发明了一套用点和短划代表字母的编码系统。电报不久就向商业界提供了前所未有的最快捷的通讯工具。扩大了的邮政系统也加快了信息的流通。

印刷业的发展将信息传播给前所未有的大量人群。更高速的印刷机降低了报纸印刷的成本。1835年以后，许多报纸出版商将报纸的售价降至一分钱，甚至连穷人都买得起。

塞缪尔·莫尔斯

3. The Age of Jackson

杰克逊时代

Andrew Jackson was a dominant figure of the early 19th century. He won fame as an Indian fighter and as a hero in the War of 1812. He was nicknamed "Old Hickory" because of his toughness and endurance. Western farmers and pioneers, city laborers and craftworkers disliked wealthy Easterners who controlled governmental and economic policy, gathered around Jackson, and helped elect him President in 1828 and again in 1832. Jackson took steps to reduce the power of wealthy Easterners and aid the "common man". Under Jackson's leadership, his followers tried to win reforms in the states. They fought for the right of workers to organize labour unions, and called for a 10-hour workday. They sought adoption of the secret ballot in elections. They worked for such social reforms as women's rights, improvements in education, and the abolition of slavery. When Jackson was reelected President in 1832, he became the first President who had been nominated by a party convention. The period of his influence in American history is often called the *Age of Jackson*. By the end of the era, the United States was a

安德鲁·杰克逊是 19 世纪初的重要人物。他赢得了印第安人的克星和 1812 年战争中的英雄的美誉。由于他坚忍不拔的意志，被人用绰号称呼为"老核桃木"。西部农民和拓荒者、城市劳工和手工业工人不喜欢控制政治和经济政策的东部富人，他们团结在杰克逊周围，支持他在 1828 年和 1832 年当选总统。杰克逊采取措施削弱东部富人的势力、扶助所谓的"老百姓"。在他的领导下，他的追随者们在各州努力进行改革。他们开展斗争，争取工人组织工会的权利，号召 10 小时工作制。他们主张在选举中采取秘密投票制。他们致力于争取妇女权益、改善教育、废除奴隶制等社会改革活动。杰克逊于 1832 年再次当选总统时，他成为由政党代表大会提名的头一位总统。他在美国历史上发挥影响的时期常被称为

安德鲁·杰克逊

more democratic nation than it had been before. Historians often use the term *Jacksonian Democracy* to describe the reforms and reform movements of the period from 1828 to 1850.

When Jackson became President, many wealthy Easterners held federal government offices. Jackson dismissed many of these people from office, replacing them with his supporters. Some historians consider this action the start of the spoils system in the federal government.

Jackson's fight against the Bank of the United States became the major issue of his first Administration. In 1816, Congress had granted the bank a 20-year charter. Jackson was strongly opposed to this bank. He felt it helped the wealthy people at the expense of ordinary people. In 1832, Congress voted to renew the bank's charter, but Jackson vetoed the bill. He soon withdrew the government's money from the bank, and the bank later collapsed.

The other great issue of Jackson's Administration involved the tariff and nullification. In 1828, Congress passed a bill that placed high tariffs on goods imported into the United States. Some Southerners protested because the tariff increased the cost of the manufactured goods they bought. Speaking for South Carolina, Calhoun (then the Vice President) argued that the tariff unconstitutional and any state could nullify it. In 1832, South Carolina threatened to break away from the Union if the federal government tried to collect tariffs in the state. Jackson believed in states' rights, but maintained the Union must be preserved. In 1833, he persuaded Congress to pass the Force Bill, which allowed him to use the

"杰克逊时代"。这一时代结束时，美国比以往任何时候都更加民主。历史学家常用"杰克逊式民主"一词来概括从1828年至1850年间的改革和改革运动。

杰克逊就任总统后，许多东部富人把持着联邦政府机构。杰克逊解除了许多人的职务，代之以自己的支持者。某些历史学家将这一举措视为联邦政府分赃制的起源。

杰克逊与美国银行的斗争是他第一任期中的大事。国会于1816年给予这家银行以为期20年的特许权。杰克逊强烈反对这家银行，认为它帮助富人，剥削普通民众。1832年，国会投票赞成延长这家银行的特许权，但杰克逊否决了这一提案。他不久便将政府的存款从银行里提出，致使银行在不久后垮台。

杰克逊执政时期的另一件大事涉及关税和否认原则。1828年，国会通过一项法案，向进口美国的货物收取高额关税。一些南方人对此提出抗议，因为高额关税增加了他们购买工业品的开支。卡尔霍恩（当时的副总统）替南卡罗莱纳州说话，声称这一关税违反宪法，任何州均可否认其在本州有效性。1832年，南卡罗莱纳州发出威胁，称如果联邦政府试图在该州征税，该州将退出美利坚合众国。杰克逊主张各州享有自主权，但坚持认为合众国的统一必须加以维护。1833年，他说服国会通过强制法案，允

armed forces to collect tariffs. But Congress lowered tariffs to a point acceptable to South Carolina, and the nullification crisis ended.

As a Westerner, Jackson had always been for the settlers and against the Indians. In 1819 the state of Georgia began trying to remove the Cherokee people from their lands in the southeastern United States. In 1832, the Supreme Court decided in a lawsuit that it was illegal for the state of Georgia to remove the Cherokee nation from their land. Georgia did not obey the Court's decision, but Jackson refused to enforce it. As a result, in 1838 federal soldiers forced most of the Cherokee to march about 1,285 km from Georgia to an area in what is now Oklahoma. Thousands died on the march, later known as the "Trail of Tears".

Two new parties took form during the age of Jackson. The Democratic-Republican Party split into several groups. One group, under the leadership of Jackson, formed the *Democratic Party*. Those who supported John Quincy Adams first took the name *National Republicans* and then in the early 1830s, joined with other groups against Jackson to form a new party, the *Whigs*.

By the end of his second term, Jackson chose Martin Van Buren to be the party's candidate in the 1836 presidential election. Most Whigs supported William Henry Harrison to oppose Van Buren. Because of the influence of Jackson over the voters, Van Buren easily won the election.

No sooner had Van Buren taken office than United States suffered a depression called "the Panic of 1837". It was largely the result of the

许总统动用军队征收关税。但国会将关税降低到了南卡罗莱纳可以接受的水准，否认危机才结束。

作为一个西部人，杰克逊一贯支持移民而反对印第安人。1819年，佐治亚州开始试图将切罗基人从他们在美国东南部的故土上迁出。1832年，最高法院在一项诉讼案中判决佐治亚州将切罗基民族从他们故土上迁出为非法行为。佐治亚州没有服从法院判决，但杰克逊拒绝强制执行。结果，联邦军队于1838年迫使大多数切罗基人跋涉1,285公里，从佐治亚迁到现在的俄克拉何马。数千人死于途中，这次大迁移后来被称为"泪水之旅"。

在杰克逊时代，两个新的政党开始形成。民主-共和党分裂成几个派别。其中一派在杰克逊的领导下形成民主党。那些支持约翰·昆西·亚当斯的人先取名为"国民共和党"，然后于30年代初与其他反对杰克逊的派别联合形成一个新的政党，即"辉格党"。

在第二任期将近结束时，杰克逊选择马丁·范布伦为党的候选人参加1836年的总统选举。大多数辉格党人支持威廉·亨利·哈里森与范布伦竞选。由于杰克逊在选举人中的影响，范布伦轻易获胜。

范布伦刚一就任，美国就进入了经济萧条期，这个时期被称为"1837年经济恐慌"。萧条在很大程度上要归咎于杰克逊执政期间的经济政策。虽然后来经济恢复了繁

economic policies of Jackson's administration. Though prosperity returned later, the Whigs blamed Van Buren for the country's hard time. As a result, in the presidential election of 1840, Van Buren lost and Harrison became the new president.

荣，辉格党指责范布伦应对国家的困难局面负责。结果，在 1840 年的总统选举中，范布伦落选，哈里森当选新总统。

题外话

如果有谁应当对切罗基人的悲惨的"泪水之旅"负责，此人非杰克逊莫属。但他对驱逐印第安人有一番妙论。他说："有哪个善良的人宁愿要一个覆盖着森林的国家，任几千个野蛮人游荡其中，而不愿要我们这个广大的共和国，遍布着城镇和繁荣的农庄，被技艺所能设计、工业所能创造的一切所美化，居住着 1200 多万幸福的人民，享受着自由、文明和宗教带来的一切福祉？"这是白人殖民者的霸权口吻，既无理又有理。面对历史的潮流，既弱小又无法适应现代生活的印第安人又能拿什么来反驳？

4. Social Reform

社会改革

The democratic spirit of the Age of Jackson was reflected not only in political reforms but also in efforts to correct social abuses and improve American society.

A number of reforms were made to ease human distress. Dorothea Dix, a Boston schoolteacher, visited a Massachusetts house of correction in 1841, and was shocked to see the mentally ill living in chains. She asked the legislature to provide better care, and started the reform in that state. She later carried her message to

杰克逊时代的民主精神不但体现在政治改革中，也反映在对社会陋习的矫正、对美国社会的改良中。

有几项改革的目的是减轻人类的苦难。波士顿教师多萝西·迪克斯于 1841 年参观了马萨诸塞州的一所教养院，看到精神病患者竟然戴着镣铐，不禁感到震惊。她要求立法机构立法，改善那里的护理方式。她就此发起了马萨诸

多萝西·迪克斯

other states. During the next few years, 15 states built mental hospitals where patients could be properly treated. Dix was also concerned about the treatment of criminals in prison. She and other reformers improved prison conditions so that prison became a place not only for punishment but also for teaching the criminals how to lead useful lives after they were freed.

As industry began to develop, more and more Americans became workers in factories. But they were at first very badly treated. Men, women and children usually worked long hours but their pay was low and working conditions were often poor and even dangerous. During the 1820s and 1830s, skilled workers established organizations in their cities in order to obtain better pay. The democratic spirit of the Age of Jackson helped this movement to grow. In 1834, the first American labour organization National Trade Union formed. An important gain won by organized labour in this period was the ten-hour workday.

Before the 1830s, Americans did not have much opportunity to go to school. Many people learned to read and write, but they did so at religious or other private schools. As political democracy grew, Americans began to feel the need for better education in order to take offices in government. As a result, more public schools were opened, the number of subjects taught was increased and the school year extended.

In the early 19th century, the position of women in American society was far inferior to that of men. They could not vote, they were paid less than men doing the same job, and discouraged from acquiring advanced education, learning a

塞州的改革，后来又到其他各州宣传自己的改革主张。在其后的几年里，15个州建立了精神病院，使病人得到适当的护理。迪克斯还关心监狱里囚犯的待遇。经过她和另外几个改革者的努力，监狱的条件得到改善，使监狱不再仅仅是一个惩戒的场所，同时也是一个教育罪犯的学校，使他们在刑满释放后能够过有益的生活。

随着工业的发展，越来越多的美国人走进工厂。但他们的待遇起初很差。无论男人还是女人，成人还是儿童，他们通常要工作很长时间，而报酬却很低，工作条件恶劣甚至危险。二三十年代，熟练工人在自己所在的城市里组织起来，以争取较高的报酬。杰克逊时代的民主精神促进了这场运动的开展。1834年，美国的第一个劳工组织，即全国工会成立。在这一时期，工会取得的一个重要成就是10小时工作制。

30年代以前，美国人上学的机会不多。许多人是在教会或其他私立学校学会读书写字的。随着政治民主的发展，美国人开始感到需要接受更良好的教育，以便在政府部门任职。结果更多的公立学校开办了，教授的科目增加了，学期也延长了。

19世纪初，妇女在美国社会中的地位远比男人低下。她们没有选举权，与男人们同工而不同酬，接受高等教育、学习从事脑力劳动、当众演说等都受到非议。这时，争

profession, or speaking in public. Then a women's rights movement developed, and brought about some changes. Maria Mitchell discovered a new comet in 1847 and became the first woman member of the American Academy of Arts and Sciences. Although she was largely self-educated, she served as professor of astronomy at Vassar College from 1865 to 1888. In 1849, Elizabeth Blackwell became the first woman in the United States to receive a medical degree. She helped break down prejudice against women in medicine. In 1857, she and her younger sister Emily Black-well, a surgeon, opened their own hospital in New York City. The hospital was staffed entirely by women. The sisters later expanded the hospital to include a medical school for women. In 1848, a group of feminists organized a Woman's Rights Convention in Seneca Falls, N.Y. The convention

伊丽莎白·布莱克韦尔

取妇女权益的运动开展起来，使妇女的处境发生了一些变化。玛利亚·米切尔于 1847 年发现了一颗新的彗星，成为美国艺术与科学院的

Contemporary Anti-Slavery Propaganda. This also appeared as "Am I Not a Woman and a Sister?"

反对奴隶制的宣传画，画上的文字是："难道我不是一个男人，一个兄弟吗?"

"Am I Not a Woman and a Sister?" A popular appeal. (Garrison's *Liberator*.)

画上的文字是："难道我不是一个女人，一个姊妹吗?"

issued the first formal appeal for woman suffrage (the right to vote).

The most stirring reform activity of the early 19th century was the abolition movement. This movement involved people of different aims and backgrounds, black and white. They often disagreed about how to end slavery, but all of them believed that slavery was evil and had to be ended. The American Colonization Society, founded in 1816, led antislavery protests during the early 19th century. It tried to send freed slaves to Liberia in Africa. One of the most famous fighters in the cause of abolition was William Lloyd Garrison. In 1831, Garrison began publication of his newspaper, *The Liberator,* through which he demanded immediate freedom for slaves. Two

威廉·劳埃
德·加里森

头一位女性会员。虽然她主要是通过自学成材的，她仍被聘任为天文学教授，从 1865 年开始在瓦萨女子学院执教，直至 1888 年。1849 年，伊丽莎白·布莱克韦尔成为美国头一位领取医学学位的女性。她打破了妇女不得从事医务工作的偏见。1857 年，她与妹妹外科医生埃米莉·布莱克韦尔在纽约市开办了自己的医院。医院的职员都是妇女。姊妹两人后来将医院扩充，建立了一所附属女子医学校。1848 年，一群女权运动积极分子在纽约州的塞尼卡福尔斯举行了妇女权利大会，发表了要求妇女选举权的头一份正式呼吁。

19 世纪初最激动人心的改革运动是废奴运动。卷入这场运动的人们目的不同、背景各异，既有黑人又有白人。他们对于如何废除奴隶制意见不一，但所有的人都一致认为奴隶制是罪恶的，应当予以废除。成立于 1816 年的美国殖民协会在 19 世纪初领导了废奴抗议活动。这个组织试图将被解放了的奴隶运往非洲的利比里亚。废奴事业中最著名的战士之一是威廉·劳埃德·加里森。1831 年，加里森创办了自己的《解放者》报，鼓吹立即让奴隶们获得自由。两年后，他参与建立了美国反奴隶制协会。此后废奴运动逐渐在北方各州开展起来，尽管遭到南方奴隶主和北方赞成奴隶制的人们的强烈反对。废奴主义者们筹建了一个交通网络，即

社会改革

奴隶拍卖

南方黑奴

years later, he helped found the American Anti-Slavery Society. The abolition movement gradually spread throughout the Northern States despite bitter and violent opposition by Southern slaveholders and Northerners who favored slavery. Abolitionists organized a network, the *underground railroad*, to guide slaves from one house ("station") to another. Local abolitionists acted as "conductors". The "end of the line"was usually the free states or Canada. Two leaders of this activity were Levi Coffin, a Quaker, and Harriet Tubman, a former slave.

"地下铁路",将逃奴们从一个人家("车站")引领到另一个人家。所到之地的废奴主义者充当"列车员",将逃奴们送一程。铁路的"终点站"通常是北部各州或加拿大。"地下铁路"的两个领导者是公谊会会员列维·科芬和获释女奴哈丽特·塔布曼。

"地下铁路"领导者之一哈丽特·塔布曼

贩奴船

5. Texas Became Part of the United States

得克萨斯并入美国

As the westward movement continued, pio-

随着西进运动的持续开展,拓

neers passed the Great Plain and travelled either to the Rockies and beyond or to the area south and west of the Red River. In doing so, many of them settled in areas claimed by foreign nations. Conflicts inevitably followed.

In 1820s, Stephen Austin led 300 American families to Texas, a province of Mexico, and established a colony. Later, more Americans moved in to establish colonies. By 1835, the number of settlers had reached 30,000. Before long, troubles developed between the Americans and Mexicans. In 1834, General Antonio Lopez de Santa Anna, a Mexican politician and soldier, overthrew Mexico's constitutional government and made himself dictator. The American colonists in Texas soon rebelled and declared their independence in 1836. Santa Anna assembled a large army and surrounded a small group of Texan rebels in the Alamo, an old Spanish mission in San Antonio. Santa Annas forces attacked the Alamo for 12 days and it finally fell. All its defenders, including William B. Travis, Jim Bowie, and Davy Crockett, were killed in the battle. But the Texans did not give up fighting. In April of 1836, an army of Texans under Samuel Houston defeated the Mexicans in the Battle of San Jacinto and captured Santa Anna. Mexico had to agree to recognize the independence of the Republic of Texas. Texas soon asked to be admitted

荒者们跨过了大平原。此后，部分人进入落基山，到达山脉以西地区；部分人则前往红河的西南地区。这样，许多移民就在外国的领土上定居下来，发生冲突在所难免。

20 年代，斯蒂芬·奥斯汀率领 300 户美国人来到墨西哥的一个省份得克萨斯，建立了一个殖民地。后来更多的美国人迁入得克萨斯，建立更多的殖民地。到了 1835 年，移民总数已达 3 万人。不久，美国人和墨西哥人之间的摩擦激化了。1834 年，墨西哥的政治家和军人安东尼奥·罗佩兹·德·圣安纳将军推翻了墨西哥的合法政府，成为独裁者。得克萨斯的殖民者们不久发动叛乱，并于 1836 年宣布独立。圣安纳调集了一支大军，在圣安东尼奥包围了西班牙传教地旧址阿拉莫的一小股叛军。圣安纳的部队攻击阿拉莫长达 12 天，最终攻下了这一据点。守军战士全部阵亡，其中包括威廉·B.特拉维斯、吉姆·鲍伊和戴维·克罗克特。但得克萨斯人没有放弃斗争。1836年4月，塞缪尔·休斯敦率

塞缪尔·休斯敦

into the Union as a new state. Nine years later, the United States annexed Texas and made it a state.

⊕ 题 外 话

得克萨斯州的最大城市休斯敦即以塞缪尔·休斯敦的名字命名。

领的一支军队在圣哈辛托一战中打败了墨西哥人，俘获了圣安纳。墨西哥被迫承认得克萨斯共和国独立。得克萨斯不久要求以一个新州的身份加入联邦。9 年后，美国吞并了得克萨斯，使之成为得克萨斯州。

6. Oregon Country Became Part of the United States

俄勒冈地区并入美国

At the same time, the United States also came into conflict with Great Britain over Oregon Country. An 1818 treaty allowed both nations to occupy the territory, lying between 42 degrees and 54 degrees 40 minutes north latitude. As the number of American settlers increased in the 1830s and 1840s, the U.S. government felt it necessary to settle the boundary dispute with Britain. In 1846, President James K. Polk signed a treaty with Britain, which set 49 degrees as a boundary, except for Vancouver Island. The United States secured the land south of the line, and Britain obtained the land to the north. In this way, the United States acquired what is now Washington, Oregon, Idaho, and parts of Montana and Wyoming.

与此同时，美国就俄勒冈问题与英国发生冲突。1818 年签订的条约允许两国共同占有这片北纬 42 度和 54 度 40 分之间的领土。随着三四十年代美国移民的人数增长，美国政府觉得有必要与英国解决领土争端。1846 年，美国总统詹姆斯·K. 波尔克与英国签署条约，认定北纬 49 度为边界，温哥华岛例外。美国和英国分别获得了此纬线以南和以北的土地。这样，美国获得了现在的华盛顿、俄勒冈、爱达荷三州和蒙大拿、怀俄明两州的部分地区。

7. The Mexican War

墨西哥战争

After the United States annexed the Republic

美国于 1845 年吞并得克萨斯

of Texas in 1845, tension between the United States and Mexico increased.

In 1846, President Polk ordered troops under General Zachary Taylor to occupy land near the Rio Grande that both the United States and Mexico claimed. Fighting broke out between Taylor's troops and Mexican soldiers. Polk asked Congress for a declaration of war, and Congress passed it on May 13, 1846. This war broke out and became known as the Mexican War. The United States quickly defeated its weak neighbor. The *Treaty of Guadalupe Hidalgo*, signed in 1848, officially ended the war. The treaty gave the United States a vast stretch of land from Texas west to the Pacific and north to Oregon. The vast territory later became California, Nevada, Utah, and parts of Arizona, New Mexico, Colorado, and Wyoming.

In 1853, in the *Gadsden Purchase*, America bought from Mexico the strip of land that makes up the southern edge of Arizona and New Mexico. The United States then owned all the territory of its present states except Alaska (purchased from Russia in 1867) and Hawaii (annexed in 1898).

詹姆斯·K·波尔克

共和国后,与墨西哥的关系日趋紧张。

1846 年,美国总统波尔克命令扎卡里·泰勒将军的部队占领格兰德河附近地区。当时美国和墨西哥都宣称对该地区拥有主权。泰勒的军队与墨西哥军队交火。波尔克向国会请求宣战,国会于 1846 年 5 月 13 日通过了他的请求。战争随之爆发,史称墨西哥战争。美国迅速打垮了弱小的邻国。1848 年,交战双方签署瓜达卢佩伊达尔戈和约,战争正式结束。和约使美国得到了得克萨斯以西直至太平洋、以北直抵俄勒冈的一片广阔的领土。这片广阔的地域日后成为加利福尼亚、内华达和犹他三州,以及亚利桑那、新墨西哥、科罗拉多和怀俄明四州的部分地区。

1853 年,通过加兹登购地,美国从墨西哥购得一条狭长地带,这条地带构成亚利桑那和新墨西哥的南部边缘。此时,美国已拥有了除去阿拉斯加 (1867 年购自俄国) 和夏威夷 (1898 年吞并) 以外的所有各州的领土。

题外话

在墨西哥战争中美国获取领土的方式纯属赤裸裸的掠夺。这一事件暴露了美国对待弱国的傲慢态度。但美国也并非铁板一块。东部的辉格党人就公开表示反对墨西哥战争，指责其为恃强凌弱的不义之战，而且其目的是为了扩张奴隶制。

　　购买加兹登为的是修建一条从南方各州到太平洋的最便捷的铁路，为此美国向墨西哥支付了 1000 万美圆。比较一下购买庞大的路易斯安那（1803 年）的价钱（1500 万美圆）和购买后来成为美国面积最大的州的阿拉斯加（1867 年）的价钱（720 万美圆），这笔钱应当不算少。有美国人称之为"良心钱"，因为美国人自己也为侵略墨西哥感到内疚。至此，在短短的半个世纪里，美国领土比独立时扩大了 7 倍。

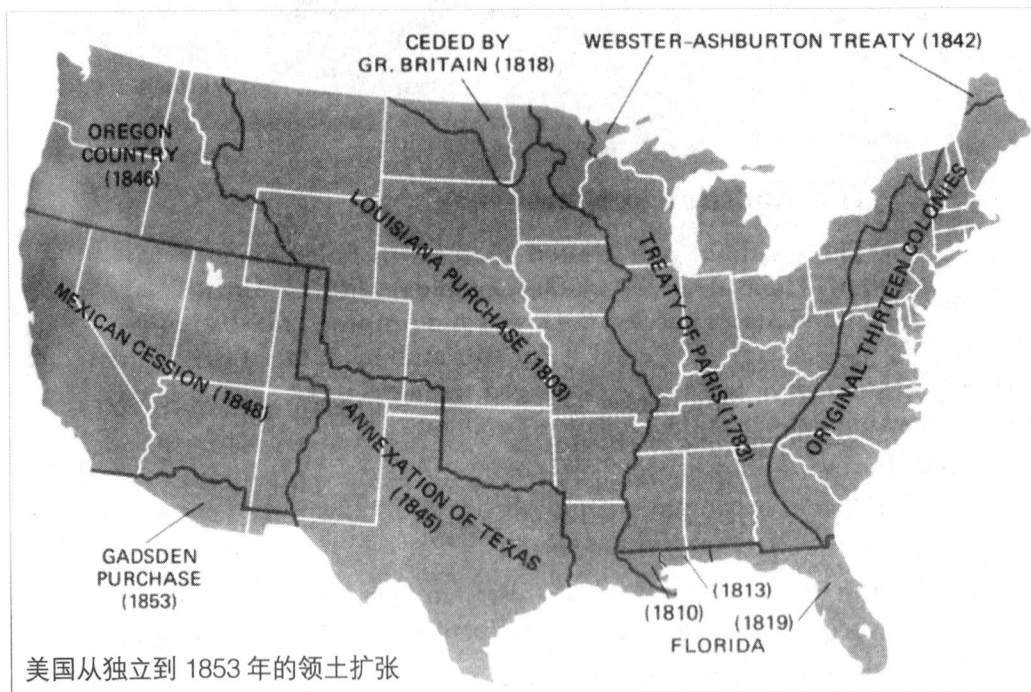

美国从独立到 1853 年的领土扩张

8. The Gold Rush

淘金热

Early in 1848, shortly before the United States and Mexico signed the peace treaty, gold was discovered in California. The first pieces of gold were found at the sawmill on the American River in the Sacramento Valley. News of the discovery spread, and thousands of people rushed to California.

　　1848 年初，在美国与墨西哥签订和约前不久，加利福尼亚发现了黄金。头一批金块是在萨克拉门托河谷阿美利加河上的锯木厂附近发现的。发现黄金的消息不胫而走，成千上万的人拥向加利福尼亚。由

These people were called "forty-niners", since most of them arrived in 1849. San Francisco, the nearest port, grew from a small town to a city of 25,000 in a year's time as people arrived from all over the world. By the end of 1849, California's population had increased to more than 100,000. A few forty-niners found gold and became rich overnight. Others made fortunes by selling the miners food, supplies, and services at high prices. Those miners who were not so lucky in the gold fields became farmers and ranchers, raising cattle and growing fruit in the Central Valley. By 1850, California had enough people to be admitted to the Union as a state.

Gold rushes also brought people to Colorado, Alaska, Arizona, Idaho, Montana, Nevada, New Mexico, South Dakota, Utah, and Wyoming. These people built cities, transportation systems, and brought in varied economies. Gold rushes played an important role in the development of the West.

于他们大多在第二年到达，被称为"四九佬"。随着人们从世界各地蜂拥而至，离矿区最近的港口旧金山在一年之中就从一个小镇扩大成一个25000人口的城市。到1849年末，加利福尼亚的人口已猛增至10万。少数"四九佬"找到了黄金，一夜暴富。还有些人通过向矿工出售高价食品和用品、提供高价服务而发了财。那些在金矿上不走运的矿工则改行成了农夫或农场主，在中央谷地养牛、种植果树。到了1850年，加利福尼亚已有足够的法定人口，被接纳成为美国的一个州。

淘金热也使人们拥向科罗拉多、阿拉斯加、亚利桑那、爱达荷、蒙大拿、内华达、新墨西哥、南达科他、犹他和怀俄明等州。淘金者们建立了城市、交通系统，引入了多种经济。淘金热在西部的开发中起到重要作用。

9. The Mormons in Utah

摩门教徒在犹他

Joseph Smith founded The Mormon Church (The Church of Jesus Christ of Latter-day Saints) in New York in 1830. The church grew rapidly, and had 1,000 members by the end of the first year. During the early 1830s the Mormons left New York and tried to establish their communities first in Ohio and then in Missouri and Illinois. In each place their attempts to settle failed because as their

1830年，约瑟夫·史密斯在纽约州创立了摩门教（耶稣基督后期圣徒教）。教会很快扩大，到当年年底就发展教徒1000人。30年代初，摩门教徒离开纽约州先后试图在俄亥俄、密苏里和伊利诺伊州建立了自己社区。但每到一处，他们定居的企图均告失败，因为随着摩

population grew, their neighbours became suspicious of their economic and political power, as well as their practice of polygamy.

In 1844, Joseph Smith and his brother were shot and killed by a mob. Brigham Young was chosen to be the new church leader. In 1847, Young began to move his followers to the Great Basin in the Rocky Mountains. Some 80,000 Mormons travelled from the Missouri River to the Great Basin and more than 6,000 died along the way. They settled in what is now Salt Lake City. The population of the region grew rapidly, and by 1849, the Mormons had set up a civil government. Under Young's guidance, the Mormons carried out great plans for developing industry, agriculture, commerce, and education in their new home.

门教徒人口的增长，他们实行的多妻制以及他们的经济和政治势力引起当地人的猜忌。

1844 年，约瑟夫·史密斯和他的弟弟被一群暴民枪杀。布里格姆·扬被推选为新的教会首领。1847 年，扬开始率领教徒迁往落基山的大盆地。大约 8 万摩门教徒长途跋涉从密苏里河前往大盆地，6000 余人死于途中。他们在盐湖城所在的地方定居下来。这一地区的人口迅速增长，到了 1849 年，摩门教徒成立了市政府。在扬的指导下，摩门教徒制定了在新家乡发展工业、农业、商业和教育的庞大计划，并加以实施。

题外话

据约瑟夫·史密斯自称，大约在 1820 年，当他 14 岁时，看到了天父和耶稣基督的幻象，他们告诉他，世上尚无真正的教会。1827 年，他宣称一位叫做摩罗尼的天使向他显灵，责令他建立教会，并指引他去到纽约州他家附近的一座山里，找到埋藏了千年之久的金页。金页上镌刻着一种古代的语言，纪录了北美古代居民的宗教生活。他靠着"上帝赋予的异能"翻译了金页，并在 1830 年将译文发表，称之为《摩门经》。史密斯和他的同伴于 1830 年 4 月 6 日创立摩门教。

摩门教首领布里格姆·扬

CHAPTER SEVEN
The Slavery Controversy
奴隶制引起的争议

1. The Missouri Compromise

密苏里妥协方案

Beginning in colonial times, many Americans had demanded an end to slavery. By the early 19th century, every Northern state had outlawed slavery. But the plantation system had spread throughout the South, and the economy of the Southern States depended more and more on slaves as a source of cheap labor.

The question of whether to outlaw or allow slavery became an important political and social issue in the early 19th century. Of the original 13 states, 7 were free states (where slavery was prohibited) and 6 were slave states (where slavery was allowed). Between 1791 and 1819, 9 new states were admitted to the Union. Of these, 4 were free and 5 slave. This meant that both sides would have an equal number of representatives in the United States Senate.

When the Territory of Missouri, a slaveholding area, applied for admission to the Union in 1818, bitter controversy broke out over whether to admit it as a free or slave state. In either case,

早在殖民时代，许多美国人就要求废除奴隶制。到了19世纪初，北方各州均已宣布奴隶制为非法。但庄园经营的体制盛行于南方，南方各州的经济越来越依赖奴隶的廉价劳动来维持。

是禁止还是许可奴隶制，成为19世纪初一个重要的政治和社会问题。最初建立的13个州里，有7个是自由州（禁止奴隶制的州），6个是蓄奴州（奴隶制合法的州）。在1791～1819年间，美国接纳了9个新州。其中4个是自由州，5个是蓄奴州。这意味着自由州和蓄奴州双方在美国参议院里的代表人数相等。

当允许奴隶制的密苏里准州于1818年申请加入联邦时，它究竟应以自由州还是蓄奴州的身份纳入联邦，引发了激烈的争议。无论以哪种身份加入联邦，其结果都会威胁

the admission of Missouri threatened to destroy the balance between free and slave states. But in 1820, Maine also applied for admission to the Union. Congress worked out the *Missouri Compromise*. The compromise admitted Maine as a free state and Missouri as a slave state so that there were 12 free and 12 slave states. The balance was thus temporarily maintained. The compromise also banned slavery from the Louisiana Purchase north of the southern boundary of Missouri, except in the state of Missouri. The Missouri Compromise satisfied many Americans as an answer to the slavery question. But large numbers of people still called for complete abolition.

In the 1830s and 1840s, the North and South continued to have equal representation in the Senate. Six more states were added to the Union—Michigan, Iowa, Wisconsin, Arkansas, Florida, and Texas. The first three were free states, and the other three, slave states. The balance was thus kept at 15 states each.

打破自由州和蓄奴州的均势。但在1820年，缅因州也要求加入联邦。国会达成了所谓的"密苏里妥协方案"。这一妥协方案允许缅因以自由州的身份，密苏里以蓄奴州的身份加入联邦。结果，自由州和蓄奴州各有12个，均势暂时得到维持。这一妥协方案同时禁止密苏里南部边界以北的路易斯安那购地实行奴隶制，密苏里州除外。密苏里妥协方案作为解决奴隶制问题的一个方法使许多美国人感到满意。但是仍有很多人号召彻底废除奴隶制。

在30年代和40年代，南北双方在参议院的代表人数一直保持均等。又有6个州加入联邦——密歇根、艾奥瓦、威斯康星、阿肯色、佛罗里达和得克萨斯。前3个是自由州，后3个是蓄奴州。每方各15州，均衡仍然维持着。

2. The Compromise of 1850

1850年的妥协方案

Soon after the Missouri Compromise was made, however, the United States acquired a vast area in the West as a result of the Mexican War. This created a new problem. Southerners demanded that slavery be permitted in the new territories and states. Northerners wanted the federal government to outlaw slavery in the newly acquired lands.

The issue of slavery came to a head in 1850

然而，不久后，墨西哥战争使美国获得一大片领土。新的问题随之产生。南方人要求在新建的准州和州里允许实行奴隶制。北方人则希望联邦政府宣布在新获得的领土上奴隶制为非法。

1850年，加利福尼亚要求作为自由州加入联邦，使奴隶制问题再次尖锐化。激烈的争吵爆发了。肯

when California asked to be admitted as a free state. Bitter quarrelling broke out. Henry Clay, a senator from Kentucky, and others suggested a plan known as the *Compromise of 1850* to settle the argument. This Compromise was passed as a series of laws that made concessions to both the North and South. As part of the Compromise, California was admitted to the Union as a free state. At the same time, Congress created the territories of New Mexico and Utah, and when these territories became states, the settlers in each territory would decide whether or not to allow slavery. To satisfy the South, the Compromise gave Texas $10 million to give up its claims to eastern New Mexican territory. The Compromise also set up a stricter federal law for the return of runaway slaves. To please the North, the slave trade was abolished in Washington, D.C.

塔基州参议员亨利·克雷等人提出一个被称为"1850年的妥协方案"的建议以解决争端。这个方案以一系列法案的形式获得通过，对北南双方均做了让步。作为妥协方案的一部分，加利福尼亚作为自由州加入联邦，与此同时，国会创建新墨西哥和犹他两个准州，当这两个准州升格为州时，由当地居民决定是否允许奴隶制存在。为使南方满意，妥协方案拨给得克萨斯州1000万美圆，使之放弃对于新墨西哥准州东部的领土要求。妥协方案还制订了针对遣返逃亡奴隶的更为严格的法律。为了安抚北方，华盛顿特区的奴隶贸易被取消。

3. The Kansas-Nebraska Act

堪萨斯－内布拉斯加法案

The Compromise of 1850 eased the relations between North and South only for a while. A new conflict broke out in 1854 when the Congress passed *Kansas-Nebraska Act*. Senator Stephen Arnold Douglas of Illinois was largely responsible for this act. At the time plans were being made to build a railroad across the continent. The railroad would cross Indian land that lay roughly between Missouri and present-day Idaho. For building the railroad, this land would need to be organized into two new territories. Douglas proposed a bill to organize this land into two territories: Nebras-

1850年的妥协方案只是暂时缓和了北南双方的矛盾。1854年，当国会通过堪萨斯－内布拉斯加法案时，新的冲突发生了。这一法案主要是伊利诺伊州参议员斯蒂芬·阿诺德·道格拉斯提出的。当时，一条贯穿北美大陆的铁路正在筹划之中。这条铁路将穿过大致位于密苏里州和现在的爱达荷州之间的印第安人居住区。为了修建铁路，这片地区必须组建两个新的准州。道格拉斯提出一项法案，在北边建立内

ka in the north and Kansas in the south. To gain Southern support, the bill stated that all questions of slavery in the new territories were to be decided by the settlers rather than by Congress. This meant that the Missouri Compromise, which banned slavery from the Louisiana Purchase north of the southern boundary of Missouri, except in the state of Missouri, was abolished.

Angered by the Kansas-Nebraska Act, a group of antislavery Americans formed the Republican Party in 1854. Many Democrats and Whigs who opposed slavery left their parties and became Republicans. The new party called for repeal of Kansas-Nebraska Act and the Fugitive Slave Law, and the abolition of slavery in Washington, D.C. Few Southern voters supported the Republicans, because almost all Southerners wanted to expand slavery, not restrict it. Many Northerners supported the party. The new party soon replaced the Whig party and became dominant in the North.

布拉斯加准州，在南面建立堪萨斯准州。为获得南方的支持，该法案规定新准州里的奴隶制问题将由当地居民决定，国会将不再干预。密苏里妥协方案曾禁止密苏里南部边界以北的路易斯安那购地实行奴隶制，密苏里州除外；而新法案意味着密苏里妥协方案被废止。

一群废奴主义者被堪萨斯－内布拉斯加法案所激怒，他们于1854年成立了共和党。许多民主党和辉格党人离开了本党，加入了共和党。这个新成立的政党呼吁撤消堪萨斯－内布拉斯加法案和逃亡奴隶法，在华盛顿特区废除奴隶制。南方选民很少有支持共和党的，因为几乎所有的南方人都希望推广奴隶制，而不是限制它。许多北方人则支持共和党。这个新党不久便取代了辉格党，成为北方的最大党。

题外话

美国女作家、废奴主义者哈丽特·比彻·斯托的小说《汤姆叔叔的小屋》在启发美国民众的反奴隶制情绪方面起了重要作用。在小说中，斯托提供了奴隶制罪恶的生动例子，证明了奴隶制如何腐蚀了本性善良的奴隶主，使他们变得冷酷无情。这部小说出版当年(1852)售出30万册，第二年夏已售出120万册。

哈丽特·比彻·斯托

4. Bleeding Kansas

The other result of the Kansas-Nebraska Act was an outbreak of violence in Kansas. Since the questions of slavery were left for the settlers to decide, both Northerners and Southerners rushed into Kansas to make sure that they could control the legislature. Violence soon broke out, and many people were killed.

In 1856, supporters of slavery attacked an antislavery stronghold at Lawrence and burned part of the town. John Brown, a man who hated slavery, led a raid on a town of slavery supporters and killed five men. In 1859, Brown and his followers planned to stir up a slave uprising in the South. They attacked and seized the federal arsenal in Harpers Ferry, Virginia (now West Virginia). John wanted to obtain weapons for the slaves he hoped would join his force. But no uprising took place, and Brown and his men were soon killed or captured. Brown was tried, found guilty of treason and hanged. Many Southerners saw the raid as evi-

堪萨斯内战

堪萨斯–内布拉斯加法案的另一后果是堪萨斯发生的暴乱。由于奴隶制的问题归当地人决定，北方人和南方人纷纷拥入堪萨斯，以确保自己一方控制议会。不久便发生了暴力冲突，许多人被杀死。

1856年，奴隶制的支持者攻击了设在劳伦斯市的废奴主义势力的大本营，焚毁了该市的部分建筑。一个痛恨奴隶制的人约翰·布朗率领反奴隶制的人袭击了一座奴隶制支持者的城市，杀死5个人。1859年，布朗及其追随者们策划挑起南方的奴隶暴动。他们攻占了弗吉尼亚州（现在的西弗吉尼亚州）哈珀斯费里的军火库。他希望奴隶们会愿意加入他们队伍，因而企图夺取武器分发给奴隶们。但是奴隶暴动并没有发生。不久后，布朗一伙儿人有的阵亡，有的被俘。布朗本人受到审判，以叛国罪被处以绞刑。许多南方人将这次袭击视为一个

约翰·布朗

dence of a Northern plot to end slavery by force.

证据，表明北方酝酿着一个用武力结束奴隶制阴谋。

题外话

布朗的计划几乎毫无成功的希望，因为力量的对比过于悬殊。所以许多人怀疑他攻击哈珀斯费里的军火库时精神是否正常。但即使如此，许多北方人仍把他当做为争取人类自由而斗争的烈士看待。他后来在一首著名歌曲《约翰·布朗的遗体》里受到人们的颂扬。歌中唱道："约翰·布朗的遗体在墓中化为尘土，然而他的精神一往无前。"这首歌曲在南北战争开始时成为联邦军的战歌。美国著名作家拉尔夫·沃尔多·爱默生说布朗使他的绞刑架"犹如十字架一般光辉四射"。

5. The Dred Scott Decision

德雷德·斯科特裁决

In 1857, the Supreme Court of the United States tried to settle the slavery issue with its decision about a slave named Dred Scott.

Dred Scott was the slave from Missouri, a slave state. In 1834, Scott went with his master to live in Illinois, a free state, and later in the Wisconsin Territory, where slavery was forbidden by the Missouri Compromise. In 1838, Scott returned to Missouri with his master. His master died there in 1843, and Scott then sued his master's widow for his freedom, arguing that he had lived for a time in a free state and territory and was no longer a slave. The court denied Scott's claim and declared that no black could be a United States citizen. It further ruled that laws limiting the spread of slavery were unconstitutional. The ruling aroused anger in the North and led the nation a step closer to civil war.

1857年，美国最高法院就一个名叫德雷德·斯科特的奴隶的身份问题做出裁决，试图以此解决奴隶制问题。

德雷德·斯科特是来自蓄奴州密苏里的奴隶。1834 年，他随主人到自由州伊利诺伊居住，后来又到威斯康星准州居住。根据密苏里妥协方案，威斯康星禁止奴隶制。1838 年，斯科特随主人返回密苏里。他的主人于 1843 年去世。斯科特此时对主人的遗孀提起诉讼，要求获得自由，理由是他曾在自由州和自由准州生活过，因而不再是奴隶。法院驳回了斯科特的要求，宣称黑奴不具有美国公民资格。法院还进一步判决，限制奴隶制推广的立法由于违宪而无效。这一判决激怒了北方，使整个国家向内战迈进了一步。

6. The Lincoln-Douglas Debates

The slavery controversy remained the greatest issue in 1858. When Democrat Stephen Arnold Douglas, a U.S. senator from Illinois ran for reelection to the Senate, his Republican opponent was Abraham Lincoln, a man then almost unknown outside Illinois. Douglas was a popular and skillful American orator. He and Lincoln held a series of public debates on the problem of slavery. These meetings attracted the attention of the entire country. Douglas defended the policy of the Kansas-Nebraska Act. He believed that the people of the territories should decide for themselves whether they wanted slavery. He argued that the people of any territory could keep slavery out of that territory simply by refusing to pass local laws protecting it. Lincoln insisted that there was a fundamental difference between Douglas and himself. Douglas ignored the moral question of slavery, but Lincoln regarded slavery "as a moral, social, and political evil". Douglas won his reelection to the Senate, but some of his speeches in the debates displeased Southern Democrats. When Douglas ran for President in 1860, he lost the support of Southern Democrats. Lincoln lost the election to the Senate, but he gained a national reputation that won him the Republican nomination for President in 1860.

林肯-道格拉斯辩论

到了 1858 年，关于奴隶制的争议仍然是最重大的问题。当年，来自伊利诺伊州的美国参议员、民主党人斯蒂芬·阿诺德·道格拉斯竞选连任参议员，其共和党竞选对手是亚伯拉罕·林肯，一个在伊利诺伊以外几乎毫无名气的人。而道格拉斯则是在美国颇受欢迎的老练演说家。道格拉斯与林肯就奴隶制问题举行了一系列的公开辩论会。两人的辩论吸引了全国的关注。道格拉斯为堪萨斯－内布拉斯加法案辩护。他主张准州本地人应当有权决定是否采取奴隶制。他辩称任何准州只要拒绝制订地方法规保护奴隶制，均可将奴隶制拒之门外。林肯则坚持说道格拉斯与自己之间有着根本的分歧。道格拉斯将奴隶制的道德问题置之度外，而林肯则认为奴隶制是"道德上、社会上和政治上的一桩罪恶"。道格拉斯获胜连任参议员，但他在辩论中发表的某些言论使南方民主党人感到不快。当道格拉斯于 1860 年竞选总统时，他失去了南方民主党人的支持。林肯竞选参议员虽然失利，但他在全国名声大振，他的名气使他获得 1860 年的共和党候选人提名。

斯蒂芬·阿诺德·道格拉斯

亚伯拉罕·林肯

🔘 题 外 话

　　道格拉斯是个矮个子，大脑袋、宽肩膀，绰号"小巨人"，在辩论中杀伤力极强。在参议院中他以自己的干练、勇气和充沛的精力赢得尊敬。当他和林肯辩论时，两人的外观形成戏剧性反差。道格拉斯身材矮墩墩的，嗓音洪亮如公牛，而且衣冠楚楚、精心修饰过自己；林肯则身材颀长，嗓音尖锐，衣服松松垮垮，皮鞋也未擦亮。

　　南北战争爆发后，道格拉斯支持林肯总统和联邦。他说："在这场战争中没有中立者。要么当爱国者，要么当叛国者。"

7. The Secession of the South　南方退出联邦

During the 1850s, the North and South drew further and further apart over the issue of slavery. Early in 1860, many Southern leaders threatened to withdraw their states from the Union if Lincoln

　　在整个 50 年代，北南双方在奴隶制问题上分歧越来越大。1860 年初，南方领导人威胁说如果林肯当选总统，南方各州将退出联邦。

should win the election. Lincoln had earned a reputation as an outspoken opponent of slavery, and his election was unacceptable to the South. Southerners feared the new President would restrict or end slavery. After Lincoln's victory, South Carolina declared on December 20, 1860 that it withdrew from the Union. By the time Lincoln became President, Alabama, Florida, Georgia, Louisiana, and Mississippi had left the Union. The six seceded states formed the *Confederate States of America* in February 1861. They elected Jefferson Davis of Mississippi as president and Alexander H. Stephens of Georgia as vice president. In March, Texas joined the Confederacy. Later in that year, when the Civil War started, Arkansas, North Carolina, Tennessee, and Virginia joined the Confederacy. However, Virginians in the western part of the state remained loyal to the Union and formed the new state of West Virginia in 1863.

Lincoln took office on March 4, 1861. In his inaugural address, the new President warned that he would use the full power of the nation to hold the Union together. To him, the states that had left the Union were still part of the United States, and there was yet hope for reconciliation. But a little more than a month later, the North and South were at war.

林肯早以奴隶制直言不讳的反对者著名，他的当选对于南方是不可接受的。南方人担心新总统会限制或废止奴隶制。林肯在选举中获胜后，南卡罗莱纳州于 1860 年 12 月 20 日宣布退出联邦。到了林肯就任时，亚拉巴马、佛罗里达、佐治亚、路易斯安那和密西西比也已脱离联邦。6 个退出联邦的州于 1861 年 2 月成立了美利坚诸州联盟（南部邦联）。他们选出密西西比州的杰斐逊·戴维斯为总统，佐治亚州的亚历山大·H.斯蒂芬斯为副总统。3 月，得克萨斯加入南部邦联。当年晚些时候，南北战争爆发后，阿肯色、北卡罗莱纳、田纳西和弗吉尼亚加入了南部邦联。然而，弗吉尼亚西部居民仍然忠于联邦，他们于 1863 年成立了一个新的州，即西弗吉尼亚州。

林肯于 1861 年 3 月 4 日就职。在就职演说中，新总统发出警告，说他将动用国家的全副力量以维护联邦的完整。在他看来，那些脱离了联邦的州仍是美国的一部分，和解的希望依然存在。但仅仅过了一个月，南北战争就爆发了。

杰斐逊·戴维斯

CHAPTER EIGHT

The Civil War and Reconstruction
南北战争与战后重建

1. The Attack on Fort Sumter

炮轰萨姆特要塞

As the Southern States seceded, they seized most of the federal forts within their boundaries. One federal fort that had not been seized was Fort Sumter, in Charleston Harbor, South Carolina. Late in March, the troops at the fort run short of supplies. Since now the fort became a symbol of an indivisible Union, Lincoln decided to send provisions to the troops there, even though he knew that the South would consider this an act of war. When the supply ships came close to their destination, on April 12, Confederate guns opened fire on the fort and forced it to surrender the next day. The attack on Fort Sumter marked the start of the Civil War.

南方各州退出联邦的同时，它们夺取了边界内的大多数联邦军队的要塞。但南卡罗莱纳州查尔斯顿港的萨姆特要塞仍在联邦军队手中。3 月下旬，萨姆特要塞的军需供应出现短缺。由于此时这一要塞成为联邦不可分割的象征，林肯决定向那里的驻军运送粮食，即使他知道南方会将此举视为战争行动。当供给船于 4 月 12 日接近目的地时，南部邦联军队用炮火轰击萨姆特要塞，迫使要塞中的联邦军在次日投降。炮轰萨姆特要塞标志着南北战争的爆发。

2. First Battle of Bull Run

第一次布尔溪战役

In July 1861, a Union force of about 31,000

1861 年 7 月，一支大约 31000

under General Irvin McDowell moved into eastern Virginia to capture the Confederate capital Richmond. It met a Confederate army under Beauregard at a creek called Bull Run, a few kilometers south of Washington, D.C. Both armies had had too little training to fight well, but the Confederates had better leaders. The North launched several attacks without success. When the South launched a counterattack, the tired Union forces fled to Washington, D.C. In the battle, the Confederate General Thomas J. Jackson stood his ground so firmly that he received the nickname "Stonewall". The defeat at Bull Run made the North realize that it faced a long fight. The war would not be over in three months, as many Northerners had predicted.

人的联邦军在欧文·麦克道尔将军的率领下进入弗吉尼亚东部,试图夺取邦联首府里士满。这支军队在华盛顿南方几公里远的一条称为布尔溪的河边与博雷加德率领的南部邦联军相遇。两支军队都由于缺乏训练而不能有效打击对方,但南部邦联军却有较好的统帅。北军发动数次进攻,均未奏效。待南军发起反攻时,筋疲力尽的联邦军逃回华盛顿特区。在战斗中,南部邦联军的托马斯·J.杰克逊将军固守阵地,寸土不让,赢得了"石壁"的绰号。布尔溪战役的失利使北方意识到它所面对的将是一场持久战。这场战争不会像许多北方人所预想的,在三个月内结束。

3. The War at Sea

海上的战斗

At the outbreak of the war, Lincoln ordered Union ships to blockade the Southern coast. The blockade was so successful that it cut off the South's main source of income. The south tried to break the blockade. In 1861, the Confederates covered the wooden ship, the *Merrimack*, with iron plates four inches thick. On March 8, 1862, the *Merrimack* attacked Northern ships off the coast of Virginia and destroyed two ships made of wood. The next day, however, it faced the *Monitor*, an ironclad ship designed especially for the Northern Navy, with a flat deck and a revolving turret with two guns. A fierce sea battle followed. It was the

战争一爆发,林肯立即命令联邦军舰封锁南方海岸。封锁产生了预想的效果,切断了南方的重要收入来源。南方试图打破封锁。1861年,南部邦联军用4英寸厚的铁甲覆盖了一艘木船"梅里麦克"号。1862年3月8日,"梅里麦克"号向弗吉尼亚海岸附近的北方军舰发起攻击,摧毁两艘木船。但在次日,"梅里麦克"号遇到了"莫尼特"号。"莫尼特"号是一艘专为北方海军设计建造的铁甲舰,甲板低平,配有旋转炮塔,两门火炮。

first's battle in naval history between ironclad warships. The *Monitor* forced the *Merrimack* to withdraw. The battle saved the Northern blockade and showed that ironclad vessels were superior to wooden ones.

激烈的战斗随之打响。"莫尼特"号迫使"梅里麦克"号撤退。这场战斗使北方能够继续其对南方海岸的封锁，并证明铁甲舰的作战性能优于木船。

"莫尼特"号与"梅里麦克"交火

4. Fighting in the West in 1862

1862年的西部战斗

One of the main aims of Northern forces in the West was to seize the Mississippi River. In February 1862, Union troops under Ulysses S. Grant, with the help of a Union gunboat fleet, captured Fort Henry on the Tennessee River. Then they took Fort Donelson on the Cumberland River. The Confederates retreated southwards but then attacked Grant at Shiloh, in southwestern

北军在西部的重要军事目标之一是控制密西西比河。1862 年 2 月，联邦军在尤利西斯·S. 格兰特的率领下，依靠一艘联邦炮舰的支持，夺取了田纳西河上的亨利要塞。联邦军继而攻占了坎伯兰河上的唐奈尔森要塞。南部邦联军向南退却，但在田纳西西南部的夏洛向

Tennessee. In one of the bloodiest fights in the war, Grant's army suffered heavy losses, but it finally defeated the enemy. These victories gave the Union control of western Tennessee and the upper Mississippi River.

Meanwhile, Northern forces were moving up the Mississippi River from the South. In April, a fleet of warships under David G. Farragut sailed from the Gulf of Mexico into the mouth of the Mississippi River. They defeated the gunboats sent to stop them and captured New Orleans on May 1. Since then New Orleans and southern Louisiana were in the hands of Northerners until the end of the war.

5. Further Drives on Richmond

In the East, the Union army was still trying to capture Richmond. In April 1862, General George B. McClellan landed on the peninsula between the York and James rivers with more than 100,000 men, and drove on the Southern capital. He first captured Yorktown and advanced along the York River. By late May 1862, McClellan was within 10 kilometers of Richmond. There he stopped to wait for reinforcements. The Confederates under Johnston launched an attack against McClellan on May 31, but were driven back toward Richmond.

The Confederates feared that McClellan would receive reinforcements from the numerous troops that had stayed behind to protect Washington. Stonewall Jackson therefore launched a campaign in the Shenandoah Valley. He planned to

格兰特发起进攻。这里进行了南北战争中最血腥的战斗之一，格兰特的部队损失惨重，但最终打败了敌军。西部的胜利使联邦控制了田纳西的西部和密西西比河的上游。

与此同时，北军从南面沿密西西比河逆流而上。4月，戴维·G.法拉格特率领的一支舰队从墨西哥湾开入密西西比河口。北军击溃了前来拦截的炮艇，于5月1日攻占了新奥尔良。从此以后，新奥尔良和路易斯安那的南部一直处于北军控制之下，直至战争结束。

再攻里士满

在东部，联邦军仍在尝试攻占里士满。1862年4月，乔治·B.麦克莱伦将军率军10万余人，在约克河和詹姆斯河之间的半岛登陆，直逼南方首府。他们先占领了约克敦，沿约克河北上。到了1862年5月末，麦克莱伦距里士满只有不到10公里远。他在那里停下来等候增援。5月31日，南部邦联军在约翰斯顿的率领下向麦克莱伦发起进攻，但被逐回里士满。

南部邦联军担心麦克莱伦会得到在后方保卫华盛顿的大部队的增援，于是"石壁"杰克逊在谢南多厄河谷发起进攻。他想给北方制造错觉，以为他即将进攻华盛顿。从

make the Northerners think he was going to attack Washington, D.C. From May 4 through June 9, 1862, Jackson advanced about 560 kilometers up the Shenandoah Valley toward the Potomac River. Jackson won four battles against the Union armies. He reached the Potomac but soon had to retreat. However, he had kept the Northern troops too busy to give the powerful reinforcements that McClellan had needed.

Robert E. Lee, the great general who commanded the Confederate Army in the Civil War, planned to destroy McClellan's army. With his forces reinforced by Jackson's men to about 95, 000 men, Lee fell on McClellan in a series of attacks, called the Battles of the Seven Days, from June 25 to July 1, 1862. Lee forced McClellan to retreat to the James River, and then northwards. Richmond was saved from capture.

1862年的5月4日到6月9日，杰克逊沿谢南多厄河谷向北推进大约560公里，向波托马克河逼近。杰克逊在四次战斗中打败联邦军。但他抵达波托马克河后不久就被迫撤军。然而，他使北军无暇向急需兵力的麦克莱伦派出强大的增援部队。

南北战争中南部邦联军的伟大统帅罗伯特·E.李将军计划摧毁麦克莱伦的军队。得到杰克逊部队的增援后，李将军率领兵力大约95000人向麦克莱伦频频发起攻击。这一系列的战斗从6月25日进行到7月1日，称为"七天战役"。李将军迫使麦克莱伦撤退到詹姆斯河，然后继续向北撤退。对里士满的威胁解除了。

6. The Second Battle of Bull Run

第二次布尔溪战役

After the Battles of the Seven Days, McClellan was ordered to bring his men back to Washington, D.C., where he was to join with the forces under General John Pope. Lee moved rapidly northward to attack Pope, stationed at Manassas, the site of the First Battle of Bull Run, before McClellan's men could join him. Lee sent Jackson ahead to move behind Pope's army and force a battle. In August 1862, Pope attacked Jackson. Meanwhile, Lee and General James Longstreet moved up to reinforce Jackson. Pope's troops were thoroughly beaten and fled back to Washington, D.C.

七天战役后，麦克莱伦接到命令将部队撤回华盛顿，与约翰·波普将军的部队会师。李将军趁麦克莱伦与波普会师之前迅速北上，攻击驻扎在第一次布尔溪战役的发生地马纳萨斯的波普的部队。李将军派杰克逊迂回到波普部队的后方，迫使波普交战。1862年8月，波普向杰克逊发动进攻。与此同时，李将军和詹姆斯·朗斯特里特将军北上增援杰克逊。波普的部队惨败，逃回华盛顿。

7. The Battle of Antietam

安提塔姆战役

After the second battle of Bull Run, Lee invaded Maryland in September. McClellan's forces of about 90,000 men met Lee at a town on Antietam Creek in Maryland. McClellan launched a series of attacks, and Lee's force of about 40,000 men suffered heavy losses and had to retreat to Virginia. The Battle of Antietam was the bloodiest of the Civil War. About 5,000 men from both sides were killed and approximately 19,000 men were wounded, of which about 3,000 later died. Neither side really won, but because Lee retreated, the North called Antietam a Union victory.

第二次布尔溪战役后，李将军于9月入侵马里兰。麦克莱伦的大约9万人与李将军的军队在马里兰州安提塔姆河上的一座小镇上相遇。麦克莱伦发动一连串的攻击，李将军指挥的4万人损失惨重，被迫撤回弗吉尼亚。安提塔姆战役是南北战争中的最血腥的一战。双方共阵亡大约5000人，近19000人负伤，其中后来又有3000人不治身亡。双方都未能真正打赢这场战役，但由于李将军自动撤军，北方称安提塔姆战役为联邦的胜利。

安提塔姆战役中南军的阵亡士兵

北方军士兵

麦克莱伦将军

8. Battle of Fredericksburg

弗雷德里克斯堡战役

After the Battle of Antietam, McClellan refused to take the offensive against Lee's army. Lincoln, who had long felt that McClellan was not aggressive enough, replaced him with General Ambrose E. Burnside as commander of the Army of the Potomac. Burnside decided to attack Lee at Fredericksburg, Virginia. The Confederates, about 73,000 strong, placed in strong defensive positions on the hills near Fredericksburg. In December 1862, Burnside's troops launched an attack. In the bloody fighting, Union losses amounted to 12,600, as opposed to Confederate losses of 5,300. In January 1863 Lincoln relieved Burnside and

安提塔姆战役之后，麦克莱伦拒绝主动攻击李将军的军队。林肯长期以来就对麦克莱伦行动不够果敢感到不满，于是撤换了他，任命安布罗斯·E.伯恩赛德将军为波托马克兵团的指挥官。伯恩赛德决定在弗吉尼亚的弗雷德里克斯堡进攻李将军。南部邦联军大约73000人，在弗雷德里克斯堡附近的山上布置了牢固的防御阵线。1862年12月，伯恩赛德的军队发起进攻。一场血战之后，联邦军兵力损失多达12600人，而南部邦联军只损失5300人。1863

put General Joseph Hooker in command of the army.

9. The Homestead Act

Perhaps the most important act passed by Congress during the war was the *Homestead Act.* According to the law passed in May 1862, any person over 21, who was the head of a family, and either a citizen or an alien who intended to become a citizen, could apply for 160 acres of public land. If he or she lived there and farmed the land for five years he or she would become the owner of the land. Or, the settler could pay $1.25 per acre to become the owner of the land if they did not want to live there and farmed the land for five years. The Homestead Act attracted thousands of settlers to the West. From 1862 until 1900, it provided farms and new homes for between 400,000 and 600,000 families.

年 1 月，林肯免去伯恩赛德的职务，任命约瑟夫·胡克将军指挥军队。

《宅地法》

在战争期间，国会通过的最重要立法应算是《宅地法》。根据这项于 1862 年 5 月通过的法律，任何年满 21 岁的户主，无论是美国公民或是有意成为美国公民的人，均可以申请得到 160 英亩的公有土地。在该地生活并耕作 5 年以上，便可自动成为土地的所有者。若不愿在该地生活并耕作 5 年，在交纳每英亩 1.25 美圆的购地款后，亦可成为该地的所有者。《宅地法》吸引了成千上万的移民前往西部定居。从 1862 年至 1900 年，《宅地法》为 400000 至 600000 个家庭提供了耕地和宅地。

移民在大平原上建立的草泥屋

10. The Emancipation Procla-mation

《解放宣言》

Lincoln had been waiting for a Northern victory as a good time for freeing slaves. The Battle of Antietam served this purpose. On September 22, 1862, Lincoln declared that all slaves in states of the Confederacy that were still in rebellion against the Union would be forever free at the beginning of the new year.

The Emancipation Proclamation was issued on January 1, 1863. Its immediate effect was limited. The Proclamation did not actually free a single slave, because it affected only areas under Confederate control. It did not apply to slaves in border states and in such Southern areas under Union control as Tennessee and parts of Louisiana and Virginia. But the proclamation provided for the use of blacks in the Union Army and Navy. As a result, about 200,000 black soldiers and sailors, many of them former slaves, served in the armed forces. They helped the North win the war. Besides, the proclamation gave the Northern cause a moral force by making the war a fight against slavery. Most British and French citizens opposed slavery, and so they gave their support to the Union. Most importantly, the proclamation was a historic document that led to the 13th Amendment to the Constitution, which abolished slavery throughout the nation.

林肯一直在等待着一场北方的胜利作为解放奴隶的良机。安提塔姆战役提供了这一机遇。1862 年 9 月 22 日，林肯宣布正在与联邦为敌的邦联各州中所有的奴隶从新的一年开始将永远成为自由人。

《解放宣言》于 1863 年 1 月 1 日正式发布。其效果一时并不明显。《宣言》实际上没有解放任何奴隶，因为它仅适用于南部邦联控制之下的各州，而不适用于边界各州以及联邦控制下的区域，如田纳西、路易斯安那及弗吉尼亚部分地区。但是《宣言》规定可以接纳黑人参加联邦陆军和海军。结果，大约有 200000 名黑人士兵和水手，其中许多曾经是奴隶，到军队里服役。他们为北方赢得战争做出了贡献。此外，《宣言》使这场战争成为一场反对奴隶制的战争，从而使北方的事业在道义上占了上风。英国和法国的公民大多反对奴隶制，因而支持北方。最重要的是，《宣言》是个具有重大历史意义的文件，它促使制订了宪法的第 13 条修正案，在全国范围内废除了奴隶制。

南卡罗莱纳庄园上的黑奴家庭

11. Battle of Chancellorsville

When Union General Joseph Hooker replaced General Ambrose Burnside as commander of the army in the spring of 1863, the Army of the Potomac numbered about 138,000 men. Lee had only about 60,000 men and still held the line of defense at Fredericksburg. Hooker planned to keep the attention of the Southern army at Fredericksburg, while sending another force to attack the Confederate flank. At first the attack seemed about to succeed. But then, Hooker hesitated. On May 1, he withdrew his flanking troops to a defensive position at Chancellorsville, a settlement just west of Fredericksburg. The next day, Lee left a small force at Fredericksburg and boldly moved to attack Hooker. He sent Stonewall Jackson to attack Hooker's right flank, while he struck in front. After three days of fierce fighting, Hooker was forced to withdraw. During the battle, Jackson was shot accidentally by his own men and died later. The Army of the Potomac had again failed to reach Richmond.

钱瑟勒斯维尔战役

1863年春，当约瑟夫·胡克将军替代了安布罗斯·伯恩赛德将军指挥军队时，波托马克军团兵力大约有13.8万人。李将军只有6万人，固守弗雷德里克斯堡防线。胡克计划吸引弗雷德里克斯堡南军的注意力，然后派遣另一支部队袭击邦联军的侧翼。起初，袭击似乎即将取得成功，但此时胡克犹豫了。5月1日，他将袭击邦联军侧翼的部队撤回到弗雷德里克斯堡西面的一个居民点钱瑟勒斯维尔，进入防守阵地。次日，李将军将一小股部队留在弗雷德里克斯堡，大胆向胡克发起进攻。他派遣"石壁"杰克逊攻打胡克的右翼，而自己从正面出击。经过三天的激烈战斗，胡克被迫撤退。在战斗中，杰克逊被自己人偶然击中，不久死去。波托马克军团再次失利，未能抵达里士满。

12. Battles in the West in 1863

In the spring of 1863, Grant launched a fierce attack on the last key Southern city that guarded the Mississippi River. In a brilliant campaign, Grant scattered Confederate forces in the field and drove toward Vicksburg. After direct at-

1863年的西部战斗

1863年春，格兰特向保卫密西西比河的最后一个南方重镇发起猛烈进攻。他打了一场出色的战役，驱散了战场上的南部邦联军，朝着维克斯堡急进。直接进攻未能奏

tacks failed, he began a siege of the city in mid-May. Vicksburg finally surrendered on July 4. Four days later, the Northern forces took Port Hudson. The North now got complete control of the Mississippi River, and the states west of the river were cut off from the rest of the Confederacy.

In September 1863, a Union force of about 55,000 men under William S. Rosecrans advanced on Chattanooga in eastern Tennessee. The Confederates withdrew from the city. Rosecrans followed them into Georgia where the two sides fought at the Battle of Chickamauga. The Union army was saved from total defeat only because General George H. Thomas bravely held his line. His bravery won him the nickname "The Rock of Chickamauga". In the end, Rosecrans' entire army had to retreat to Chattanooga. The Battle of Chickamauga was the Confederacy's last important victory in the Civil War. In late September 1863, the Confederates surrounded Chattanooga. Starvation threatened Rosecrans' army. But the North had enough troops available in the West to meet any threat. In October, Grant was given command of all Union forces in the West. He replaced Rosecrans with Thomas. Grant then went to Chattanooga with part of his own army. From November 23 to 25, the Union troops launched an attack and quickly defeated the Southerners. By the end of 1863, almost all Tennessee was in Union hands.

效，5 月中旬他开始围困维克斯堡。维克斯堡终于在 7 月 4 日投降。4 天后，北军占领哈得孙港。北方现在完全控制了密西西比河，密西西比河以西的州与邦联其他各州的联系被切断。

1863 年 9 月，一支大约 5.5 万的联邦军在威廉·S.罗斯克兰斯的率领下向田纳西东部的查塔努加进军。南部邦联军从该市撤出，罗斯克兰斯追逐他们进入佐治亚，双方在奇克莫加战役中交火。联邦军险些被彻底击溃，多亏乔治·H.托马斯将军英勇地守住了阵地。托马斯的勇敢使他赢得了"奇克莫加之岩"的绰号。最后，罗斯克兰斯的整个军队不得不撤退到查塔努加。奇克莫加战役是南北战争中南部邦联军取得的最后一场胜利。1863 年 9 月末，南部邦联军包围了查塔努加。饥荒威胁着罗斯克兰斯的部队。但北方在西部有足够的兵力来对付任何威胁。10 月，格兰特受命指挥所有在西部的联邦军。格兰特用托马斯替换了罗斯克兰斯，然后亲自率领部分兵力前往查塔努加。从 11 月 23 日至 25 日，联邦军发动了一次进攻，很快打败了南军。到了 1863 年末，整个田纳西几乎都落入联邦手中。

13. Battle of Gettysburg

葛底斯堡战役

In June 1863, Lee's army moved up into southern Pennsylvania. He was met by George G. Meade, a general Lincoln had just put in command of the Union troops. For the first three days of July, a Northern army of about 85,000 men fought a Southern army of about 65,000 in the greatest battle ever fought in the Western Hemisphere. Lee had to withdraw his army after it suffered over 25,000 casualties. Much to Lincoln's disgust, Meade made little effort to follow Lee's army, even though his troops greatly outnumbered Lee's. Lee's army thus escaped.

Gettysburg became a turning point in the war. Never again would the South have the troop strength to launch a major offensive. Gettysburg is also linked with one of the most famous speeches in American history — Lincoln's Gettysburg Address.

1863年6月，李将军的部队北上侵入宾夕法尼亚南部。与他相遇的是林肯刚刚任命的联邦军总指挥乔治·G.米德将军。在7月的3天里，北军的大约85000人和南军的大约65000人展开了西半球历史上最大规模的战斗。李将军的部队伤亡多达25000人，不得不撤军。使林肯大为恼火的是，米德竟没有尽力追逐李将军的军队，虽然他的军队人数大大超过李将军的军队，结果让李将军的军队逃脱了。

葛底斯堡战役成为南北战争的转折点。此后南方再没有足够的兵力发动大规模的进攻。葛底斯堡也与美国历史上最著名的演说之一，即林肯的《葛底斯堡演说》联系在一起。

葛底斯堡战役中北军的阵亡士兵

14. The Richmond Campaign

Early in 1864, Lincoln gave Grant command of all the Union armies. Grant planned to destroy Lee's army and capture Richmond. In May, the Northern Army moved into an area of northern Virginia called the Wilderness. Grant, with about 118,000 men, planned to march through the Wilderness and force the Confederates into a battle that would have a clear winner. Lee, with only about 62,000 troops, met Grant on May 5, and the Battle of the Wilderness fought for two days. Soldiers fought blindly in the densely wooded area, and both sides suffered heavy losses.

In spite of his losses, Grant pushed on. Lee marched to meet him, and they clashed again at Spotsylvania Court House, Virginia, from May 8 to 19, 1864. The battle, like that of the Wilderness, brought large losses but no victory for either side.

By June 1, Grant had reached Cold Harbor, a town just north of the Confederate capital. There, on June 3, he made another attempt to smash Lee. Lee showed superb defensive skill, and Northern losses were enormous. In a month of fighting, Grant had lost almost 40,000 men. Grant had to change his strategy. He marched south and crossed the James River, planning to attack Richmond from the south. Lee gathered his troops at Petersburg, which Grant surrounded for nine months.

To relieve the pressure of Richmond, Lee sent Jubal Early north through the Shenandoah Valley to attack Washington, D.C. Grant put all Union

里士满战役

1864年初，林肯将整个联邦军队的指挥权授予格兰特。格兰特计划摧毁李将军的军队，攻占里士满。5月，北军开进弗吉尼亚北部称为莽原的一片地区。格兰特率领大约118000人，计划穿过莽原，迫使邦联军队与之决一胜负。李将军只有军队62000人，于5月5日与格兰特的军队相遇，在莽原战役中战斗两天。士兵们在茂密的丛林中盲目作战，双方损失都很惨重。

格兰特不顾损失，继续向前推进。李将军前去迎战，双方军队在1864年5月8日和9日会战于弗吉尼亚的斯波特瑟尔韦尼亚县府。这场战斗，与莽原战役一样，损失巨大而不分胜负。

6月1日，格兰特抵达冷港，邦联首府北部的一座小镇。6月3日，格兰特再次尝试粉碎李将军的部队。李将军以其高超的防御技巧使北军蒙受巨大损失。在一个月的战斗中，格兰特损失了近4万人。格兰特不得不改变战略。他向南前进，跨过詹姆斯河，企图从南面攻打里士满。李将军将军队聚集在彼得斯堡，格兰特围困彼得斯堡长达9个月。

为减轻里士满的压力，李将军派遣朱巴尔·厄尔利北上沿谢南多厄河谷攻打华盛顿。格兰特将谢南

forces in the Shenandoah Valley under Philip H. Sheridan. Sheridan's forces outnumbered the Confederates 2 to 1 and drove them from the valley in a series of victories. Sheridan then devastated the area so thoroughly that its rich farms could no longer send food and supplies to Lee's troops.

多厄河谷的全部联邦兵力由菲利普·H.谢里登指挥。谢里登的部队比邦联军队的人数多一倍，连续打了几场胜仗，将南部邦联军队逐出河谷。谢里登将这一地区彻底破坏，使富庶的农庄无法再向李将军的军队提供粮食和物资。

15. Sherman's Drive

谢尔曼长驱

In May 1864, while Grant drove into the Wilderness, William T. Sherman's army of about 100,000 men advanced on Atlanta, Georgia, from Chattanooga. General Joseph E. Johnston opposed him with a force of about 62,000. After a series of small battles, President Jefferson Davis, decided Johnston fought too cautiously and replaced him with General John B. Hood. Hood attacked the Union troops as Sherman approached Atlanta. But Hood's attacks failed, and he took up a position in the city. Sherman's army moved to the south of the city, and seized its railroad to cut its supply line. The enemy had to leave Atlanta, and Sherman took the city in September 1864.

Hood decided to invade Tennessee in the hope that Sherman would follow him. He felt sure that he could beat Sherman in the mountains. But instead of following him, Sherman sent more troops to Thomas at Nashville, Tennessee, and ordered him to keep Hood out of the state. When Hood took a position outside Nashville, Thomas, with an army of about 55,000, attacked Hood in December, 1864, and won one of the biggest

1864年5月，当格兰特的军队进入莽原时，威廉·T.谢尔曼的军队大约100000人从查塔努加出发向佐治亚的亚特兰大推进。约瑟夫·E.约翰斯顿率领大约62000人迎战谢尔曼。几场小规模的战斗之后，杰斐逊·戴维斯总统认为约翰斯顿作战过于谨慎，用约翰·B.胡德将军替代了他。在谢尔曼逼近亚特兰大时，胡德向联邦军发起进攻。但进攻被击退，胡德返回城里坚守阵地。谢尔曼的军队绕到城的南面，夺取了铁路，切断了城市的供给。敌军不得不离开亚特兰大，谢尔曼于1864年9月攻占了亚特兰大。

胡德决定入侵田纳西，希望谢尔曼紧随其后。他自觉有把握在山区击败谢尔曼。但谢尔曼没有跟随他，却派遣军队增援田纳西州纳什维尔的托马斯，命令他阻止胡德进入田纳西。胡德在纳什维尔城外布阵时，托马斯率领55000人于1864年12月向胡德发起进攻，取得南

victories of the war.

In November, Sherman burned Atlanta, and with a force of about 62,000 men, swept across Georgia to Savannah, near the Atlantic coast. The Union troops burned crops, killed cattle, and tearing up railroads so that the South could not produce or move any of the food that it needed to continue fighting.

Sherman occupied Savannah in December. From Savannah, Sherman moved quickly north into South Carolina. Along the way, Sherman's troops destroyed everything in their path, including civilian property that could be of use to the Confederates. The town of Columbia, the capital of South Carolina, was burned, although Sherman tried to prevent its destruction.

Sherman and his troops then moved on into North Carolina. Johnston tried to oppose them, but he had only one-third as many men. Sherman drove on toward Virginia to link up with Grant.

北战争中又一场最重大的胜利。

11 月，谢尔曼将亚特兰大付之一炬，率领大约 62000 人横扫佐治亚，推进到大西洋岸边的萨凡纳。联邦军一路上烧毁庄稼、杀死牲畜、破坏铁路，使南方无法生产和运送继续作战所需要的粮食。

谢尔曼于 12 月占领萨凡纳，再从萨凡纳迅速向北推进，突入南卡罗莱纳。谢尔曼的军队沿途破坏一切，包括南部邦联军可能利用的平民财产。南卡罗莱纳州的首府哥伦比亚市也被焚毁，虽然谢尔曼曾试图阻止破坏它。

谢尔曼的军队然后进入北卡罗莱纳。约翰斯顿试图抵抗，但他的兵力只有谢尔曼军队的三分之一。谢尔曼继续朝弗吉尼亚推进，去与格兰特会师。

威廉·T.谢尔曼将军

16. The End of the War

战争结束

In April 1865, Grant seized the railroads supplying Richmond. Lee had to take his troops out of Petersburg and Richmond. Lee retreated

1865年4月，格兰特夺取了里士满的铁路供给线。李将军不得不将军队撤出彼得斯堡和里士满。李

westward with nearly 50,000 men. He hoped to join forces with Johnston in North Carolina. But Grant overtook him and barred his way with an army of almost 113,000 troops. Lee realized that further resistance would mean useless loss of lives. He wrote to Grant and asked for an inter-view to arrange surrender terms. On April 9, 1865, the two great generals met at Appomattox Court House, Virginia. Grant offered generous terms, and Lee accepted them with deep appreci-ation. The Confederate soldiers received a day's rations and were released. They were allowed to keep their horses and mules to take home. Offi-cers could keep their side arms. A few weeks later, Johnston surrendered to Sherman. The war to preserve the American Union was over.

将军率领近 50000 人向西撤退，希望能与在北卡罗莱纳的约翰斯顿的部队会师。但格兰特赶上了他，以一支将近 113000 人的大军拦住他的去路。李将军意识到进一步的抵抗将意味着浪费生命。他给格兰特写了一封信，请求会见，安排投降事宜。1865 年 4 月 9 日，两位伟大的将军在弗吉尼亚的阿波马托克斯县府会见。格兰特提出了宽大的条件，李将军带着深切的感激之情接受了这些条件。邦联士兵领取了一天的给养后被释放了。他们被允许保留骡马，带回家乡。军官可以保留随身武器。几周后，约翰斯顿向谢尔曼投降。为维护美国联邦完整的战争至此结束。

李将军

格兰特将军

格兰特将军与李将军会面

题外话

格兰特与李在阿波马托克斯县府的会面是美国历史上最富于戏剧性的一幕。格兰特身着满是泥污的普通士兵的军服，只有肩章表明他的军衔；李将军则身着将军服，一尘不染，并带有佩剑。

遭战争破坏的里士满

17. The Assassination of Lincoln

林肯遇刺

A few days after Lee's surrender at Appomattox, on April 14, 1865, Lincoln went to see a play at Ford's Theatre in Washington. During the performance, John Wilkes Booth, a Southern actor, shot the President in the head from the rear of the presidential box. Booth leaped onto the stage, and escaped (but was later killed). Lincoln was carried unconscious to a neighboring house. He died next morning, on April 15, 1865.

Before his death, Lincoln delivered his second inaugural address on March 4, 1865. In this eloquent speech, Lincoln emphasized the need for reconciliation between the North and the South. He advised his countrymen: "With malice toward none, with charity for all, with firmness in the right as God gives us to see the right, let us strive on to finish the work we are in, to bind up the nation's wounds, to care for him who shall have borne the battle and for his widow and his orphan, to do all which may achieve and cherish a just and lasting peace among ourselves and with all nations."

李将军在阿波马托克斯县府投降几天后，1865 年 4 月 14 日，林肯前往华盛顿的福特剧场观剧。在演出中，一个名叫约翰·威尔克斯·布斯的南方演员从总统包厢后面朝总统头部开了一枪。布斯跳上舞台，逃跑了（但后来被杀死）。失去知觉的林肯被抬进临近的一所房子里。他在次日上午，即 1865 年 4 月 15 日去世。

林肯去世前，曾在 3 月 4 日发表第二任总统就职演说。在这篇雄辩的演说中，林肯强调了北南双方和解的必要性。他劝告自己的同胞们：“我们对任何人不怀恶意，对所有的人都抱有善心，对上帝使我们认识到的正义信念坚定。让我们努力完成我们未竟的事业，包扎起国家的战争创伤，关怀参战的将士，关怀他们的遗孀与遗孤，竭尽全力争取并维护我国及全世界的正义的、持久的和平。

题外话

南北战争是美国历史上争议颇多、最令史学家感兴趣的问题之一，也是无数文学和艺术作品的题材。南北战争的原因何在？许多人认为奴隶制的争议是最根本的原因。林肯也是这样认为的。但大多数历史学家则认为，战争的起因有多种。首先，北南双方存在着巨大的地区差异，即经济上的、观念上的以及生活方式上的差异。其次，北南双方对于联邦和州政府的权利分配上一直存在着分歧。此外，政治家们缺乏远见及决策失误等等也有很大影响。然而，所有这些解释都直接或间接地与奴隶制有关。

这场战争是美国历史上最大规模的战争，共死亡 60 余万人，大致相当于从革命战争到越南战争美国阵亡将士的总和，而当时美国的总人口不过 3000 万。参战人员的阵亡率为四分之一强。阵亡率如此之高的原因之一是战术上的落后。当时兵器的杀伤力已很高，但大多数指挥官仍沿用陈旧的战术，如在开阔地正面冲击，一仗下来，往往尸横遍野。这是林肯，也是许多认为三个月结束战争的北方人未曾料到的。一位北方参议员在看到战场的血腥场面后说，"如果战前我能看到这个景象，即使再想维护联邦，也会说：'代价实在太大了，误入歧途的姊妹们，和平地离开联邦吧。'"生命无价。用 60 万条性命换取国家的完整，是否可取？提出这一问题，只有在战前才有意义。后人只能反思这一问题而已，而且无法征求那已死去的 60 万人的意见。

从交战双方的地域大小、人口多寡和工业先进与落后来看，显然北方具有绝对优势。而且，颇具讽刺意味，南方素来反对强大的中央政府，这种各自为政的传统在战争这一非常时期显然是一种弊端。它大大削弱了南方政府的协调和调度能力。尽管有所有这些不利因素，弱小的南方竟然撑持了 4 年才被打败，而且在历次大战役中南方伤亡人数一般要少于北方，这不能不说是个奇迹。究其原因，一是南方将领显然具有更高的军事才能；另外，战争主要在南方的土地上进行，供给线较短，南方人更熟悉自己的家乡，更易于获得当地人民的支持。

战争中最伟大的军事天才无疑是李将军。只可惜他效劳的是几乎没有获胜希望的南方。而格兰特之所以取胜，与其说靠其才能，不如说靠北方的军事实力、自己的勇气和决心。南方的另一个伟大的军事领袖是"石壁"杰克逊。可惜他过早阵亡了。在西部战区，优秀的统帅都在北军方面，其中包括格兰特、谢尔曼和托马斯。

南北战争证明美国民主也有它失败的时候。这场战争，用林肯的话来说，是"抛弃选票，诉诸大炮"（"appeal from the ballot to the bullet"）。美国的国家格言是"合众为一"（E Pluribus Unum）。但美国人在"众"与"一"之间徘徊了很长一段时间。北方的胜利使他们做出了抉择：任何州无权退出联邦。

18. Reconstruction

Reconstruction was the period in United States history that followed the Civil War. The word also refers to the process through which the South returned to the Union after their defeat. Reconstruction lasted from 1865 to 1877 and was a time of bitter political quarrels and disappointed hopes.

By the end of the war the political leaders of the North and South faced a set of difficult questions. For example, what was the relationship between the former Confederate states and the

重建时期

在美国历史上，南北战争之后的一段时期称为"重建时期"，指的是南方战败后重新返回联邦这一过程。重建时期从 1865 年持续到 1877 年，这一时期的特点是在政治问题上争吵不休，美好的希望归于落空。

战争末期，北南双方的政治领袖有一系列的难题亟待解决。例如，前南部邦联州和联邦的应是什么样的一种关系？曾退出联邦的 11

Union? How should the 11 states that had with-drawn from the Union be readmitted? How should Southern whites be treated? Who, if anyone, should be punished for the Confederate rebellion? What should be the position of the newly-freed slaves? How should the war-torn South be rebuilt?

Northerners divided over Reconstruction policy. Some people wanted to end the bitterness between the North and South and disapproved of harsh treatment of the rebels. But those radicals insisted that the South be punished. They also wanted a policy that would make sure that blacks would be better treated in the South than they had been before the war.

President Lincoln had already announced his plan for Reconstruction before his death. His plan was mild and generous to the South. When An-drew Johnson succeeded Lincoln and became President, he tried to carry out Lincoln's policy, but the radicals in Congress rejected his Recon-struction programs. Many of the most powerful Republicans controlled enough votes in Congress to pass their own Reconstruction poli-cy over Johnson's vetoes.

Johnson was almost removed from his of-fice for dismissing a radical official in his gov-ernment. In 1868, the House of Representatives impeached him. The Senate, sitting as a court, tried Johnson on the Impeachment charge in the spring of 1868. By the margin of a single vote, the radicals failed to get the two-thirds vote necessary to remove Johnson. Congress actually

个州应以何种方式重新加入联邦？怎样对待南方的白人？如果要惩罚南方的反叛，那么谁应当承担罪责？新解放的奴隶的地位如何？战争破坏了的南方将如何重建？

北方人对重建政策产生了分歧。有些人希望结束北南双方的仇恨，不赞成苛待那些反叛过联邦的人。但是那些激进分子则坚持要惩罚南方。他们希望制订一项政策，确保黑人比战前得到更好的待遇。

林肯总统在去世前已宣布了他的重建计划。他的计划对南方温和而宽大。安德鲁·约翰逊继任总统后试图按林肯的方针办，但国会里的激进分子否定了他重建规划。许多最有影响力的共和党人在国会控制了足够的票数，推翻了约翰逊的否决，而通过了他们自己的重建方针。

安德鲁·约翰逊总统

controlled Reconstruction, and it developed its own policies for the South.

Congress insisted that the Confederate States agree to follow all federal laws before being read-mitted to the Union. Between 1866 and 1870, all the Confederate States eventually met various requirements and all returned to the Union by 1870. Newly formed state governments in the South began to rebuild the ruined regions.

Some of the problems were solved during Reconstruction. First, Congress passed new laws to give blacks their rights. The 13th Amendment to the Constitution (1865) outlawed slavery throughout the United States. The 14th Amendment (1868) confirmed the citizenship of blacks, and the 15th Amendment (1870) made it illegal to deny the right to vote on the basis of race. The last two amendments had lasting significance. Starting in the middle of the 20th century, the 14th and 15th amendments became the legal basis of the civil rights movement, the struggle of black Americans for equality.

In 1865, Congress created the Freedmen's Bureau to protect the interests of Southern blacks. The bureau helped blacks find jobs and set up hospitals and schools for blacks in the South.

Thousands of blacks voted in the elections to form the new Reconstruction governments. These voters helped the Republicans win power throughout the South. But no state elected a black governor, and only 17 blacks won election to Congress during Reconstruction. South Carolina, where blacks made up more than half the population, was the only Southern state with a black majority in its legislature.

约翰逊由于将一名激进的政府官员解职而险些丢掉总统职位。1868年，众议院对总统提出弹劾。当年春天，参议院成立法庭，审讯弹劾案。在投票判决时，激进分子仅以一票之差未能获得将总统解职所需的三分之二的多数票。国会实际上控制了重建，制订了自己的南方政策。

国会坚持南方承诺遵守所有的联邦法律后才能重新加入联邦。1866年至1870年间，所有前邦联州都最终满足了各种条件，在1870年前已全部返回联邦。南方新成立的州政府开始重新建设被战争破坏的地区。

一些问题在重建时期得到解决。首先，国会通过新的法律给黑人以公民权。1865年通过的宪法第13条修正案在全美国废除了奴隶制。1868年通过的第14条修正案肯定了黑人的公民身份；1870年通过的第15条修正案，规定以种族原因剥夺任何人的选举权为非法。后两项修正案产生了持久的影响。从20世纪中叶开始，第14和15两条修正案成为美国黑人为争取平等而发动的民权运动的法律基础。

1865年，国会成立了被解放黑奴事务管理局，以保护南方黑人的利益。管理局帮助黑人找工作，并为南方黑人建立医院和学校。

成千上万的黑人参加投票，选举出新的重建政府。这些选举人帮助共和党在南方取得控制权。但在

One of the most significant achievements of the Reconstruction governments was the establishment of the first public school systems in most states of the South. Blacks, both young and old, went to these schools. At first, many whites refused to attend. Most of the Southern states then attracted white students by educating blacks and whites separately, even though many laws prohibited this action.

However, Reconstruction failed to solve the economic problems of either the blacks or the South as a whole. Farms, cities, railroads, and factories were destroyed during the war, and thousands of soldiers had lost their lives, and thousands more suffered from wounds and illness. Though state governments helped develop the South's natural resources and expand its railroad network, the South long remained the poorest, most backward section of the country. The living and working conditions of the blacks improved only slightly. Few blacks got land and economic independence. Instead, most of them continued to pick cotton on land that was owned by whites, the same job they had done as slaves.

In politics, Reconstruction made most Southern whites firm supporters of the Democratic Party. During Reconstruction, Republicans, protected by the troops, took control of local Southern governments. Most Southern whites considered these governments illegal. For more than 40 years after Reconstruction, no Republican presidential candidate received a majority of the votes in any Southern state.

Reconstruction also failed to bring racial harmony to the South. White Southerners remained

重建时期没有一个州选出黑人州长，只有17名黑人选入国会。黑人人口过半的南卡罗莱纳州是州议会中黑人占多数的唯一的南方州。

重建政府取得的最重要的成就之一是在南方大多数州首创了公立学校体系。黑人们无论长幼，都去学校上学。起初，许多白人拒绝入学。大多数南方州采取将黑人和白人隔离教学的措施以吸引白人学生，虽然许多法律禁止这种措施。

然而，重建未能解决黑人和整个南方的经济问题。战争期间，农庄、城市、铁路和工厂被摧毁了，千千万万的士兵阵亡，千千万万的士兵负伤或患病。虽然各州政府帮助开发南方的自然资源并扩大铁路网，但南方在很长一段时期都是全国最贫穷落后的地区。黑人的生活和工作条件只是略有改善。极少数黑人获得了土地和经济独立。大多数黑人仍在白人的地里摘棉花，与他们当奴隶时的工作一样。

在政治上，重建使大多数南方白人成为民主党的坚定支持者。在重建时期，共和党人在军队的护卫下控制了南方的地方政府。大多数白人认为这些政府是非法政府。重建时期以后的40年间，没有一个共和党总统候选人在任何一个南方州获得过多数选票。

重建也未能给南方带来种族和谐。南方白人维护着他们旧有的社会秩序，认为白人优越于黑人，拒绝与黑人分享政治权力。许多白人

loyal to their old social order and believed whites were superior to blacks, and refused to share important political power with blacks. Many of them joined the Ku Klux Klan, a secret society. Members of the society wore white robes and hoods and draped white sheets over their horses. The Ku Klux Klan grew rapidly and spread terror across the South. Klan members beat and even murdered blacks and their white sympathizers to keep them from exercising their rights. Blacks set up their own churches and other institutions rather than attempt to join white society. As the North gradually lost interest in Reconstruction and "the Negro question", Southern whites regained control of their state governments and took away many of the rights that blacks had won during Reconstruction. By the early 20th century, every Southern state had passed laws limiting voting rights. These laws gave the vote only to males who could pass certain educational tests or pay special taxes called poll taxes. Such laws effectively prevented most blacks from voting.

加入了秘密组织三 K 党。三 K 党徒披白袍、戴头罩，用白色床单罩住马匹。三 K 党发展很快，在南方散播恐怖气氛。党徒们殴打、乃至杀害黑人和同情黑人的白人，使他们不敢行使自己的权利。黑人建立了他们自己的教堂和其他机构，而不是试图加入白人的社会。随着北方逐渐对重建和"黑人问题"失去兴趣，南方白人重新控制了州政府，再次剥夺了黑人在重建时期取得的许多权利。到了 20 世纪初，各南方州都通过了限制选举权的法律，规定只有通过了某些教育水平测试，或缴纳称为"人头税"这一特殊税种的男性才有选举权。这些法律有效地阻止了大多数黑人参加选举。

19. Abraham Lincoln

Abraham Lincoln (1809-1865), the 16th President of the United States, stands in world history as one of the greatest men. Lincoln helped keep the American Union together during the Civil War and abolished slavery in the United States. Remembered for his honesty, compassion, and strength of character, Lincoln remains one of the most respected presidents in American history.

亚伯拉罕·林肯

美国第 16 位总统亚伯拉罕·林肯(1809-1865) 是世界历史中最伟大的人物之一。由于他的努力，经过南北战争，联邦的统一得以维护，美国的奴隶制得以废止。人们怀念他的正直、仁慈、和坚强的个性，他一直是美国历史上最受人景仰的总统之一。林肯是一个通过个人奋

Lincoln is a perfect example of a self-made man. His life shows how an honest and hardworking man in America can rise from humble origin to the nation's highest office. Lincoln was also an orator. His language was both simple and powerful. His Gettysburg Address, second inaugural address, and many of his other speeches and writings are classic statements of democratic beliefs and goals.

Lincoln was born on February 12, 1809, in a log cabin on a small farm in Kentucky. His parents, Thomas Lincoln and Nancy Hanks were poor and uneducated, but they sent Abraham and his sister Sarah to the local log schoolhouse to learn reading, writing, and arithmetic.

In 1816, when Abraham was seven, his family moved to Indiana. There, Thomas Lincoln began the task of changing 160 acres of forest into farmland. Life was harder in Indiana than in Kentucky. They arrived early in winter, and needed shelter at once. Thomas and his son built a three-sided shelter made of logs. A fire on the fourth side burned night and day to keep the family warm. Soon after finishing this shelter, the boy and his father began to build a log cabin. The family moved into it in February 1817. Then Abraham began to work with the rest of the family to cut trees and clear fields so that a crop could be planted. Although Abraham was only 8, he was large for his age and had enough strength to swing an ax. One of his chores with an axe was to make fence rails by splitting poles. Later, as a presidential candidate, Lincoln was known as the "Railsplitter".

Slowly, life became happier on the farm. But

斗而成功的典型。他的一生表明，在美国，一个正直而勤奋的人尽管出身卑微，仍可以上升到国家的最高职位。林肯也是一个演说家。他的语言简洁而有力。他的葛底斯堡演说、第二次就职演说以及许多其他的演说和文章是民主信念和理想的经典阐述。

林肯于 1809 年 2 月 12 日出生在肯塔基州一座小农庄上的一间小木屋里。他的父母托马斯·林肯和南希·汉克斯家境贫穷而且没有受过教育，但他们将亚伯拉罕和他的姐姐萨拉送到当地的木屋小学学习识字、写字、算算术。

1816年，林肯 7 岁时，全家迁到印第安纳。在这里托马斯·林肯开始苦干，将 160 英亩的森林改造成农田。印第安纳的生活比肯塔基更艰苦。他们于初冬到达，马上需要栖身之所。托马斯和儿子用圆木盖起了一个三面环绕的临时避风处，在第四面升起一堆火，日夜燃烧，供全家人取暖。有了这个避风处后，父子二人开始建造木屋。1817 年 2 月，全家迁入新居。然后，亚伯拉罕开始与全家人一起砍伐树木，为种植庄稼清理田地。亚伯拉罕只有 8 岁，但个头很高，有足够的力气挥动斧头。他每天要做的事情之一是用斧头劈木头，用木条做篱笆栏杆。后来，当他成为总统候选人时，被称为"劈栏杆的人"。

在这个农庄上，一家人的生活

in October 1818, Nancy Lincoln died after drinking poisoned milk from cows that had eaten the wild snakeroot plant. The next year, Thomas Lincoln returned to Kentucky for a visit, and married Sarah Bush Johnston, a widow with three children. Abraham Lincoln was very much attached to his kind stepmother.

Abraham Lincoln grew from a boy of 7 to a man of 21 on the wild Indiana frontier. When he had spare time, he attended a local school. At the time schools were held in log cabins, and often the teachers were barely more educated than their pupils. Including a few weeks at a similar school in Kentucky, Lincoln had less than one full year of formal education in his entire life. But he had a strong desire to learn. He would often read at night by the light of the fire in his family's cabin. Books were scarce on the frontier. He would walk a great distance for a book. The few he could borrow were good ones. He came to know the Bible thoroughly. He often quoted from the Bible in his later writings and speeches. The few other books he read included *Robinson Crusoe, Pilgrim's Progress, Aesop's Fables* and Mason Locke Weems's *Life and Memorable Actions of George Washington*. The biography of George Washington made a lasting impression on Lincoln.

By the time Lincoln was 19 years old, he had reached his full height of 193 centimeters. He was lean and strong, with long arms and legs, big hands and feet, which made him look awkward. He had a homely face and dark skin. His hair was black and coarse, and stood on end.

In 1828, he was hired by the local merchant

逐渐改善了。1818 年 10 月，南希·林肯喝了吃过美蛇根草的奶牛的奶，中毒身亡。第二年，托马斯·林肯回肯塔基探亲，娶了萨拉·布什·约翰斯顿，一个带着三个孩子的寡妇。亚伯拉罕·林肯对他和善的后母颇为眷恋。

林肯在印第安纳边境的蛮荒之地从一个 7 岁的孩子长成一个 21 岁的青年。当他有时间时，就去学校上学。当时的学校都设在木屋里，教师们受过的教育往往并不比学生们多多少。算上在肯塔基的类似学校里学习过的那几个星期，林肯一生中受过的正式教育不足一年。但他十分好学。他常常在家里的木屋里借着火光在深夜读书。在边境地区书籍很难找到。他常常为了借到一本书跑很远的路。他借到的那几本书都是好书。他对《圣经》内容了如指掌，在日后的文章和演讲中经常引用《圣经》。他读过的另外几本书包括《鲁宾逊漂流记》、《天路历程》、《伊索寓言》和梅森·洛克·威姆斯的《乔治·华盛顿传》。这部传记给林肯留下了永久的印象。

林肯 19 岁时，他的身高就达到了 193 厘米。他身材瘦削，但很健壮，长胳膊长腿，大手大脚，显得有些笨拙。他貌不出众，皮肤发暗，一头黑发又粗又硬。

1828 年，当地的一个商人雇林肯押送一艘满载货物的平底船沿密西西比河到新奥尔良。这趟旅行使

to take a cargo-laden flatboat down the Mississippi River to New Orleans. The trip gave him his first view of the world beyond his own community.

In 1830 the Lincoln family moved again and settled in Illinois. Lincoln helped his father build a log cabin and fence in 4 hectares to grow corn. Then he hired out to neighbors, helping them to split rails. That year, Lincoln attended a political rally and was persuaded to speak on behalf of a local candidate. It was his first political speech.

In the spring of 1831, a trader named Denton Offutt hired Lincoln and the two other young men to take a flatboat with a load of cargo down the Mississippi to New Orleans. According to legend, Lincoln saw for the first time how slaves were sold at auctions in New Orleans. What he saw filled him with indignation. This trip gave Offutt a good impression of his lanky boat hand. He hired Lincoln as a clerk in his new store in the village of New Salem, Illinois.

Lincoln lived in New Salem almost six years, from July 1831 until the spring of 1837. In the spring of 1832, Chief Black Hawk led a band of several hundred Indians back across the Mississippi River to try to regain their lands. The governor called out the militia, and Lincoln volunteered for service. Because of his popularity, Lincoln was elected captain. His comrades liked his friendliness, his honesty, and his skill at storytelling. When his term expired, he reenlisted as a private. In all, he served three months, but saw no actual fighting. However, Lincoln took great pride in this brief military career.

During the years in New Salem Lincoln

他看到了外面的世界。

1830年，林肯全家再次迁居，来到伊利诺伊定居。林肯帮助父亲建起一座木屋，用木栅围起4公顷的土地种植玉米。然后他受雇于邻人，帮助他们劈木头做栏杆。当年，林肯参加了一场政治集会，被人劝说为当地的候选人讲话。这是他头一次就政治问题当众讲话。

1831年春，一个名叫丹顿·奥法特的商人雇林肯和另外两个年轻人押送一艘载货的平底船顺密西西比河到新奥尔良。据说林肯在新奥尔良头一次见到奴隶如何在市场上拍卖。他所见到的景象使他充满义愤。这次旅行使奥法特对这个瘦高的船夫产生好感，于是雇林肯做店员，在伊利诺伊的新塞勒姆村他新开张的一家商店里卖货。

林肯在新塞勒姆住了将近6年，从1831年7月直至1837年春。1832年春，黑鹰酋长率领数百名印第安人渡过密西西比河，试图夺回他们失去的土地。州长号召组织民兵，林肯自愿加入民兵。由于他颇得人心，被推选为队长。他的战友们喜欢他的友善、诚实和讲故事的口才。服役期结束后，他重新加入民兵，成为列兵。他一共服役3个月，但没有参加过真正的战斗。然而，林肯仍为自己短暂的军事生涯感到自豪。

在新塞勒姆居住期间，林肯研读了语法书，并对英国诗人和剧作家莎士比亚和苏格兰诗人罗伯特·

studied books on grammar and acquired a life-long taste for the poetry of English poet and play-wright William Shakespeare and Scottish poet Robert Burns.

Lincoln decided to enter politics in the spring of 1832 and announced that he would be a candidate for the Illinois legislature. But the Black Hawk War prevented him from making much of a campaign. He arrived home in July, only two weeks before the election. Lincoln received a great many votes, but they were not enough to elect him.

The next year Lincoln went into business with a man named Berry, and the partners bought a New Salem store. The business failed, leaving them with a debt of about $1,100. When Berry died, Lincoln assumed the debt and eventually paid it off. His integrity helped him earn the nickname "Honest Abe".

In 1834, Lincoln again ran for the legislature. He had become better known by this time, and won election as a Whig. He served four successive two-year terms in the lower house of the Illinois General Assembly. During his first term, he met a young Democratic legislator, Stephen A. Douglas. It was the beginning of a rivalry between the two men that lasted for years. Lincoln quickly became noted in the legislature, because he was witty and ready in debate. His skill in party management enabled him to become the Whig floor leader at the beginning of his second term.

At the same time Lincoln began to study law by reading law books borrowed from John T. Stuart, a lawyer in Springfield, the capital of the

彭斯的诗歌产生了毕生的爱好。

1832年春,林肯决定从政,宣布他将竞选伊利诺伊州议会席位。但黑鹰战争使他无法全力竞选。他7月回家,离选举还有两周时间。林肯获得很多选票,但票数仍不足以使他当选。

第二年,林肯开始与一个名叫贝里的人合伙做生意,两人买下了新塞勒姆的一家商店。但生意亏了本,两人欠下大约1100美圆的债务。贝里去世后,林肯承担了所有的债务,最终将它全部偿还。他正直的人品为他赢得了"老实人亚伯"的绰号。

1834年,林肯再次竞选议员。这次他的名气更大,以辉格党员的身份当选。他在伊利诺伊议会的下院4次连任任期两年的议员。在头一任期中,他见到了年轻的民主党议员斯蒂芬·A.道格拉斯。这是两人多年竞争的开端。林肯在议会里很快引起人们的关注,因为他在辩论中头脑机敏,出口成章。他在党务管理方面的能力使他在第二任期成为辉格党领袖。

与此同时,林肯向伊利诺伊州首府斯普林菲尔德的一位律师约翰·T.斯图亚特借书,开始学习法律。林肯于1837年获得从事律师业的执照,先是在斯普林菲尔德的斯图亚特和林肯法律事务所担任初级律师,然后又为伊利诺伊州最著名的律师之一斯蒂芬·T.洛根担任初级律师。1844年,林肯与一个名叫

state. Lincoln received his license to practice law in 1837, and first became the junior partner in the law firm of Stuart and Lincoln in Springfield, and then the junior partner of Stephen T. Logan, one of the greatest lawyers who ever practiced in Illinois. In 1844 Lincoln formed a lifelong partnership with a young lawyer named William H. Herndon.

In 1840, soon after Lincoln moved to Springfield, he met a cultured, highly sensitive Kentucky woman named Mary Todd, who was staying with a married sister in Springfield. They got married in 1842, when Lincoln was 33 and his bride was 23. The couple had four sons, but only the eldest reached adulthood.

Lincoln's storytelling abilities and his skill and honesty as a lawyer made him well known throughout Illinois. He could argue a case strongly. He took only cases that he believed to be honest and fair. He sometimes persuaded clients to settle their differences out of court, which meant a smaller fee, or no fee at all, for him.

In 1846, Lincoln won the Whig nomination for the U.S. House of Representatives. Throughout his term, Lincoln supported the Whig policy of having the federal government pay for internal improvements.

When Lincoln's term ended in March 1849, he returned to Springfield. Now he appeared more often in the higher courts and handled more important cases. He represented corporations and big businesses frequently in lawsuits, and soon became one of the most respected lawyers in the state.

A sudden change in national policy toward

威廉·H.赫恩登的年轻律师结成毕生的合伙关系。

1840 年，林肯到斯普林菲尔德居住后不久就遇到了一个有良好教养的、十分敏感的肯塔基女子玛丽·托德，当时玛丽正在斯普林菲尔德已婚的姐姐家小住。林肯与玛丽·托德于 1842 年结婚，当年林肯 33 岁，新娘 23 岁。夫妻生下 4 个儿子，但只有最大的一个长大成人。

林肯讲故事的口才、他作为律师的技巧以及诚实的人品使他在伊利诺伊全州闻名。他对案子的辩护令人信服。他只接受那些他认为诚实与公正的案子。他有时劝说当事人庭外解决争端，尽管这样意味着他只能收取很少费用，或不收费用。

1846 年，林肯获得国会众议院辉格党的代表提名。在整个任期中，林肯一贯支持辉格党的政策，主张由联邦政府出资改善国计民生。

1849 年 3 月林肯任期期满，返回斯普林菲尔德。现在他更经常地出现在高等法院里，处置更重要的讼案。他常常在诉讼中代表大公司和大企业，不久就成为州内最受人尊重的律师之一。

联邦政府对奴隶制政策的突然改变，使林肯回到伊利诺伊政治活动的中心。1854 年初，伊利诺伊州参议员斯蒂芬·A.道格拉斯提出一项组建堪萨斯和内布拉斯加的法

slavery brought Lincoln back into the center of political activity in Illinois. Early in 1854, Senator Stephen A. Douglas of Illinois introduced a bill to organize the territories of Kansas and Nebraska. As approved by Congress, this Kansas-Nebraska Act abolished the old dividing line between free and slave states as set by the Missouri Compromise. It provided that the settlers of new territories should decide for themselves whether they wanted slavery. Lincoln believed that the new policy gave new life to slavery, and it outraged him. Lincoln never became an abolitionist, but he always opposed slavery and wanted the people to realize that slavery was evil, and should be abolished sooner or later. Now he became a forceful spokesman for the antislavery forces.

In the congressional election campaign of 1854 Lincoln help a candidate who opposed the Kansas-Nebraska Act. When Senator Douglas returned to Illinois to justify the new law, Lincoln opposed him by making powerful speeches at Springfield, Peoria, and Chicago. To Lincoln, slavery was incompatible with American democracy. "When the white man governs himself," he said, "that is self-government; but when he governs himself, and also governs another man—that is despotism. If the Negro is a man, why then my ancient faith teaches me that 'all men are created equal,' and that there can be no moral right in connection with one man's making a slave of another." Lincoln became known as the leader of the Illinois forces opposing the Kansas-Nebraska Act.

In 1856, Lincoln joined the antislavery Republican Party. During the presidential election

案，在国会获得通过。堪萨斯－内布拉斯加法案废止了密苏里妥协方案划定的自由州和蓄奴州的老分界线，规定新准州里是否允许奴隶制将由当地居民自行决定。林肯认为这项新政策延长了奴隶制的寿命，这使他感到义愤。林肯从来不是废奴主义者，但他一贯反对奴隶制，希望人民意识到奴隶制是一种罪恶，迟早应被废除。现在，他成为反对奴隶制势力的强有力的代言人。

在1854年的国会选举中，林肯支持一个反对堪萨斯－内布拉斯加法案的候选人。但参议员道格拉斯返回伊利诺伊为新的法案辩护时，林肯在斯普林菲尔德、皮奥里亚和芝加哥发表雄辩的演说反对道格拉斯。在林肯看来，奴隶制与美国民主水火不容。他说："当白人治理他自己时，是自治；但当他治理自己时，又统治着另外一个人——这就成了专制。如果黑人也是人的话，我多年以来的信仰告诉我'一切人生而平等'；一个人迫使另一个人成为奴隶，毫无道德的正义可言。" 林肯成为伊利诺伊州反对堪萨斯－内布拉斯加法案力量的著名领袖。

1856年，林肯加入了反对奴隶制的共和党。在当年的总统竞选中，他为共和党候选人约翰·C.弗里蒙特的竞选做了一百多场演说。虽然弗里蒙特竞选失利，林肯通过无私的工作加强了自己在党内的地

campaign that year, he made more than a hundred speeches on behalf of John C. Fremont, the Republican candidate. Though Fremont lost the election, Lincoln had strengthened his own position in the party through his unselfish work.

In 1858, Lincoln was nominated to run against Douglas for the U.S. Senate. He accepted the honor with a speech that caused severe criticism. Many politicians viewed Lincoln's speech as radical. Lincoln said: "A house divided against itself cannot stand. I believe this government cannot endure permanently half slave and half free. I do not expect the Union to be dissolved—I do not expect the house to fall—but I do expect it will cease to be divided."

Lincoln challenged Douglas to a series of debates. Douglas accepted, and seven meetings were arranged. The debates continued for nearly two months. Large crowds attended each debate. Newspapers reported the debates, and the two men drew national attention. Douglas defended the policy of the Kansas-Nebraska Act. He believed that the people of the territories should decide for themselves whether they wanted slavery. He argued that the people of any territory could keep slavery out of that territory simply by refusing to pass local laws protecting it. Lincoln insisted that there was a fundamental difference between Douglas and himself. Douglas ignored the moral question of slavery, but Lincoln regarded slavery "as a moral, social, and political evil". Douglas won his reelection to the Senate, but some of his speeches in the debates displeased Southern Democrats. When Douglas ran for President in 1860, he lost the support of Southern

位。

1858年，林肯被提名与道格拉斯竞选国会参议员。他接受提名时发表一篇演说，但遭到强烈批评。许多政客认为他的讲话过于激进。林肯说："分裂之屋不可久立。我认为政府不能永远容忍一半自由一半奴役的状态。我不希望联邦分裂——我不希望房屋倒塌——我只希望结束分裂状态。"

林肯提出要与道格拉斯进行一系列的辩论。道格拉斯接受了挑战，双方安排了7场辩论。辩论进行了近两个月。每场辩论都有大群听众。报纸报道了这些辩论，两人吸引了全国的关注。道格拉斯为堪萨斯–内布拉斯加法案的政策辩护。他主张准州本地人应当有权决定是否采取奴隶制。他辩称任何准州只要拒绝制订地方法规保护奴隶制，均可将奴隶制拒之门外。林肯坚持说道格拉斯与自己之间有着根本的分歧。道格拉斯将奴隶制的道德问题置之度外，而林肯则认为奴隶制是"道德上、社会上和政治上的一桩罪恶"。道格拉斯获胜连任参议员，但他在辩论中发表的某些言论使南方民主党人感到不快。当道格拉斯于1860年竞选总统时，他失去了南方民主党人的支持。林肯竞选参议员虽然失利，但他在全国名声大振，他的名气使他获得1860年的民主党候选人提名。

在1860年的竞选中，伊利诺伊州的共和党人提名林肯为总统候

Democrats. Lincoln lost the election, but he gained a national reputation that won him the Republican nomination for President in 1860.

During the election campaign of 1860, the Illinois Republicans named Lincoln as its choice for president. The Democratic Party broke into two groups, which greatly helped Lincoln. Senator Douglas, the nation's leading Democrat, had displeased the supporters of slavery of his party. Lincoln held moderate views on the slavery question. His humble background increased his popularity. Lincoln won election easily. But all of his electoral votes, and nearly all his popular votes, came only from the North.

Before Lincoln took his office, South Carolina declared it withdrew from the Union. By the time Lincoln became President, six other Southern States had withdrawn from the Union. Four more states followed later. The seceded states organized themselves into the Confederate States of America.

On March 4, 1861, Lincoln took the oath of office and became the 16th President of the United States. In his inaugural address, Lincoln warned that he would use the full power of the nation to hold the Union together. To him, the states that had left the Union were still part of the United States, and there was yet hope for reconciliation. But a little more than a month later, the North and South were at war.

During the first two years of the war, the Union suffered one defeat after another. Two days after Fort Sumter fell, Lincoln appointed General Irvin McDowell as commander of the Northern army. But in the first Battle of Bull Run

选人。民主党人则分裂成两派，造成大大有利于林肯的态势。民主党全国领袖参议员道格拉斯已使民主党内奴隶制的支持者感到不快。林肯对奴隶制则采取温和的态度。他的卑微的出身也增加了他的声望。林肯轻而易举地赢得了选举。但是他获得的全部选举人票和几乎全部民众票，只来自北方。

林肯就职前，南卡罗莱纳宣布退出联邦。到了林肯就职时，已有另外 6 个南方州退出联邦。后来又有 4 个州效尤。退出联邦的州组建了美利坚诸州联盟。

1861 年 3 月 4 日，林肯宣誓就职，成为美国第 16 位总统。在他的就职演说中，林肯警告说他将动用国家的全副力量维护联邦的完整。在他看来，那些脱离了联邦的州仍是美国的一部分，和解的希望依然存在。但仅仅过了一个月，南北战争就爆发了。

在战争的头两年，联邦屡战屡败。萨姆特要塞失守后两天，林肯任命欧文·麦克道尔将军为北方军指挥官。但在第一次布尔溪战役中，麦克道尔的军队被打败。林肯然后选派乔治·B.麦克莱伦为陆军总司令，但麦克莱伦发动的半岛攻势又以失败告终。林肯解除了麦克莱伦的大部分指挥权。约翰·波普将军受命为弗吉尼亚部队指挥官，又在第二次布尔溪战役中失利。林肯命令麦克莱伦保卫华盛顿，麦克莱伦在安提塔姆战役中迫使罗伯特·

McDowell's troops were defeated. Lincoln then selected General George B. McClellan as commander in chief of the army, but McClellan's Peninsular Campaign of 1862 ended in failure. Lincoln relieved McClellan of much of his command. General John Pope was made commander of troops in Virginia. He was defeated in the second Battle of Bull Run. Lincoln called on McClellan to defend Washington, D.C. McClellan turned back the army of General Robert E. Lee in the Battle of Antietam. Then McClellan refused to move. Lincoln removed him for the second time, and put General Ambrose E. Burnside in command. Burnside met defeat in the Battle of Fredericksburg. His successor, General Joseph Hooker, lost the Battle of Chancellorsville in May 1863.

Only in the west, Union forces made some progress. In the valley of the Mississippi River General Ulysses S. Grant took Fort Henry and Fort Donelson in February 1862. In early April, Grant's troops forced a Confederate army to retreat in the Battle of Shiloh, but only after the Union army had suffered enormous losses.

The hardship, tragedy, and bitterness of the war touched Lincoln deeply. He shared the suffering of those who were wounded and of those who lost husbands, sons, and brothers. The death of his own small son, Willie, in the darkest years of the war, added to the sympathy and grief he felt for the war victims. He once said, "I feel as though I shall never be glad again." Late at night, he sometimes found solace by reading works of Shakespeare or the Bible. But his official duties left little time for diversion.

E.李将军退兵。此后麦克莱伦便拒绝追击。林肯第二次将他解职，任命安布罗斯·E.伯恩赛德将军为指挥官。伯恩赛德在弗雷德里克斯堡战役中失利。他的继任者约瑟夫·胡克将军在1863年5月的钱瑟勒斯维尔战役中败绩。

只有在西线，联邦军取得了一些进展。在密西西比河流域，尤利西斯·S.格兰特将军于1862年2月夺取了亨利要塞和唐奈尔森要塞。4月初，格兰特在夏洛战役中迫使邦联军退却，但联邦军也损失惨重。

战争的艰苦、悲惨和血腥深深触动了林肯。他与伤兵们体味着同样的伤痛，与那些丧失了丈夫、儿子和兄弟的人忍受着同样的悲伤。在战争最黑暗的岁月里，他的幼子威利夭折，增添了他对战争受害者们的同情。他说："我觉得自己永远不会再快活起来了。"他有时会在深夜读莎士比亚的作品或《圣经》，试图从中找到慰藉。但政务缠身，他很少有时间消愁。

北方在安提塔姆战役中取得胜利后，林肯发布了《解放宣言》，宣布反叛的各州或州内部分地区的所有的奴隶将在1863年1月1日获得自由。《解放宣言》意义深远。在其他国家的心目中，北方正在进行一场反对奴隶制的正义之战。在北方，共和党统一了思想和组织，赢得了人心，执掌政权直至1884年。

1863年，形势发生转变而有利

After the North's victory in the Battle of Antietam, Lincoln issued the Emancipation Proclamation. He declared that all slaves in states, or parts of states, that were in rebellion, would be free on January 1, 1863. The Emancipation Proclamation had a far-reaching effect. In the eyes of other nations, the North was fighting a just war against slavery. In the North, the Republican Party became unified in principle and in organization, and it became so popular that it could hold power until 1884.

The tide turned in favor of the North in 1863. Union armies won two great victories in the year. General George G. Meade's Union forces defeated the Confederates under Lee at Gettysburg, Pennsylvania, during the first three days of July. On July 4, Vicksburg, Mississippi, fell to Grant's troops. On November 19, 1863, Lincoln presented his famous Gettysburg Address at the dedication of the Gettysburg National Cemetery, honoring those who died in the Civil War Battle of Gettysburg. Today, the Gettysburg Address is generally recognized not only as a classical model of the noblest kind of oratory but also as one of the most moving expressions of the democratic spirit ever uttered.

In March 1864, Lincoln put Grant in command of all the Union armies. The Army of the Potomac started to march toward Richmond two months later. At the same time, General William T. Sherman began his famous march from Tennessee to Atlanta, and then to the sea. Grant met stubborn resistance in the South, and suffered heavy casualties. Many people called him "the butcher", and condemned Lincoln for supporting

于北方。联邦军取得两场重大胜利。乔治·G.米德将军率领的联邦军于7月的头三天在宾夕法尼亚的葛底斯堡击败李将军率领的邦联军。7月4日，密西西比州的维克斯堡落入格兰特军队之手。1863年11月19日，林肯在葛底斯堡国家公墓落成典礼上发表了著名的葛底斯堡演说，纪念那些在葛底斯堡战役中阵亡的将士。今天，举世公认，这篇演说辞是风格最崇高的演说的经典范例，也是民主精神最动人的表达。

1864年，林肯任命格兰特指挥联邦所有的军队。两个月后，波托马克军团开始进军里士满。威廉·T.谢尔曼将军开始了他从田纳西到亚特兰大，再到海边的著名进军。格兰特在南方遇到顽抗，伤亡惨重。许多人称他为"屠夫"，指责林肯袒护他。当年6月，林肯再次被提名为总统候选人。民主党推选乔治·B.麦克莱伦将军为该党总统候选人。联邦在1864年取得的胜利为林肯的重新当选提供了支持。

1865年3月4日林肯第二次宣誓就职时，战争即将结束。他现在可以致力于重新统一国家了。在他的第二次就职演说中，他宣布说北南双方将共同为奴隶制付出代价。他结束演说时发出动人的呼吁，要以慈悲之心对待南方，对待所有的战争受害者。

1865年4月9日，李将军在弗吉尼亚的阿波马托克斯县府向格兰

him. In June that year, Lincoln was nominated again for President. The Democrats chose General George B. McClellan as their candidate for President. The Union victories in 1864 helped Lincoln win reelection.

The end of the war was clearly in sight when Lincoln took the oath of office a second time, on March 4, 1865. He could now concentrate on reuniting the nation. In his second inaugural address, he declared that the North and South together pay the price for slavery. He closed his speech with a moving plea for merciful treatment for the South and for all victims of the war.

On April 9, 1865, Lee surrendered to Grant at Appomattox Court House in Virginia. Under authority from Lincoln, Grant extended generous terms to Lee and his army. A great wave of joy swept the North when the fighting ended.

On the evening of April 14, 1865, Lincoln attended a performance at Ford's Theatre in Washington. A Southern actor named John Wilkes Booth shot the President in the head from the rear of the presidential box. Lincoln was carried unconscious to a neighboring house. He died the next morning.

特投降。格兰特得到林肯的授权，向李将军和他的军队提出宽大条件。战争结束的消息传来，北方一片欢腾。

1865年4月14日晚，林肯前往华盛顿的福特剧场观剧。一个名叫约翰·威尔克斯·布斯的南方演员从总统包厢后面朝总统头部开了一枪。失去知觉的林肯被抬进临近的一所房子里。他在次日上午去世。

林肯在第二次就职仪式后不久拍摄的照片显示出4年的战争给林肯造成的精神压力。他面部瘦削，眼窝深陷。在战争中的危机时刻，他睡眠很少，他进餐时间没有规律，几乎没有时间放松一下

华盛顿特区林肯纪念堂里的林肯像

题 外 话

在葛底斯堡国家公墓落成典礼上，主要演讲人是爱德华·埃弗雷特，当时美国最伟大的演说家之一。他的演说措辞优美，滔滔不绝。他的葛底斯堡演说是他的精心杰作。演说是这样开头的："站在明净的长天之下，从这片岁末安然憩息的广阔田野放眼望去，那雄伟的阿勒格尼山脉隐约耸立在前方，兄弟们的坟墓就在我们的脚下，我不敢贸然用我这微不足道的声音打破上帝与大自然意味深长的肃静。……"他一连讲了两个小时。林肯应邀讲几句话，他只讲了10句话，总长不过两三分钟。有人传说林肯是在前往葛底斯堡的火车上匆匆写下演说辞的。但这并非事实。他的演说辞是精心准备的，讲话前还做了某些修改。埃弗雷特听罢林肯的演说，马上意识到林肯气壮山河的宣言 "民治、民有、民享的政权将永世长存（government of the people, by the people, for the people, shall not perish from the earth）"也将永世长存，铭记人心。第二天，埃弗雷特写信给林肯说："如果我两小时的讲话能像您两分钟的讲话那样切题，我就感到十分欣慰了。"林肯回信说："昨天，就我们各自的身份来说，你没有理由作简短发言，我则不能长篇大论。你认为我那三言两语还不是彻底失败，我为此感到十分高兴。"

林肯是个自学成材的人。他一生在学校里学习的时间总共不足一年。对于那些误认为只有坐在教室里听课才能学到知识的人，他的话发人深省："如果你下定决心要使自己成为一名律师，事情已经完成了一多半了。你是否跟任何人学习则无关紧要。我就没有跟任何人学习。把书找来，钻研它们，直到你弄懂了其中的基本内容为止，这是最紧要的。读书学习不一定要在大城市里。我就是在新塞勒姆读书学习的，那里的人口从未超过三百。书籍，还有你对书籍的理解力，无论在那里都是一样的。……永远牢记，你必获成功的决心比任何其他条件都更重要。"

20. Robert Edward Lee

罗伯特·爱德华·李

Robert Edward Lee (1807-1870) was a great general who commanded the Confederate Army in the Civil War. He is one of the best-loved and respected figures in American history. His military genius probably contributed mostly to keeping the Confederacy alive through the four years of the American Civil War. He won the admiration and respect of Northerners as well as Southerners. Union General Ulysses S. Grant said about Lee: "There was not a man in the Confederacy whose influence with the whole people was as great as his."

Unlike President Abraham Lincoln, Lee was not a self-made man. Lee was a member of the leading family of Virginia, and one of the most distinguished in the United States. His father, Henry Lee, was a brilliant cavalry commander in the Revolutionary War, and several other members of his family were important government officials. Two of them, Francis Lightfoot Lee and Richard Henry Lee, had been statesmen and soldiers in Revolutionary War, and had signed the Declaration of Independence.

Robert E. Lee was a tall, handsome man, looking dignified and intelligent. He was well-bred gentleman, never known to smoke, drink alcohol, or use swearwords.

Lee was born on January 19, 1807, in Virginia, and was educated at the U.S. Military Academy at West Point. He graduated second in his class in 1829, receiving a commission as

罗伯特·爱德华·李 (1807-1870) 是南北战争中南部邦联军的伟大将领，美国历史上最受人爱戴和尊敬的人物之一。他的军事天才可能是使南部邦联得以在南北战争中维持 4 年之久的最重要原因。他不但在南方，而且在北方都赢得了赞扬和尊敬。联邦军的尤利西斯·S.格兰特将军这样评价李："南部邦联方面没有一个人能像他那样对全体人民产生如此巨大的影响。"

与亚伯拉罕·林肯不同，李不是一个靠个人奋斗取得成就的人。李出身弗吉尼亚的一个世家，他的家族是美国最著名的家族之一。他的父亲亨利·李是革命战争中出色的骑兵指挥官，家族中数名其他成员是重要政府官员。其中两人，弗朗西斯·莱特伏特·李和理查德·亨利·李在革命战争中是政治家和军人，都在《独立宣言》上署过名。

罗伯特·E.李身材魁梧，仪表堂堂，相貌威严而聪颖。他是个教养良好的绅士，不抽烟、不喝酒、不说脏话。

李于 1807 年 1 月 19 日出生在弗吉尼亚，在西点军校受教育。1829 年以班里第二名的优异成绩毕业，在工兵部队任少尉。1836 年升任中尉，1838 年升任上尉。他在墨西哥战争中一举成名。1852 年他任

second lieutenant in the engineers. He became first lieutenant in 1836, and captain in 1838. He distinguished himself in the battles of the Mexican War. He became superintendent of West Point in 1852, and later was appointed colonel of cavalry. When John Brown raided Harpers Ferry in 1859, Lee happened to be in Washington, D.C. and was sent there to arrest Brown and restore order.

When Texas withdrew from the Union in 1861, Lee, who was then in command of an army on the Texas frontier, was recalled to Washington, D.C., to wait for further orders. President Abraham Lincoln offered him the field command of the United States Army, but Lee declined. On April 20, three days after Virginia withdrew from the Union, Lee resigned from the U.S. Army.

Though a southerner, Lee did not believe in slavery. He felt that slavery had an evil effect on masters as well as slaves. Long before the war, he had freed the few slaves whom he had inherited. Lee did not favor withdrawal from the Union, either. He hated the thought of a divided nation. He had great difficulty in deciding whether to stand by his native state or remain with the Union. He wrote to his sister: "... in my own person I had to meet the question whether I should take part against my native state. With all my devotion to the Union, and the feeling of loyalty and duty of

西点军校总监，后来又被任命为骑兵上校。当约翰·布朗于 1859 年袭击哈珀斯费里时，李恰巧在华盛顿，于是被派往哈珀斯费里，逮捕了布朗，恢复了秩序。

1861 年，得克萨斯退出联邦时，李正在得克萨斯边境指挥军队。他被召回华盛顿待命。林肯总统任命他为美国陆军野战司令，但李谢绝了。4 月 20 日，弗吉尼亚退出联邦后 3 天，李辞去美军中的职务。

李虽然是南方人，却不赞成奴隶制。他认为奴隶制不但对奴隶有害，对主人也有害。在战前很久，

李将军和他的军官

an American citizen, I have not been able to make up my mind to raise my hand against my relatives, my children, my home. I have therefore resigned my commission in the army, and, save in defense of my native state—with the sincere hope that my poor services may never be needed—I hope I may never be called upon to draw my sword."

On April 23 he became commander in chief of the military and naval forces of Virginia. For a year he was military adviser to Jefferson Davis, president of the Confederate States of America, and was then placed in command of the army in northern Virginia. In February 1865 Lee was made commander in chief of all Confederate armies; two months later the war was virtually ended by his surrender to General Ulysses S. Grant at Appomattox Court House. His great battles included those of Antietam, Chancellorsville, Fredericksburg, and Gettysburg.

After the war, Lee accepted the position of president of Washington College, which was named Washington and Lee University after his death.

Lee has long been respected as an ideal by southerners and as a military genius by all Americans. His campaigns are almost universally studied in military schools as models of strategy and tactics. January 19, Lee's birthday anniversary, is now a legal holiday in most Southern states.

题 外 话

　　对人格高尚、有军事才能的"叛将"的尊重，反映出美国人的宽容。

他就已经释放了继承下来的几个奴隶。他也不赞成退出联邦。他痛恨国家分裂。是支持自己所在的州还是留在联邦内，在做出决定前他经历了一番艰苦的思想斗争。他在给姐姐的信中写道："就我个人而言，我不得不面对是否要参与反对我的家乡州这一问题。我虽然愿为联邦效力，虽然具有美国公民的忠诚感和义务感，但始终无法下决心举起手来打我的亲属，打我的孩子们，打我的家乡。我因此辞掉了军职，并且，除了保卫我的家乡州——但愿它永不需要我的犬马之劳——我希望自己永远不会受命拔剑出鞘。"

　　4月23日，李受命担任了弗吉尼亚陆海军总司令。他为美利坚诸州联盟总统杰斐逊·戴维斯担任了一年的军事顾问，然后调任指挥北弗吉尼亚军。1865年2月，李被任命为邦联各军总司令；两个月后，他在阿波马托克斯县府向格兰特投降，战争实际上结束了。他参加的最重要战役包括安提塔姆战役、钱瑟勒斯维尔战役、弗雷德里克斯堡战役和葛底斯堡战役。

　　战后，李接受了华盛顿学院校长一职，该校在他去世后更名为华盛顿和李大学。

　　李作为南方人的典范和军事天才受到所有美国人的尊敬。他的指挥的战役几乎在所有军事院校中都作为战略和战术的经典范例来学习、研究。李的诞辰，1月19日，现在是大多数南方州的法定假日。

CHAPTER NINE

Industrialization and Reform
工业化与改革

1. The End of the Western Frontier

西部边疆的终结

In the West, frontier life was ending after the Civil War. The long process of settling the United States from coast to coast drew to a close. In 1862, Congress passed the Homestead Act, which offered public land to people free or at very low cost. Thousands of Americans and immigrants started farms in the West. They settled chiefly on the Great Plains. Miners flocked to the West. Towns sprang up near the mines. Cattle ranching spread throughout the Southwest after the Civil War. By the end of the 1870s, settlement was so widespread in the West that America's frontier had practically ended.

As white people were moving westward the American Indians were constantly pushed back. The vast buffalo herds had long served as the main source of food, clothing, and shelter for the Indians. With the extension of railroads westward, the Americans from the East killed thousands of

南北战争后，西部的边疆生活已不复存在。从大西洋至太平洋的漫长移民过程终告结束。1862 年，国会通过《宅地法》，无偿或以极低的价格向人们提供公有土地。千千万万的美国人和外国移民在西部建立了农场。他们大多数在大平原上定居下来。矿工们则拥向西部。城市在矿山附近建立起来。南北战争后，西南部到处都建起了养牛场。到了 70 年代末，居民点已遍及西部，美国的边疆实际上已经消失。

随着白人的西进，印第安人则不断被迫后退。大群的野牛曾是印第安人衣食居所的主要来源。随着铁路的向西延伸，来自东部的美国人成群地屠杀野牛以获取毛皮。到 1899 年，野牛只剩下不到一千头。

these animals for their fur. By 1899, there were only fewer than a thousand left. This brought an end to Indian way of life. Some Indians tried to defend their land and their way of life. Fierce battles took place in the 1860s and 1870s between the Indians and federal troops, and the Indian uprisings were crushed. The federal government then set aside reservations for the Indians to live on. Reservation Indians suffered from poverty and illness, and could not adjust to the new way of life forced upon them. By the end of the 19th century, the traditional Indian way of life had become a thing of the past.

印第安人的生活方式因此而难以为继。有些印第安人试图保卫家园和自己的生活方式。60 与 70 年代，印第安人和联邦军队发生激烈战斗，但印第安人的暴动被镇压下去。联邦政府划出保留地供印第安人居住。保留地的印第安人受着贫穷和疾病的折磨，无法适应强加于他们的新的生活方式。到了 19 世纪末，印第安人的传统生活方式已成历史。

2. Industrial Growth

工业的增长

The industrial growth that began in the United States in the early 19th century continued steadily up to and through the Civil War. Still, by the end of the war, the United States was mainly a land of farms, villages and small businesses. Manufacturing was concentrated in the Northeast. The typical factory was a small plant, operated by a few workers. It produced a limited amount of goods for a local market. After the Civil War, however, American industry changed dramatically.

One of the main reasons for the rapid development was improved railroads and better communications. Beginning in the 1860s, rail lines were extended across the whole country. The new network of railroads shipped raw materials to fac-

美国在 19 世纪初开始的工业增长一直持续着，南北战争期间也未曾中断。然而，战争结束时，美国仍是一个以农场、村庄和小型企业为主的国家。制造业集中在东北部。典型的工业是小作坊，由几名工人进行生产。工业品产量有限，只供应本地市场。但在南北战争后，美国工业发生了戏剧性的变化。

工业迅速发展的重要原因之一是铁路和通讯方式的改善。从 60 年代开始，铁路线已遍布全国。新的铁路网将原材料从遥远的地方快捷地运送到工厂，又将制成品发送到全国各地。电报在 50 年代已开

tories over long distances quickly and distributed finished products throughout the country. The telegraph was already in use by the 1850s. In 1866, the first underwater telegraph line was laid across the Atlantic. The telephone, invented by Alexander Graham Bell, came into use in the 1870s. Another advance in communication was the wireless telegraph. This invention made communication possible without the use of cables. These developments provided the quick communication that is extremely important to the smooth operation of business.

The most striking feature of the period was the development of entirely new industries. Steel industry developed after new, cheaper methods of making steel were discovered. Steel played a vital role in the industrialization process. It replaced iron in machines, railroad tracks, bridges, automobiles, and skyscrapers.

In the early 1850s, chemists discovered that petroleum could be made into kerosene, a cheaper and better lamp oil than whale oil. But the supply of petroleum was limited. This situation was changed, however, when the world's first successful oil well was drilled in Pennsylvania in 1859. Later, when the gasoline engine was invented, the development of oil industry led to the rise of the automobile industry in

始使用。头一条横跨大西洋的海底电报线于 1866 年敷设成功。亚历山大·格雷厄姆·贝尔发明的电话机于 70 年代开始投入使用。在通讯方面取得的另一成就是无线电报。这项发明使不用电线的通讯成为可能。这些发明提供了快捷的信息交流，而快捷的信息交流对于企业的顺利经营至关重要。

这一时期最突出的特点是新型的工业的发展。廉价的炼钢新方法发明后，炼钢业发展起来。钢材在工业化过程中发挥着至关重要的作用。它替代了铁，用于建造机器、路轨、桥梁、汽车和摩天大楼。

50 年代初，化学家发现石油可

发明家托马斯·爱迪生

the early 20th century.

In the 1870s, electricity was put into use as an energy source. The practical dynamo was designed to produce a steady flow of electric current. Thomas A. Edison invented the electric light bulb. And the electric motor came into use. Before long, power plants were built to produce electricity in large quantities. Within a short time, factories started to switch from stream power to electric power.

Of all the new industries, the automobile industry had the greatest impact on the nation's economy. The gasoline automobile was developed in 1885. At first, automobile production was low, and cars were very expensive. In the early 20th century, Ransom Eli Olds and Henry Ford began turning out cars by mass production. Automobile prices dropped, and sales increased rapidly. Even ordinary workers owned their cars.

以制成煤油，而煤油用作灯油，比鲸油价格低，质量高。但石油的供应不足。然而在1859年，宾夕法尼亚钻出了头一眼油井后，形势发生了变化。后来，汽油机发明后，石油工业的发展导致了20世纪初的汽车工业的兴起。

70年代，电力作为一种能源开始投入使用。实用的发电机被设计出来，可以产生恒定的电流。托马斯·A.爱迪生发明了电灯。电动马达也投入使用。不久，发电厂建立起来，可以大量发电。没过多久，工厂便用电力代替了蒸汽动力。

在所有的新兴工业中，汽车工业对国民经济的影响最大。汽油汽车于1885年研制成功。起初，汽车产量很低，价格高昂。20世纪初，兰塞姆·伊莱·奥尔兹和亨利·福特开始批量生产汽车。汽车价格下跌，销售量迅速增长。甚至普通工人都拥有了汽

亨利·福特坐在他于1896年造出的第一辆汽车里

The use of machines became common in manufacturing throughout American industry. With machines, workers could produce goods many times faster than they could by hand. The new large manufacturing firms hired hundreds, or even thousands, of workers. Each worker was assigned a specific job in the production process. This system of organizing laborers, called the division of labor, also sped up production. The increased production speed enabled businesses to charge lower prices for products. Lower prices, in turn, meant more people could afford the products, and so sales increased.

车。

在美国工业中，使用机器已司空见惯。有了机器，工人们的产量要数倍于手工生产。新兴的大型制造企业雇用数百乃至数千名工人。每个工人只分配从事生产流程中的一件特殊工作。这种组织劳动的体系称为"分工"，也加快了生产的速度。生产速度的加快使企业有可能降低产品价格。低廉的价格，反过来意味着更多的人买得起产品，从而使销售增长。

3. New Business Structure

新的经营结构

Industrial growth after the Civil War was greatly influenced by a group of business leaders. They not only gained control of the nation's leading industries but also changed the structure of American business. The government did little to regulate business during the 19th century. Without restriction, these business leaders struggled to wipe out competition and gain complete control of their industries. They brought together the various stages of production, from raw materials to finished products.

Individual companies not only grew in size and wealth but also formed combination. Companies in the same industry united to form a single company to gain control over a product or service. In this way they created monopoly, that is, they could demand and get high prices. Some business

南北战争后的工业增长受到一群工商企业界领袖的重大影响。他们不但控制了国家的主要工业，而且改变了美国工商企业的经营结构。在19世纪，政府很少规范工商企业的经营行为。由于没有限制，工商企业界领袖尽力消除竞争，完全控制了相关产业。他们将生产的各个阶段，从原材料到成品的生产，都集中在自己手中。

工业公司不但扩大了规模与财富，而且组成了联合体。同一行业的公司联合起来组建唯一的一家大公司，以控制一种产品或服务。这样，它们制造了垄断，也就是说，它们可以为自己的产品定高价。有些工商企业界领袖组成了托拉斯。

leaders formed trusts. A trust was giant business combination consisting of a number of corporations in the field or in related fields. The first successful trust was organized by John D. Rockefeller. After starting an oil refining business in the 1860s, he bought out competitors or ruined them by sharply lowering his own prices. He finally formed the Standard Oil Trust, which controlled 90 percent of the oil refining business. In the 1880s, trusts were formed in many other industries. One of the biggest trusts was the American Tobacco Company, formed by James B. Duke and his brother Benjamin.

Monopoly had some favorable effects on the economy. Giant corporations are usually more efficient. Monopoly also enabled businesses to avoid sharp rises and falls in price and output, and thus keep sales steady. On the other hand, monopoly gave some business leaders so much power that they could take unfair advantage of others or demand goods from suppliers at low cost, while charging high prices for the finished product.

A new type of business was corporations. A corporation is owned by all the people who buy shares in it. There may be thousands of these shareholders. They elect a board of directors to manage the business. Each shareholder receives a share of the profits in the form of dividends. An important advantage of the corporation is its ability to raise a large amount of capital to build huge factories, buy expensive machinery, and expand its operations rapidly. By 1900, corporations controlled more than two-thirds of all manufacturing.

In the age of industrialization, bankers played an important role. They supplied the huge amounts

托拉斯是巨型的企业联合体，由业界和相关行业的数家大公司组成。约翰·D.洛克菲勒组建了头一个成功的托拉斯。洛克菲勒于60年代成立炼油企业后，就收购竞争者或采用猛降油价的方法使竞争者破产。他最终建立了美孚石油托拉斯，控制了炼油业的90%。80年代，许多其他工业部门都成立了托拉斯。最大的托拉斯之一是美国烟草公司，由詹姆斯·B.杜克和他的兄弟本杰明建立。

垄断对经济有正面影响。巨型的公司通常效率更高。垄断也能使企业避免价格和产量的大起大落，从而使销售保持稳定。另一方面，垄断赋予某些企业的领袖过大的权力，使他们能够从他人身上牟取不正当利益，或以压低的价格从供应商进货，以抬高的价格出售成品。

一种新型的公司是有限公司。有限公司为所有购买其股票的人所拥有。股东可能多达成千上万。他们选举董事会来管理企业。每个股东以红利的形式分得利润。有限公司的最大优点是能够筹集大量资本建设巨大的工厂、购买昂贵的机器，迅速扩大经营规模。到了1900年，有限公司控制的制造业超过了三分之二。

在工业化时代，银行扮演着重要角色。它们提供企业领袖扩大经

of money that business leaders needed to expand their operations. New banks sprang up throughout the country. Some bankers of the era, especially J. P. Morgan, assumed key positions in the American economy because of their ability to provide huge sums of capital.

Improved sales methods also aided economic growth. Owners of big businesses sent salespeople to all parts of the country to promote their products. Some companies opened chain stores. Chains could sell goods at lower prices because of centralized management and large-scaled purchasing. Other companies opened huge department stores in the growing cities. The stores offered a wide variety of products at reasonable prices.

营所需的巨额资金。新银行在全国各地纷纷成立。这一时代的某些银行家，特别是 J.P.摩根，在美国经济中占据关键地位，因为他们有能力提供巨额资本。

销售方法的改进也促进了经济的成长。大企业主派销售人员到全国推销他们的产品。有些公司开办连锁店。连锁店由于集约化的管理和规模化的采购可以降低货物的价格。其他公司在不断扩大的城市里开办巨型百货公司。百货公司以可以接受的价格提供多种多样的商品。

约翰·D.洛克菲勒

J.P.摩根

4. The Growth of Cities

城市的扩大

In the period from the Civil War to 1900, cities grew by leaps and bounds. In 1860, less than 15 per cent of all Americans lived in cities. By 1916, almost 50 per cent did. Cities, with their jobs, excitement, entertainment, educational opportunities and conveniences, attracted not only Americans from farms, but immigrants. Between 1870 and 1916, more than 25 million immigrants entered the United States. Population growth helped the economic boom in two ways. It increased the number of consumers, and thus enlarged the market for products. It also provided the additional workers needed for the jobs created by the new business activity.

Until the 1880s, most immigrants to the United States came from northern and western Europe. Then, more and more people came from eastern and southern Europe—Poland, Russia, the Austro-Hungarian Empire, the Balkan states, and Italy. Some Americans wanted the government to limit immigration, because poor immigrants were often willing to work for less than the normal wage and take jobs as strikebreakers. The government did not do much about this, however. The main exception to free immigration involved the Chinese. Competition for jobs between white workers and the increasing number of Chinese workers became so intense, particularly in California, that Congress passed the *Chinese Exclusion Act*, which prohibited all Chinese laborers from immigrating to the United States.

从南北战争到1900年，城市迅速发展。1860年，不到15%的美国人居住在城市里。到了1916年，城市居民已接近50%。城市里有工作，有丰富多彩的生活，有娱乐场所，有受教育的机会，有方便的设施等等，不但吸引了农场的美国人，也吸引了外来移民。1870～1916年间，2500多万的移民进入美国。人口增长从两方面促进了经济的繁荣。一方面增加了消费者的数量，从而扩大了产品的市场；另一方面提供了新兴行业所需要的劳动力。

80年代前，来到美国的大多数移民来自北欧和西欧。接着，越来越多的人来自东欧和南欧——来自波兰、俄国、奥匈帝国、巴尔干国家和意大利。有些美国人要求政府限制移民，因为贫穷的移民常常甘愿为了挣得低于正常标准的薪酬而做工，并在罢工期间干活，成为罢工的破坏者。然而，政府对此并没有过多干预。自由移民的例外主要是针对华人的。白人工人与越来越多的华工之间的竞争变得如此激烈，特别是在加利福尼亚，以致国会通过《排华法案》，禁止所有华工移民美国。

工业增长主要集中在北方。被战争破坏了的南方在经济上落后于

The industrial growth centered chiefly in the North. The war-torn South lagged behind the rest of the country economically. Some industry developed in the region, but the South remained an agricultural area throughout the period of industrialization.

其他地区。南方的某些工业也有所发展，但在整个工业化期间，南方仍以农业为主。

到美国寻梦的欧洲移民

5. City Life During the Industrial Era

工业化期间的城市生活

There were great economic and social contrasts between the rich and the poor in cities. A small percentage of business leaders and investors were able to gather enormous wealth and enjoyed lives of luxury. They built enormous mansions, wore the finest clothing, ate in the best restaurants, and could afford to buy almost anything

城市中的富人和穷人在经济和社会地位上存在着重大差别。占人口少数的企业界大亨和投资者能够积聚巨量的财富，过着豪华的生活。他们建起豪宅，穿最华丽的衣服，在最高档的餐馆里进餐，买得起几乎任何他们想要的东西。在积

they desired. Among the millionaires who accu-
mulated fortunes of more than $100 million each
were Andrew Carnegie, Marshall Field, J. P.
Morgan, John D. Rockefeller, and Cornelius
Vanderbilt.

Some city people belonged to the middle
class. These included owners of small businesses,
and such workers as factory and office managers.
They had enough money to live comfortably.

But at the bottom of the economic ladder
were those poor laborers. They usually worked
long hours for low pay. Unemployment was an
ever-present threat. Business leaders felt little
pressure to raise their workers' wages, because
there was job competition, and poor people
would work under almost any conditions. Poor
people lived crowded together in slums. Disease
spread quickly because sewage and water systems
did not keep up with the growing cities. The
frightful living conditions in the slums ruined the
health of the thousands. Many poor children received little or no education, because they had to
work to help support their families. Ignorance and
poverty encouraged crime. In spite of harsh living
conditions, hope made the lives of many of the
poor tolerable. The poor believed that economic
growth would improve their lives sooner or later.

As cities grew, so did their influence on life
of the American people. Cities played a key role
in the expansion of education, the rise of professional sports, the spread of popular newspaper,
and the growth of literature and the visual arts.

累了上亿家资的富翁里，有安德
鲁·卡内基、马歇尔·菲尔德、J.P.
摩根、约翰·D.洛克菲勒和科尼利
厄斯·范德比尔特。

有些城市居民属于中产阶级。
这些人中有小企业主、工厂和机关
里的管理人员。他们有足够的钱过
舒适的生活。

但在经济阶梯的底层则是穷苦
的劳工。他们劳动时间长而报酬
低。失业是一种无时不在的威胁。
企业界的领袖们感受不到提高工人
工资的压力，因为存在着就业竞
争，穷人几乎不讲条件，任何工作
都愿意干。穷人居住在拥挤的贫民
窟里，由于下水道和供水系统的建
设赶不上城市的发展，疾病迅速流
行。贫民窟的可怕生活条件损害了
千千万万人的健康。许多穷人家的
孩子只接受很少或完全不接受教
育，因为他们必须干活帮助养家。
无知与贫困造成了犯罪。尽管生活
条件恶劣，许多穷人仍对未来抱有
希望，这使他们能够忍受自己的生
活。穷人们相信经济增长早晚会使
他们的生活得到改善。

随着城市的发展，城市对美国
人生活的影响也越来越大。在教育
的发展、职业运动的兴起、通俗报
刊的普及、文学和视觉艺术的发展
中城市扮演了重要角色。

6. Labor Movement

Industrialization and growth of cities created many problems, but political and government leaders showed little interest in solving them. They largely ignored such issues as the growing power of corporation or big-city political corruption. They made little effort to close the gap between the rich and poor. Protest movements did arise, however, and their demands for reform led to some improvements during the late 19th century and early 20th century. Many Americans called for changes in the country's economic, political, and social systems. They wanted to reduce poverty, improve the living conditions of the poor, and regulate big business. They worked to end corruption in government and make government more responsive to the people.

Early reform efforts included movements to organize labourers. As the United States industrialized, American workers realized that the only way they could change their bad situation was to band together into labor unions. In 1886, skilled labourers formed the *American Federation of Labour* (AFL) — now the *American Federation of Labour-Congress of Industrial Organizations* (AFL-CIO). Samuel Gompers was the union's president from 1886 to 1924. He believed that unions should not aim to reform society, but rather seek to win immediate benefit for their members. Under his leadership, this union bargained with employers and gained better wages and working conditions for its members.

劳工运动

工业化与城市的发展中出现了许多问题，但政治家和政府官员们对解决这些问题没有多少兴趣。他们在很大程度上忽视了诸如日益增长的公司的力量和大城市的政治腐败。他们没有尽力弥合贫富之间的巨大鸿沟。然而抗议运动还是兴起了，抗议运动提出的改革要求导致了19世纪末与20世纪初的某些社会改良。许多美国人要求改变国家的经济、政治和社会体制。他们希望减少贫困、改善穷人的生活条件，规范大企业的经营行为。他们采取行动制止政府的腐败，使政府更加关心人民的愿望。

早期的改革包括组织劳工。随着美国工业化的进展，美国工人意识到改变他们恶劣生存条件的唯一办法是组织工会。1886年，技术工人组建了美国劳工联合会（劳联）——现在的美国劳工联合会－产业工会联合会（劳联－产联）。塞缪尔·龚帕斯从1886年至1924年任这个工会的主席。他认为工会的目标不是改造社会，而是为工会会员谋取目前的利益。在他的领导下，工会与顾主谈判，为工会会员提高了工资，改善了工作条件。

Unskilled labourers had less success in organizing than did skilled labourers. They formed Knights of Labor, the first important national union, aiming to unite all workers, skilled and unskilled, into one large union. The members hoped not only to better the worker's lot but also to reform society in general. This union gained a large membership during the 1880s. In 1886, a serious labour disturbance occurred in Chicago. Thousands of workers went on strike, seeking an eight-hour workday. Violence broke out between strikers and police, and two men were killed. When police arrived to break up the crowd, someone threw a bomb during a meeting of workers in Haymarket Square in Chicago. The bomb killed and injured a number of people, including some policemen. Although the Knights of Labor had not been involved in the Haymarket affairs and had actually condemned it, many Americans blamed the disaster on the labour movement. As a result, its membership fell off sharply and its importance declined.

非技术工人在组织工会方面不如技术工人那样成功。他们组建了头一个重要的全国组织劳动骑士团，旨在将所有的工人，无论是技术工人还是非技术工人，团结起来，组成一个大工会。劳动骑士团不但希望改善工人的境遇，而且希望改造社会的各个方面。这个工会在80年代发展了大批会员。1886年，芝加哥发生了严重的劳工骚乱。成千上万的工人罢工，要求实行8小时工作制。罢工者和警察之间发生了暴力冲突，两人丧命。当警察前来驱散人群时，有人在芝加哥的秣市广场举行的工人聚会上投掷了一枚炸弹，炸死炸伤数人，包括几名警察。虽然劳动骑士团没有卷入秣市事件，而且实际上谴责了它，许多美国人仍然认为劳工运动应对这场灾难负责。结果，劳动骑士团的成员人数骤减，其重要性也随之降低了。

7. Struggle for Women's Right to Vote

争取妇女选举权的斗争

Movements for women's rights became strong after the Civil War. In 1869, Susan B. Anthony and Elizabeth Cady Stanton founded the National Woman Suffrage Association. For many years after that the association struggled for women's right to vote. Owing to its effort, a few states

南北战争后，争取妇女选举权的运动日益强大。1869年，苏曾·B.安东尼与伊丽莎白·卡迪·斯坦顿建立了全国妇女选举权协会。此后，该协会为争取妇女选举权进行了多年的斗争。结果，有几个州允

allowed women to vote, though only in local elections. Stanton persuaded Senator Aaron A. Sargent of California to sponsor a woman suffrage amendment to the U.S. Constitution in 1878. The amendment was reintroduced every year until Congress finally approved it in 1919, granting women the right to vote.

许妇女参加选举，虽然只是地方选举。斯坦顿劝说加利福尼亚的参议员阿伦·A.萨金特于 1878 年提出给予妇女选举权的宪法修正案。从此，这一修正案年年再次提出，直至 1919 年国会最终通过了它。

1913 年美国妇女在纽约游行，要求选举权

8. The Civil Service Reform

公务员体制改革

One of the most important reforms was civil service reform. The earliest Presidents generally sought qualified individuals for jobs, though they tended to favor their own political supporters. But

最重要的改革之一是公务员体制的改革。最早的总统通常任命有资格的人担任公职，虽然他们倾向于照顾在政治上支持自己的人。但

since the early 19th century, the spoils system was commonly used in governments. This system gave public offices as political rewards to faithful party members, and thus led to much corruption. Many people hired through the spoils system had little or no training for their work and no interest in it. Many were dishonest. After the Civil War, the practice came under heavy attack. Government had become increasingly complex, requiring more and more workers with special skills. Reformers argued that government jobs should be given on the basis of merit, rather than political connections. In 1883, their efforts led to passage of the *Civil Service Act*. The *Civil Service Act* called for examinations open to all citizens. It provided for selection of new workers from among those making the highest grades on these examinations. The law banned the firing or lowering the rank of workers for political reasons.

At first, the Civil Service Act covered only about 10 percent of the federal positions. But more were added in the years that followed. By 1900, about 40 percent of all federal jobs were covered.

是自从 19 世纪初开始，政府通常采取分赃制。这一体制将公职分给忠实的党员，作为一种酬劳。许多通过分赃制受雇的人很少或没有受过从事该项工作的训练，对该项工作没有兴趣。许多人不够正直。南北战争后，分赃制受到猛烈攻击。政府变得越来越复杂，需要越来越多的有专门技能的工作者。改革者主张政府部门的职务应依照任人唯贤的原则分配，而不是依照政治上的关系分配。1883 年，经过改革者的努力，国会通过了《公务员法》。《公务员法》要求举办对所有公民开放的考试，规定从那些在考试中获得最高分数的人中选择新的工作人员。这项法律禁止由于政治原因解雇工作人员或降低他们的职位。

起初，《公务员法》仅适用于 10%的联邦政府职务。但后来逐年有所增加。到了 1900 年，《公务员法》覆盖了大约 40%的联邦政府职务。

9. The Sherman Antitrust Act

《谢尔曼反托拉斯法》

In 1890, the federal government passed the *Sherman Antitrust Act*. This act made illegal trusts and other businesses that eliminate free competition. It also prohibits any person or business from monopolizing or attempting to monopolize any market. But the act had little effect at

1890年，联邦政府通过了《谢尔曼反托拉斯法》。这项法案规定托拉斯和其他消除竞争的工商企业为非法。法律同时禁止任何个人或企业垄断或企图垄断任何市场。但这项法案起初没有产生多少影响。

first. Presidents at the time were not interested in enforcing the act. After Theodore Roosevelt became President in 1901, he decided to regulate big businesses whenever they operated against the public interest. In 1903, he established the Bureau of Corporations, an agency that collected information on businesses. When the bureau found that a business was violating the Sherman Antitrust Act, the government sued. During Roosevelt's presidency, the government brought suits against more than 40 companies. The most famous suit broke up John D. Rockefeller's Standard Oil Company in 1911.

当时的总统们对实施这项法律不感兴趣。西奥多·罗斯福1901年就任总统后，决定规范大型工商企业触犯公众利益的任何经营行为。1903年，罗斯福成立了公司管理局，搜集公司的情报。一旦发现一家工商企业违反了《谢尔曼反托拉斯法》，政府就会起诉它。在罗斯福任总统期间，政府对40余家公司提起诉讼。最著名的一次诉讼于1911年分割了约翰·D.洛克菲勒的美孚石油公司。

10. Reforms in Cities

城市里的改革

After 1890 many middle-class and some upper-class Americans were alarmed by the sharp economic contrast between the rich and the poor, the power of big business, corruption in government, violent strikes, and the increasing influence of socialism. They regarded all these as a threat to American democracy. They began to support social reforms.

Reformers in local and state government passed many laws to help the poor and improve living condition in the slums. With their effort many cities built public parks and playgrounds in poorer sections, and established kindergartens and improved schools.

Some reform governments expanded public education and forced employers to protect workers against fires and dangerous machinery in factories.

1890年后，许多中产阶级和某些上流社会的美国人对贫富之间的巨大经济差异、大企业的霸权、政府的腐败、导致暴力冲突的罢工和社会主义日益增长的影响感到不安。他们将所有这些现象视为对美国民主的威胁。他们开始支持社会改革。

改革者们在地方和州一级政府中通过了许多法律帮助穷人改善他们在贫民窟里的生活条件。通过他们的努力，许多城市在穷人的居住区开辟了公园和运动场，建立了幼儿园，改善了学校的条件。

有些致力于改革的政府扩大了公共教育的范围，强迫顾主在工厂里采取防护措施，使工人们不致受

Wisconsin went so far as to pass an income tax, a measure bitterly opposed by the wealthy Americans.

At the beginning of the 20th century, two new types of city government were created. One was the commission plan. Under this plan, voters elect a small group of non-partisan commissioners. Each one heads a government department. Together, they carry out both the executive and legislative duties of the city. The other new form of city government was the city-manager plan. Under this system, the voters elect commissioners, who, in turn, hire a professional manager to run the city.

到火灾和危险机器的伤害。威斯康星州走得更远，它通过立法征收所得税，遭到有钱人的强烈反对。

20世纪初，两种新的城市行政体制创造了出来。一种是委员市政制。根据这一体制，选举人选出数名不受党派控制的委员。每个委员领导一个政府部门。委员们在一起履行市政府的行政和立法职能。另一种新型的城市行政体制是市行政官制。根据这一体制，选举人选出委员会，委员会再雇用有专业知识的行政官治理城市。

11. Reforms under Roosevelt

罗斯福任期内的改革

Theodore Roosevelt became the first President to help labourers in a strike against employers. In 1902, the United Mine Workers went on strike for more pay and better working conditions. Roosevelt proposed that the miners and the mine owners settle their differences through arbitration, but the mine owners refused. Roosevelt threatened to have the Army take over the mines. The owners gave in, and reached a compromise with the miners.

In 1902, Roosevelt's government sued the Northern Securities Company on charges of trying to reduce competition. This firm had been formed by J. P. Morgan and other financiers to control key railroads in the West. The department of Justice succeeded in breaking up the Northern Securities Company. During Roosevelt's presidency,

西奥多·罗斯福是在工人罢工中帮助劳工反对顾主的头一位总统。1902年，美国联合矿工工会举行罢工，要求提高工资，改善工作条件。罗斯福建议通过仲裁解决矿工与矿主之间的分歧，但遭到矿主们的反对。罗斯福威胁动用军队接管矿山。结果矿主做出让步，与矿工达成妥协。

1902年，罗斯福政府起诉北方证券公司，指控它试图减少竞争。这家公司由 J.P.摩根等金融家建立，旨在控制西部的重要铁路。结果司法部成功地将北方证券公司分割开来。在罗斯福的任期内，政府对另外43家大公司提起诉讼，结束了约翰·D.洛克菲勒的石油业托拉斯

the government sued 43 other corporations. It ended John D. Rockefeller's oil trust and James B. Duke's tobacco trust.

In 1906, Upton Sinclair published *The Jungle*, a novel about unsanitary conditions in the meat-packing industry. Among the book's vivid details was a description of sausage ingredients, including moldy meat, dirt, and dead rats. Roosevelt ordered an investigation of Sinclair's charges, and found they were true. At Roosevelt's urging, Congress passed the *Meat Inspection Act* of 1906. It gave the federal government power to enforce sanitary regulations in meatpacking plants. The *Pure Food and Drugs Act*, another law passed in the same year, banned the sale of harmful and impure foods and medicines. It also required truthful labels on foods and drugs.

Some of Roosevelt's most important and lasting contributions were in the field of conservation. He was the first president to take an active interest in preserving the environment. He stopped the public sale of about 80 million acres of mineral land and 1.5 million acres of land suitable for waterpower sites. During his administration, nearly 150 million acres of public land were set aside as national forest reserves.

和詹姆斯·B.杜克的烟草业托拉斯。

1906年，厄普顿·辛克莱发表了小说《丛林》，揭露肉类加工业中不卫生的状况。小说生动地描写了香肠里混入的杂物，包括霉变的肉、脏土和死老鼠。罗斯福下令调查，结果发现辛克莱的指控属实。在罗斯福的敦促下，国会于当年通过《肉检法》，授权联邦政府强制肉类加工厂遵守卫生法规。同年，国会还通过了《洁净食品药品法》，禁止销售有害健康的不洁食品与药品。这项法律还规定食品与药品必须附有内容真实的标签。

罗斯福的贡献中具有最重大、最持久意义的，是他的环保措施。他是头一个对保护环境持积极态度的总统。他制止拍卖8000万英亩的矿区和150万英亩适于建造水电设施的土地。在他的任期内，近15000万英亩的公共土地划为国家森林保护地。

西奥多·罗斯福总统

题外话

罗斯福退休后，有人问起他在任期间的最大成就是什么。罗斯福答道，是他的资源保护政策。罗斯福为后代保存了公园、矿藏、石油、煤田和水利资源，大大减轻了美国工业化中出现的生态问题。罗斯福是个鸟类学家，环保意识强烈。想到 21 世纪初仍有很多人为了眼前的私利无限制地开发土地、矿产和水利资源，我们越发佩服罗斯福的英明远见。他对生态问题的关注，比很多其他国家的领导人早了一个世纪。

12. Reforms under Taft and Wilson

塔夫脱和威尔逊任期内的改革

Republican William Howard Taft succeeded Roosevelt in 1909. Although a conservative, Taft helped further the cause of reform. He took action against many trusts and brought twice as many suits against businesses as Roosevelt did. He also extended civil service and called for a federal income tax.

During the election of 1912, the Republican Party was badly split. Conservative Republicans backed Taft as their party's presidential candidate, and liberal Republicans supported Roosevelt. Taft won the nomination. The liberals then formed the Progressive Party and nominated Roosevelt for President. The Republican split helped Democrat candidate Woodrow Wilson win the presidency.

The reform movement further developed under Wilson. The 16th Amendment, ratified in 1913, gave the federal government the power to levy an income tax. The 17th Amendment provided for the election of U.S. senators by the people, rather than by state legislatures. The *Clayton Antitrust Act*, passed in 1914, struck a blow against

1909年，共和党人威廉·霍华德·塔夫脱继罗斯福后任总统。他虽然是个保守主义者，但仍然进一步推行了改革。他采取措施制裁了许多托拉斯，针对工商企业提起的诉讼是罗斯福提起的两倍。他扩大了公务员制度的适用范围，并呼吁联邦政府征收所得税。

在 1912 年的选举中，共和党严重分裂。保守派共和党人支持塔夫脱为党的总统候选人，自由派则支持罗斯福。结果塔夫脱赢得提名。自由派然后成立了进步党，提名罗斯福为总统候选人。共和党的分裂使民主党候选人伍德罗·威尔逊赢在总统选举中获胜。

威尔逊任期内，改革运动继续发展。1913 年通过的第 16 条修正案授权联邦政府征收所得税。第 17 条修正案规定美国参议员将由人民选举，不再由州议会选举。1914 年通过的《克莱顿反托拉斯法》，给垄

monopolies. It broadened the Sherman Antitrust Act by clearly defining unfair business practices and gave the federal government more power to deal with business combination. It also helped labour by making it impossible to prosecute unions under antitrust laws. In 1914, the government set up the Federal Trade Commission (FTC) to handle complaints about unfair business practices. It is an independent U.S. government agency that works to maintain free and fair competition in the economy and protect consumers from unfair or misleading practices. The FTC also issues trade regulation guides for business and industry and conducts a variety of consumer-protection activities. The other reform measures passed during Wilson's presidency included the *Underwood Tariff Act* of 1913, which lowered a high tariff that protected American business from foreign competition.

断企业以沉重的打击。它扩大了《谢尔曼反托拉斯法》的范围，给不正当企业经营行为下了明确的定义，给联邦政府更多的权力对付企业合并。这条法律也对劳工有利，因为它使人不再能够援引反托拉斯法来起诉工会组织。1914 年，政府成立了联邦商务委员会处理不正当企业经营行为的投诉。这是一个独立的美国政府机构，它致力于维护经济领域里的自由和公正的竞争，保护消费者，使他们免受不公正和误导行为的伤害。联邦商务委员会还针对工商业发行了商务法规手册，举办了各种各样的消费者保护活动。威尔逊任期内通过的其他改革措施中还有 1913 年的《安德伍德关税法》，该法降低了旨在保护美国工商企业，使之免受国外商家竞争的高额关税。

威尔逊和塔夫脱

CHAPTER TEN

Overseas Expansion
海 外 扩 张

1. Acquiring New Territories

获得新领土

The first new land acquired after the Civil War was Alaska. Russian explorers first established their settlement in Alaska. The Russians tried to develop several industries, including coal mining, shipbuilding, and whale hunting. But by the 1850s, the fur trade had declined and the other enterprises had begun to fail. After Russia lost the Crimean War against the British and French, the government felt it could hardly afford to keep so large a colony that had so little value. They offered to sell it to the United States. United States Secretary of State William H. Seward agreed to buy the region for $7,200,000, about 2 cents per acre (5 cents per hectare). In 1867, he signed the Treaty of Cession of Russian America to the United States.

南北战争后获得的第一块新领土是阿拉斯加。俄国人最先在阿拉斯加建立了居民点。俄国人试图发展几种产业，包括采煤、造船和捕鲸。19 世纪 50 年代，毛皮生意已不景气，其他企业也开始衰落。俄国在反对英法的克里米亚战争中失利后，感到继续维持这块价值不大的巨大殖民地已力不从心。俄国政府向美国提出出售这片土地。美国国务卿威廉·H.西沃德同意以 720 万美圆的价格买下这片领土，约合每英亩两美分（每公顷 5 美分）。1867 年，西

美国国务卿威廉·H.西沃德

Some Americans considered the region worthless and opposed the purchase. They called Alaska "Seward's Folly", and "Seward's Icebox". After the purchase, Alaska was largely neglected until gold deposits were discovered there in 1880.

By the late 19th century, as the output of American factories increased, Americans began to show interest in lands beyond their borders. Industrialists wanted to export their products to new markets abroad. They also needed to import raw materials. Businessmen wished to take advantage of investment opportunities overseas. And farmers were trying to find foreign markets to sell their surplus crops. An oversea area that attracted American attention was Hawaii.

In the latter part of the 19th century, American and European business leaders had become very powerful in Hawaii. In 1887 a group of American and other white business leaders, backed by an armed militia they had founded, imposed on the king a new constitution that sharply limited his powers. When Queen Liliuokalani took the throne in 1891, she attempted to regain some of the power the monarchy and native Hawaiians had lost. In 1893, after the queen attempted to impose a new constitution, powerful white leaders occupied the government office building in Honolulu and overthrew the monarchy. The rebels were helped by the official United States representative in Hawaii, who ordered troops from a U.S. warship to land in Honolulu, on the pretext of protecting American lives and property. The rebels established a provisional government headed by Sanford B. Dole, the son of an American missionary.

沃德签署了将俄属美洲割让给美国的条约。有些美国人认为这块领土一文不值，反对购买。他们称阿拉斯加为"西沃德的蠢举"，或"西沃德的冰箱"。购买之后，阿拉斯加很大程度上被人们遗忘，直至1880年在当地发现金矿。

19世纪末，随着美国工业品产量的增长，美国人开始对海外感兴趣。工业家希望向新的海外市场出售他们的产品。他们也需要进口原材料。商人们希望利用机会到海外的投资。农民们正在寻找海外市场出售他们多余的粮食。引起美国人关注的一个海外地区是夏威夷。

19世纪后半期，美国和欧洲的工商界领袖在夏威夷的势力已十分强大。1887年，一群美国和其他国家的白人工商界领袖靠着他们所建立的武装民兵的支持，将一部新的宪法强加给夏威夷国王，大大限制了国王的权力。当利留卡拉尼女王于1891年登基后，她试图恢复君主和夏威夷土著人丧失了的某些权利。1893年，女王试图颁布新宪法，势力强大的白人领袖占领了火奴鲁鲁的政府机关大楼，推翻了君主制。叛乱者受到美国官方驻夏威夷代表的协助，这位代表命令美国军舰上的军队在火奴鲁鲁登陆，借口要保卫美国公民的生命与财产。叛乱者建立了一个临时政府，由一个美国传教士的儿子桑福德·B.多尔担任政府首脑。

Two days after taking over, the new government sent representatives to Washington to negotiate a treaty of annexation. President Grover Cleveland, who strongly opposed imperialist enterprises, supported efforts to return Liliuokalani to the throne. The revolutionaries, however, refused to yield to Cleveland's pressures. Instead, they established an independent republic in 1894. William McKinley, who succeeded Cleveland as president of the United States in 1897, favored the annexation of Hawaii. The next year both houses of Congress approved a joint resolution to annex Hawaii.

During this period, Americans also gained control over other Pacific islands, some 50 in all. Midway Island, 2,090 kilometers northwest of Hawaii in the Pacific Ocean, was annexed in 1867. Part of Samoa, an island group southwest of Hawaii, became a possession of the United States in 1900.

夺取政权后两天，新政府派代表到华盛顿谈判缔结夏威夷并入美国的条约。格罗弗·克利夫兰总统强烈反对帝国主义野心，支持扶持利留卡拉尼复位。但革命者们拒绝屈服于克利夫兰的压力。他们反而于1894年建立了一个独立的共和国。威廉·麦金利于1897年继克利夫兰后出任总统，赞成吞并夏威夷。第二年，国会两院通过联合决议，吞并夏威夷。

在同一时期，美国人还控制了其他太平洋岛屿，共达50个。夏威夷西北2090公里远太平洋里的中途岛，于1867年被吞并。夏威夷西南的萨摩亚群岛的一部分也于1900年成为美国的领土。

利留卡拉尼女王

2. The Spanish-American War   西—美战争

During the 1870s and 1880s, the United States

在19世纪70和80年代，美

paid relatively little attention to foreign affairs. During the 1890s and early 1900s, however, it developed into a world power and took a leading role in international affairs.

The Spanish-American War of 1898 marked a turning point in United States foreign policy and the emergence of the United States as a world power. Spain ruled Cuba, Puerto Rico, the Philippines, and other overseas possessions during the 1890s. In 1895, the Cubans revolted against their Spanish rulers, and the struggle between them and the Spaniards became bitter and violent. Many Americans demanded that the United States help the rebels. To protect American lives and property in Cuba, the battleship *Maine* arrived in Havana harbor in January 1898. On February 15, an explosion blew up the ship and killed about 260 persons on board. The American public immediately blamed the Spaniards for the disaster, but today many

国对外交很少关注。然而，到了19世纪90年代和20世纪最初10年，美国已发展成为一个世界强国，在国际事务中开始扮演重要角色。

1898年的西－美战争标志着美国外交政策的一个转折点，也标志着美国已成为一个世界强国。在90年代，西班牙统治着古巴、波多黎各、菲律宾等海外领地。1895年古巴人起义反对西班牙统治者，与西班牙人的斗争渐趋激烈。许多美国人要求美国帮助起义者。为保卫古巴的美国人的生命与财产，战舰"缅因"号于1898年1月抵达哈瓦那港。2月15日，战舰上发生爆炸，炸死大约260人。美国公众立即将灾难归咎于西班牙。但今天，许多历史学家认为这是一场事故，爆炸发生于战舰内部。要求对西班牙采

战舰 "缅因" 号发生爆炸之后

historians believe it was accidental and occurred inside the ship. Demands for action against Spain grew, and "Remember the *Maine*" became a nationwide war cry. In April Congress passed a resolution asserting that Cuba was independent, and authorized the president to use of the army and navy to force the Spaniards to leave the island. A few days later, both Spain and the United States declared war on each other.

The first important battle of the war took place in the Philippines. Immediately after war was declared, George Dewey, commander of the American navy in the Pacific, sailed from Hong Kong to Manila Bay, where a Spanish fleet was stationed. On May 1, 1898, Dewey's warships destroyed or captured all the Spanish ships without the loss of an American life or serious damage to any American ship. Then Dewey blockaded Manila harbor. After American troops arrived later, Manila fell and the Spanish land forces in the Philippines surrendered.

In the Caribbean, American warships blockaded a Spanish fleet in the Cuban harbor of Santiago, on the southeastern part of the island. In June 1898, the United States landed 15,000 soldiers southeast of Santiago and marched on the city. By early July, the American troops had defeated Spanish land forces and taken a stone fort at El Caney and San Juan Hill, two strategic heights overlooking the city. The most famous fight was Lieutenant Colonel Theodore Roosevelt's charge up Kettle Hill during the Battle of San Juan Hill. At the outbreak of the Spanish-American War, Theodore Roosevelt had formed a group of volunteers that became the First United States Cavalry Volunteers.

取行动的呼声日高，"切莫忘记'缅因'号"成为全国的动员口号。4月，国会通过决议，承认古巴独立，授权总统动用陆军和海军迫使西班牙人离开古巴。几天后，西班牙和美国相互宣战。

西－美战争的头一个战役发生在菲律宾。宣战后不久，太平洋的美国海军指挥官乔治·杜威从香港出发驶向西班牙舰队碇泊的马尼拉湾。1898年5月1日，杜威的战舰摧毁或俘获了所有的西班牙军舰，而美军则没有损失一兵一卒，美国军舰也未严重受损。杜威接着封锁了马尼拉港。美国军队抵达后，马尼拉陷落，西班牙在菲律宾的陆军投降。

在加勒比海，美国军舰封锁了古巴东南部圣地亚哥港的西班牙舰队。1898年6月，美军15000人在圣地亚哥东南登陆，向该市进军。7月初，美军打败了西班牙陆军，夺取了两个俯视该市的战略高地埃尔坎内的石堡和圣胡安山。最著名的一场战斗是西奥多·罗斯福中校在夺取圣胡安山过程中率领军队冲上凯特尔山。在西－美战争爆发时，西奥多·罗斯福募集了一群志愿者，组建了美国第一志愿骑兵团。罗斯福将骑兵团命名为"莽骑兵"。凯特尔山的冲锋使莽骑兵闻名全国。

Roosevelt gave them the title of the Rough Riders. The charge up Kettle Hill made the Rough Riders nationally famous.

As soon as Santiago was surrounded, the Spanish fleet tried to break the blockade and escape from the Harbor. In the sea battle that followed, the entire Spanish fleet was destroyed. After days of negotiations, Santiago surrendered.

The *Treaty of Paris* of December 10, 1898, officially ended the war. Under the treaty, Spain granted Cuba its freedom. The United States received Guam, Puerto Rico, and the Philippines from Spain.

圣地亚哥被围困后不久，西班牙舰队试图突围逃出港口。在随后发生的海战中，西班牙舰队全军覆没。经过几天谈判，圣地亚哥投降。

1898 年 12 月 10 日签署的巴黎条约正式结束了战争。根据条约，西班牙放弃古巴。美国从西班牙得到关岛、波多黎各和菲律宾群岛。

西奥多·罗斯福中校和他的"莽骑兵"战士

3. A New World Power

一个新的世界强国

Now United States had become a new colonial power. But it met new problems. The nation had to increase its military spending and become more involved in foreign affairs. The Americans also had to find ways of dealing with colonial peoples with cultures they did not understand.

此时，美国已成为一个新的殖民大国。但它也遇到了新的问题。国家必须增加军事开支并更多地卷入国际事务。美国人还必须找到与殖民地人民打交道的方式，因为他们对当地人的文化缺乏了解。

An immediate difficulty was the Philippines. The Americans who were against imperialism pointed out that it would be foolish to take responsibility for a foreign people living thousands miles away in Asia. But those who were in favour of expansion stressed the economic and strategic importance of the Philippines to the United States. Mckinley supported expansion and declared that Americans had a duty to "educate the Filipinos, and uplift and civilize and Christianize them".

Many Filipinos resented U.S. occupation of their country. They had expected to be independent after Spain was defeated. Now, they were to be ruled by another foreign power. Emilio Aguinaldo, who had helped the American attack on the Philippine Islands during the Spanish-American War, now began guerrilla warfare against the United States forces in 1899. The United States had to fight a long and bloody war in the Philippines until March 1901, when Emilio Aguinaldo was captured.

After acquiring the Philippines, the United States began to focus its attention on China. The Chinese government had long resisted Western influence. But a disastrous war with Japan in 1894 and 1895 showed that China was too weak to say no to great powers. Britain, France, Germany, and Russia then forced the Chinese empire to give them more trading rights and territory. It seemed likely that China would soon be divided into a number of spheres of influence into which other trading nations would not have right to enter. But two things prevented the division of

在菲律宾当下就遇到了困难。反对帝国主义的美国人指出，为居住在数千英里外的一个亚洲民族承担责任是愚蠢的。但那些赞成扩张的人则强调菲律宾对美国在经济和战略上的重要性。麦金利支持扩张，宣布说美国人有义务"教育菲律宾人，提升他们，教化他们，使他们成为基督徒"。

许多菲律宾人憎恨美国占领他们的国家。他们本来希望打败西班牙后获得独立。现在，他们却被另一个大国统治。埃米里奥·阿奎纳多曾在西一美战争中协助美军攻打菲律宾群岛，从 1899 年开始却开展了打击美军的游击战。美军不得不在菲律宾打一场长期的血腥战

菲律宾起义领袖埃米里奥·阿奎纳多

the country. One was the growth of nationalism in China; the other was rivalry among the foreign powers. None of the foreign powers would allow any of the others to become dominant in China.

American business leaders now hoped to expand their trade in the Far East. But they were at a disadvantage in areas where the other powers had special commercial privileges. To protect American interests, the United States proposed the Open-Door Policy to the other foreign powers in 1899. This policy made sure that all nations had equal rights to trade with China. All the leading powers accepted this proposal, though somewhat reluctantly.

But not all the Chinese welcomed Western and Christian influences. Some Chinese formed secret societies to fight these influences and wanted to drive the "foreign devils"out of their country. The best-known society was the Boxers. In 1900, the Boxers and other secret societies attacked and killed more than 200 foreigners. An international army from eight nations came to rescue their people and put down the Boxer Rebellion. The army included some 2,500 Americans.

The powers forced China to pay a large indemnity for foreign losses during the rebellion. The United States returned a large part of its share of the indemnity to China, which used the money to aid Chinese students who studied at American colleges.

In Latin America, the United States did not withdraw its troops from Cuba as it had promised. It occupied the island until 1902. Even after that, the United States kept its naval bases

争，直到 1901 年阿奎纳多被俘为止。

得到了菲律宾以后，美国开始将注意力转向中国。中国政府长期反抗西方的影响。但是 1894 和 1895 年中日战争中中国的惨败表明，中国无力拒绝强国提出的要求。英、法、德、俄此时迫使中华帝国让给他们更多的贸易特权和领土。中国似乎不久将被瓜分成若干势力范围，其他贸易国无权进入。但瓜分中国有两个障碍。一个是中国正在增强的民族主义，另一个是列强之间的竞争。哪一个强国都不肯让其他列强在中国称霸。

现在，美国工商界领袖希望在远东扩张贸易。但在列强享有贸易特权的地区，他们处于不利地位。为了维护美国的利益，美国于 1899 年对列强提出了门户开放政策。这项政策确保所有国家享有与中国贸易的同等权利。所有的列强都接受了这一建议，虽然多少有些勉强。

但是并非所有的中国人都欢迎西方和基督教的影响。有些中国人结成秘密社团，对抗这些影响，希望将"洋鬼子"赶出他们的国家。最著名的是义和团。1900 年，义和团与其他秘密社团攻击并杀死 200 多名洋人。由 8 个国家组成的国际联军赶来救助自己人，镇压了义和团。这支军队中有 2500 名美国士兵。

列强迫使中国为在骚乱期间外国人的损失偿付大笔赔款。美国将

in Cuba, and had right to intervene in Cuba's internal affairs.

Events in Venezuela and the Dominican Republic made the United States further involved in the Caribbean area. In 1902, Germany, Great Britain, and Italy blockaded Venezuela in an attempt to collect debts from that Latin American nation. Citing the Monroe Doctrine, Roosevelt forced the Europeans to withdraw. Then America took over the management of the finances of the Dominican Republic in 1905 to keep that country stable and free from European intervention. In 1916, during Wilson's Administration, American troops occupied the Dominican Republic to keep order there. These and other actions showed that the United States had become a world power.

镇压义和团的美军进入北京

自己得到的赔款中的大部分返还中国，用以资助中国学生留学美国。

在拉丁美洲，美国没有按照自己的诺言从古巴撤军。美军占领古巴直到1902年。甚至在1902年以后，美国仍在古巴保留了海军基地，并有权干涉古巴内政。

委内瑞拉与多米尼加共和国发生的事件使美国进一步卷入加勒比海地区事务。1902年，德国、英国和意大利封锁了委内瑞拉，试图从这个拉美国家讨回债务。罗斯福援引门罗主义，迫使欧洲国家撤军。接着，美国于1905年接管了多米尼加共和国的财政，以保持该国的稳定，免受欧洲的干涉。1916年，威尔逊执政期间，美国军队占领了多米尼加共和国，以维持那里的秩序。诸如此类的行动表明美国已成为世界强国。

题外话

美国之所以向海外不断扩张，与当时某些美国人的种族主义有关。如参议员艾伯特·贝弗里奇就认为菲律宾人，乃至所有的亚洲人，都没有民主自治的能力。因而他反对让菲律宾人自治，主张吞并菲律宾。他确信盎格鲁－撒克逊人是优秀的种族，肩负着白人的责任，即"教化""野蛮的"种族。

4. The Panama Canal

巴拿马运河

The United States had for some time wanted a shorter sea route between the Atlantic and Pacific for trade and military purposes. During the Spanish-American War in 1898, one U.S. battleship was sent from San Francisco to Cuba to reinforce the Atlantic Fleet. The ship had to sail nearly all the way around the tip of South America. This long voyage helped convince the United States Congress that a canal was essential for national defense.

In 1899, Congress authorized a commission to survey possible canal routes. The commission favored Nicaragua, because a canal there would require less digging than one across Panama. But a French company, which had already begun but could not continue the construction of a canal in Panama, offered to sell its Panama rights and property and the Panama Railroad for $40 million. In 1902, Congress gave President Theodore Roosevelt permission to accept the French offer if Colombia would give the United States permanent use of a canal zone. The United States negotiated a treaty with Colombia for rights to build the canal. Under the agreement, the United States would obtain a strip of land across the isthmus and build a canal. But the Colombian senate refused to ratify the treaty. Panama, encouraged by the United States, then revolted against Colombia. It became an independent nation in November 1903. The United States sent ships and troops to prevent Colombia from defeating the rebels.

美国长期以来一直想开辟一条连接大西洋与太平洋的较短的海上通道，为贸易和军事目的提供方便。在 1898 年的西-美战争中，一艘美国战舰受命从旧金山出发到古巴增援美国舰队。这艘船不得不长途奔波，绕过南美洲的南端。这一漫长的航行向美国国会证明，出于国防上的考虑，开辟一条运河至关重要。

1899 年，国会任命了一个委员会考察开凿运河的可能的路线。委员会倾向于选择尼加拉瓜，因为在那里开凿运河，用工将少于在巴拿马开凿运河。但一家法国公司早已开始在巴拿马开凿运河，而工程又无法继续进行，此时提出要价 4000 万美圆，出让其在巴拿马的各项权利、财产以及巴拿马铁路。1902 年，国会决定如果哥伦比亚允许美国永远使用运河区，总统可以接受法国人的建议。为获得巴拿马运河的开凿权，美国与哥伦比亚谈判签订了条约。按照条约，美国将获得贯穿巴拿马地峡的狭长地段并开凿运河。但哥伦比亚的参议院拒绝批准条约。巴拿马在美国的怂恿下，发动反对哥伦比亚的叛乱，并于 1903 年 11 月宣布独立。美国派军舰和军队到巴拿马，防止哥伦比亚镇压叛乱。

Two weeks later Panama signed a treaty with the United States giving permission for the canal project. Under the agreement, the United States acquired a permanent lease on a section of central Panama 16 kilometers wide, where the canal would be built; the right to take over more Panamanian land if needed; and the right to use troops to intervene in Panama. The United States agreed to guarantee Panama's independence and pay $10 million, plus an annual fee of $250,000. On Panama's side, the treaty was negotiated and signed not by Panamanians but by Philippe Bunau-Varilla, a French citizen who represented the French canal company. The treaty terms were resented by Panamanian nationalists and became a source of continuing controversy in Panama's history.

两周后，巴拿马与美国签订条约，允许美国开凿运河。根据条约，美国获得了巴拿马中部16公里宽的运河区的永久租让权；在需要的情况下，有权占据更多的巴拿马土地；有权使用军队干涉巴拿马。美国同意保障巴拿马的独立，并向巴拿马支付1000万美元，外加每年租赁费25万美元。在巴拿马方面，谈判签约的不是巴拿马人，而是一个代表法国公司的法国公民菲利普·比诺-瓦里亚。条约引起巴拿马民族主义分子的反对，成为巴拿马历史上一个不断引起争议的问题。

开凿巴拿马运河

题外话

美国在19世纪末的海外扩张也与美国海军军官、历史学家艾尔弗雷德·塞耶·马汉的理论有关。马汉在其主要著作是《海上力量对1660-1783年历史的影响》和一系列的讲座中宣扬海权在国家政策中的重要性。他的理论使美国脱离了传统的孤立主义，开始向扩张主义政策倾斜。马汉认为，为了与其他国家展开竞争以扩大影响，美国必须建立一支庞大的海军，并在海外取得海军基地。马汉对西奥多·罗斯福总统的影响尤其大。罗斯福使美国在20世纪初骤然卷入国际事务中。

CHAPTER ELEVEN

World War I
第一次世界大战

1. The Cause of the War

战 争 的 起 因

World War I was one of the most violent and destructive wars in European history. It lasted four years, and involved many of the countries of Europe as well the United States and other nations throughout the world. It took the lives of nearly 10 million troops.

World War I began in 1914. The two sides that fought each other were called the *Allies* and the *Central Powers*. The Allies included Britain, France, Russia and Serbia. Later Italy, Rumania, Greece, Japan, the United States and other countries joined the Allies. The Central Powers were Germany, Austria-Hungary, the Ottoman Empire, and Bulgaria.

During the years before 1914 the important countries of Europe got into political and economic rivalry and more and more suspicious of one another. European countries had divided into two groups, which were called the *Triple Entente* (England, France and Russia) and the *Triple*

第一次世界大战是欧洲历史上最残酷、破坏性最大的战争之一。战争持续了四年，欧洲许多国家参与其中，美国和全世界其他国家也卷入其中。此次战争中有近 1000 万人阵亡。

第一次世界大战始于 1914 年。交战双方称为协约国和同盟国。协约国包括英国、法国、俄国和塞尔维亚。后来意大利、罗马尼亚、希腊、日本、美国等国家也加入了协约国。同盟国包括德国、奥匈帝国、奥斯曼帝国和保加利亚。

1914 年以前，欧洲的大国就开始了政治和经济的角逐，相互之间越来越缺乏信任。欧洲国家分成两个集团，称为三国协约 (英、法、俄) 和三国同盟 (德、奥、意) 。由于每个集团都害怕另一集团发动战

Alliance (Germany, Austria, and Italy). Because each group was afraid that the other would start a war, every nation made preparations by building up armed forces.

In 1914, the great countries came into conflict in the Balkans, in the southeastern part of Europe. The people of the little country of Serbia were Slavic and they hated Austria because Austria ruled Slavic territories. Serbia was too weak to fight Austria, but expected the great Slavic country of Russia to give support. Germany, the most powerful European country, was the old enemy of France and wanted Austria as an ally. Great Britain was afraid of Germany because Germany was building a great fleet of warships that might threaten British control of the sea.

On June 28, 1914, Archduke Francis Ferdinand, heir to the throne of Austria-Hungary, went to Sarajevo, the capital of Austria-Hungary's province of Bosnia-Herzegovina. As he and his wife rode through the streets in their automobile, a young Serbian nationalist fired two shots at them and they died almost instantly. Austria-Hungary believed that Serbia's government was behind the assassination. It seized the opportunity to declare war on Serbia.

Though the assassination touched off the war, the war had deeper causes. It resulted chiefly from the growth of nationalism among various European peoples, an enormous increase in European armed forces, competition for colonies, and the formation of military alliances. By the late 19th century, Germany had the best-trained army in the world. In 1898, Germany began to develop a naval force big enough to challenge the British

争，所以所有的国家都扩军备战。

1914 年，这些大国在欧洲南部的巴尔干卷入了冲突。小国塞尔维亚的居民是斯拉夫人，他们仇恨奥地利，因为奥地利统治着斯拉夫人的领土。塞尔维亚太弱小，没有能力反抗奥地利，但指望斯拉夫大国俄国维护它的利益。欧洲最强大的国家德国是法国的夙敌，希望奥地利成为盟国。英国害怕德国，因为德国正在建立一支强大的舰队，可能威胁到英国的制海权。

1914 年 6 月 28 日，奥匈帝国王储弗朗西斯·斐迪南大公前往奥匈帝国的波斯尼亚－黑塞哥维那省的首都萨拉热窝访问。当他和妻子乘车穿过大街时，一个年轻的塞尔维亚民族主义分子朝他们开了两枪，二人很快死去。奥匈帝国认为塞尔维亚政府策划了刺杀，借机向塞尔维亚宣战。

虽然战争的导火索是刺杀，战争有更深层的原因。主要原因有欧洲各民族民族主义情绪的高涨，欧洲军事力量的迅猛增长，对殖民地的争夺以及军事联盟的形成。到了19 世纪末，德国拥有了世界上训练最良好的军队。1898 年，德国开始加强海军力量，使之强大到足以挑战英国海军。德国决心成为海上强

navy. Germany decided to become a major sea power because it was struggling with Britain for colonies in Africa. These colonies supplied both countries with raw materials for factories, markets for manufactured goods, and opportunities for investment. But the competition for colonies strained their relations and made them enemies. Germany's naval build-up alarmed Britain and made it feel the need for allies. In 1904, Britain and France settled their past disagreements over colonies and signed the Entente Cordiale (Friendly Agreement). In 1907, Russia joined the Entente Cordiale, and it became known as the Triple Entente. Although the alliance provided protection for the three countries, it left Europe divided into two opposing camps, and so increased the danger of war.

国，是因为它要与英国争夺非洲的殖民地。这些殖民地为英德两国提供了工业原材料、工业产品的市场和投资的机会。但对殖民地的争夺恶化了两国的关系，使它们成为敌人。德国海军实力的增长使英国感到不安，感到需要盟友。1904年英法两国解决了以往在殖民地问题上的争端，签署了友好协约。1907年，俄国加入友好协约，该协约遂被称为三国协约。虽然结盟为三国提供了保护，但它也使欧洲划分为两个对立的阵营，因而增加了战争的危险。

2. The Stalemate on the Western Front

西线的僵局

When the fighting began, the Allies, including France, Britain and Russia were on the side of Serbia. They opposed the Central Powers made up of Austria-Hungary and Germany. Britain entered the war in August 1914, when German troops marched through the small country of Belgium to attack France. Great Britain had promised to protect Belgium and so declared war on Germany and Austria. Italy broke its alliance with Germany and a year later joined Britain and France in the war.

战争开始时，协约国，即法国、英国和俄国都站在塞尔维亚一边。他们反对同盟国奥匈帝国和德国。英国于1914年8月参战，当时德国军队穿越小国比利时向法国发动进攻。英国曾许诺要保护比利时，所以向德奥宣战。意大利脱离与德国的联盟，一年后加入英法一方作战。

The war was fought on three main fronts. One was in the east, along the Russian border. Another was in the south, along the Italian border. The third, which was the main front, was in the west, in Belgium and northern France.

Germany won early victories on the Western Front. German armies swept through Belgium in less a month. By the beginning of September 1914, the Germans had occupied northern France, and approached Paris. But then they were forced to move back until they stopped near the Aisne River. From there, the Germans and the Allies fought a series of battles. Germany wanted to seize ports on the English Channel and cut off supply lines between France and Britain. But the British stopped the German advance to the sea.

For the next three and half years, the war was fought basically along the same line. The opposing armies dug trenches to protect themselves from enemy bullets and shells, until there were two continuous lines of trenches running from the coast of the North Sea across Belgium and northeastern France to the border of Switzerland. Soldiers lived a terrible life in the mud of the trenches, never knowing when the enemy would bombard them with shells or when they would be ordered to make an attack.

Both the Allies and the Central Powers developed new weapons, which they hoped would break the stalemate. Machine guns, poison gas, and tanks began to be used, and they could kill hundreds of soldiers in a minute. Attacks all failed and millions of lives were lost for the purpose.

大战主要在三个战线上进行。一个是东线，沿俄国边界；另一个南线，沿意大利边界，第三个，也是最主要的一个，是西线，在比利时和法国北部。

德国在西线取得了最初的胜利。在不到一月的时间里德国军队横扫比利时。1914年9月初，德国已占领了法国北部，逼近了巴黎。但他们此时受阻，被迫后撤，直到埃纳河附近才停下来，与协约国军展开一系列战斗。德军企图占领英吉利海峡上的港口，切断法国和英国之间的供应线。但英军阻挡住德军向海边的推进。

在以后的三年半里，战争处于胶着状态。交战双方挖掘壕堑以防御敌人炮火的袭击，阵地上形成了一条东起北海海岸，穿越比利时和法国北方直至瑞士边界的连续不断的壕堑线。在壕堑的泥水里，士兵们的生活极其艰苦。他们不知道敌人会何时轰炸他们，也不知道何时会接到命令发起进攻。

协约国和同盟国都研制了新武器，企图打破胶着状态。他们开始使用机枪、毒气和坦克。新武器能够在很短时间里杀死大量士兵。但进攻都未能成功，数百万士兵阵亡。

3. American Neutrality

Soon after the war began, Woodrow Wilson, President of the United States, declared that his country would be neutral. But few Americans were truly neutral. Most Americans sympathized with the Allies. The United States showed its sympathy for the Allies by carrying food and war supplies across the Atlantic to them.

During the war Britain had the most powerful navy in the world. With it Britain tried to stop any food and supplies from reaching Germany. Germany's navy was strong, but not as strong as Britain's. So most of the time Germany's big ships had to stay in its home waters, and the Germans sent out their submarines, called U-boats, to sink neutral ships that were carrying supplies to the Allies. On May 7, 1915, a U-boat sank without warning the British passenger liner *Lusitania* off the coast of Ireland. Among the 1,198 passengers who died were 128 Americans. After the U.S. government protested sharply, Germany promised to limit submarine warfare and for a while the Germans stopped attacking neutral or passenger ships.

Relations between the United States and Germany were relatively calm until early 1917. Since the German navy failed to defeat the British navy and take control of the seas, now it seemed to the Germans that the only way to win the war was to build more submarines and again begin sinking neutral ships, so as to starve Britain into surrender. So it then announced a return to

美国的中立

战争开始后不久，美国总统伍德罗·威尔逊宣布美国中立。但真正持中立态度的人很少。大多数美国人同情协约国。美国人对协约国的同情体现在渡过大西洋向它们运送粮食和战争物资。

在战争中，英国拥有世界上最强大的舰队。英国试图利用这支舰队阻断德国的粮食和物资的供给。德国的海军也很强大，但实力仍比不上英国舰队。所以德国的大型舰只大部分时间都不得不停留在自己的海域里，而派出称为 U- 潜艇的潜水艇击沉向协约国运送物资的中立国的船只。1915 年 5 月 7 日，一艘 U- 潜艇未加警告便在爱尔兰海岸附近击沉英国客轮卢西塔尼亚号，1198 名乘客死难，其中有 128 名美国人。美国政府提出强烈抗议，德国答应限制潜艇战，暂时停止攻击中立国船只或客轮。

美国和德国的关系保持相对平静直至 1917 年初。由于德国海军未能打败英国而取得制海权，在德国人看来，现在唯一打赢战争的办法就是建造更多的潜艇，重新开始攻击中立国船只，用饥饿迫使英国投降。于是德国宣布重新开始无限制的潜艇战。又有几艘美国船只被击沉后，美国人愤怒了。美国政府于 1917 年 4 月 6 日向德国宣战。

unlimited submarine warfare. After several more American ships were sunk the Americans became angry, and on April 6, 1917, the United States declared war on Germany. A huge American army was sent to France. In the end, about 2 million Americans served in Europe.

一支美国大军派往法国，最后，在欧洲服役的美国人达到大约 200 万。

客轮卢西塔尼亚号

4. U.S. Troops on the Western Front

美国军队在西线

The first American troops, in small numbers, went into action in the autumn of 1917 on the western front. In early 1918, Germany launched a series of offensives. The Allied forces fought stubbornly, and both sides suffered heavy losses. In May German troops again approached Paris.

美国小股部队于 1917 年秋在西线加入战斗。1918 年初，德国发动一系列攻势。协约国军顽强抵抗，双方兵力损失惨重。5 月，德国军队再次逼近巴黎。6 月，兵力得到增强的美国军队将德军逐出马

1918 年美国士兵
在前线壕堑中

During June, U.S. troops, now in large numbers, drove the Germans out of Belleau Wood, a wooded area near the Marne. On July 18 the Allied forces launched a counterattack with forces that included several American divisions. One of the centers of fiercest battle was at Chateau-Thierry, where the American troops won their first decisive victory. The German armies were forced back. On September 26, 1918 the Allied forces launched the last great offensive of World War I. A fierce battle, known as the Battle of the Meuse-Argonne, was fought between the Argonne Forest and the Meuse River. About 60,000 U.S. troops took an active part in the fighting. The battle finally broke down German resistance. After Bulgaria, Turkey and Austria surrendered to the Allies one after another,

恩河附近的贝洛林地。7 月 18 日，协约国军队发起反攻，美军的几个师也投入战斗。战斗最激烈的地点之一是蒂耶里堡，美军在这里取得首次决定性胜利。德军被迫后撤。1918 年 9 月 26 日，协约国军队发动了第一次世界大战中最后一次大规模进攻。在阿尔贡森林和默兹河之间发生激烈战斗，这场激战称为默兹-阿尔贡战役。大约 6 万美军也积极投入了战斗。战斗最终粉碎了德军的抵抗。保加利亚、土耳其和奥地利先后投降协约国之后，德国要求停战议和。第一次世界大战结束。

Germany asked for an agreement to stop fighting. World War I was over.

美国士兵在法国前线欢呼停战

5. The Paris Peace Conference 巴黎和会

In the early morning on November 11, 1918, the Germans signed the agreement, accepting the terms demanded by the Allies. Germany agreed to withdraw all its troops from the territories it had taken during the war; to give up large numbers of arms, ships, and other war materials; and to allow the Allied powers to occupy German territory along the Rhine River.

In January 1919, representatives of the victorious powers gathered in Paris to draw up the peace settlement. The meeting was called the Paris Peace Conference.

From the beginning, Wilson had viewed the

1918年11月11日清晨，德国签署和约，接受了协约国提出的条件。德国同意德军从在战争中夺取的所有领土上撤出；放弃大批武器、军舰和其他战争物资；允许协约国占领莱茵河地区。

1919年1月，各战胜国代表会集巴黎起草和约。这次会议称为巴黎和会。

从一开始，威尔逊就从理想主义的观点来看待这场战争。他说，协约国的目标是"没有胜利的和平"，"各国地位平等的和平"。1918

war in idealistic terms. The aim of the Allies, he said, should be "peace without victory," a "peace between equals". In January 1918 Wilson presented Congress with his *Fourteen Points* as a guide for a peace settlement. The most important points are summarized as follows:

1. Abolition of secret international agreements.

2. Freedom of the seas outside territorial waters in peace and in war.

3. Removal of barriers to trade among nations.

4. Reduction of arms.

5. Fair settlement of all colonial claims.

6. Recognition of the right of national groups to self-government.

7. Formation of an association of nations to help keep world peace.

At the Peace Conference, however, Wilson met with much opposition to the Fourteen Points. The other leading Allies were chiefly interested in gaining territory and war payments from Germany. They adopted the *Treaty of Versailles*, which ignored almost all of Wilson's proposals. Wilson was only able to soften some of the Allies' more extreme demands.

In May, the peace conference approved the treaty and presented it to Germany. Germany agreed to it only after the Allies threatened to invade. The treaty was signed in the Palace of Versailles near Paris on June 28, 1919. Under the Treaty of Versailles, Germany gave up territory to France, Poland, Belgium, and Denmark, and lost its overseas colonies to the Allied powers. An Allied military force, paid for by Germany, was to occupy the west bank of the Rhine River for

年 1 月，威尔逊就向国会提交了"十四点和平纲领"，作为和平解决冲突的指导原则。十四点纲领的要点如下：

1．废除国际秘密协议。

2．无论平时与战时，公海航行自由。

3．撤消贸易壁垒。

4．裁军。

5．公正调整对殖民地的权利主张。

6．承认民族自治权。

7．成立国际联合组织以维护和平。

然而，在巴黎和会上，十四点纲领遭到不少国家的反对。其他协约国所感兴趣的是向德国索取领土与赔款。它们通过了凡尔赛和约，几乎忽视了威尔逊的全部建议。威尔逊所能做到的只是软化协约国的某些更为强硬的要求。

5 月，和会通过条约，交给德国。德国在协约国入侵的威胁下，接受了条约。条约于 1919 年 6 月 28 日在巴黎附近的凡尔赛宫签署。根据凡尔赛和约，德国向法国、波兰、比利时、丹麦割让了领土，海外殖民地被协约国列强瓜分。一支协约国军队将占领莱茵河东岸 15 年，军队的开支由德国支付。德国还被迫为战争造成的破坏和损失支付一大笔赔款。根据和约，一个国际联合组织，称为国际联盟，建立了起来。凡尔赛和约对德国惩罚之严厉出乎德国人的预料。它为阿道

15 years. Germany was forced to pay a huge sum of money for the destruction and loss caused by the war. A new international organization, called the *League of Nations*, was established. The Treaty of Versailles punished Germany more severely than it had expected. It created conditions that helped Adolf Hitler gain power in Germany, which led to World War II.

Wilson knew that the Versailles Treaty was far from perfect. But he believed strongly in the League of Nations. He hoped that it would prevent aggression and war. But U.S. senators were totally opposed to the League. They feared that American democracy would suffer if the nation joined an international organization. The Versailles Treaty failed to pass the Senate, and the United States did not become a member of the League of Nations.

夫·希特勒在德国上台和第二次世界大战创造了条件。

威尔逊明白，凡尔赛和约远远不够完善。但他对国际联盟的作用信心十足。他希望这个组织能防止侵略与战争。然而国会参院却根本不赞成国际联盟。他们担心如果美国加入国际组织，美国的民主会受到限制。凡尔赛和约未能在参议院通过，美国因而也未能成为国际联盟的成员。

题外话

林语堂这样评价凡尔赛和约："凡尔赛和约岂止是不公平，简直是粗鄙和缺乏'涵养'。如果法国人在他们胜利之际有一点道家修养的话，他们就不会将凡尔赛和约强加于人，因而现在他们的头枕在枕头上要安稳得多。""凡尔赛会议如果请老子去做主席，今日就不会有个希特勒。"

1919年巴黎和会开幕式

CHAPTER TWELVE

The Twenties
二十年代

1. The Roaring Twenties

沸腾的 20 年代

The tempo of life in the 1920s seemed so much faster than it had been earlier that the period came to be called the "Roaring Twenties". Other nicknames for this period included the "Jazz Age" and the "Dollar Decade". After the war ended, large numbers of Americans wanted to forget about the troubles of Europeans. Instead, they simply wanted to enjoy life. In many ways, the decade marked the point at which the United States began developing into the modern society it is today. By the end of the decade, such features of modern life as the automobile, telephone, radio, and electric washing machine had become part of millions of American households.

Developments of the 1920s broadened the experiences of millions of Americans. More and more urban people could enjoy such activities as movies, plays, and sporting events. The new role of women also changed society. Many women found careers outside the home and began think-

20 世纪 20 年代的生活节奏似乎比先前大大加快，因而得名"沸腾的 20 年代"。这段时期的其他绰号有"爵士时代"和"金元年代"。战争结束后，大批美国人希望忘却欧洲的纷扰，他们只想享受快乐的生活。从许多方面看，这 10 年标志着美国开始进入现代社会。20 年代末，现代生活的特征如汽车、电话、收音机和洗衣机已进入千千万万个美国家庭。

20 年代的发展开阔了千千万万美国人的眼界。越来越多的城市居民可以观看电影、戏剧和体育竞赛。妇女扮演的新角色也改变了社会。许多妇女走出家庭，从事职业，开始自认为与男人们地位平等，而不再仅仅是家庭主妇和母亲。

沸腾的 20 年代是有才华的美

ing of themselves more as the equal of men, and less as housewives and mothers.

The Roaring Twenties was the age when talented Americans emerged in large numbers and won admiration for their accomplishments. In 1927, Charles A. Lindbergh received a hero's welcome after making the first solo nonstop airplane flight across the Atlantic Ocean. Sports superstars of the 1920s became household names for their exceptional ability. Movie stars' lives made the front-pages of newspapers. Many American writers and artists became worldly famous. Even attitudes toward big business changed during the 1920s. Despised by many in earlier days, business leaders gained widespread admiration for their accomplishments.

国人大批涌现，由于成就卓著而备受赞扬的时代。1927年，查尔斯·A.林白首创单人驾机不着陆飞越大西洋的纪录，受到英雄般的欢迎。20年代的运动明星由于他们非凡的技艺而家喻户晓。电影明星的生活成为报纸的头版新闻。许多美国作家和美术家扬名世界。20年代，人们对大工商企业的态度也发生了变化。一度遭到许多人蔑视的工商界领袖如今也由于他们的成就而受到赞扬。

It was 1927. A young air-mail pilot named Charles Lindbergh was about to become famous by making the first nonstop solo flight across the Atlantic.

一九二七年，一位名叫查尔斯·林白的不着陆飞机驾驶员，首次创下单人不停飞越大西洋的飞行纪录，一举成名。

查尔斯·A.林白与他不着陆飞越大西洋的飞机"路易斯精神"号

2. The Growth of Economy

During the 1920s, the American economy began to develop rapidly. Wartime government restrictions on business ended. The government raised tariff duties to the highest level ever in order to keep foreign goods from competing with American products. This and other measures did much to help American business flourish.

With the help of new technology American manufacturers developed new products and turned out goods much faster and more cheaply than ever before. Sales of such items as electric washing machines, refrigerators, and radios rose.

Probably the best symbol of industrial growth in the 1920s was the automobile. Early automobiles were so expensive that only a few people could afford them. Henry Ford changed car manufacture. He developed a simple car, the popular black Model T, and mass-produced it. In his factory, a moving belt brought interchangeable parts to workers who performed one of more specific operations again and again. These new techniques made cars less expensive so that large numbers of people would be able to afford them. The cost of automobiles continued to drop and sales rose. In just 10 years between 1920 and 1930, the number of cars in the United States grew from about 8 million to 23 million.

The thriving automobile industry contributed a great deal to the growth of national economy. It provided jobs for millions of people in such related industries as steel, road construction, gasoline

经济的增长

20年代，美国的经济开始迅速增长。战时政府对工商业的限制取消了。政府将关税提升到了前所未有的高度，使外国产品无力与美国产品竞争。诸如此类的举措大大促进了工商业的繁荣。

由于采用了新的技术，美国的制造业开发了新产品，生产效率比以往任何时候都更高，产品的价格也更低廉。洗衣机、电冰箱和收音机一类的产品的销售量增长了。

20年代工业增长的最佳标志应当是汽车。早期的汽车价格昂贵，只有少数人买得起。亨利·福特改变了汽车生产技术。他研制出一种构造简单的汽车，即广受欢迎的黑色 T 型车，然后批量生产。在他的工厂里，传送带将可替换的零件送到工人手里，而工人只反复进行一两件特殊的操作。这些新技术大大降低了汽车的价格，使普通大众都能买得起。汽车的成本持续下降，销量则持续上升。从 1920 年到 1930 年的仅仅 10 年内，美国的汽车占有量从大约 800 万辆增加到 2300 万辆。

繁荣的汽车工业对国民经济的增长做出了重大贡献。它为千千万万的人在钢铁、公路建设、汽油销售、石油和旅游等相关行业提供了职业。遍布全国的道路和公路网建

sales, oil production, and tourism. Networks of roads and highways across the country were built. With their own cars, many people could live in single-family homes on small plots of land in the suburbs of cities. The construction industry developed as a result.

As industry developed, jobs were easy to find, and the average city income had a larger increase than ever before. Families spent larger part of their incomes to buy home appliances such as refrigerators, washing machines, and vacuum cleaners; things previously considered luxuries now became necessities.

But in spite of its growth and apparent strength, the economy was on shaky grounds. Only manufacturing industries prospered. Workers in the coal, railroad, and textile industries failed to share in the prosperity of the 1920s. They became worse off instead. Throughout the decade, farmers were struggling with surplus crops, heavy debts and dropping income. Thousands of them went bankrupt. These poor people had little demand for manufactured goods. This unhealthy growth finally led to a stock market crash that toppled the economy like a house of cards in 1929.

起来了。许多人有了私家车，就可以到城郊居住在小片地产上盖起的独栋住宅里。结果，建筑工业得到发展。

随着工业的发展，工作较容易找到，城市的人均收入比以往有了较大的增长。家庭将收入的大部分用于购买电冰箱、洗衣机和吸尘器等家用电器。曾被视为奢侈品的东西，现在成了必需品。

然而，尽管经济增长很快，而且看上去很强劲，但其根基却不牢固。只有制造业繁荣起来了。煤矿、铁路和纺织工业并没有分享到20年代的繁荣，它们的处境反而更糟了。在这10年里，农民们由于多余的粮食、沉重的债务和下降的收入而苦苦挣扎。成千上万的农民破产。穷人对工业品的需求很少。这一不健康的经济增长最终导致1929年股票市场的崩溃，进而使整个经济像纸牌搭成的小屋一样轰然倒塌。

福特汽车生产线在生产T型车

20年代美国人乘私车出游时的盛况

3. Political Conservatism

政治保守主义

Many Americans of the 1920s became conservative in politics and economics. All three Presidents elected during the 1920s—Warren G. Harding, Calvin Coolidge, and Herbert Hoover—tended to favor big business in domestic policy and isolationism in foreign policy. Throughout the 1920s, most Americans regarded big business as the foundation of society. Under Harding and Coolidge, tariffs were raised, and income taxes fell for people who were most well off. And the United States never became a member of the

许多 20 年代的美国人在政治和经济上趋于保守。20 年代选出的三位总统——沃伦·G. 哈定、卡尔文·柯立芝和赫伯特·胡佛——在国内政策上倾向于袒护大型工商企业，在外交政策上则倾向于孤立主义。整个 20 年代，大多数美国人将大型工商企业视为社会的基础。在哈定和柯立芝的任期内，关税提高了，对于最富裕的人征收的所得税却降低了。而且，美国一直未能

League of Nations. Many Americans believed that League membership could involve the United States in future European wars.

While staying away from international political affairs, the United States began to close its doors to immigrants. Protests against unlimited immigration came from labour organizations, which feared the loss of jobs to newcomers, and from patriotic organizations, which feared foreign radicalism. In 1924 the U.S. Congress passed the *National Origins Act*, which limited immigration into the country.

Distrust of foreigners also set off a nationwide panic called the Red Scare. Many Americans blamed what they regarded as an international Communist conspiracy for various protest movements and union activities in 1919 and 1920.

Many rural Americans joined a secret organization called the Ku Klux Klan. The Ku Klux

成为国际联盟的成员国。许多美国人认为，加入国联会使美国卷入未来的欧洲战争。

避开国际政治事务的同时，美国也开始对移民关闭国门。对无限制移民的抗议来自劳工组织和爱国组织。劳工组织担心新来的移民抢走工作岗位；爱国组织则担心国外激进主义的传播。1924年，美国国会通过《移民法》，限制移民进入美国。

对外国人的猜疑还引起了全国范围的"红色恐慌"。许多美国人将1919年和1920年发生的各种各样的抗议运动和工会活动归咎于他们所谓的国际共产主义阴谋。

许多美国乡下人加入了秘密组织三K党。三K党在19世纪70年代已销声匿迹，但在20世纪20年代党徒大大增加。新的三K党将现代社会的种种问题归咎于"局外人"，包括黑人、犹太人、天主教徒、外国人和政治激进分子。这个组织最多时有党徒200多万。

保守主义还表现在宗教的原教旨主义。原教旨主义是一种宗教运动，其成员坚持认为《圣经》字字句句都是真理。1925年田纳西的一个学校教师约翰·T.斯科普斯受到审判，原因是他违反了田纳西州在公立学校里禁止讲授进化论的法律。原教旨主义分子称进化论与

1925年三K党在华盛顿举行4万人的游行

Klan had died out in the 1870s, but a new Klan gained a large following during the 1920s. The new Klan blamed all the problems in modern society on "outsiders", including blacks, Jews, Roman Catholics, foreigners, and political radicals. At its height, the organization had more than 2 million members.

Conservatism can also be seen in religious fundamentalism. Fundamentalism is a movement whose members insist that words of the Bible should be taken literally. In 1925 John T. Scopes, a Tennessee schoolteacher, was tried for breaking a Tennessee law that made it illegal to teach the theory of evolution in public schools. Fundamentalists said that this theory contradicted the story of creation in the Bible. Scopes and the American Civil Liberties Union believed that the law violated freedom of speech. The trial attracted worldwide attention. Scopes was fined $100, but the conviction was later reversed because of a small legal error.

During the 1920s social criticism became weaker, and some intellectuals fled the United States and settled in Paris.

《圣经》里的创世故事相矛盾。斯科普斯和美国公民自由联盟则认为田纳西的法律危害了言论自由。这一审判引起了全世界的关注。斯科普斯被罚款 100 美圆，但后来由于司法上的小过失而被免于追究。

在 20 年代，对社会的批判减弱了，一些知识分子离开美国到欧洲定居。

卡尔文·柯立芝和赫伯特·胡佛

题外话

1924年的《移民法》实际上依移民的种族与文化对他们加以区别对待。对来自北欧和西欧的移民，限制相当宽松。对来自俄国的移民（其中犹太人居多），以及意大利人则限制较严，对亚洲人实际上是大门紧闭。第二次世界大战中，美国为了向其盟国中国表示友好，才于 1943 年决定每年允许区区 105 名中国人移居美国。

田纳西州在公立学校里禁止讲授进化论的法律一直维持到 1967 年，当年州议会废除了这一法律。

4. Prohibition

Prohibition refers to the laws that forbid the manufacture, sale, or transportation of alcoholic drinks, including beer, gin, rum, vodka, whiskey, and wine. In the United States, prohibition became so popular in the early 20th century that, in 1920, a prohibition amendment was added to the U. S. Constitution. This amendment, the 18th Amendment, caused the use of alcoholic drinks to decline sharply.

However, most Americans who drank alcohol continued doing so. Some people made their own beer, wine, or distilled liquor at home illegally. Large numbers of otherwise law-abiding citizens considered prohibition a violation of their rights. They bought alcoholic drinks in illegal bars. Neither federal agents nor state and local officials could stop the widespread violation of national prohibition.

Since the alcoholic trade was highly profitable, competition for control of the business led to organized crimes. Many people argued that prohibition gave the government too much power over people's personal lives, and besides, it took away jobs and deprived the government of badly needed revenues from taxes on liquor.

In the 1932 presidential campaign, the Democratic Party promised to repeal prohibition. The Democratic presidential candidate, Franklin Delano Roosevelt, won the election by a large margin. In February 1933, Congress proposed the 21st Amendment to the Constitution to repeal the 18th Amendment.

《禁酒令》

《禁酒令》指禁止制造、销售、或贩运酒精饮料，包括啤酒、金酒、朗姆酒、伏特加、威士忌和葡萄酒的一系列法令。20世纪初，禁酒在美国受到极其广泛的支持，以至于禁酒的修正案写入了美国宪法。这条修正案，即第18条修正案，使酒精饮料的消费锐减。

然而，有饮酒习惯的美国人大多继续饮酒。有些人在自己家里非法自制啤酒、葡萄酒或蒸馏酒。许多在其他方面守法的公民认为禁酒剥夺了他们的权利。他们在非法的酒吧里购买酒精饮料。无论是联邦特工还是州和地方官员都无法阻止广泛的违反联邦禁酒令的行为。

由于私酒贸易利润很高，试图控制私酒行业的竞争导致有组织的犯罪。许多人争辩说，《禁酒令》使政府的权力过大，干涉了公民的私生活；此外，它还使许多人失业，使政府无法通过向酒类征税而得到急需的财政收入。

在1932年的总统竞选中，民主党许诺废除《禁酒令》。民主党候选人富兰克林·德拉诺·罗斯福以压倒多数在选举中获胜。1933年2月，国会提出第21条宪法修正案，废除了第18条修正案。

5. Changes in Life Style

生活方式的改变

In an effort to be modern, many young men and women of the Roaring Twenties adopted a life style that earned them the nickname of the Flaming Youth.

Before World War I, women had worn ankle-length dresses, long cotton stockings and long hair. But in the 1920s, they began wearing short skirts and tight dresses and rolled their silk stockings down to their knees. They cut their hair in a boyish style called the bob. They also used lipstick and rouge, and smoked cigarettes. They and their beaus (boyfriends) enjoyed such new thrills as speeding around in cars. Women who looked and behaved in this way became known as flappers.

Young people — along with many of their elders — often visited secret nightclubs, drank illegal alcoholic drinks, listened to jazz, the latest craze in popular music, and danced the Charleston and other modern steps.

Women's lives were also changing greatly during the 1920s. The 19th Amendment to the Constitution, which became law in 1920, gave women the right to vote in all elections. Many new opportunities for education and careers opened up to women during the decade.

为了追求时尚，沸腾时代的许多青年男女改变了自己的生活方式，使他们得到了"激情青年"的绰号。

第一次世界大战前，妇女穿长至脚踝的裙装和长筒棉袜，留长发。但在20年代，她们开始穿短裙和紧身裙装，丝袜向下翻卷至膝盖。她们将头发剪短成男孩子的式样。她们还使用唇膏和胭脂，并且吸烟。她们和男友们 (beaus) 喜欢开快车兜风。如此举止打扮的妇女被称为"时尚女"(flappers)。

青年人，还有他们的不少长辈，常常到秘密的夜总会去喝非法的酒精饮料，听最时兴的流行音乐爵士乐，跳查尔斯顿舞和其他摩登舞蹈。

在20年代，妇女的生活也发生了重大变化。1920年通过的第19条宪法修正案使妇女在所有的选举中获得选举权。许多受教育和就业的机会对妇女敞开了。由于电

在1920年的时尚女

Women's housekeeping chores became easier as electric appliances became available. In addition, women had fewer children to raise.

器的使用，妇女的家务减轻了。此外，妇女抚养的孩子也少了。

6. Popular Culture

大众文化

Radio became very popular in the 1920s. Americans listened on the radio to the same popular music, comedy shows, and commercials, broadcast by new radio networks such as National Broadcasting Company (NBC) and Columbia Broadcasting System (CBS). Another mass medium was the motion picture, which gained vast urban audiences. By 1920, Hollywood had become the world's movie capital. It turned out hundreds of full-length films. These early movies were silent, and black and white, shown to the accompaniment of piano music. The movies provided the public with daring fictional heroes, including good, strong cowboys who always defeated bad Indians or outlaws. Fans followed the life-style of movie stars in film magazines.

The 1920s have been called the golden age of jazz. Radio stations gave live performances by the growing number of jazz musicians. New Orleans, Memphis, St.

20年代，收音机大大普及。美国人通过收音机听同样的流行音乐，同样的喜剧演出和广告节目，这些节目都是由全国广播公司(NBC)和哥伦比亚广播公司(CBS)的新建的广播网播出的。另一种大众传媒是电影，城市里观众人数众多。到了 20 年代，好莱坞已成为世界影都。那里生产了数以百计的故事片。早期的电影是无声的，黑白两色，上映时有钢琴音乐伴奏。影片内容多是好勇斗狠的传奇英雄，包括善良、强健的牛仔，他们总会打败邪恶的印第安人和非法之徒。电影迷们阅读电影杂志，模仿影星的生活方式。

20 年代又有爵士乐的黄金时代之称。

20年代的一个杂志封面

Louis, Kansas City, Chicago, Detroit, and New York City were all important centers of jazz. During the late 1920s and early 1930s, jazz advanced from relatively simple music played by performers who often could not read music to a more complex and sophisticated form. Jazz influenced several classical composers, notably George Gershwin. His *Rhapsody in Blue* and *An American in Paris*, both composed in the 1920s, made jazz respectable.

爵士乐手越来越多，电台直播他们的演奏。新奥尔良、孟菲斯、圣路易斯、堪萨斯城、芝加哥、底特律和纽约市都是重要的爵士乐中心。20 年代末和 30 年代初，爵士乐由往往不识乐谱的乐手演奏的相对简单的音乐发展成一种复杂而精致的音乐形式。爵士乐影响了几位古典作曲家，其中最著名的是乔治·格什温。他的《蓝色狂想曲》和《一个美国人在巴黎》都创作于 20 年代，这些作品使爵士乐登上大雅之堂。

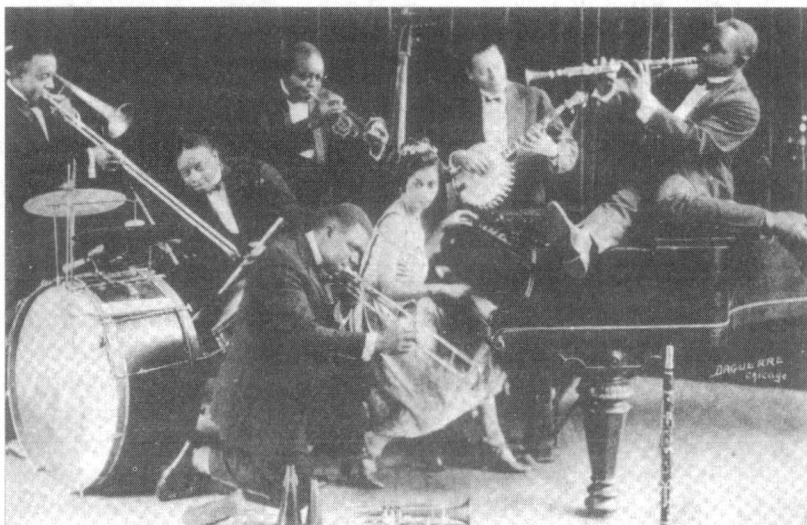

20年代初的一个爵士乐队

7. Literature

文　学

In literature, Sinclair Lewis, in his novel *Main Street*, reveals the monotony and lack of spiritual and intellectual values in American middle-class life. And in *Babbitt*, he characterizes the small-town American businessman who conforms blindly to the materialistic social and ethical standards of his environment. Theodore Dreiser was

在文学方面，辛克莱·路易斯的小说《大街》揭露了美国中产阶级生活的单调和精神价值的匮乏。在《巴比特》里，路易斯刻画了一个小城市的商人，盲目地认同环境所推崇的物质主义的社会和道德标准。西奥多·德莱塞是自然主义运

the most famous American writer in the natural-ism movement. In his *Sister Carrie* and *An American Tragedy*, Dreiser described his charac-ters as victims of social and economic forces, and of fate, all of which conspire against them.

One group of Americans, who disliked the materialism they saw in the United States, spent years abroad. Gertrude Stein, an experimental writer who lived most of her life in France, called these Americans a "lost generation". One of the best known, Ernest Hemingway, wrote of Ameri-cans living in Europe in *The Sun Also Rises*. His novel *A Farewell to Arms* is a tragic love story set in Italy and Switzerland during World War I.

The novelist who probably best captured the spirit of the time was F. Scott Fitzgerald. *The Great Gatsby*, his best novel, creates fictional characters whose plea-sure-seeking lives won public admiration, and presents a penetrating criticism of the moral emptiness of wealthy so-ciety in the United States during the 1920s.

动中最著名的美国作家。在他的《嘉莉妹妹》和《美国的悲剧》中，他将人物描写成社会和经济力量以及命运合谋迫害的牺牲品。

一群美国人不喜欢他们在美国所见到的物质主义，因而多年侨居国外。格特鲁德·斯泰因，一位一生大部分时间侨居法国的实验作家，称这些美国人为"迷惘的一代"。其中最著名的作家是厄内斯特·海明威。他在《太阳照样升起》里，描写了一群旅居欧洲的美国人。他的小说《别了，武器》讲述的是第一次世界大战中发生在意大利和瑞士的一个悲剧爱情故事。

或许最能捕捉时代精神的小说家要算是 F. 司各特·菲兹杰拉德。他的杰作《大款盖茨比》创造了以寻欢作乐的生活方式博得公众赞美的人物，对美国 20 年代富裕社会的道德空虚做了深刻的批判。

F. 司各特·菲兹杰拉德和妻子齐尔达

CHAPTER THIRTEEN

Depression and the New Deal
大萧条与新政

1. The Great Depression

大萧条

Great Depression was the period of high unemployment and low business activity during the 1930s. The Great Depression began in October 1929, when stock prices in the United States began to fall sharply. Thousands of stockholders lost large sums of money. Banks and businesses closed their doors, people lost their jobs, homes, and savings, and many people had to depend on the government or charity to provide them with food.

The depression was caused by a number of serious weaknesses in the economy. The 1920s appeared on the surface to be a prosperous time, but income was unevenly distributed. The wealthy made large profits, but more and more Americans

大萧条指 30 年代高失业率以及经济低迷的一段时期。大萧条开始于 1929 年 10 月，当时美国的股票价格猛跌。千千万万的股东损失惨重。银行与工商企业纷纷关闭，人们失去了工作、房产和储蓄，许多人不得不依靠政府和慈善机构来获得食物。

大萧条是经济中的几种严重缺

纽约的失业工人等待救济

spent more than they earned, and farmers were struggling with surplus crops, heavy debts and dropping income. Industrial production kept rising, but wage earners' incomes did not. People could not afford to buy all the cars, appliances, and other goods being manufactured. Foreign demand for American products was limited, too. Europe was still struggling to pay war debts and reparations. High protective tariffs further slowed down international trade.

Continuing throughout the 1930s, the depression ended in the United States only when massive spending for World War II began.

陷造成的。20 年代表面上看是一个繁荣的时代，但收入的分配并不均匀。富人赚取了大笔的利润，但是越来越多的美国人过着透支的生活，农民们由于多余的粮食、沉重的债务和下降的收入而苦苦挣扎。工业生产不断增长，但人们的薪金却没有增加。人们无力购买正在制造出来的所有的汽车、电器和其他工业品。国外对美国产品的需求也很有限。欧洲正在挣扎着偿还债务和战争赔款。高额关税进一步制约了国际贸易的发展。

大萧条一直持续到 30 年代末，只有开始为第二次世界大战投入巨额开支时，它才在美国结束。

银行倒闭，人们失去存款

人们戏称为"胡佛镇"的贫民窟

2. The New Deal

Hoover's administration took some measures to fight the depression, but most Americans felt that the President did not do enough. They elected Franklin D. Roosevelt President in 1932.

Roosevelt believed the federal government had the chief responsibility of fighting the depression. He called Congress into a special session on March 5, 1933. From March 9 to June 16, Congress passed a series of important laws to provide relief for victims of the depression, to help economic recovery, to reform financial, business, agricultural, and industrial practices. Most laws passed quickly without much opposition. Never before had Congress approved so many important laws so quickly. The session then became known as "The Hundred Days". Roosevelt called his program the New Deal.

During "The Hundred Days" Congress created the Federal Emergency Relief Administration

新 政

胡佛的政府采取了一些措施来克服萧条，但大多数美国人觉得他的行动不够有力。1932 年，他们选举富兰克林·D. 罗斯福为总统。

罗斯福认为联邦政府应在克服萧条中承担主要责任。他要求国会于 1933 年 3 月 5 日召开特别会议。从 3 月 9 日至 6 月 16 日，国会通过了一系列的重要法案为大萧条的受害者提供救济，促进经济复苏，改革金融、商业、农业和工业的经营方式。大多数法案没有遇到太大阻力便得以通过。国会从来没有如此迅速地批准如此众多的重要法案。这个会期史称"百日"。罗斯福将他的计划称为"新政"。

在"百日"里，国会建立了联邦紧急救济署(FERA)，向各州拨款直接救济失业者。数以百万计的家

(FERA) to give the states money for direct relief to the unemployed. Millions of families received cash for food, clothing, and shelter. The Civilian Conservation Corps (CCC) hired thousands of young men for such conservation projects as replanting forests, controlling floods, and improving national parks. The Public Works Administration (PWA) created jobs for large numbers of people. Thousands of schools, courthouses, bridges, dams, and other useful public works projects were built through PWA projects. Congress also created several agencies to manage economic recovery programs and supervise banking and labour reforms. The government tried to help recovery by spending large sums of money. It also increased trade by lowering tariffs on certain imported goods. In return, other nations lowered tariffs on some United States products that they imported.

One of the most successful reforms of the New Deal was the Tennessee Valley Authority (TVA). This was a giant public power project in the valley of the Tennessee River. The many dams built not only controlled floods, but also provided cheaper electricity for residents of the Ten-

罗斯福总统

庭得到了现金以购买食品、衣物和住房。公共资源保护队(CCC)雇用成千上万的青年人从事诸如植树、治水、改善国家公园的工作。公共工程署(PWA)为大批的人创造了工作。成千上万的学校、县府、桥梁、堤坝和其他有用的公共工程建设都通过 PWA 的计划得以完成。国会还建立了几个机构主管经济复苏计划，监督银行系统和劳工组织的改革。政府试图靠大量支出的办法刺激经济复苏。政府还通过降低某几种进口商品关税的办法促进贸易。作为回应，其他国家也对它们进口的某些美国商品降低了关税。

新政中最成功的改革之一是设立了田纳西河流域管理局(TVA)。这是一个田纳西河流域的庞大的公共水利工程。建起的许多水坝不但可以防洪，而且为田纳西河流域的居民提供了廉价的电力。

1935 年，罗斯福宣布开始实行所谓的"第二新政"。主要

nessee River Valley.

In 1935, Roosevelt launched the so-called "second New Deal". A major relief and recovery measure was a huge public work program, to be managed by the Works Progress Administration (WPA). The WPA provided jobs building highways, bridges, streets, hospitals, schools and parks. It also created work for artists, writers, actors, and musicians. The WPA provided some work for about 8.5 million people.

In addition, Congress passed two reform bills. One was the *National Labor Relations Act*, which guaranteed workers the right to organize unions. The other was the *Social Security Act*, which provided pensions for retired workers and insurance for the jobless. The law also provided money for the handicapped, and families with dependent children.

的救济和复苏措施是实施一项庞大的公共工程计划，由工程进度管理署 (WPA) 负责实施。WPA 提供修建公路、桥梁、街道、医院、学校和公园的工作，还为美术家、作家、演员和音乐家创造了就业机会。WPA 为大约 850 万人提供了工作。

此外，国会还通过了两项改革法案。一项是《全国劳工关系法》，保障工人组织工会的权利。另一项是《社会保障法》，为退休工人提供养老金，为失业工人提供保险。这项法案还为残疾人和有未成年子女的家庭提供救助。

罗斯福视察公共资源保护队(CCC)的营地

3. The Effects of the New Deal

新政的效果

The New Deal did not end the depression. It was military spending for World War II that brought back prosperity. But the New Deal relieved much economic hardship and gave Ameri-

新政并没有结束大萧条。带来了繁荣的是为第二次世界大战投入的军费。但新政减轻了经济困难，在其他遭受萧条打击的国家转向独

cans faith in the democratic system at a time when other nations hit by the depression turned to dictators. The New Deal had also some lasting effects. The most important one, perhaps, is the adoption of a new political philosophy, liberalism, to which many Americans remained attached for decades to come. The New Deal elevated the social status of minority groups. Until the 1930s, the most influential members of American society were white, Anglo-Saxon Protestants (so-called WASPs). Roosevelt's government began to hire more blacks, Catholics, and Americans of other ethnic and religious backgrounds. The New Deal caused major political changes. The Democratic Party, generally a minority party since the Civil War, became the largest political party. Its main strength shifted from the rural South to the urban North. Immigrants, union members, urban intellectuals, and reformers gained a stronger voice in party decisions. The New Deal created a welfare state, in which the government had a duty to provide economic security for the people and the economic growth of the nation. After the New Deal, the government's role in banking and public welfare grew steadily. Also, organized labour became an important force in national affairs.

Roosevelt's efforts to end the depression made him one of the most popular U.S. Presidents. The voters elected him to four terms. No other President won election more than twice. Roosevelt's New Deal was a turning point in American history. It marked the start of a strong government role in the nation's economic affairs that has continued and grown to the present day.

裁时，使美国人建立起对民主制度的信心。新政也产生了某些持久的影响。或许其中最重要的是采用了一种新的政治哲学，即自由主义。许多美国人在未来的几十年中一直奉行这一哲学。新政提升了少数群体的社会地位。30 年代以前，美国社会最有影响的成员是白人盎格鲁－撒克逊新教徒（即所谓的 WASPs）。罗斯福的政府开始雇用更多的黑人、天主教徒和其他种族和宗教背景的美国人。新政也引起了重大的政治变革。自从南北战争以来一贯处于少数党地位的民主党，成为最大的政党。民主党的主要力量从南方农业地区转向北方的都市。移民、工会会员、城市知识分子、主张改革的人在党的决策中有了更有力的发言权。新政创造了一个福利国家，政府在其中承担了为人民提供经济保障、为国家的经济发展提供条件的职责。新政之后，政府在银行业和公共福利方面发挥的作用稳步扩大。此外，有组织的劳工在国内事务中也成为一股重要力量。

罗斯福克服萧条所做的努力使他成为美国最得人心的总统之一。选举人选举他连任 4 届总统。没有任何其他总统在选举中获胜超过两次。罗斯福的新政是美国历史上的一个转折点。他标志着政府在经济事务中发挥强大作用的开端，这种作用一直持续并发展到今天。

CHAPTER FOURTEEN

World War II
第二次世界大战

1. The Cause of World War II

战争的起因

World War II was the biggest and most destructive war that has ever been fought. Some 1,700 million people, about three-fourths of the world's population, from 61 nations were involved in the war, which was fought on the land, on the sea, and in the skies of Europe, East and Southeast Asia, North Africa, and the islands of the Pacific Ocean. About 70 million people served in the armed forces and about 17 million of them lost their lives. The war caused more destruction, cost more resources, and probably had more far-reaching consequences than any other war in history.

The causes of World War II can be found in the political and economic problems left unsolved by World War I. First, many nations were dissatisfied with the treaties that ended the war. The defeated nations thought the treaties unfair, because they imposed too harsh punishment on them, forcing them to give up territory and re

第二次世界大战是历史上规模最大、破坏力最强的战争之一。约占世界总人口四分之三、来自 61 个国家的 17 亿人卷入战争。战火遍及欧洲、东亚、东南亚、北非以及太平洋岛屿的海洋、陆地和天空。大约 7000 万人在军队服役，其中大约有 1700 万人死于战场。战争造成的破坏、浪费的资源及其深远影响，是任何其他战争所无法相比的。

第二次世界大战的原因根植于第一次世界大战后未能解决的政治和经济问题。首先，许多国家对和约不满。战败国认为条约不够公正，对它们的惩罚过于苛刻，不但要它们割让土地和资源，还要它们支付大笔赔款。有些战胜国也不喜

sources and pay large sums of money. Some winning nations also disliked the treaties, because the treaties did not let them gain as much as they had expected. Secondly, World War I seriously damaged the economies of European countries. Both the winners and the losers came out of the war in poverty. Before their economies could return to the normal, an economic crisis, called the Great Depression, struck them in the early 1930s. Millions of people lost their jobs, and they were poorer and filled with despair. Democratic governments lost support and extreme political movements became stronger because they promised to end the economic problems.

As the political and economic problems became more serious, nationalism grew stronger. Many nationalists viewed foreigners and members of minority groups as inferior. They thought they had good reason to conquer other countries and treat minorities badly. Nationalism grows especially when a people feel they are unfairly treated by other peoples. Many Germans felt humiliated by their country's defeat in World War I and the harsh treatment they received under the Treaty of Versailles. They wished to see their country powerful and able to insist on its rights. During the 1930s, they enthusiastically supported a violently nationalistic organization called the Nazi Party. The Nazi Party declared that Germany had a right to become strong again. Nationalism also gained strength in Italy and Japan.

Nationalistic leaders in several countries took advantage of the political and economic problems to seize power. During the 1920s and 1930s, dictatorships came to power in Italy, Germany, and

欢和约，因为它们未能得到想要的东西。其次，第一次世界大战严重破坏了欧洲的经济。无论战胜国还是战败国，战后都成了穷国。在经济恢复正常之前，一场称为"大萧条"的经济危机在30年代初袭击了这些国家。数百万人失业，他们更加贫困，充满绝望情绪。民主政府失去支持，极端政治组织开始壮大，因为它们许诺解决经济问题。

政治和经济问题日趋严重，民族主义情绪随之高涨。许多民族主义者歧视外国人和少数民族。他们认为自己有理由征服其他国家，虐待少数民族。当一个民族受其他民族的欺侮时，民族主义会变得特别强烈。许多德国人对国家在一战中的失败和凡尔赛和约强加于他们的苛刻条件感到屈辱。他们希望看到自己的国家强大起来，能够主张自己的权利。在30年代，他们热心支持一个叫做纳粹党的极端民族主义的组织。纳粹党宣称德国有权强大起来。民族主义势力在意大利和日本也增强了。

有几个国家的民族主义组织的领袖利用政治和经济问题来夺取政权。在20和30年代，意大利、德

Japan. In these countries one person or a small group of people had absolute power and used force to stop people from criticizing their rule. The dictators in Germany, Italy, and Japan all had ambition to conquer more territory.

国和日本都建立了独裁政权。在这些国家里，个人或一小撮人掌握绝对权力，使用暴力禁止人们对他们的批评。德国、意大利和日本的独裁者都有扩张领土的野心。

2. Aggressions Before the War

大战前的局部侵略战争

Japan, Italy and Germany began to invade weak countries in 1930s. Japan seized control of northeast China in 1931, and began to attack the rest of China in 1937. It occupied most of eastern China by the end of 1938. Italian troops invaded Ethiopia in 1935, and conquered the country the next year. In 1936, Hitler sent troops into the Rhineland, violating the Treaty of Versailles, which forbade German troops to go into that area.

While Germany and Italy took aggressive actions, Great Britain and France were hesitating, afraid of fighting another war so soon after World War I. This attitude actually encouraged the aggressors.

The aggressors soon formed an alliance. In 1936, Germany and Italy agreed to support one another's foreign policy. The alliance was known as the *Rome-Berlin Axis*. Japan joined the alliance in 1940, and it became the *Rome-Berlin-Tokyo Axis*. Six other nations eventually joined the Axis. During the war, countries fighting the Axis were called the *Allies*. The Allies included 50 nations by the end of the war.

In March 1938, German soldiers marched into Austria and united it with Germany. A few

日本、意大利和德国于30年代开始入侵弱国。日本于1931年夺取了中国东北，并于1937年开始进攻中国的其余部分。到1938年末，日本已占领中国东部大部分地区。意大利军队于1935年入侵埃塞俄比亚，次年占领该国。1936年，希特勒派军进入莱茵兰地区，破坏了凡尔赛和约，因为和约禁止德军进入该地区。

当德国和意大利采取侵略行动时，英法两国犹豫不决，害怕一战刚刚结束，就打另一场战争。这一态度实际上鼓励了侵略者。

侵略者们不久便结成联盟。1936年，德国和意大利约定支持彼此的外交政策。联盟称为罗马—柏林轴心。日本于1940年加入联盟，联盟成为罗马—柏林—东京轴心。最终有六个国家加入轴心。战争期间，与轴心国作战的称为同盟国。到战争结束时，同盟国增加到50个国家。

1938年3月，德军开入奥地利，将其并入德国。几个月后，希

months later Hitler said he wanted to take Sudetenland region of Czechoslovakia, because most people living there were Germans. Hitler and Mussolini met Chamberlain and Daladier, the heads of the governments of Great Britain and France, in the German city of Munich to discuss the matter, and Hitler was allowed to have exactly what he wanted. Chamberlain and Daladier thought they could prevent a war by just giving in. This policy is called appeasement. But it turned out to be a bad policy.

特勒声称他想要夺取捷克斯洛伐克的苏台德地区，因为当地大多数居民是日尔曼人。希特勒和墨索里尼在德国城市慕尼黑会见英法政府首脑张伯伦和达拉第讨论此事，结果希特勒得到了他想要的东西。张伯伦和达拉第认为仅仅通过让步就可以防止战争。这一政策称为绥靖政策，结果证明它是很糟糕的政策。

纳粹占领捷克斯洛伐克

3. Early Years of the War

大战初年

In March 1939, Germany broke the Munich Agreement and seized the rest of Czechoslovakia. On September 1, Germany invaded Poland. This event is generally considered to be the start of World War II. Great Britain and France saw that appeasement would not work, and two days later they declared war on Germany. In April 1940, German troops invaded Denmark and Norway. Chamberlain resigned in May, and Winston Churchill became prime minister. Churchill told the British people he had nothing to offer them

1939年3月，德国撕毁慕尼黑协定，占领了捷克斯洛伐克的其余地区。9月1日，德国入侵波兰。一般认为这一事件是第二次世界大战的开端。英法两国看到绥靖政策已告失败，两天后向德国宣战。1940年4月，德国军队入侵丹麦和挪威。张伯伦于5月辞职，温斯顿·丘吉尔继任首相。丘吉尔告诉英国人民，他所能奉献的没有别的，只有"热血、辛劳、眼泪和汗

but "blood, toil, tears, and sweat" to win "victory at all costs". That same day, Germany attacked Belgium, Luxembourg, and the Netherlands and advanced toward France.

After the fall of France, Great Britain stood alone against Hitler. The United States sent guns, planes and supplies to help the British, but was not in the war. Now Hitler wanted to conquer Great Britain. Before the Germans could invade England, however, they had to defeat Britain's Royal Air Force. The Battle of Britain began in July 1940. All through that year German planes bombed the cities of England, killing thousands of people, but the British people became more determined than ever to win the war. The Royal Air Force shot down 2,000 German planes in three months, until Hitler had to give up his attempts to defeat Britain from the air.

When Germany attacked France, Italy entered the war on Germany's side. In August 1940 Italian army went to North Africa to invade British Somaliland (now northern Somalia) and Egypt. The Axis wanted to control Egypt so as to cut Britain off from oil fields in the Middle East and from the Suez Canal. Britain struck back at the Italians in December 1940, sweeping them out of Egypt. Early in 1941, Hitler sent tank units led by General Erwin Rommel to help the Italians in northern Africa. During the spring, Rommel recaptured the territory the Italians had lost and drove into Egypt until he reached El Alamein, not far away from the Suez Canal. But his troops were defeated by the British army under General Bernard Law Montgomery. The Battle of El Alamein proved to be the turning point of the war

水",要"不惜一切代价赢得胜利"。同一天,德国占领了比利时、卢森堡与荷兰,并向法国进军。

法国陷落后,只剩下英国与希特勒对抗。美国运送大炮、飞机和物资援助英国,但没有加入战争。希特勒开始盘算征服英国。但在入侵英国之前,德国必须先打垮英国皇家空军。不列颠战役于1940年7月打响。当年德国飞机不断轰炸英国城市,炸死数千人,但英国人民更坚定了打赢战争的决心。皇家空军在三个月内击落2000架敌机,直至希特勒放弃从空中击败英国的计划。

德国进攻法国时,意大利加入德方作战。1940年8月,意大利军队进入北非,入侵英属索马里兰(即现在的索马里)和埃及。轴心国企图控制埃及以切断英国与中东油田和苏伊士运河的联系。1940年12月英军向意军发起反攻,将意军逐出埃及。1941年初,希特勒派遣隆美尔将军率领的坦克部队援助北非的意大利军。当年春天,隆美尔夺回意大利军的失地,然后开入埃及,直抵离运河不远的阿拉曼。但他的军队被蒙哥马利将军率领的英军击败。阿拉曼战役是北非战争的一个转折点。

in North Africa.

In 1940 and 1941, Hitler forced Hungary, Romania and Bulgaria into joining the Axis. Then the German forces invaded and occupied Yugoslavia and Greece.

On June 22, 1941, the Germans suddenly invaded the Soviet Union, even though they had made a treaty of friendship with that country. At first the Germans did very well. They captured and killed hundreds of thousands of Soviet troops, and came very close to Moscow and Leningrad. Then the extremely cold Russian winter began, the German advance was stopped, and the Russians were able to win back some of the territory they had lost.

1940～1941年间，希特勒迫使匈牙利、罗马尼亚和保加利亚加入轴心国。然后，德国入侵并占领了南斯拉夫和希腊。

1941年6月22日，德军突然入侵苏联，尽管事先与苏联签署了友好条约。起初德国战事进展顺利。他们俘获、击毙了苏军数十万人，逼近莫斯科和列宁格勒。此时俄国的严冬开始了，德军的推进受阻，俄军收复了一些失地。

4. United States Neutrality

美国的中立

After World War II began in Europe in 1939, the United States had remained neutral. Yet most Americans hoped for an Allied victory. President Roosevelt persuaded Congress to provide the nations fighting the Axis powers with ships, tanks, planes, and other war materials. By late 1940, when Britain had nearly run out of their money, Congress approved the Lend-Lease Act, which allowed the president to supply weapons and equipment to the nations fighting the Axis powers. In return, the United States obtained the right to use certain Allied bases. In all, 38 nations received a total of about $50,000 million in aid under Lend-Lease.

二战于1939年在欧洲爆发时，美国保持中立。但大多数美国人希望同盟国取胜。罗斯福总统说服国会为与轴心国作战的国家提供军舰、坦克、飞机和其他战争物资。1940年末，当英国的财力已近枯竭，国会通过租借法案，允许总统为与轴心国作战的国家提供武器和装备。作为交换，美国获得盟国军事基地的使用权。依据租借法案，总共有38个国家接受了总价值约500亿美圆的援助。

5. Pearl Harbour

It was Japan that finally brought the United States into World War II. The United States opposed Japan's expansion in Southeast Asia. The Japanese military leaders believed that only the United States Navy had the power to check Japan's expansion. They decided to damage the U.S. Pacific Fleet with one forceful blow. On December 7, 1941, Japanese planes attacked without warning United States military bases at Pearl Harbor in Hawaii. The bombing of Pearl Harbor damaged much of the Pacific Fleet and destroyed many planes. But this event made all Americans angry and determined to fight until Japan was beaten. Early next year, Japanese forces rapidly conquered much of Southeast Asia and many islands in the Pacific.

The United States, Canada, and Great Britain declared war on Japan on December 8, 1941. The next day, China declared war on the Axis. Germany and Italy declared war on the United States on December 11. World War II had become a global conflict.

珍珠港美军基地遭到袭击

珍珠港事件

是日本最终使美国卷入大战。美国反对日本在东南亚的扩张。日本军队统帅们认为只有美国海军有力量阻止日本的扩张。他们决定出重拳一举摧毁美国的太平洋舰队。1941年12月7日，日本飞机偷袭了夏威夷的珍珠港美军基地。对珍珠港的轰炸重创了太平洋舰队，摧毁了许多飞机。但这一事件却激怒了所有的美国人，他们决心不打败日本决不罢休。次年年初，日本军队迅速攻克东南亚的大部分地区和许多太平洋岛屿。

美国、加拿大和英国于1941年12月8日向日本宣战。次日，中国向轴心国宣战。德国和意大利

于 12 月 11 日向美国宣战。第二次
世界大战演变成一场全球冲突。

罗斯福向日本宣战

6. The American Home Front

战时的美国国内

The American people mobilized for war even more completely in World War II than thcy had in World War I. All men between 18 and 45 were subject to military service. About 15 million American men and 338,000 women served in the armed forces. At home, automobile plants and other factories were converted into war plants to produce airplanes, tanks, ships, weapons, and other war supplies. War plants operated 24 hours a day, 7 days a week. Since the country had a shortage of civilian men, thousands of women worked in the plants to do jobs that had previously been done only by men.

To finance the war, Americans invested billions of dollars in war bonds. The government rationed food and other scare things, such as shoes, gasoline and fuel oil. Even children took part in the war effort. Boys and girls collected

在第二次世界大战中，美国人民比第一次世界人战更为彻底地动员了起来。18 岁至 45 岁之间的所有男人都有服兵役的义务。大约有 1500 万名男性、33.8 万名女性在军队里服役。在国内，汽车厂和其他工厂改装成军工厂，生产飞机、坦克、军舰、武器和其他战争物资。军工厂一周 7 天，每天 24 小时不间断生产。由于国家缺少男性公民，成千上万的妇女在工厂里从事过去只有男人才做的工作。

为了筹集战争所需资金，美国人将数十亿美圆投资战争债券。政府对食品和其他短缺物资，如鞋子、汽油和燃油实行配给制。甚至儿童们也为战争做出贡献。他们搜集罐头盒、旧轮胎和别的废品，使

used tin cans, old tires, and other "junk" that could be recycled and used for war supplies.

之加工后重新用于战争。

7. The Battle of Stalingrad

斯大林格勒战役

In 1942, the Germans started to advance again in Russia. They got as far as Stalingrad (now Volgograd). In North Africa the German forces went very close to the Suez Canal before they were stopped. In the Atlantic Ocean, German submarines sank so many Allied ships that the British nearly ran out of war supplies and food.

Then the tide turned. At Stalingrad the Russians stopped the German army and started a counterattack in mid-November 1942, and in February 1943, the last German troops in Stalingrad surrendered. The Battle of Stalingrad marked a turning point in World War II. It halted Germany's eastward advance. About 300,000 German troops were killed or captured.

1942年，德国再次开始进攻俄国。他们向俄国纵深推进，远达斯大林格勒(现在的伏尔加格勒)。在北非，德军已逼近苏伊士运河时才受阻。在大西洋，德国潜艇击沉了大量同盟国的船只，补给缺乏的英国几乎用光了战争物资和粮食。

这时战局发生了转变。在斯大林格勒，俄国军队阻止了德军的推进，并于1942年11月中旬发起反攻。1943年2月，斯大林格勒的最后一支德军投降。斯大林格勒战役是二战转折的标志。它阻止了德国在东线的攻势。大约30万德军战死或被俘。

8. Battles in Africa and Italy

北非和意大利的战役

In North Africa Montgomery struck the Axis forces at El Alamein in October 1942. He won a great victory and began driving the German and Italian forces into Tunisia. Soon after that the Allies invaded French colonies in northern Africa. Vichy French forces in northern Africa fought back for a few days and then joined the Allied side. After a battle in Tunisia the last Axis forces

在北非，蒙哥马利于1942年10月在阿拉曼向轴心国发起进攻。他取得了重大胜利，开始将德意军队驱逐到突尼斯。不久后，盟军入侵了北非的法国殖民地。维希政府在北非的法国军队抵抗数日后，加入盟军一方。北非的轴心国残余部队在突尼斯打过一仗后，于1943

in northern Africa surrendered in May 1943. By clearing the Axis forces from northern Africa, the Allies obtained bases from which to invade southern Europe.

In July, Allied forces landed on the island of Sicily. After a month's bitter fighting they captured it. In September, the Americans and British invaded Italy. Italy surrendered immediately but the Germans in Italy continued to fight until they surrendered in May 1945.

年5月投降。肃清了北非的轴心国军队后，盟军获得了进攻南欧的立足点。

7月，盟军在西西里岛登陆。经过一个月的激战，夺取了该岛。9月，美英军队攻入意大利。意大利立即投降，但在意大利的德军则继续作战，直至1945年5月才投降。

9. The Invasion of France

登陆法国

Meanwhile thousands of American troops were arriving in England, and American and British planes began bombing German cities and factories. The Russians were winning back all the territories they had lost to Germany.

On June 6, 1944 (known as D-Day), about 2,700 ships carried 176,000 Allied troops crossed the English Channel. They landed on the coast of Normandy in northern France. Other soldiers were dropped by parachute behind German lines to

同时，成千上万的美军抵达英国，美英两国的飞机开始轰炸德国的城市和工厂。俄国正在收复所有被德国占领的领土。

1944年6月6日（称为D日），大约2700艘船载着盟军176000人渡过英吉利海峡。他们在法国北部的诺曼底海岸登陆。还有一些士兵

诺曼底登陆

capture bridges and railroad tracks to prevent the Germans from bringing fresh troops to stop the landing. D-Day took the Germans by surprise. But they fought back fiercely. After much hard fighting the Allies cleared the Germans out of most of northwestern France during August, and advanced eastward toward Paris. The French people in Paris rose up against the occupying German forces. American and Free French forces liberated Paris on August 25.

空降到敌军战线后方占领桥梁和铁路，以防止德国运送后续部队阻止盟军登陆。D日行动出乎德国人预料，使之措手不及。但他们随即展开凶猛的反击。一番艰苦的战斗之后盟军在8月清除了法国西北部所有的德国人，然后向东进军巴黎。巴黎人民起义反抗德国占领军。美军和自由法国军队于8月25日解放巴黎。

10. The Last Stage of the War in Europe

战争在欧洲的最后阶段

The Russians launched a counterattack after their victory in the Battle of Stalingrad. Their troops moved slowly forward during the summer and autumn of 1943, and finally drove the Germans out of the Soviet Union by August 1944. In September, Soviet troops forced Bulgaria, Romania and Finland to surrender. In October the Russians and the forces of Tito liberated Belgrade. The Germans withdrew from the Balkans.

At the beginning of 1945, the Russians advanced through Poland, took Czechoslovakia, Budapest, the capital of Hungary, and Vienna, the capital of Austria. Soviet troops then entered eastern Germany.

After liberating the whole France and Belgium, the allied forces cleared the Germans out of the Netherlands and moved into northern Germany. They crossed the Rhine River into the

在斯大林格勒战役中取得胜利后，俄国人发起反攻。他们的军队在1943年夏季和秋季缓慢向前推进，到1944年8月终于将德国人逐出苏联领土。9月，苏军迫使保加利亚、罗马尼亚和芬兰投降。10月，苏军和铁托的军队解放贝尔格莱德。德军退出巴尔干。

1945年初，俄国人已穿越波兰，占领捷克斯洛伐克、匈牙利首都布达佩斯、奥地利首都维也纳。苏军然后进入德国东部。

盟军解放整个法国和比利时后，扫除了荷兰的德军，然后突入德国北部。他们渡过莱茵河，于1945年3月进入德国中部地区。4月，他们在易北河上与自东而来的俄军会师。1945年4月25日，苏

heart of Germany in March 1945, and the next month they met on the Elbe River the Russian Army, which was coming from the other direction. By April 25, 1945, Soviet troops had surrounded Berlin and as they took the city, Hitler killed himself. On May 8, 1945, a day called V-E Day, or Victory in Europe Day, the German government signed a statement of unconditional surrender. World War II had ended in Europe.

军包围柏林，在夺取这座城市时，希特勒自杀。1945 年 5 月 8 日，德国政府签署无条件投降声明。这一天被称为 V-E 日，即欧洲胜利日。第二次世界大战在欧洲到此结束。

美军和俄军会师

11. Japanese Successes Early in the War

战争初期日军的胜利

In the East, after the attack on Pearl Harbor on December 7, 1941, Japanese forces swept across Southeast Asia and the western Pacific Ocean. By the end of the year, they had taken the British colony of Hong Kong, Thailand and two U.S. islands in the Pacific Ocean — Guam and

在东方，日军于 1941 年 12 月 7 日袭击珍珠港后，横扫东南亚和太平洋西部。到了年底，日军已占领英国殖民地香港、泰国、美国在太平洋上的两个岛屿，即关岛和威克岛。日军不久又从泰国推进到马

Wake. From Thailand, Japanese forces soon advanced into Malaya (now part of Malaysia) and Burma, driving Allied forces from most of the region. By late January 1942, the Japanese had pushed British forces back to Singapore, an island off the tip of the Malay Peninsula. The Japanese attacked the island on February 8, and Singapore surrendered a week later and about 85,000 British soldiers were captured. Then Japan's navy defeated the Allied warships that protected the Netherlands Indies (now Indonesia) in the Battle of the Java Sea and took those islands in early March. Japanese forces also defeated American and Philippine forces and conquered the Philippines early in the same year.

来亚 (现在的马来西亚) 和缅甸，将盟军逐出大部分地区。到 1942 年 1 月末，日军已迫使英军退回到新加坡，马来半岛尖端的一座岛屿。日军于 2 月 8 日进攻该岛，一周后新加坡投降，大约 85000 名英军被俘。在爪哇海战中日本海军打败了保卫荷属东印度 (现在的印度尼西亚) 的盟军舰只，于 3 月初占领这一群岛。日军还打败了美军和菲律宾军队，当年上半年占领菲律宾。

12. Stopping the Japanese Advance in the Pacific

日军在太平洋受阻

Now Japan seemed to have the intention of invading Australia and India. But in May 1942, the American warships met the Japanese fleet in the Coral Sea, not far from Australia. Neither side won a clear victory in the battle, but the Japanese threat to Australia was checked. In June, a large Japanese fleet sent to capture Midway Island was defeated by the U.S. Pacific Fleet in the Battle of Midway. The Japanese lost 4 aircraft carriers and more than 200 planes and skilled pilots. The Battle of Midway was the first clear Allied victory over Japan in World War II.

这时，日本似乎有意入侵澳大利亚和印度。但在 1942 年 5 月，美国军舰与日本舰队在距澳大利亚不远的珊瑚海相遇。在战斗中双方都未取得明显胜利，但日本对澳大利亚的威胁被止住了。6 月，日本派出一支庞大的舰队去夺取中途岛，但在中途岛战役中被美国太平洋舰队击败。日军损失 4 艘航空母舰，200 多架飞机和 200 多名技术熟练的飞行员。中途岛战役是二战中盟军对日本取得的头一个明显的胜利。

13. Taking the Offensive

After the Battle of Midway, the Allies were determined to stop Japanese expansion in the South Pacific. In August 1942, U.S. marines invaded the island of Guadalcanal, where the Japanese were building an air base from which to attack Allied ships. After a fierce battle that was fought for six months, the Allies drove the Japanese out of the Island. After taking Guadalcanal, for three years American forces captured one island after another, always getting closer to Japan.

Allied forces invaded the island of Leyte in the central Philippines in the autumn of 1944. The Battle for Leyte Gulf was fought in October 1944, and it ended in a major victory for the United States. Japan's navy was so badly damaged that it was no longer a serious threat for the rest of the war. Early in the next year, the Allies took back most of the Philippines. By the end of 1944, Allied forces had fought their way through northern Burma and reopened a supply route to China in January 1945. With the war supplies China tied down hundreds of thousands of Japanese troops, and greatly helped the Western Allies who were fighting in other parts of Asia.

中途岛战役后，盟军决心遏止住日本在南太平洋的扩张。1942年8月，美国海军陆战队在瓜达尔卡纳尔岛登陆，日军正在当地建造空军基地用以攻击盟军舰只。经过6个月的激烈战斗，盟军将日军逐出该岛。夺取瓜达尔卡纳尔岛之后，美军夺取一个又一个岛屿，逐渐逼近日本本土。

1944年秋，盟军攻上菲律宾中部的莱特岛。在当年10月的莱特湾战役中，美国取得重大胜利。日本海军遭受重创，此后无力对盟军造成严重威胁。第二年初，盟军夺回菲律宾的大部分地区。1944年底，盟军攻入缅甸北部，并于1945年1月重新打开对中国的供给线。得到战争物资的供应后，中国牵制了数十万日军兵力，有力地支援了在亚洲其他地区作战的西方盟军。

14. The Final Attack

In the spring of 1945, the Allies captured the

1945年春，盟军夺取了日本的

Japanese islands of Iwo Jima and Okinawa. These islands were valuable as bases, because they are very close to the main Island of Japan. But the loss of Allies was heavy. 75 thousand of American soldiers were killed or wounded.

By the summer of 1945, Japan had lost nearly all of the islands in the Pacific, and its navy and air force had been beaten. But there was still a big army in Japan waiting to fight the Allies if they invaded. It looked as if many more Americans might be killed before Japan was beaten.

However, the Allies found another way to end the war. On August 6, 1945, an American bomber dropped the first atomic bomb on the Japanese city of Hiroshima. The explosion killed 70,000 people. 3 days later the United States dropped another atomic bomb on Nagasaki. It killed about 40,000 people. Meanwhile, on August 8, the Soviet Union declared war on Japan and invaded Manchuria. On August 14, Japan offered to surrender.

On September 2, 1945, representatives of Japan signed the official statement of surrender aboard the U.S. battleship *Missouri*, which lay at anchor in Tokyo Bay. Representatives of all the Allied nations were present. Truman declared September 2 as V-J Day, or Victory over Japan Day. World War II had ended.

硫黄岛和冲绳岛。这两个岛屿非常接近日本本土，作为军事基地有重要价值。但盟军也付出了沉重代价。美军士兵死伤 75000 人。

1945 年夏天，日本丧失了几乎所有太平洋上的岛屿，海军和空军已无力再战。但在日本本土仍有一支大军等待着与入侵的盟军决战。看来，在彻底打败日本之前，美军还会有大批士兵阵亡。

然而，盟军找到结束战争的另一个途径。1945 年 8 月 6 日，一架美国轰炸机在日本城市广岛投下第一枚原子弹。7 万人在爆炸中身亡。三天后美国在长崎投下第二枚原子弹，炸死 4 万人。与此同时，苏联于 8 月 8 日向日本宣战，侵入中国东北。8 月 14 日，日本宣布投降。

1945 年 9 月 2 日，日本代表在停泊在东京湾上的美国战舰密苏里号上签署了正式的投降书。所有的盟国代表出席了签字仪式。杜鲁门宣布 9 月 2 日为 V-J 日，即战胜日本日。第二次世界大战到此结束。

美国旗插上硫黄岛

题外话

第二次世界大战的开始一般以德国进攻波兰算起，但也有人认为，应当从 1931 年日本占领中国东北三省算起。

原子弹在长崎爆炸

日本代表签署投降书

15. **Wartime Conferences**

战时会议

Allied leaders met from time to time during the war, not only to devise military strategy but also to discuss the future. In 1941, four months before the Pearl Harbour, President Franklin D. Roosevelt and Prime Minister Winston Churchill met at a series of conferences aboard a warship in the North Atlantic off the coast of Newfoundland. The result of the meeting was a joint declaration known as the *Atlantic Charter*. The charter expressed certain common principles of the United States and the United Kingdom in their postwar policies. These included the right of all peoples to choose their own form of government and not to

在战争期间，同盟国领袖经常会面，不但设计军事战略，而且讨论未来计划。1941 年，珍珠港事件之前 4 个月，富兰克林·D.罗斯福总统与温斯顿·丘吉尔首相在纽芬兰海岸附近的北大西洋军舰上举行了一系列的会议。会后发表了被称为"大西洋宪章"的联合声明。宪章表述了美英两国在战后将奉行的某些共同政策。这些政策包括：各国人民有选择自己政府形式的权利；未经有关民族之同意，不改变各国领土现状；所有国家都有获得地球自然资源的权利。宪章希望，在打败纳粹之后，所有民族将安居乐业，既无恐惧，亦无贫困；所有民族都能够在公海上自由航行；所有民族都将放弃使用暴力。

美国参战后，美国、英国和苏联三国首脑多次举行重要会议。德黑兰会议是三国首脑在第二次世界大战中的头一次会议。三国首脑，号称"三巨头"，是美国总统富兰克林·D.罗斯福、英国首相温斯顿·丘吉尔、苏联部长会议主席约瑟夫·斯大林。会议上做出的两个重

罗斯福总统与丘吉尔首相在纽芬兰海岸附近的北大西洋军舰上

have boundary changes imposed on them and the right of all nations to get the earth's natural resources. The charter expressed the hope that, after the defeat of the Nazis, all peoples would be able to live free from fear and want. All peoples would be able to cross the seas and oceans without being hindered. All peoples were to give up the use of force.

After the United States entered the war, there were several important meetings of the leaders of the United States, Great Britain and the Soviet Union. Teheran Conference was the first of their meetings during World War II. These leaders, called the "Big Three", were U.S. President Franklin Delano Roosevelt, British Prime Minister Winston Churchill, and Soviet Premier Joseph Stalin. The two main military decisions made at the conference were that the United States and Britain would launch an invasion of France in 1944 and that the Soviet Union would enter the war against Japan after Germany's defeat. The leaders also discussed plans for establishing a United Nations organization, for dividing and disarming Germany, and for moving Poland's borders westward after the war.

The three leaders met again at Yalta, a famous Black Sea resort in the Crimea, in February

要军事决议是美英两国将在 1944 年入侵法国，苏联在打败德国后将对日本宣战。首脑们还讨论了建立联合国组织、分区占领德国并解除其武装、战后波兰边界西扩等计划。

1945 年 2 月，三国首脑在克里米亚的黑海疗养胜地雅尔塔再次聚会。这一次，欧洲的战争即将结束，战后计划成为中心议题。三巨头就战后对德国的联合军事占领达成一致意见。他们承诺支持自由选举、在被解放的国家建立"有广泛代表性"的政府。斯大林承诺德国投降后苏联将在三个月内对日本宣战。

1945 年 7 月，德国战败大约两个月后，三巨头的最后一次会议在德国柏林附近的波茨坦举行。出席

丘吉尔、罗斯福和斯大林在雅尔塔

1945. Now, with the war in Europe nearly over, postwar planning was the focus. The Big Three agreed on a joint military occupation of Germany after the war. They promised to support free elections and the establishment of "broadly representative" governments in liberated countries. Stalin promised that the Soviet Union would go to war against Japan within three months after Germany surrendered.

A final Big Three meeting took place at Potsdam, Germany, near Berlin. The conference was held in July 1945, about two months after Germany's defeat in the war. Present at the opening were U.S. President Harry S. Truman, British Prime Minister Winston Churchill, and Soviet Premier Joseph Stalin. Clement Attlee succeeded Churchill as prime minister on July 26 and represented Great Britain for the rest of the conference. At this meeting, the Allied leaders made plans for the occupation and control of the recently defeated Germany and set up a council of foreign ministers to drew up peace treaties.

丘吉尔、杜鲁门和斯大林在波茨坦

开幕式的有美国总统哈里·S.杜鲁门、英国首相温斯顿·丘吉尔和苏联部长会议主席约瑟夫·斯大林。7月26日，克莱门特·艾德礼接替丘吉尔代表英国参加会议的其余部分。会上，同盟国的首脑制订计划占领并控制新近战败的德国，成立一个由各国外长组成的委员会起草和约。

题外话

德黑兰会议仍留下一些问题没有妥善解决。三国首脑对解决德国问题的态度不明确；对于战后成立国际组织的建立，观点也含糊不清；对待波兰问题，美英与苏联则有尖锐分歧。此时已能看出冷战苗头。

雅尔塔会议上也留下不少有争议的问题，如波兰问题。美英两国一直支持设在英国的波兰流亡政府；而苏联却只承认共产党领导的波兰民族解放委员会。双方均不肯让步，结果同意两个组织一起协商，以待自由选举。雅尔塔会议承认苏联支持的外蒙古独立，使中国领土缩小160万平方公里。会后，美国有些支持波兰、德国和国民党中国的人对会议达成的许多协议提出批评，认为罗斯福手太软，受到国务院内亲苏分子的影响。

前两次会议上美英与苏联之间的态度大体上是友好和睦的，但波茨坦会议上则发生了改变。双方都猜疑对方的企图，在涉及切身利益问题上寸步不让。意识形态上的纷争更加明显。

16. The Founding of the United Nations

联合国成立

As early as 1941, when Roosevelt and Churchill met to work out the Atlantic Charter, they had also discussed plans for establishing a United Nations organization. Then on January 1, 1942, at a conference held in Washington, D.C., representatives of 26 nations then at war with the Axis powers declared that they approved the aims of the Atlantic Charter, and signed the *Declaration by United Nations*. This was the first official use of the words *United Nations* (UN).

In 1944, representatives of Britain, China, the Soviet Union, and the United States held a series of meetings at the Dumbarton Oaks estate in Washington, D.C. There they drew up plans for a peacekeeping organization to replace the League of Nations. The most important part of the plan was a Security Council of which Britain, China, France, the Soviet Union, and the United States would be permanent members.

Delegates from 50 nations met in San Francisco in the spring of 1945 to work out a charter for the United Nations. In June, all 50 nations present at the conference voted to accept the charter. The United Nations formally came into being on October 24, 1945, a date celebrated every year as United Nations Day.

The United States had refused to join the League of Nations after World War I, but now the Americans were willing to become a member of UN. Experience had told them isolationism could not guarantee their peace and security.

早在 1941 年，罗斯福和丘吉尔在制订大西洋宪章时，就讨论了建立联合国组织的计划。然后在 1942 年 1 月 1 日，在华盛顿举行的一个会议上，与轴心国交战的 26 国的代表宣布他们同意大西洋宪章提出的目标，签署了《联合国宣言》。这是正式场合首次使用"联合国"一词。

1944 年，英、中、苏、美四国在华盛顿敦巴顿橡树园举行了一系列会议，起草计划建立一个维护和平的组织以替代国际联盟。计划中最重要的部分是建立安全理事会，由英、中、法、苏、美五国任常任理事国。

1945 年春，50 个国家的代表团会聚旧金山制订《联合国宪章》。6 月，与会的所有 50 个国家投票接受了宪章。联合国于 1945 年 10 月 24 日正式成立。10 月 24 日遂成为每年庆祝的联合国日。

美国曾在第一次世界大战后拒绝加入国际联盟，但美国人这次却很愿意成为联合国成员。经验告诉他们，孤立主义无法保障和平与安全。

CHAPTER FIFTEEN

The Cold War

冷 战

1. The Beginning of the Cold War

冷战的开端

The United States and the Soviet Union both fought on the side of the Allies during World War II. After the war, however, serious tension developed between the two superpowers. Since the Communist Revolution in Russia, Soviet leaders had been calling for world revolution to overthrow capitalism, the economic system of the West. The United States, as the world's most powerful capitalist country, took on the role of defending any nation threatened by Communism.

During World War II the Russians had suffered more casualties than any other country. They were determined to protect themselves from future attack by making sure that all the countries around their borders were under their control. The Soviet Union had taken over the Baltic states of Latvia, Estonia, and Lithuania; and when the war ended, the Russian troops had occupied a third of Germany and all of Bulgaria, Hungary,

在第二次世界大战中，美国和苏联都在同盟国一边作战。然而在战后，两个超级大国之间的关系变得极为紧张。俄国发生共产主义革命后，苏联领导人号召发动世界革命推翻资本主义，即西方的经济制度。美国作为世界上最强大的资本主义国家，承担义务保护受到共产主义威胁的任何国家。

第二次世界大战中，俄国人的伤亡大于任何其他国家。他们决心将周围邻国置于自己的控制之下，以保卫自己，免受未来的敌国的攻击。苏联已占领了波罗的海三国，即拉托维亚、爱沙尼亚和立陶宛；到战争结束时，苏军已攻占了德国的三分之一，保加利亚、匈牙利、波兰和罗马尼亚的全部。此后不久，苏联切断了与西方的一切联

Poland, and Romania. Soon after that, the Soviet Union cut off nearly all contacts between the West and the occupied territories of Eastern Europe. In March 1946, Churchill warned that "an iron curtain has descended across the Continent" of Europe. Later, the phrase *Iron Curtain* became a popular term to refer to Soviet barriers against the West. Behind these barriers, the Soviet Union helped Communists take control of most of the countries. These countries became known as satellites, since they were under the control of the Soviet Union. Two other Eastern European countries, Albania and Yugoslavia also established Communist governments.

The struggle between the non-Communist nations led by the United States and the Communist allies led by the Soviet Union became known as the *Cold War*. The conflict was so named because it was not a "hot" war, or fighting with guns, but mainly with economic, political, and diplomatic weapons. The major allies of the United States during the Cold War included Britain, France, West Germany, Japan, and Canada. On the Soviet side were many of the countries of Eastern Europe, including Bulgaria, Czechoslovakia, Hungary, Poland, East Germany, and Romania. And, during parts of the Cold War, Cuba and China also belonged to the Soviet side.

系，占领了东欧各国的领土。1946年3月，丘吉尔警告说，"一条横贯欧洲的铁幕已经落下。"后来，"铁幕"一词就流行开来，特指苏联为遏制西方而设置的屏障。在这一屏障的后面，苏联扶植共产主义者控制了其中的大多数国家。这些国家被称为卫星国，因为它们处于苏联的控制之下。另外两个东欧国家阿尔巴尼亚和南斯拉夫也建立了共产党政权。

以美国领导为首的非共产主义国家和以苏联为首的共产主义盟国之间进行的斗争称为"冷战"。之所以称之为"冷战"，是因为它不是动用枪炮的"热战"，而主要是在经济、政治和外交方面进行的较量。冷战时期美国的重要盟国包括英国、法国、西德、日本和加拿大。站在苏联一方的是许多东欧国家，包括保加利亚、捷克斯洛伐克、匈牙利、波兰、东德和罗马尼亚。此外，在冷战时期，古巴和中国有一段时期也属于苏联阵营。

2. The Containment Policy

遏制政策

During the Cold War period, which lasted from the mid-1940s until the end of the 1980s,

冷战从40年代一直持续到80年代末。在这段时期，遏制共产主

the containment of Communism became the major goal of U.S. foreign policy. Truman and Dwight D. Eisenhower, the first two Presidents of the Cold War era, promised to give military support to any nation threatened by Communism.

Containment was first put into action in Greece and Turkey. In the autumn of 1946, Greek Communists revolted against the Greek government. Turkey was also under the threat of the Soviet Union. In March 1947, President Truman declared that the United States would help any free nation resisting Communist attack. At his request Congress granted $400 million to aid Greece and Turkey. With this aid, both Greece and Turkey successfully resisted Communism. The new American policy became known as the *Truman Doctrine*. Aimed at Soviet expansion in Europe, the Truman Doctrine developed into the *Containment* Policy. This Policy was designed to contain (hold back) the expansion of Communism throughout the world.

义是美国的主要外交政策。冷战时期的头两位总统杜鲁门和德怀特·D.艾森豪威尔承诺给任何受到共产主义威胁的国家以军事支持。

遏制政策首先在希腊和土耳其实施。1946 年秋，希腊共产党发动起义，试图推翻希腊政府。土耳其也受到苏联的威胁。1947 年 3 月，杜鲁门总统宣布美国将帮助任何自由国家抵抗共产主义的进攻。在杜鲁门的请求下，国会拨出 4 亿美圆援助希腊和土耳其。结果希腊和土耳其成功地抵抗住了共产主义。美国的这一新政策被称为"杜鲁门主义"。针对苏联在欧洲的扩张，杜鲁门主义发展成为"遏制政策"。遏制政策的目的是遏制共产主义在全球的扩张。

哈里·S.杜鲁门

3. Marshall Plan

马歇尔计划

The United States believed that a strong, stable Western Europe would block the spread of Communism. In June 1947, the United States promised to give aid to all European nations that

美国认为，一个强大稳定的西欧将会阻挡共产主义的蔓延。1947 年 6 月，美国承诺援助愿意共同努力以恢复经济的所有欧洲国家。这

would work together for their economic recovery. The official name of the plan was the *European Recovery Program*. But it is commonly known as the *Marshall Plan*, because Secretary of State George C. Marshall first suggested it. Marshall Plan began in 1948 and ended in 1952. During the four years, the United States sent more than $13 billion in food, fuel, raw material and machinery to Europe. Only western countries took part in the plan, because the Soviet Union and its satellites rejected it as a form of "American imperialism". This economic aid helped the participating countries raise their industrial and agricultural production above prewar levels. It greatly stimulated their international trade. The Marshall Plan also helped the United States, because it enlarged the European market for American goods.

项计划的正式名称是"欧洲复兴计划",但通称"马歇尔计划",因为是国务卿乔治·C.马歇尔首先提出来的。马歇尔计划1948年开始实行,1952年结束。在这4年期间,美国向欧洲运送了价值超过130亿美圆的粮食、燃料、原材料和机械设备。只有西欧国家参加了这项计划,因为苏联及其卫星国斥之为"美帝国主义"的一种表现形式。这一经济计划帮助参与国的工农业生产提高到战前水平之上,大大地促进了国际贸易。马歇尔计划也有利于美国,因为它为美国的产品扩大了欧洲的市场。

4. The Berlin Blockade and Airlift

柏林封锁与空运

By the time the war in Europe ended, Soviet troops had advanced far into eastern Germany. This area became the Soviet zone of occupation. Western Germany was divided into three zones, and occupied respectively by Great Britain, US and France. Berlin, located in the Soviet zone, was subdivided into four parts.

By 1948, it was clear that the Western countries and the Soviet Union could not agree on the establishment of a unified German government. In June the Western Allies announced plans to unify their German occupation zones and establish

欧洲的战争结束时,苏军已进入德国东部纵深地区。这片地区成为苏联占领区。德国西部被一分为三,分别由英国、美国和法国占领。柏林位于苏占区,被一分为四。

到了1948年,西方国家和苏联显然已无法就建立一个统一的德国政府达成一致意见。6月,西方盟国宣布它们计划将各自在德国的占领区合并,建立德意志联邦共和国(西德)。西德于1949年9月正

the German Federal Republic (West Germany). West Germany was formally established in September 1949.

To defeat the West's plans for West Germany, Soviet troops blocked all railroad and highway traffic through East Germany to West Berlin. Two million people in West Berlin faced starvation. The Soviet leaders thought their blockade would force the West to leave Berlin. Instead of pulling out of West Berlin, the Western Allies answered the blockade with a massive airlift of supplies to West Berlin. For 11 months, beginning in June 1948, huge cargo planes flew tons of food and fuel and other supplies into West Berlin. The Soviet Union finally lifted the blockade in May 1949.

式成立。

为挫败西方建立西德的计划，苏联军队封锁了穿过东德到西柏林的所有铁路和公路交通。西柏林的200万人民面临饥饿的威胁。苏联领导人希望他们的封锁会迫使西方撤离柏林。但西方盟国没有从西柏林撤出，而是采用向西柏林大量空运物资的办法来回应封锁。从1948年6月开始，在11个月里，大型运输机将成吨的食品、燃料和其他物资空运到西柏林。1949年5月，苏联最终解除了封锁。

柏林居民仰望空运救济物资的美国运输机

5. Military Alliances

军事联盟

The Cold War was also reflected in the establishment of two opposing military alliances. To check the spread of Communism in Europe and to defend West Germany the United States, Canada, and 10 Western European nations signed a treaty and established the North Atlantic Treaty Organization (NATO). The NATO nations agreed to treat an armed attack on one member as an attack on all. They set up a unified military force, and each member contributed funds and soldiers to it. Greece and Turkey became members in 1952. As a response to the creation of NATO, the

冷战也表现在两个对立的军事同盟的建立上。为阻止共产主义在欧洲的蔓延并保卫西德不受侵犯，美国、加拿大以及 10 个欧洲国家签约成立了北大西洋公约组织（北约）。北约国家同意将对任何一个成员国的武装进攻视为对所有成员国的进攻。它们建立了一支联合军事部队，各成员国都向其提供资金和军事人员。希腊和土耳其也于 1952 年加入北约。作为对成立北约的回应，苏联和东欧共产党国家也

艾森豪威尔将军在北大西洋公约组织会议上讲话

Communist bloc announced the formation of its own military alliance, the *Warsaw Pact*. The Soviet Union kept strict control over the other countries in the pact.

Both the United States and the Soviet Union built up arsenals of atomic bombs, more powerful hydrogen bombs, and other nuclear weapons. The nuclear weapons made each nation capable of destroying the other. The threat of nuclear war made both sides cautious. As a result, Cold War strategy emphasized threats of force, propaganda, and aid to weak nations. The United Nations provided a forum where the nations could try to settle their Cold War disputes.

宣布成立自己的军事同盟，即"华沙条约组织"。苏联对签约国实行严密控制。

美国和苏联都建立了核武库，储存原子弹、威力更大的氢弹及其他核武器。核武器使每个国家都可能摧毁另一个国家，核战争的威胁使双方均保持谨慎。结果，冷战战略强调的是武力威胁、宣传和对弱小国家的援助。联合国提供了一个讲坛，使各国能够试图解决冷战争端。

CHAPTER SIXTEEN

Postwar American Society
战后美国社会

1. McCarthyism

麦卡锡主义

As the Cold War went on, it affected domestic affairs. Many Americans feared not only Communism around the world but also disloyalty at home. Charges that Americans had served as Soviet spies received wide attention. The federal government began to search for secret Communists among its employees. In 1947, President Truman established agencies called loyalty boards to investigate government workers and fire those found to be disloyal. The government dismissed hundreds of employees, and thousands more felt compelled to resign. In 1949 the Justice Department prosecuted 11 leaders of the Communist Party, who were convicted and jailed under the Smith Act of 1940. The law prohibited groups from conspiring to advocate the violent overthrow of the government.

One of the most important figures of this period was Senator Joseph McCarthy of Wisconsin, who gained national attention in 1950, when he charged that Communists dominated the State

在冷战过程中，美国国内也受到了影响。许多美国人不但对世界上的共产主义满怀恐惧，也担心美国人的背叛行为。美国人为苏联担任间谍的指控引起广泛关注。联邦政府开始在其雇员中查找秘密的共产党人。1947 年，杜鲁门总统建立了称为"效忠委员会"的机构，调查政府工作人员，解雇那些被发现有不忠行为的人。结果，政府解雇了数百名雇员，另有数千人被迫辞职。1949 年，司法部对 11 名共产党领袖提出指控，依照 1940 年的《史密斯法》，他们被判有罪入狱。《史密斯法》规定凡鼓吹以暴力推翻政府的社团均属非法。

这一时期的一个重要人物是威斯康星州的参议员约瑟夫·麦卡锡。1950 年，麦卡锡指控共产党控制了国务院，引起全国对他的关注。参议院对外关系委员会调查了国务

Department. The Senate Foreign Relations Committee investigated the department but found no Communists or Communist sympathizers there. Nevertheless, McCarthy made many more accusations and gained many followers. The accusations and investigations affected thousands of people. Librarians, college professors, entertainers, journalists, clergy, and others came under suspicion. Some firms refused to hire people accused of Communist associations. Many employees, to keep their jobs, were required to take oaths of loyalty to the government. McCarthy even accused the army of harboring Communists.

McCarthyism gradually declined after 1954, when the Senate finally officially reprimanded him for his conduct. However, it had damaged or destroyed the reputations and careers of many innocent Americans. From 1955 to 1958, the Supreme Court of the United States made a series of decisions that helped protect the rights of people accused of sympathizing with Communists.

McCarthyism came to mean hysterical anticommunism and false charges of disloyalty to the United States.

院，但并没有发现共产党或共产党的同情者。然而麦卡锡提出更多的指控，并赢得了很多支持者。指控和调查涉及了数千人。图书馆管理员、大学教授、演员、记者、神职人员及其他各色人等受到怀疑。一些公司拒绝雇用被控与共产党有牵连的人。许多雇员，为了保住饭碗，按要求宣誓忠于政府。麦卡锡甚至指控军队窝藏共产党分子。

1954年后，参议院最终正式谴责麦卡锡及其行径，此后麦卡锡主义逐渐偃旗息鼓。然而麦卡锡主义毁了许多清白的美国人的声誉和职业生涯。从1955年至1958年，美国最高法院做出一系列判决，以保护受控同情共产主义的人的权益。

此后，麦卡锡主义成为反共歇斯底里和诬告背叛美国的代名词。

题外话

麦卡锡的反共歇斯底里的教训是，听任一种意识形态操控一切，对不同政见缺乏宽容，会使人近于疯狂。

麦卡锡指责军队包庇"红色分子"

2. The Warren Court

沃伦法院

In 1953 President Eisenhower appointed Earl Warren (1891-1974), former governor of California, as Chief Justice of the United States. The Warren Court, which lasted from 1953 to 1969, was one of the most liberal and influential in American history. It made a lot of changes in civil rights laws and in criminal procedures.

The first major case to be decided under Warren involved racial segregation. A black girl, Linda Brown, had been turned away from a public school in Kansas, because it was a school for whites. Her father sued on the grounds that she was being denied equal protection of the law. In *Brown v. Board of Education* (1954), the Court reversed the "separate but equal" decision made by the Supreme Court in 1896. The justices unanimously ruled that segregation in public schools denied black students equal protection of the law under the 14th Amendment, and therefore it was unconstitutional. The Court decision aroused a storm of protest, especially in the South, where separate school systems were com-

1953 年，艾森豪威尔总统任命前加利福尼亚州长厄尔·沃伦 (1891-1974) 为美国首席大法官。沃伦法院，从 1953 年持续到 1969 年，是美国历史上自由主义倾向最强、影响最大的一届法院。它使民权立法和刑事诉讼程序发生了很多变化。

沃伦主持下的法院处理的头一个重要讼案涉及种族隔离。一个名叫林达·布朗的黑人女孩向堪萨斯的一所公立学校申请入学，却遭到拒绝，原因是该校是白人学校。女孩的父亲对当地教育局提起诉讼，理由是该女孩被拒绝给予人人平等的法律保护。在这桩布朗诉教育局案（1954 年）中，法院改变了 1896 年最高法院"隔离而平等"的判决。大法官们一致裁决，公立学校里的种族隔离拒绝给予黑人学生宪法第十四条修正案所赋予的人人平等的法律保护，因而是违宪的。法院的裁决引起了一阵抗议的风暴，特别是在南方，因

厄尔·沃伦大法官

mon. In 1957, when some black students were refused entry into the Central High School, Little Rock, Arkansas, rioting broke out. President Eisenhower sent federal troops into the city to preserve order. Under their protection, the black students completed the school year.

In criminal procedures the Court made some far-reaching decisions. One decision was that persons accused of a serious crime have a right to free legal service if they are too poor to pay for a lawyer. Another decision was that a criminal suspect cannot be denied a lawyer during questioning. One of the most important decisions to protect the rights of the accused came in 1966 in *Miranda v. State of Arizona*. The Court ruled that criminal suspects had to be informed of their rights. Since then, when American police make an arrest, they must read the Miranda (Rule) to the suspect, explaining his or her legal rights during questioning, especially those of remaining silent and being represented by a lawyer.

Some of the decisions of the Warren Court met widespread opposition. One of these decisions forbade organized prayer and Bible reading in public schools. Conservative groups even demanded Warren's impeachment.

为那里普遍实行黑白分校。1957年，当堪萨斯州小石城的中心中学阻止黑人学生入校时，骚乱爆发了。艾森豪威尔总统派遣联邦军队进入该市维持秩序。在士兵的保护下，黑人学生完成了当年的学业。

在刑事诉讼程序上，法院做出几项意义深远的裁决。一项是被控犯有重罪的人如果雇不起律师，有权获得免费的法律援助。另一项裁决是在刑讯过程中，犯罪嫌疑人若要求律师陪同，不得拒绝这一要求。保护被告权益的最重要的一项裁决是1966年的米兰达诉亚利桑那州案。法院裁决犯罪嫌疑人必须被告知他们的权利。从那以后，当美国警察实施逮捕时，必须对犯罪嫌疑人宣读"米兰达忠告"，向他们说明在刑讯过程中他们所具有的权利，特别是保持沉默和聘请律师的权利。

沃伦法院的某些裁决遭到广泛的反对。有一项裁决禁止在公立学校里进行有组织的祈祷和阅读《圣经》。为此，保守组织甚至要求弹劾沃伦。

🔘 题 外 话

"米兰达忠告"的全文是："你有权保持沉默，你说的话可能会在审判中用做不利于你的证据；你有权会见律师，如果你请不起，政府可以免费为你提供。"该规则公布之后，美国的执法人员怨声不断，因为获得证据的难度大增。但该规则迫使执法人员运用心理科学、行为科学和其他科学手段进行讯问，而不仅仅依靠口供，从而减少了误判。

德怀特·D.艾森豪威尔

一个白人妇女在怒骂头一个进入小石城中心中学
的黑人学生

3. Progress Against Discrimination

反对种族歧视取得的进展

Progress against discrimination was made not only in schools. Eisenhower completed the desegregation of the armed forces, begun under Truman. In 1957, Congress passed the first federal civil rights law since Reconstruction. It removed some of the obstacles that prevented blacks from voting. It also created the Civil Rights Division in the Department of Justice to protect the civil rights of blacks.

But black Americans still had to struggle hard for equal rights. In 1955 Rosa Parks was arrested for disobeying a segregation law in Montgomery, Alabama, because she refused to give up her seat on a bus to a white person. Her bold action helped to stimulate protests against

反对种族歧视的斗争不只在学校里取得了进展。杜鲁门执政时期就已开始在军队里取消种族隔离，艾森豪威尔完成了这一进程。1957年，国会通过了重建时期以来头一个联邦民权法。该法取消了对黑人参加选举的种种阻碍，在司法部成立了民权处，以保护黑人的民权。

但是美国黑人仍不得不为争取与白人的同等权利进行艰苦斗争。1955年，罗莎·帕克斯由于违反了亚拉巴马州蒙哥马利市的种族隔离法而被逮捕，原因是她在公共汽车上拒绝给白人让座。她的大胆的行动激起反对权利不平等的抗议活动。

inequality. The bus boycott, led by Martin Luther King, Jr., received national attention and forced city officials to repeal the segregation law.

马丁·路德·金领导的对公共汽车的抵制运动引起全国的关注，迫使市政当局取消了种族隔离法。

4. Postwar Prosperity

战后的繁荣

Military spending during World War II drew the United States out of the Great Depression. After the war, the nation entered the greatest period of economic growth in its history. Major industries, such as automobile manufacturing and housing construction, which had all but stopped during the war, resumed production on a much larger scale than ever. Consumer goods had been in short supply during the war. Now there was a vast market for American products. Postwar "baby boom" caused the nation's population to grow about 20 per cent between 1950 and 1960, and increased the number of consumers. Relatively new industries such as electronics, plastics, frozen foods and jet aircraft became booming businesses. More people shared in the prosperity than ever before, creating a huge, well-to-do middle class with their own houses, cars and household appliances. New highways, cheap gasoline and open spaces encouraged many middle class families to moved to suburbs.

However, not all people shared in the prosperity. Millions of Americans, especially a high percentage of the nation's blacks, continued to live in poverty. The existence of poverty amid prosperity brought on a period of active social protest that has continued to the present day.

第二次世界大战的军事开支将美国拉出了大萧条的泥潭。战后，美国进入了有史以来最快的经济增长时期。汽车制造和住宅建筑等重要工业在战争期间几乎陷于停顿，现在以从未有过的大规模恢复了生产。战争期间消费品一直处于短缺状态，现在美国产品有了巨大的市场。战后的"婴儿潮"使美国人口在 1950～1960 年十年间增加了大约 20%，同时也增加了消费者的数量。电子、塑料、食品和喷气式飞机等相对较新的工业发展最快。从繁荣中获益的人比以往更多，形成了一个庞大而富裕的中产阶级，他们拥有自己的住宅、汽车和家用电器。新的公路、廉价的汽油和广阔的空间鼓励许多中产阶级家庭迁移到了郊区。

然而并非所有的人都从繁荣中得到了益处。数百万美国人，其中黑人比例较高，则继续生活在贫困之中。繁荣之中的贫困使美国进入一个持续至今的社会抗议活跃期。

5. The Development of Science and Technology

科技的发展

The most important development of science and technology was the peaceful uses of nuclear energy. The United States made the world's first full-scale use of controlled nuclear energy in 1954. That year, the U.S. Navy launched the first nuclear-powered vessel, the submarine *Nautilus*. It sailed across the North Pole, under the polar icecap, in 1958. In 1957, the first large-scale nuclear plant in the United States opened in Pennsylvania.

A brand new application of science and technology was the conquest of space. In 1957, the Soviets shocked the world by launching the first artificial satellite, *Sputnik*. The United States then speeded up its own program. In 1958, a civilian space agency called the National Aeronautics and Space Administration (NASA) was

科技领域最重要的发展是和平利用核能。1954 年，美国开创了大规模利用可控核能的世界先例。当年，美国海军的第一艘核动力潜艇"鹦鹉螺"号下水。"鹦鹉螺"号于1958 年在冰盖下穿过北极。1957年，美国的第一座大型核电站在宾夕法尼亚开始发电。

科学技术在征服空间方面开拓了一个新的运用领域。1957 年，苏联发射了第一颗人造卫星，震惊了全世界。美国随之加速了自己的研究计划。1958 年，一个民用空间机构国家航空航天局成立。航空航天局聚集了各种航空领域里的研究者和军用空间实验室的力量。同年，美国的第一颗人造卫星"探险者一号"升空。

1961 年，苏联空军飞行员尤里·A.加加林乘宇宙飞船环绕地球一周，安全返回地面。美国紧随其后，小约翰·H.格伦成为第一个在轨道上环绕地球的美国人。1965 年，副驾驶员爱德华·H.怀特第二成为第一

美国海军的第一艘核动力潜艇"鹦鹉螺"号

格伦在乘飞船环绕地球飞行之前

established. NASA absorbed various aviation researchers and military space laboratories. In the same year, the first United States satellite, *Explorer 1*, was launched.

In 1961, a Soviet air force pilot named Yuri A. Gagarin orbited the earth once in a spacecraft and returned safely. The United States followed up, and in the next year, John H. Glenn, Jr., became the first American to orbit the earth. 1965, copilot Edward H. White II became the first American to walk in space. On March 16, 1966, Gemini 8 completed the world's first docking of two space vehicles when it linked up with an Agena rocket in space.

The race to the moon dominated the space race of the 1960s. In a 1961 address to Congress, President John F. Kennedy called for the United States to commit itself to "landing a man on the moon and returning him safely to the earth" before the 1960s ended. This goal was intended to overtake the Soviet Union in the race to dominate space exploration.

In the mid-1960s, NASA began to carry out its Apollo Program, American manned lunar-space program designed to land an astronaut on the moon and return him safely to earth. A total of 16 unmanned Apollo missions were flown between October 1960 and April 1968 to test all the systems. Apollo 11 was the first mission to land astronauts on the moon. It blasted off on July 16, 1969, carrying three astronauts — Neil A. Arm-

个在太空行走的美国人。1966 年 3 月 16 日,"双子座 8 号"在空间与阿金纳火箭连接,完成了世界上首次两个空间飞行器的对接。

登月竞赛是 60 年代空间竞赛的主题。约翰·F. 肯尼迪总统在 1961 年对国会发表的一次讲话中,号召美国争取在 60 年代结束前"将人类送上月球并安全返回地球"。确定这一目标是为了在空间探索领域的竞赛中领先于苏联。

60 年代中期,国家航空和航天局开始实施载人登月的阿波罗计划,目标是将一位宇航员送上月球并使之安全返回地球。在 1960 年 10 月至 1968 年 4 月间,共进行了 16 次不载人的阿波罗计划飞行,测试所有的系统。阿波罗 11 号首次将宇航员送上月球。火箭于 1969

strong, Edwin E. Aldrin, and Michael Collins. Armstrong and Aldrin became the first humans to set foot on the moon's surface. Said Armstrong: "That's one small step for a man, one giant leap for mankind."

NASA began to develop a reusable space shuttle while the Apollo program was still underway. The shuttles were designed to blast off like a rocket and land like an airplane. After ten years of preparation, the first space shuttle, Columbia, was launched on April 12, 1981. The 54-hour mission went perfectly.

One invention that made space travel possible was the computer. The first commercial digital computers were manufactured in the 1950s. In the late 1970s, the computer industry's rate of growth increased dramatically. The United States had the largest computer industry in the world. Advances in both computer technology and manufacturing technology enabled the United States to sell computers worth more than $30 billion in 1981. By 1990, the U. S. computer industry's annual revenues had topped $100 billion, and they continued to grow.

美国宇航员登月

年 7 月 16 日点火升空，飞船上载有三名宇航员，即尼尔·A.阿姆斯特朗、埃德温·E.奥尔德林和麦克尔·柯林斯。阿姆斯特朗和奥尔德林是将脚踏上月球的头两个人。阿姆斯特朗说："对于个人来说，这仅仅是一小步；对于整个人类来说，这是一个巨大的飞跃。"

当阿波罗计划正在实施过程中，国家航空和航天局就开始研发可重复使用的航天飞机。根据设计，航天飞机将像火箭一样升空，像飞机一样着陆。经过 10 年的准备，首架航天飞机哥伦比亚号于 1981 年 4 月 12 日升空。这次 54 小时的飞行一帆风顺。

使空间旅行得以成功的一项发明是计算机。第一台商业数码计算机制造于 50年代。70 年代末，计算机工业的增长率陡然上升。美国拥有世界上最大的计算机工业。在计算机技术和计算机制造技术的领先地位使美国在 1981 年出售了价值 300 多亿美圆的计算机。到了 1990 年，美国计算机工业的年收入高达 1000 亿美圆，而且还在不断增长。

CHAPTER SEVENTEEN

The United States in the 1960s
20 世纪 60 年代的美国

1. The Cuban Missile Crisis

古巴导弹危机

John F. Kennedy became President of the United States in January 1961. Cold War tensions were high, not only in Europe, in Asia, but also in Cuba, a neighbor of the United States.

The Cuban government of Fidel Castro had become openly an ally of the Soviet Union in 1960. Castro condemned the United States and began to receive military aid from the Soviet Union and other Communist countries. The Cuban government seized millions of dollars' worth of American property in Cuba. The United States ended diplomatic relations with Cuba in January 1961.

The United States trained an army of anti-Castro Cubans to overthrow Castro. In April 1961, this army invaded Cuba at the Bay of Pigs. The attack was poorly planned and failed badly. The unsuccessful invasion strengthened Castro's control of Cuba.

In October 1962, the United States discov-

约翰·F. 肯尼迪于 1961 年 1 月就任美国总统。冷战仍然处于紧张状态, 不但在欧洲、亚洲, 而且在美国的邻国古巴。

菲德尔·卡斯特罗领导的古巴政府于 1960 年公开成为苏联的盟国。卡斯特罗谴责美国, 并开始接受苏联和其他共产党国家的援助。古巴政府没收了美国人在古巴的价值数百万美圆的财产。1961 年 1 月, 美国中断了与古巴的外交关系。

美国训练了一支由反对卡斯特罗的古巴人组成的军队, 试图推翻卡斯特罗。1961 年 4 月, 这支军队在猪湾登陆, 入侵古巴。由于进攻计划不周, 结果一败涂地。这次入侵失败巩固了卡斯特罗在古巴的统治。

1962 年 10 月, 美国发现苏联正秘密地在古巴建立导弹基地, 一些导弹已经安装到位。这些导弹可

ered that the Soviet Union was secretly building missile bases in Cuba, and some missiles had already been in place. The missiles could have been used to launch nuclear attacks on American cities. The crisis was one of the most serious incidents of the Cold War. President Kennedy immediately set up a blockade of Cuba by ordering U.S. navy to turn back any ship delivering Soviet missiles to Cuba. He also demanded that the Soviet Union remove the missiles. The Soviet Union said that it would not remove the missiles unless the United States removed its nuclear missiles from Turkey. Kennedy privately agreed to the proposal. Then the Soviet Union offered to remove the missiles if the United States would promise not to invade Cuba. Publicly Kennedy agreed to this Soviet proposal. After a week of extreme tension, Khrushchev removed the Soviet missiles.

From the Cuban missile crisis both sides learned that it was simply too dangerous to achieve political aims in the Cold War at the risk of a nuclear war. It was the last time during the Cold War that either side would take this risk.

以用来对美国城市发动核打击。这次危机是冷战期间最严重的事件。肯尼迪总统立即下令封锁古巴，并派遣美国海军将运送苏联导弹的任何船只驱逐回去。他还要求苏联将导弹拆除。苏联宣称，作为交换条件，美国须将其核导弹从土耳其撤出。肯尼迪私下里同意了这一建议。然后苏联提出如果美国承诺不再入侵古巴，苏联将拆除导弹。肯尼迪公开同意了苏联的建议。剑拔弩张的局势持续了一周后，赫鲁晓夫下令拆除了苏联的导弹。

冷战双方从古巴导弹危机中得出了一个教训，即在冷战中以核战争相威胁来达到政治目的是极其危险的。

题外话

肯尼迪和赫鲁晓夫的协议之所以没有公开，是因为许多美国人反对这样的交易。结果，几乎所有的美国人都认为肯尼迪仅仅是通过战争威胁来迫使苏联拆除导弹的。有些专家认为，古巴导弹危机之后美国的外交政策更加趋于强硬和更多的武力威胁。

2. Civil Rights Movement

民权运动

In the early 1960s, the black civil rights movement became the main domestic issue in the nation. Martin Luther King, Jr., an African-American Baptist minister, was the main leader of the

60 年代初，黑人的民权运动成为美国国内的主要问题。非裔美国人、浸礼会牧师马丁·路德·金是民权运动的主要领导。1963 年 8 月

civil rights movement. On August 28, 1963, King and other civil rights leaders organized a massive march in Washington, D.C. This event, called the March on Washington, was intended to urge Congress to pass Kennedy's bill for equal rights for blacks. Over 200,000 Americans, including many whites, gathered at the Lincoln Memorial in the capital. The high point of the rally, King's stirring "I Have a Dream" speech, eloquently expressed the ideals of the civil rights movement.

The movement won a major victory in 1964, when Congress passed the civil rights bill that Kennedy and his successor, President Lyndon B. Johnson, had proposed. The Civil Rights Act of 1964 was the strongest civil rights bill in U.S.

马丁·路德·金在演讲

28日，金与其他民权运动领导人在华盛顿组织了一场大规模游行。这一事件，史称华盛顿大游行，旨在敦促国会通过肯尼迪提出的黑人同权的法案。20余万美国人，包括许多白人，聚集在首都的林肯纪念堂前。大会的高潮是金发表的题为"我有一个梦想"的激动人心演说。演说表达了民权运动的理想。

1964年，民权运动取得了一项重大胜利。国会通过了肯尼迪和他的继任者林登·B.约翰逊提出的民权法案。1964年的民权法案是美国历史上最彻底的民权法。该法规定公共场所须对所有的人提供服务，不论种族、肤色、宗教信仰和国籍。该法还要求给不同的人以受聘任和受教育的同等机会。金后来获得了1964年的和平奖。

1965年，金参与组织了从塞尔

华盛顿大游行

history. It ordered public places to serve all people without regard to race, color, religion, or national origin. It also called for equal opportunity in employment and education. King later received the 1964 Nobel Peace Prize.

In 1965, King helped organize a march from Selma to Montgomery, the state capital of Alabama. The goal of the march was to draw national attention to the struggle for black voting rights in the state. But the police used tear gas and clubs to break up the group. The bloody attack, broadcast nationwide on television news shows, shocked the public. Two weeks later, more than 3,000 people marched again from Selma to Montgomery. They arrived in Montgomery five days later, where King addressed a rally of more than 20,000 people. Soon after that Johnson went before Congress to request a bill that would elimi-

马到亚拉巴马州首府蒙哥马利的游行。游行的目的是将全国的注意力引向该州争取黑人选举权的斗争。但是警察用催泪瓦斯和警棍驱散了人群。这场血腥的镇压在全国的电视新闻中播出，震惊了公众。两周后，3000 余人再次从塞尔马出发，向蒙哥马利游行。他们 5 天后到达蒙哥马利，金在该市对两万多人发表演说。约翰逊不久后到国会讲话，要求通过一项法案，一举消除对南方黑人参加选举的一切限制。几个月内，国会通过了 1965 年的选举权法。这项法案废除了南方许多州实行的文化水平测试。

在 60 年代，许多其他的人群，包括美洲印第安人、墨西哥裔美国人和妇女也开始要求得到充分权

马丁·路德·金领导从塞尔马到蒙哥马利的游行

nate all barriers to Southern blacks' right to vote. Within a few months, Congress approved the Voting Rights Act of 1965. This act outlawed literacy tests in many Southern states.

In the 1960s many other groups, including American Indians, Mexican Americans and women, also began demanding fuller rights. In the mid-1960s, many Americans began challenging U.S. foreign-policy decisions. Protesters of all kinds staged demonstrations to try to bring about change. Most demonstrations were conducted peacefully. But in some cases, they led to violence.

利。60 年代中期，许多美国人开始对美国的对外政策提出挑战。各种各样的抗议者举行抗议活动试图改变现状。大多数示威活动都是和平进行的。但也有某些示威引起了暴力冲突。

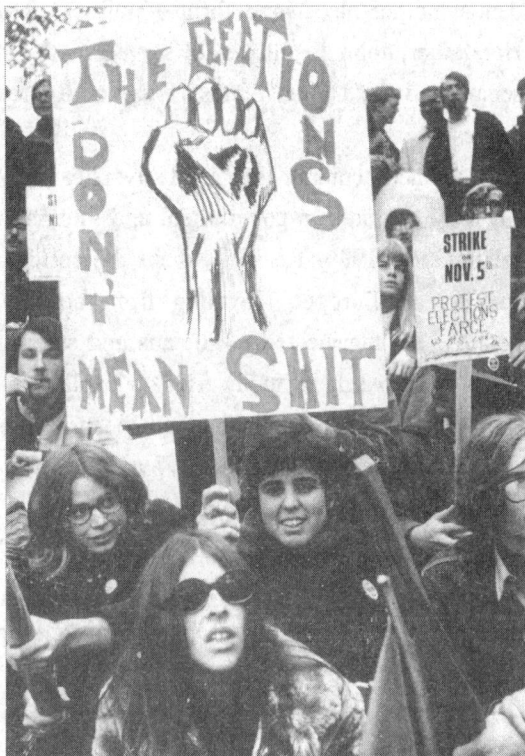

1968年的学生示威游行

3. John Fitzgerald Kennedy 约翰·菲茨杰拉德·肯尼迪

John Fitzgerald Kennedy (1917-1963), President of the United Stares from January 1961 to November 1963, was the youngest man and the only Catholic ever elected President.

Kennedy came from a distinguished family.

约翰·菲茨杰拉德·肯尼迪 (1917-1963) 自 1961 年 1 月至 1963 年 11 月任美国总统。他是美国最年轻的一位，也是唯一的一位信奉天主教的总统。

His great-grandfather left Ireland during the great potato famine of the 1840s and settled in Boston. The President's grandfather became a state senator and his father, Joseph Patrick Kennedy, a very rich banker and investor, served as U.S. ambassador to Britain from 1937 to 1940. The President's mother also came form a political family. Her father, John F. Fitzgerald served in the state senate and the United States House of Representatives.

Kennedy entered Harvard University in 1936. There he majored in government and international relations. In 1939, Kennedy spent the spring and summer in Europe. Traveling from country to country, he interviewed politicians and statesmen. Back at Harvard, Kennedy tried to explain in his senior thesis why Britain had not been ready for war. His thesis, published as *Why England Slept*, was well received by reviewers.

Kennedy was graduated cum *laude* in 1940. He then enrolled in the Stanford University graduate business school, but dropped out six months later, and enlisted as a seaman in the U.S. Navy.

When the U.S. was attacked at Pearl Harbor in 1941, Kennedy applied for sea duty and was assigned to a PT boat squadron late in 1942. After learning to command one of the small craft, he was commissioned as an ensign.

Kennedy's PT boat was assigned to patrol duty in the South Pacific. One night in August 1943, his boat was rammed by a Japanese destroyer and cut in two. 2 of the 13 men aboard were killed. Kennedy and the other survivors clung for hours to the wreckage, hoping for rescue. When none came, they swam to a small

肯尼迪出身名门。他的曾祖父在 19 世纪 40 年代马铃薯饥荒时离开爱尔兰，定居波士顿。总统的祖父当上了州参议员，父亲约瑟夫·帕特里克·肯尼迪是一个富有的银行家和投资家，于 1937～1940 年间任美国驻英国大使。总统的母亲也来自一个官宦之家。她的父亲约翰·F.菲茨杰拉德曾任州参议员和美国众议员。

肯尼迪于 1936 年进入哈佛大学学习，主修政治学和外交关系。1939 年的春夏两季，肯尼迪在欧洲云游各国，访问政治家和国务活动家。回国后，他在自己的四年级论文里试图解释为什么英国没有为战争做好准备。他的论文，以《英国为何酣睡》为书名发表，受到好评。

1940 年，肯尼迪以优等成绩毕业，进入斯坦福大学商业研究生院，但 6 个月后退学，加入美国海军。

1941 年美国在珍珠港遭受袭击后，肯尼迪申请出海执行任务，于 1942 年末被派往一个鱼雷快艇中队。学会指挥一艘鱼雷艇后，他被任命为少尉。

肯尼迪的鱼雷艇受命在南太平洋执行巡逻任务。1943 年 8 月的一天夜里，他的快艇被一艘日本驱逐舰撞成两截。艇上有 13 名士兵，死亡两人。肯尼迪和其他幸存者在被毁的船上坚持了数小时，等待救援。救援无望，他们开始游向 5 公

island 5 km away. Despite an injured back, Kennedy towed a wounded crewman by clenching the long strap of the injured man's life jacket between his teeth. Kennedy and his crew were rescued five days later. For his heroism and leadership, Kennedy received the Navy and Marine Corps Medal. For being wounded in combat, he was awarded the Purple Heart.

Kennedy began his political career in 1946. He was elected to the House of Representatives first and then to the Senate.

Kennedy got married in 1953. His wife, Jacqueline Lee Bouvier, was the daughter of a wealthy Wall Street broker. They had four children, but two of them died at birth.

In 1957, Kennedy was appointed to the Senate Foreign Relations Committee, a key assignment in Congress. He criticized the foreign policy of the Republican administration, and supported a program of increased aid to underdeveloped countries.

In 1960, Kennedy became the Democratic nominee for President, with Lyndon B. Johnson as his running mate. The Republicans chose Vice President Richard M. Nixon to oppose Kennedy for the presidency. At first, most experts believed Nixon would win. He had the advantage of being Vice President under Eisenhower, an unusu-

里外的一个小岛。尽管背部受了伤，肯尼迪用牙齿咬住一个受伤士兵救生衣的长带，拖着他向前游。5天后，肯尼迪和他的部下获救。由于他表现出的勇气和领导才能，肯尼迪获得海军和海军陆战队奖章。由于在战斗中负伤，他获得紫心勋章。

1946年，肯尼迪开始了自己的从政生涯。他先后被选入众议院和参议院。

肯尼迪于1953年结婚。他的妻子，杰奎琳·李·布维尔，是华尔街的一个富裕的股票经纪人的女儿。他们有4个孩子，但两个在出生时死去。

1957年，肯尼迪被任命为参议院外交关系委员会委员，这是国会的重要任命。他批评共和党政府的外交政策，支持对不发达国家增加援助的计划。

1960年，肯尼迪成为民主党总统候选人，林登·B.约翰逊为其竞选伙伴。共和党选择副总统理查德·M.尼克松与肯尼迪竞争总统职位。起初，大多数专

肯尼迪在1960年竞选总统

ally popular President. But Kennedy also had his advantages. His good looks, wealth, and attractive wife had made him a popular subject for articles in newspapers and magazines. His better appearance during his four televised debates with Nixon also helped him greatly. Kennedy promised to lead Americans to a "New Frontier". He charged that, under the Republicans, the United States had lost ground to the Soviet Union in the Cold War.

Kennedy won the election by a small margin over Nixon. He was inaugurated President on January 20, 1961. In his inaugural address, President Kennedy declared that "a new generation of Americans" had taken over leadership of the country. He said Americans would "... pay any price, bear any burden, meet any hardship, support any friend, oppose any foe to assure the survival and the success of liberty." He told Americans: "Ask not what your country can do for you—ask what you can do for your country."

As President, Kennedy launched a plan that was widely called "the New Frontier". In domestic affairs, he asked for stronger laws to protect civil rights, especially of blacks, and for more medical care for the aged. He persuaded Congress to lower taxes so as to improve business. In foreign affairs, he was firm opposing the spread of communism, and successfully cut tariffs so the United States could trade freely with the European Common Market.

One of the most successful of Kennedy's programs was the U.S. Peace Corps. The corps sent thousands of Americans abroad to help people in developing nations raise their standards of living.

家看好尼克松。尼克松的优势是在艾森豪威尔任职期间当过副总统，而艾森豪威尔又是一位极得人心的总统。但肯尼迪也有他的强项。他英俊的长相、财富和漂亮妻子使他成为报刊杂志文章的流行话题。在他与尼克松进行的 4 次电视辩论中，他表现略高一筹，这也有助于提高他的声望。肯尼迪承诺要领导美国人民跨越"新边疆"。他指责在共和党执政期间，美国在冷战中输给了苏联。

肯尼迪发表就职演说

肯尼迪以微弱多数险胜尼克松。1961 年 1 月 20 日，在他的就职演说中，肯尼迪宣称"新一代美国人"已承担了国家的领导职责。他说美国人将愿意"付出任何代价、承担任何责任、应对任何困

In 1963, demands by blacks for equal civil and economic rights increased. Racial protests and demonstrations took place across the United States. On August 28, 1963, more than 200,000 persons staged a Freedom March in Washington, D.C., to demonstrate their demands for equal rights for blacks. To meet growing demands of blacks, Kennedy asked Congress to pass laws requiring all hotels, motels, and restaurants to serve customers regardless of race.

In April 1961, Cuban rebels invaded their homeland to overthrow Fidel Castro, who were backed by Communist nations. The attack ended in disaster. Kennedy accepted blame for the ill-fated invasion, which had been planned by the United States.

Another Cuban crisis began in October 1962, when the United States discovered that the Soviet Union had installed missiles in Cuba, which could be used to launch nuclear attacks on American cities. Kennedy immediately set up a blockade of Cuba by ordering U.S. navy to turn back any ship delivering Soviet missiles to Cuba. Then the Soviet Union offered to remove the missiles if the United States would promise not to invade Cuba. Kennedy agreed to this Soviet proposal. After a week of extreme tension, Khrushchev removed the Soviet missiles.

Kennedy greatly increased United States prestige when he turned aside the threat of an atomic war with the Soviet Union while making the Soviets withdraw missiles from Cuba through negotiation. His action marked the start of a period of "thaw" in the Cold War as relations grew friendlier with the Soviet Union. In 1963, the

难、支持任何朋友、反抗任何敌人以争取和维护自由"。他劝告美国人:"莫问国家能为你们做什么,要问你们能为国家做什么。"

担任总统期间,肯尼迪开始实施一项被称为"新边疆"的计划。在国内,他要求制定更有力的法律以保障民权,特别是黑人的权利;要求向老年人提供更多的医疗服务。他说服国会降低税收以促进工商业的繁荣。在对外事物中,他坚决反对共产主义扩张,并成功地降低了关税,使美国与欧洲共同市场能够自由进行贸易。

肯尼迪制订的计划中最成功的项目之一是美国和平队。和平队向国外派遣成千上万的美国人到发展中国家,帮助人民提高生活水平。

1963年,黑人对平等民权和经济权利的要求增长了。因种族问题发生的抗议和示威运动遍及美国。1963年8月28日,20余万人在华盛顿举行了争取自由大游行,以表达他们为黑人争取同等权利的愿望。为满足黑人日益增长的要求,肯尼迪请求国会通过法律要求所有的饭店、汽车旅馆和餐馆不分种族,服务于所有的顾客。

1961年4月,古巴反叛分子入侵祖国,试图推翻共产党国家支持的菲德尔·卡斯特罗。这次进攻一败涂地。肯尼迪愿意为这次失败的入侵承担责任,因为入侵是由美国策划的。

另一次古巴危机开始于1962

United States, the Soviet Union, and over 100 other countries signed a treaty outlawing the testing of atomic bombs under water and on or above ground. On the home front, the United States enjoyed its greatest prosperity in history. Blacks made greater progress in their quest for equal rights. During Kennedy's Administration, the United States made its first manned space flights and prepared to send astronauts to the moon.

In November 1963, Kennedy visited Dallas in Texas, accompanied by his wife and Vice President and Mrs. Johnson. This trip was part of his plan for running for a second term. While the President, Mrs. Kennedy, Johnson, and others to travel in a motorcade through the streets of Dallas, three shots rang out. One bullet passed through the president's neck. A second bullet struck the president in the head. Kennedy fell forward, and his car sped to a nearby hospital. At 1:00 pm, he was pronounced dead.

题外话

自从威廉·H.哈里森以来，凡是在以"0"结尾的年头里当选的总统，大多死于任上。哈里森 1840 当选，1841 年死于肺炎；林肯 1860 年当选，1865 年第二任期内死于暗杀；加菲尔德 1880 年当选，1881 年遭枪击后不久身亡；麦金利 1900 年再度当选，1901 年遇刺身亡；哈定 1920 年当选，1923 年死于心脏病；罗斯福 1940 年当选连任，1945 年在第四任上死于脑溢血。"0"年当选的总统中没有死在任上的唯一例外是里根，他在 1980 年当选，1981 年遭枪击后康复。

肯尼迪的就职演说是演说词中的名篇。他的演说内容充实，语言生动，问题流畅而有节奏，感情奔放而有节制，有很大的鼓动性。这种风格在其他美国总统身上是不多见的。

年 10 月，当时美国发现苏联在古巴设置了导弹，可以用来对美国城市发动核打击。肯尼迪立即下令封锁了古巴，派遣美国海军将运送苏联导弹的任何船只驱逐回去。苏联提出如果美国承诺不入侵古巴，苏联将拆除导弹。肯尼迪公开同意了苏联的建议。剑拔弩张的局势持续了一周后，赫鲁晓夫下令拆除了苏联的导弹。

由于肯尼迪通过谈判迫使苏联从古巴撤除导弹，解除了与苏联发生核战争的威胁，他大大提高了美国的声望。他的行动标志着冷战"解冻"时期，即美苏关系缓和的开端。1963 年，美国、苏联和其他 100 多个国家签署了禁止水下、地上和空中进行原子弹实验的条约。在国内，美国经历着有史以来最大的繁荣。黑人争取同等权利的斗争取得了更大的进展。在肯尼迪任期内，美国实现了其最初的数次载人航天飞行，并准备将宇航员送上月球。

1963 年 11 月，肯尼迪由妻子和副总统约翰逊夫妇陪同访问得克萨斯的达拉斯市。这次旅行是他竞选连任计划中的一部分。当总统、肯尼迪夫人、约翰逊和其他人乘坐一列汽车穿过达拉斯的街道时，人们听到三声枪响。一颗子弹打穿了总统的颈部，第二颗击中总统的头部。肯尼迪向前扑倒，汽车将他火速送往附近医院。下午 1 点钟，公布了他死亡的消息。

4. Martin Luther King, Jr.

Martin Luther King, Jr. (1929-1968) was an African-American Baptist minister and Nobel Prize winner, the main leader of the civil rights movement in the United States during the 1950s and 1960s. King is also remembered as one of the greatest orators in the history of the United States.

King was born on January 15, 1929, in Atlanta, Georgia, the eldest son of Martin Luther King, Sr., a Baptist minister. In high school, Martin did so well that he skipped both the 9th and 12th grades. He entered Morehouse College at the age of 15, and graduated with a bachelor's degree in sociology in 1948. King became a minister just before he graduated from Morehouse. He entered Crozer Theological Seminary in Pennsylvania in 1951 and earned a divinity degree. King then went to graduate school at Boston University, where he got a Ph. D. degree in theology in 1955. In Boston, he met Coretta Scott, a music student. They were married in 1953 and would have four children. In 1954, King became pastor of a Baptist Church in Montgomery, Alabama.

At Morehouse, Crozer, and Boston University, King studied the teachings on nonviolent protest of Indian leader Mohandas Gandhi and the 19th century American philosopher Henry David Thoreau's essay "Civil Disobedience". The ideas of Thoreau and Gandhi greatly influenced him.

King's civil rights activities began with a protest of Montgomery's segregated bus system in

马丁·路德·金

马丁·路德·金 (1929-1968) 是非裔美国浸礼会牧师，诺贝尔奖获得者，美国 20 世纪 50 和 60 年代民权运动的主要领导人。金也作为美国历史上最伟大的演说家之一受到人们的怀念。

金于 1929 年 1 月 15 日出生在佐治亚州的亚特兰大，是浸礼会牧师老马丁·路德·金的长子。上中学时，马丁的学习成绩极佳，跳过 9 年级和 12 年级。他 15 岁进入莫尔豪斯学院学习，1948 年毕业，获得社会学学士学位。在毕业前不久他受任为牧师。1951 年他进入宾夕法尼亚州的克罗泽神学院学习，取得神学学位。然后金又到波士顿大学的研究生院学习，于 1955 年获得神学博士学位。他在波士顿遇到学习音乐的学生科蕾塔·斯科特，两人于 1953 年结婚，后来生下 4 个孩子。1954 年，金就任亚拉巴马州蒙哥马利市一座浸礼会教堂的牧师。

在莫尔豪斯、克罗泽和波士顿学习时，金研究了印度人领袖莫罕达斯·甘地的非暴力抗议学说和 19 世纪美国哲学家亨利·戴维·梭罗的论文 "论公民的不服从" 里阐述的观点。梭罗和甘地的思想对他产生了重大影响。

金的民权活动开始于 1955 年

1955. That year, a black woman named Rosa Parks was ordered by a bus driver to give up her seat to a white passenger. When she refused, she was arrested for breaking the city law and put into prison. Black leaders in Montgomery called on blacks to protest Rosa Parks' arrest by refusing to ride the city's buses. The leaders formed an organization to run the boycott, and asked King to serve as president, since he had a magnificent speaking ability. With a strong belief in the power of love and non-violent protest, King told black people: "First and foremost, we are American citizens. ... We are not here advocating violence. ... The only weapon that we have is the weapon of protest. ... The great glory of American democracy is the right to protest for right."

Terrorists bombed King's home, but King continued to insist on nonviolent protests. The black people's protest lasted over a year, ending when the United States Supreme Court ordered Montgomery to abolish the bus law.

The boycott became the first organized mass protest by blacks in Southern history. The protest made King a national figure. His eloquent speeches

对蒙哥马利市公共汽车的种族隔离制的抗议。当年，一个名叫罗莎·帕克斯的黑人妇女被公共汽车司机命令将座位让给一个白人乘客。她拒绝让座，遂以违反该市的法律的罪名被捕入狱。蒙哥马利市的黑人领袖号召黑人拒绝乘坐该市的公共汽车，以抗议逮捕罗莎·帕克斯。黑人领袖们成立了一个协会来领导抵制活动，请金担任会长，因为他有出色的演说才能。金坚信爱的力量和非暴力抗议的原则，他告诫黑人："首先切记，我们是美国公民。……我们不鼓吹暴力。……我们唯一的武器是抗议的武器。……美国民主的伟大光辉在于人民有权为争取权利而抗议。"

恐怖分子向金的住宅投炸弹，但金继续坚持非暴力抗议。黑人的抗议活动持续了一年多，直到美国最高法院命令蒙哥马利市废止公共汽车法为止。

联合抵制是美国南方历史上黑人进行的头一次抗议活动。抗议使

1955年，马丁·路德·金夫妇因组织抵制公共汽车在蒙哥马利市被捕

that expressed Christian brotherhood and American idealism created a positive impression on people both inside and outside the South.

King became the president of the Southern Christian Leadership Conference (SCLC) when it was founded in 1957. The organization encouraged the use of nonviolent, direct action to protest segregation. In 1960, King moved from Montgomery to Atlanta to devote more effort to SCLC's work.

During the early 1960s, King and his SCLC started a series of protest campaigns in Southern cities. They hoped that public disorder they created might force local white officials and business leaders to end segregation in order to restore normal business activity. Early in 1963, King and his SCLC staff organized massive demonstrations to protest racial discrimination in Birmingham, Alabama, one of the South's most segregated cities. Police used dogs and fire hoses to drive back peaceful protesters, including school children. Scenes of violence were shown throughout the nation and the world in newspapers, magazines, and most importantly, on television. Much of the world was shocked by the events, and support for black civil rights increased. Soon afterward, white leaders in Birmingham promised to end some segregation practices. Business leaders agreed to hire and promote more black employees and to desegregate some public places. More important, however, the Birmingham demonstrations urged Kennedy to propose a wide-ranging civil rights bill to Congress.

On August 28, 1963, King and other civil rights leaders organized a massive march in

金成为全国闻名的人物。他雄辩的演讲表达了基督徒的友爱精神和美国人的理想主义,给南方和南方以外的人们留下了正面的印象。

1957年,南方基督教领袖大会成立,金担任会长。这个组织鼓励使用非暴力的、直接的行动来抗议种族隔离。1960年,金从蒙哥马利迁居亚特兰大,以便将更多的精力投入到南方基督教领袖大会的工作中。

60年代初,金和南方基督教领袖大会在南方城市开展了一系列的抗议活动。他们希望搅乱公共秩序,迫使地方上的白人官员和工商业界领袖结束隔离,以恢复正常的工商业活动。1963年初,金和南方基督教领袖大会的工作人员在南方种族隔离最严重的城市之一,即亚拉巴马州的伯明翰市组织了数次大规模的示威,抗议种族歧视。警察使用警犬和高压水管驱赶和平的抗议者,其中包括学童。报纸、杂志、特别是电视使全国和全世界看到了暴力场面。世界上很多地方都对事件感到震惊,这使黑人民权运动得到了更多的支持。不久后,伯明翰的白人领袖承诺将结束某些隔离制度。工商业领袖同意雇用并提升更多的黑人雇员,并在某些公共场所取消隔离制。然而,最重要的是,伯明翰的示威促使肯尼迪向国会提出了一个涉及面广泛的民权法案。

1963年8月28日,金与其他

Washington, D.C. The event, called the March on Washington, was intended to urge Congress to pass Kennedy's bill for equal rights for blacks. Over 200,000 Americans, including many whites, gathered at the Lincoln Memorial in the capital. During the demonstration, King made his stirring "I Have a Dream" speech, eloquently expressed the ideals of the civil rights movement: "I have a dream that one day this nation will rise up and live out the true meaning of its creed: 'We hold these truths to be self-evident, that all men are created equal.' ... I have a dream that my four little children will one day live in a nation where they will not be judged by the color of their skin but by the content of their character."

The movement won a major victory in 1964, when Congress passed the civil rights bill that Kennedy and his successor, President Lyndon B.

民权运动领导人在华盛顿组织了一场大规模的游行。这一事件，史称华盛顿大游行，旨在敦促国会通过肯尼迪提出的黑人同权的法案。20余万美国人，包括许多白人，聚集在首都的林肯纪念堂前。在示威中，金做了以"我有一个梦想"为题的激动人心演说，雄辩地表达了民权运动的理想："我梦想有一天这个国家能够站立起来，实现其信条的真谛：'我们认为下面这些真理是不言而喻的：人人生而平等。'……我梦想有一天我的四个童年的孩子将生活在这样一个国家，其中对人们的价值的判断不再以肤色为准，而以他们的品性为准。"

1964 年，民权运动取得了一项重大胜利。国会通过了肯尼迪和他

1963 年，马丁·路德·金在底特律领导一次 10 万人的大游行

Johnson, had proposed. The *Civil Rights Act of 1964* end segregation in public places and called for equal opportunity in employment and education. King later received the 1964 Nobel Peace Prize for leading nonviolent civil rights demonstrations.

In 1965, King helped organize a march from Selma to Montgomery, the state capital of Alabama. The goal of the march was to draw national attention to the struggle for black voting rights in the state. But the police used tear gas and clubs to break up the group. The bloody attack, broadcast nationwide on television news shows, shocked the public. Two weeks later, more than 3,000 people marched again from Selma to Montgomery. They arrived in Montgomery five days later, where King addressed a rally of more than 20,000 people. Soon after that Johnson went before Congress to request a bill that would eliminate all barriers to Southern blacks' right to vote. Within a few months, Congress approved the *Voting Rights Act of 1965*. This act outlawed literacy tests in many Southern states.

After 1965, King increasingly turned the focus of his civil rights activities to economic issues. He became more critical of American society than ever before. He believed poverty was as great an evil as racism. King began to plan a Poor People's Campaign that would unite poor people of all races in a struggle for economic opportunity and attract lawmakers' attention to the issue of economic justice. In 1967, King began to attack U.S. support of South Vietnam in the Vietnam War. He regarded the South Vietnamese government as corrupt and undemocratic.

的继任者林登·B.约翰逊的提出的民权法案。1964年的民权法案结束了公共场所的隔离制，要求给不同的人以受聘任和受教育的同等机会。后来，金因领导了非暴力的民权示威而获得了1964年的和平奖。

1965年，金参与组织了从塞尔马到亚拉巴马州首府蒙哥马利的游行。游行的目的是将全国的注意力引向该州争取黑人选举权的斗争。但是警察用催泪瓦斯和警棍驱散了人群。这场血腥是镇压在全国的电视新闻中播出，震惊了公众。两周后，3000余人再次从塞尔马出发，向蒙哥马利行进。他们5天后到达蒙哥马利，金在该市对两万多人发表演说。约翰逊到国会讲话，要求通过一项法案，一举消除对南方黑人参加选举的一切限制。几个月内，国会通过了1965年的选举权法。这项法案废除了南方许多州实行的文化水平测试。

1965年，金越来越多地将民权活动的重点转向经济问题。他对美国社会的批评比以往更为激烈。他认为贫穷与种族主义同样是罪恶。金开始筹划一场穷人的示威运动，使各个种族的穷人联合起来，进行争取经济机会的斗争，同时吸引国会对经济公正问题的关注。1967年，金开始攻击美国在越南战争中对南越的支持。他认为南越政府是一个腐败而不民主的政府。

While organizing the Poor People's Campaign, King went to Memphis, Tennessee, to support striking black garbage workers in the spring of 1968. He was assassinated in Memphis by a sniper on April 4.

News of King's assassination caused great shock, grief, and anger throughout the nation and the world. Blacks rioted in more than 100 cities. In 1983, Congress passed a federal holiday honoring King. The day is celebrated on the third Monday in January, a day that falls on or near King's birthday of January 15. King thus became only the second American whose birthday is observed as a national holiday. The first was George Washington, the nation's first President. In 1991, the National Civil Rights Museum opened at the site of King's assassination in Memphis. The museum's exhibits cover the history of the civil rights movement.

在组织穷人示威活动的同时，金于 1968 年春前往田纳西的孟菲斯去支持黑人垃圾工的罢工。他在 4 月 4 日在孟菲斯被黑枪暗杀。

金被暗杀的消息在全国和全世界引起了震惊、悲痛和愤慨。在 100 多个城市里发生了黑人骚乱。1983 年，国会通过立法，确立联邦范围的金的纪念日。这个纪念日在 1 月的第三个星期一。此日或在金的诞辰 1 月 15 日当天，或在 15 日前后。这样，金成为第二个其诞辰被当做全国性假日的人。头一个是乔治·华盛顿，美国的首任总统。1991 年，美国国家民权博物馆在孟菲斯金遇刺的地点开馆。馆内的展品覆盖了民权运动的历史。

CHAPTER EIGHTEEN

The United States in the 1970s

20 世纪 70 年代的美国

1. Recognizing China

承认中国

During the early 1970s, Canada and several other Western nations established diplomatic relations with the People's Republic of China. The United States continued to recognize the Kuomindang government in Taiwan. But in 1971, the United States ended its long-standing opposition to United Nations membership for the People's Republic. Instead, it favored UN membership for both the People's Republic and Taiwan. In October 1971, the UN voted to admit the People's Republic in place of Taiwan.

In 1971, U.S. President Richard Nixon sent Henry Kissinger, assistant to the President for national security affairs, to Beijing. When Kissinger returned, the president announced to a startled world that he himself would visit China the following year.

In 1972, Nixon travelled to China and met with Premier Zhou Enlai and Chairman Mao Zedong. During Nixon's visit, the United States and

70年代初，加拿大和几个西方国家相继与中华人民共和国建立了外交关系。美国则继续承认台湾的国民党政权。1971 年，美国结束了其长期以来一直反对中国加入联合国的政策，代之以赞成中华人民共和国和台湾均为联合国成员的政策。1971 年 10 月，联合国投票接受中华人民共和国取代台湾成为联合国成员。

1971 年，美国总统理查德·尼克松派遣总统国家安全事务助理亨利·基辛格访问北京。基辛格返回后，总统宣布他将在第二年访问中国。这一消息震惊了世界。

1972 年，尼克松前往中国，会见了周恩来总理和毛泽东主席。在尼克松访问期间，中美两国签署了上海联合公报，宣布将建立正常关系。两国向对方首都互派了代表。

China signed the Shanghai Communique, which looked forward to the establishment of normal relations. The two nations sent representatives to serve in each other's capital. Nixon's trip began a long process of normalizing relations between the United States and China.

In 1979, during President Carter's administration, the United States established full diplomatic relations with the People's Republic of China. This action resulted in increased business, cultural, and diplomatic exchanges between the two countries.

尼克松的访问旅行开始了中美两国关系正常化的漫长过程。

1979年,在卡特总统执政期间,美国和中华人民共和国建立了完全的外交关系。此后,两国之间的贸易、文化交流和外交往来增加了。

尼克松会见毛泽东

尼克松与周恩来在北京举行的告别宴会上

2. Watergate

Nixon's presidency had many accomplishments, but it is remembered chiefly for the Watergate scandal.

In June 1972, during Nixon's campaign for reelection, police arrested five men for breaking into the Democratic Party's national headquarters in the Watergate apartment and office complex in Washington, D.C. One of the burglars was the security coordinator of the Committee for the Re-election of the President. The five men were found guilty of a number of crimes, including burglary and wiretapping.

Early in 1973, evidence was uncovered that linked several top White House aides with either the break-in or later attempts to hide information related to it. Nixon insisted that he did not participate in the break-in or the cover-up. In addition, he promised a full investigation of the case. In May, Archibald Cox, a Harvard Law School professor, was named to head the investigation as the special prosecutor.

In July, a Senate investigating committee learned that Nixon had secretly made tape recordings of conversations in his White House offices since 1971. Both Cox and the Senate committee asked to hear certain tapes that they believed could help their investigations. Nixon refused. He argued that, as President, he had a constitutional right to keep the tapes confidential. Cox and the committee sued Nixon to obtain the tapes. U.S. District Court Judge John J. Sirica decided to

水门事件

尼克松任总统期间有许多成就，但却由于水门丑闻而留在人们的记忆中。

1972年6月，在尼克松为连任竞选期间，警方逮捕了5名男子，他们试图秘密进入设在华盛顿特区水门商住综合楼里的民主党全国总部。他们当中有一人是总统竞选连任委员会的安全协调员。5人被发现犯有数项罪行，其中包括非法闯入和窃听。

1973年初，有证据表明数名白宫助理与非法闯入事件或事后试图隐瞒有关材料有牵连。尼克松坚持说自己没有参与非法闯入和隐瞒事实真相的活动。此外，他承诺要对事件进行详细调查。5月，哈佛大学法学院教授阿奇博尔德·考克斯被任命为特派独立检察官主持调查。

7月，参议院的一个调查委员会得知，自从1971年以来，尼克松在白宫办公室的谈话一直都有秘密录音。考克斯和参议院委员会都要求听取他们认为有助于调查的部分录音带。尼克松拒绝了这一要求。他的理由是，作为总统，他有宪法赋予的权利不将录音内容公开。考克斯和参议院委员为得到录音带起诉了尼克松。美国地区法院法官约翰·J.赛里卡决定亲自听取录

review the tapes himself and ordered Nixon to give them to him. Nixon appealed the order, but a U.S. court of appeals supported Sirica.

Nixon offered to supply summaries of the tapes to the Senate committee and to Cox. Cox refused, arguing that summaries would not be regarded as proper evidence in court. Nixon ordered Attorney General Elliot L. Richardson to fire Cox, but Richardson refused to do so and resigned. Deputy Attorney General William Ruckelshaus also resigned after being ordered to dismiss Cox. Nixon then named Solicitor General Robert Bork acting attorney general, and Bork fired Cox. Leon Jaworski, a noted Texas attorney, later succeeded Cox.

The President's actions raised a storm criticism. Impeachment resolutions were introduced in the House of Representatives. Later in 1973, Nixon agreed to give the tapes to Sirica. Then it was discovered that three key conversations were missing and one tape had a mysterious gap of 18 minutes.

In April 1974, Jaworski demanded to have more tapes documents relating to certain White House conversations. But Nixon only provided written versions of the tapes. Jaworski, however, insisted on receiving the original tapes and documents that he had requested. When Nixon refused, Jaworski sued the President in federal court. In July, the Supreme Court of the United States ruled that Nixon must turn over the requested tapes. Additional written versions and tapes revealed that Nixon had involved in the Watergate affair almost from the very beginning.

In July 1974, the Judiciary Committee of the

音带，命令尼克松将录音带交给他。尼克松对这一命令提起上诉，但美国上诉法院支持了赛里卡。

尼克松提出要将录音内容总结交给参议院委员和考克斯。考克斯拒绝了，声称内容总结不足以当做法庭上的适当证据。尼克松命令司法部长埃利奥特·L.理查森将考克斯撤职，但理查森拒绝服从，辞去职务。司法部副部长威廉·拉克尔肖斯接到将考克斯撤职的命令后也辞去职务。尼克松然后任命司法部副部长罗伯特·博克代理司法部部长职务，结果博克将考克斯撤职。得克萨斯著名的律师利昂·贾沃尔斯基继考克斯任特派独立检察官。

总统采取的行动激起暴风骤雨般的批评。众议院开始考虑弹劾决议案。1973 年末，尼克松同意将录音带交给赛里卡。结果发现缺少了三次关键性的谈话，其中一盘录音带上还有一段 18 分钟的神秘空白。

1974 年 4 月，贾沃尔斯基要求得到与某些白宫谈话有关的更多的录音带。但尼克松只提供了录音的文字本。但贾沃尔斯基坚持要求得到他所要求的原始录音带和文件。尼克松拒绝后，贾沃尔斯基向联邦法院起诉总统。7 月，美国最高法院判决尼克松必须按要求交出录音带。新得到的文字本和录音带表明，尼克松几乎从一开始就卷入了水门事件。

1974 年 7 月，众议院司法委员会投票通过对总统的弹劾条文。弹

House of Representatives voted articles of impeachment against the President. The articles charged Nixon with misusing his power, violating the constitutional rights of U.S. citizens, obstructing justice in the Watergate affair, and refusing to cooperate with the committee.

Facing an almost certain impeachment for his alleged involvement in the Watergate affair, Nixon resigned as President on August 9, 1974. He was the only United States President ever to resign. Vice President Gerald R. Ford took office as President that day. On September 8, Ford pardoned Nixon for all crimes that Nixon might have committed while serving as President.

尼克松宣布辞职

题 外 话

越战和水门事件使美国人对政治感到厌倦，对华盛顿的官僚们日益缺少信任。福特赦免尼克松也引起不少争议。有人认为此举违背了司法面前人人平等的宪法原则。他们问道，为什么水门事件的中心人物被免于起诉，而那些喽啰们却全被关进了监狱？

劾条文指控尼克松犯有滥用职权、侵害宪法赋予美国公民的权利、妨碍水门事件司法调查、拒绝与委员会合作等罪行。

由于被控卷入水门事件，遭受弹劾几乎已成定局，尼克松于 1974 年 8 月 9 日辞去总统职务。他是历史上唯一辞职的美国总统。副总统杰拉德·R.福特就职继任总统。9 月 8 日，福特赦免了尼克松任职期间可能犯下的所有罪行。

3. Carter's Successes and Failures

卡 特 的 成 功 与 失 败

Jimmy Carter, elected President in 1976, attracted worldwide attention in 1977 when he strongly supported the struggle for human rights. Carter limited or completely banned U.S. aid and exports to some nations in Africa, Asia, and Latin America, because he believed the governments of the nations were violating human rights. His administration barred export of advanced computers

吉米·卡特于 1976 年当选总统；次年，由于他有利地支持了争取人权的斗争，引起了世界的关注。卡特限制或完全禁止美国对某些非洲、亚洲和拉丁美洲国家提供援助和出口商品，因为他认为这些国家的政府侵犯了人权。他的政府禁止向苏联出口高级计算机，因为

to the Soviet Union because the country sup-
pressed free speech and restricted its citizen's
right to emigrate. When Soviet troops suddenly
invaded Afghanistan in late 1979, Carter cut off
sales of grain and high-technology equipment.

Carter also ended a long dispute with Panama over the Panama Canal, which the United
States had controlled since its construction in the
early 20th century. In 1977, the two nations
signed two new treaties, and in the following year
the United States Senate approved them. According to one treaty, Panama would gain control of
the canal on December 31, 1999. The other gives
the United States the right to defend the canal's
neutrality.

Carter tried to improve U.S. relations with
China and the Soviet Union. In early 1979, the
United States and China established normal diplomatic relations. Later that year, Carter and Leonid
I. Brezhnev, leader of the Soviet Communist Party, signed a treaty that would limit the use of U.
S. and Soviet nuclear arms. But relations between
the United States and the Soviet Union declined
sharply when Soviet troops invaded Afghanistan
in late 1979 and early 1980. Partly to protest the
invasion, the U.S. Senate ended consideration of
the arms treaty.

Cater also helped bring about a peace treaty
between Egypt and Israel. In 1977, he invited President Anwar Sadat of Egypt and Israel's Prime
Minister Menachem Begin to meet privately at
Camp David, the presidential retreat in Maryland.
This talk resulted in a formal treaty signed in
1979 in Washington, D.C., which ended the 30-
year state of war between Egypt and Israel.

苏联压制言论自由并限制其公民移居国外的权利。当苏联军队于1979年末突然入侵阿富汗时，卡特中断了对苏联的谷物和高技术设备的出口。

卡特也结束了因巴拿马运河问题与巴拿马的长期争端。自从20世纪初运河建成以来，美国就控制着运河。1977年，两国签订了两项新的条约，次年，美国参议院通过了条约。根据其中一项条约，巴拿马将于1999年12月31日取得运河控制权。另一项条约规定美国有权维护运河的中立地位。

吉米·卡特总统

卡特努力改善美国与中国和苏联的关系。1979年初，美国和中国建立了正常的外交关系。当年晚些时候，卡特与苏共领导人勃列日涅夫签订条约限制美国和苏联使用核武器。但在1979年末和1980年初，当苏联军队入侵阿富汗时，美苏关系急剧恶化。部分出于对这次入侵的抗议，美国参议院不再考虑

But the prestige of Carter, and also of the United States, received a heavy blow in the Iranian crisis. In February 1979, a movement led by Ayatollah Ruhollah Khomeini, a Muslim religious leader, overthrew the government of the shah of Iran. In October, Carter allowed the deposed shah to enter the United States for medical treatment since the shah had had a long close relationship with the United States. The next month, Iranian militant students took over the United States Embassy in Teheran. They seized 66 U.S. citizens, most of whom were embassy employees, and held them as hostages. Thirteen hostages were soon released, but the students announced that the remaining 53 would be released only when the United States apologized for its support of the shah and sent him back to Iran to stand

限制核武器的条约。

卡特还帮助埃及和以色列签订了和平条约。1977 年，他邀请埃及总统萨达特和以色列总理贝京到马里兰州总统休养地戴维营进行私下会谈。这次会谈的结果是在华盛顿签署了一项正式条约，结束了埃及和以色列之间长达 30 年的战争状态。

但是卡特的声誉，也包括美国的声誉，在伊朗人质危机中遭受沉重打击。1979 年 2 月，由穆斯林宗教领袖阿亚图拉·霍梅尼领导的一场运动推翻了伊朗国王的政府。10 月，卡特允许被赶下台的伊朗国王进入美国医病，因为国王与美国一直保持着密切关系。11 月，伊朗好

以色列—埃及和平条约

trial for his crimes. Carter denounced the Iranians' action as a violation of international law, and he refused to meet their demands. After negotiations failed to secure the release of the hostages, Carter authorized an armed rescue mission to free them in April 1980. But the mission ended in failure after three of its eight helicopters broke down while flying through a sandstorm. After the project had been canceled, a fourth helicopter crashed into a transport plane. Both aircraft exploded, killing eight men. In July, the former shah died in Egypt, but the Iranian revolutionaries continued to hold the hostages to protest American policies toward their country. They finally released the Americans on January 20, 1981, the day Carter left office.

Carter's administration confronted a mix of inflation and recession called stagflation—a condition in which both prices and unemployment rose. One major cause was an Arab oil embargo in the early 1970s, which caused a steep rise in oil prices. Carter failed to solve the problems of continuing high inflation and gasoline shortages. He lost the election of 1980 to former California governor Ronald Reagan.

斗的学生占领了德黑兰的美国大使馆。他们扣押了66名美国公民作为人质，其中大多数是使馆雇员。13名人质不久获释，但学生们宣布只有美国对支持伊朗国王表示歉意并将国王遣返伊朗受审，其余53人才能获释。卡特谴责伊朗的行为违反了国际法，拒绝满足他们的要求。几轮谈判未能使人质获救后，1980年4月卡特授权采取一次武装营救行动。但执行任务的8架直升飞机中的3架在穿过一场沙暴时出了故障。营救计划取消后，又有一架直升飞机与运输机发生碰撞。两架飞机爆炸，炸死8名士兵。7月，伊朗国王病逝于埃及，但伊朗革命者继续扣押人质，抗议美国对伊朗的政策。他们在1981年1月20日，即卡特离任当天最终释放了人质。

卡特执政时期，政府面临着所谓的"滞胀"，一种通货膨胀和经济衰退并发的局面，物价和失业率双双上升。一个主要原因是70年代初阿拉伯国家的石油禁运使油价陡升。卡特未能解决持续的高通胀和汽油短缺问题。在1980年的选举中，他败给了前加利福尼亚州长罗纳德·里根。

伊朗人质危机

CHAPTER NINETEEN
Since 1980
20 世纪 80 年代以来

1. The Ronald Reagan Administration

罗纳德·里根执政时期

The economy became the main concern of President Ronald Reagan, who succeeded Carter in 1981. He had to deal with high inflation, a recession, and high unemployment. Reagan and his advisers proposed a policy known as "supply-side" economics. It was based on the idea that financial benefits should be given to the suppliers of goods and services. When the suppliers had more money for investment, economy would expand, new jobs would be created, and prosperity would "trickle down" to the population at large.

To stimulate the economy, Reagan proposed the largest federal income tax reduction in U.S. history. In 1981 Congress reduced taxes, cut social programs, and increased military spending. By the end of Reagan's first term, rapid inflation had ended, unemployment had fallen, and the economy had made a strong recovery. However,

罗纳德·里根于 1981 年继卡特后担任总统，经济成为他最关注的问题。他必须对付高通胀、经济衰退和高失业率。里根及其顾问提出了一种称为"供给方经济"的政策。这一政策的制订是根据这样一种想法：财政收益应当让给货物和服务的供给方。当供给方有了更多的资金用于投资，经济就会发展，就业就会增加，繁荣就会从高端"淌下"，惠及大多数人口。

为了刺激经济，里根提出了美国历史上最大幅度的联邦政府减税计划。1981 年，国会降低了税收、削减了公益计划、增加了军费开支。里根第一任期末，飞速上升的通货膨胀停止了，失业率下降了，经济复苏势头强劲。然而，税收的

the tax cuts and heavy government defense spending helped bring about record deficits in the federal budget.

In foreign affairs, the Reagan Administration also increased U.S. involvement in Central America. Much fighting took place between rebels and government troops in Nicaragua and El Salvador. Cuba and the Soviet Union gave aid to the government of Nicaragua and rebels in El Salvador. The United States, in turn, sent advisers and arms to the rebels in Nicaragua and the government of El Salvador.

In October 1983, Reagan ordered the invasion of the Caribbean island of Grenada. He said the invasion was needed to protect Americans in Grenada and to prevent the nation from falling under Cuban Communist control. U.S. forces helped Grenada established a new government more favorable to American interests.

The Reagan Administration greatly increased military spending during the early 1980s. The United States and the Soviet Union held talks to reduce nuclear arms, but they failed to reach an agreement. The United States then began supplying nuclear weapons to its allies in Western Europe. During the late 1980s, however, relations between the two

削减和庞大的政府军费开支也使联邦政府的预算出现创纪录的赤字。

在外交方面，里根政府更深地卷入中美洲国家的事务中。在尼加拉瓜和萨尔瓦多，叛乱分子与政府军交战。古巴和苏联向尼加拉瓜政府军和萨尔瓦多的叛乱分子提供援助。作为回应，美国则向尼加拉瓜的叛乱分子和萨尔瓦多的政府军派遣军事顾问并运送武器。

1983 年 10 月，里根下令入侵加勒比海岛屿格林纳达。他宣称为了保护格林纳达的美国人，为了防止该国落入古巴共产党的控制之下，入侵乃必要之举。美军帮助格林纳达建立了一个更有利于美国利益的政府。

在 80 年代初，里根政府大幅度增加了军事开支。美国和苏联举行谈判削减核武器，但未能达成协议。美国开始向其西欧的盟国提供核武器。然而在 80 年代末，两个世界强国的关系得到了戏剧性的改善。里根和苏联领导人米哈伊尔·戈尔

罗纳德·里根总统

world powers began to improve dramatically. Reagan and Soviet leader Mikhail Gorbachev signed a treaty that led to a reduction of certain U.S. and Soviet nuclear arms. The treaty, which went into effect in 1988, helped ease fear of nuclear war.

巴乔夫签署了一项条约，削减了美国和苏联的某些核武器。这一条约于 1988 年生效，在一定程度上缓解了核战争的威胁。

题外话

里根是 50 年代人们熟悉的好莱坞演员，曾在电影和电视上频繁出现。一个演员竟然能当上总统，与美国人怀旧情绪有关。50 年代是美国经济繁荣、社会安定的黄金时代，是艾森豪威尔当政的时代。80 年代的美国人希望里根能像艾森豪威尔一样和蔼可亲，一样伴随着经济繁荣和社会安定。

里根命大，他是 "0" 年当选而没有死在任上的唯一一个总统。他 1981 年遭枪击后康复。

2. The George Bush Administration

乔治·布什执政时期

George Bush, vice president under Ronald Reagan from 1981 to 1989, ran for the United States presidency and won the election after promising to develop a "kinder, gentler" America.

One of the most important events that took place during Bush's Administration was the Persian Gulf War. The war broke out in early 1991 after Iraqi forces invaded and occupied Kuwait in August 1990. Kuwait is one of the most important producers of the petroleum used by the world's industrialized countries. In response to Iraq's action,

乔治·布什在 1981～1989 年里根任总统期间一直担任副总统。他参加了总统竞选，承诺要造就一个"更仁慈、更温和"的美国。

布什当政期间发生的最重大事件之一是 1991 年初爆发的海湾战

乔治·布什总统

the UN Security Council first imposed severe economic sanctions against Iraq and later authorized UN members to use military force to drive Iraq from Kuwait. In early 1991, the United States organized an army of a coalition of 35 nations and quickly defeated Iraq and drove it from Kuwait. The coalition's army included over 400,000 American soldiers and 265,000 soldiers from Britain, France, and several Arab countries. The Soviet Union and China did not participate directly in the war.

During Bush's administration, relations continued to improve between the United States and the Soviet Union. Bush and Gorbachev met several times and worked to increase cooperation between their countries. These improved relations further reduced fear of nuclear war. In 1991, Bush and Gorbachev signed the first Strategic Arms Reduction Treaty. The treaty required both countries to reduce the number of their long-range nuclear weapons.

海湾战争中的美军

Major changes within the Soviet Union also contributed to the improvement in relations. Gorbachev worked to decentralize the Soviet economic system to improve the nation's poor economy. He also worked to increase democracy and freedom of expression in the Soviet Union. He encouraged similar economic and political changes in Eastern Europe. As a result, non-

争。伊拉克于 1990 年 8 月入侵并占领了科威特，而科威特是西方工业国家使用的石油的最重要的生产国之一。针对伊拉克的行经，联合国安理会先通过对伊拉克采取的严厉经济制裁，然后又授权联合国成员国使用武力将伊拉克逐出科威特。1991 年初，美国组织了一支 35 个国家组成的联军，迅速打败了伊拉克，并将其逐出科威特。联军包括 400000 美军士兵和 265000 来自英国、法国及几个阿拉伯国家的士兵。苏联和中国没有直接参加战争。

布什执政期间，美苏关系继续改善。布什与戈尔巴乔夫数次会晤，以加强两国的合作。两国关系的改善进一步减少了核战争的威胁。1991 年，布什与戈尔巴乔夫签署了第一个削减战略武器条约。条约要求两国削减远程核武器的数量。

苏联内部发生的重大变化也有助于两国关系的改善。戈尔巴乔夫为了改善苏联糟糕的经济，采取措施分解苏联集中的经济体制。他同时也努力增加苏联的民主和言论自由。他鼓励东欧国家进行类似的经

Communist governments came to power in a number of Eastern European nations. In 1990, with Soviet approval, East Germany and West Germany united to form one non-Communist country. These events marked the end of the Cold War.

But many people felt President Bush had failed to deal effectively with the nation's economic problems.

3. The Bill Clinton Administration

Bill Clinton was elected President of the United States in 1992. He took office at a time when the nation's attention had shifted sharply from foreign affairs to domestic issues. By 1992, Americans were troubled chiefly by their country's economic problems. The unemployment rate had climbed to the highest level since 1984. The government's policy of deficit spending over the years had resulted in a large national debt. In addition, Americans had become increasingly worried about growing racial conflict, crime and poverty, especially in the nation's cities.

During his first year in office, Clinton focused on the economy and other domestic issues. He believed that government's huge deficit spending reduced the amount of money for private investment. Businesses could obtain capital only at high rates of interest, which discouraged

济和政治改革。结果，在一些东欧国家里，非共产党政府上台执政。1990年，经苏联政府的许可，东德和西德统一，成为一个非共产党国家。这一系列的事件标志着冷战的结束。

但是许多人认为布什总统未能有效处理经济问题。

比尔·克林顿执政时期

比尔·克林顿于1992年当选美国总统。他就任时全国的注意力已从外交事务转向国内问题。当时困扰着美国人的主要是国内经济问题。失业率已上升到1984年以来的最高水平。政府多年以来奉行的赤字开支政策使国家负债累累。此外，美国人对特别是在城市里出现的日益增长的种族冲突、犯罪和贫穷越来越感到担忧。

克林顿当政的头一年将注意力放在经济和其他国内问题上。他认为政府的巨额赤字开支减少了私人投资。工商企业只能通过高息贷款获得资本，打击了投资和企业扩张的积极性。

1993年，克林顿向国会提交了一份预算案，试图削减联邦政府的

investment and business expansion.

In 1993 Clinton submitted to Congress a budget that reduced federal spending and increased taxes. In spite of Republicans' opposition, the budget passed in both houses. Clinton's budget victory reversed the trend of rising deficits, and it stimulated the economy. When he left office, the nation was running a surplus instead of a deficit. His economic policies helped produce the longest period of economic growth in the nation's history. However, Clinton's major plan for providing low-cost health insurance coverage for all Americans failed to pass Congress.

In 1994, Clinton won a victory when Congress passed an anticrime law he supported. The law called for spending billions of dollars on crime prevention, law enforcement, and prison construction. It also outlawed the sale of certain types of assault weapons, guns that many people believe are designed specifically for killing or injuring people.

After the 1994 election, a conservative Republican majority took control of Congress. Clinton had to change his strategy. The Republicans called for larger spending cuts and said they would erase the deficit by the year 2002. Clinton believed some of the proposed Republican spending reductions were too steep, including those for education, welfare, and Medicare. Clinton responded to the Republican plan with a proposal designed to wipe out the budget deficit by 2005.

Clinton achieved one of his ma-

开支，并增加税收。尽管共和党提出反对，预算案仍在两院通过。克林顿的预算案改变了赤字上升的势头，刺激了经济的复苏。当他离任时，政府财政以赢余代替了赤字。他的经济政策促成了美国历史上持续最久的一段经济增长期。然而，克林顿为所有美国人提供低价医疗保险的计划却未能在国会通过。

克林顿于 1994 年取得的一项胜利是使国会通过了一项他鼓吹的反犯罪法。这项法律要求拨款数十亿美圆用于预防犯罪、执行法律和建设监狱。该法律还禁止出售某些类型的攻击性武器，即那些许多人认为是专门为了杀人和伤害人设计的枪支。

1994 年的选举后，保守的共和党多数控制了国会。克林顿不得不改变战略。共和党要求更大幅度地削减开支，并声称要在 2002 年消除赤字。克林顿认为共和党提出的某些削减开支的计划，包括削减教育、福利和卫生的开支的计划过于

比尔·克林顿总统

jor foreign policy goals in November 1993, when Congress approved the North American Free Trade Agreement, which will gradually eliminate tariffs and other trade barriers between the United States, Mexico, and Canada. Clinton strongly supported the pact, because he believed that the country's security and prosperity depended upon removing barriers to trade with other nations and upon stabilizing nations with economic troubles. In December 1994, Clinton won Congress's approval of an expansion of the General Agreement on Tariffs and Trade (GATT). This expanded GATT plan called for large reductions in trade barriers among many nations.

Because the Cold War had ended in the late 1980s, Clinton faced no threat to the nation's security like those of the presidents before him. Still, he had to make difficult decisions about whether to intervene in bloody conflicts in many places throughout the world. In 1994, the United States successfully reinstated Haitian President Jean-Bertrand Aristide, who had been ousted by a military coup in 1991. In 1992, a civil war began in Bosnia-Herzegovina between Bosnian Serb rebels who were supported by Serbia and the country's government, which is dominated by Bosnian Muslims. The United States did not then contribute ground troops to the country. But it used its air force to help provide relief to Bosnian Muslims under siege and to try to stop Serb aggression. In late 1995, Clinton helped bring about a meeting of representatives of the sides in the Bosnian civil war. Clinton agreed to send about 20,000 U.S. troops to Bosnia to keep peace. Clinton also played a leading role in bringing a per

极端。针对共和党的计划，克林顿提出自己的建议，计划在 2005 年消除赤字。

1993 年 11 月，克林顿达到了自己重要的外交目标之一。国会通过了北美自由贸易协定，规定将逐步消除美国、墨西哥和加拿大之间的关税和其他贸易壁垒。克林顿全力支持这项协定，因为他认为美国的安全和繁荣有赖于消除与其他国家之间的贸易壁垒，使那些发生经济困难的国家保持稳定。1994 年 12 月，克林顿提出的关税及贸易总协定的补充协定在国会获得通过。经过补充的关税及贸易总协定要求许多国家大幅度削减贸易壁垒。

由于冷战已在 80 年代末结束，克林顿不再像前任几位总统那样面临对美国安全的威胁。然而他仍不得不就是否干涉世界许多地方发生的流血冲突做出抉择。1994 年，美国成功地使在 1991 年的 场军事政变中被推翻的海地总统让-伯特兰·阿里斯蒂德恢复职位。1992 年，波黑发生内战，波斯尼亚的塞尔维亚人在塞尔维亚的支持下，发动暴乱反抗由波斯尼亚的穆斯林控制的政府。美国当时没有派遣地面部队到波黑，而是利用空中力量向被围困的波斯尼亚的穆斯林提供救助，并试图阻止塞尔维亚人入侵波黑。1995 年末，经过克林顿的努力，波斯尼亚内战各方代表举行了会议。克林顿同意派遣大约 20000 美军士兵到波斯尼亚维和。在为永久解决

manent resolution to the dispute between Palestinians and Israelis. In 1993 he invited Israeli Prime Minister Yitzhak Rabin and Palestine Liberation Organization chairman Yāsir Arafāt to Washington to sign a historic agreement that granted limited Palestinian self-rule in the Gaza Strip and Jericho.

During the Clinton administration the United States remained a target for international terrorists with bomb attacks on the World Trade Center in New York City (1993), on U.S. embassies in Kenya and Tanzania (1998), and on the U.S. Navy in Yemen (2000). At home, the most deadly terrorist attack in the history of the United States took place in Oklahoma City (1995). An American, Timothy McVeigh, killed 168 and injured more than 500 in bomb attack.

From his first months in office until his last day, Clinton struggled to clear himself of charges of financial wrongdoing. The longest-running investigation began with Whitewater, a small real-estate project in Arkansas in which Clinton and his

发生在俄克拉何马市的恐怖袭击

wife had invested during the late 1970s. The independent counsel investigating Whitewater learned in 1997 that Clinton had had a sexual affair with a young female intern at the White House. In 1998 the House of Representatives impeached the president. The House charged him

巴勒斯坦和以色列的争端的外交活动中，克林顿也起到了主导作用。1993 年他邀请以色列总理拉宾和巴勒斯坦解放组织主席阿拉法特到华盛顿签署了允许巴勒斯坦人在加沙和杰里科实行有限自治的历史性协议。

克林顿执政期间美国一直是国际恐怖分子的袭击目标。他们用炸弹袭击了纽约世界贸易中心 (1993 年)、驻肯尼亚和赞比亚的美国大使馆 (1998 年) 和驻也门的美国海军 (2000 年)。在国内，美国历史上造成伤亡最惨重的一次恐怖袭击发生在俄克拉何马市 (1995 年)。美国人蒂莫西·麦克维在一次炸弹袭击中炸死 168 人，炸伤 500 人。

从上任后的头几个月开始到任期最后一天，克林顿一直受到财政方面有不良行为的指控。他努力证明自己的清白。一场旷日持久的调查从白水开始。白水是克林顿夫妇在 70 年代末在堪萨斯投资的一个小型房地产工程。调查白水的独立委员会于 1997 年得知克林顿与白宫的一个年轻的女实习生有性关系。1998 年，众议院弹劾总统，指控他犯有作伪证、在联邦大

with perjury, for not being truthful before a federal grand jury, and obstruction of justice, for trying to influence the testimony of others. In 1999 the Senate tried Clinton but declared that Clinton was not guilty and did not remove him from office.

陪审团面前不讲实话、阻碍司法调查以及试图影响他人的证词等罪行。1999 年，参议院审讯了克林顿，但宣布克林顿无罪，没有解除他的职务。

4. The George W. Bush Administration

乔治·W.布什执政时期

In 2000, in one of the closest and most disputed elections in U.S. history, George W(alker) Bush, the Republican Party candidate, defeated Vice President Albert Gore, the Democratic candidate, became the 43rd president of the United States. Bush is the son of former president George Herbert Walker Bush. He became the first son to follow his father into the White House since John Quincy Adams followed John Adams in the early 19th century.

In 2001, when the U.S. economy showed signs of slowing down, Bush introduced a $1.96 trillion federal budget that included tax relief and increased funding for education and the military. Bush tried to persuade Congress to approve his tax cut to help stimulate the economy. Democratic leaders argued that the government surplus should

2000年，在美国历史上票数最接近、争议最大的选举中，共和党候选人乔治·沃克尔·布什战胜民主党候选人、副总统艾伯特·戈尔，当选美国第 43 位总统。布什是前总统乔治·赫伯特·沃克尔·布什的儿子。自从 19 世纪初约翰·昆西·亚当斯在约翰·亚当斯之后入主白宫以来，布什是头一个子承父业的总统。

2001 年，美国经济呈现发展趋缓的迹象。布什提出一项高达 19600 亿美圆的联邦预算案，包括减税和增加教育和军事开支。布什试图劝说国会通过他的减税计

乔治·W.布什总统

be used for government programs such as Social Security and that the tax cut would benefit only wealthy Americans. Bush, however, achieved a great success when Congress passed a $1.35 trillion dollar tax-cut bill.

In February 2001 Bush approved limited air strikes against Iraq. American and British warplanes bombed Iraqi military command sites south of the capital of Baghdād to warn Iraq that the no-fly zones established in Iraq after the Persian Gulf War (1991) were still in effect.

During Bush's first year in office, a terrorist attack in the United States shocked the world. On September 11, 2001, four commercial airliners were hijacked and used as suicide bombs. Two of the hijacked planes crashed into the twin towers of the World Trade Center in New York City, causing the collapse and destruction of both towers. Another destroyed a large section of the Pentagon outside Washington, D.C., and still another crashed in the southern Pennsylvania countryside. More than 3,000 people were killed in the series of attacks.

The 19 men who carried out the hijackings came from Saudi Arabia, Egypt and other Arab states. They were associated with the al-Qaeda ("the Base") network, a radical Islamic group led by

划以刺激经济发展。民主党领袖则争论说政府的财政赢余应当用于社会保障之类的政府的发展项目，而减税只能对美国的富人有利。然而，布什还是取得了重大胜利，国会通过了 13500 亿美圆的减税案。

2001 年 2 月，布什批准了对伊拉克的有限空中打击。美国和英国的战机轰炸了伊拉克首都巴格达以南的军事指挥基地，以警告伊拉克海湾战争 (1991 年) 后在伊拉克建立的禁飞区依然有效。

在布什就任的头一年，对美国的一场恐怖袭击震惊了世界。2001 年 9 月 11 日，4 架商用客机被劫持，用做自杀炸弹。两架被劫持的飞机撞入纽约世界贸易中心的双子塔，造成大楼坍塌。另一架飞机摧毁了华盛顿城外五角大楼的一大片区域，还有一架在宾夕法尼亚南部的乡村地区坠毁。在这一系列的袭击中，死亡 3000 余人。

实行劫机计划的 19 个人来自沙特阿拉伯、埃及和其他阿拉伯国家。他们与"基地"组织有联系。基地组

911恐怖袭击的图片

Saudi exile Osama bin Laden and dedicated to waging a holy war against the United States.

Bush responded the September 11 attacks with a call for a global war on terrorism. He built an international coalition against bin Laden and his al-Qaeda, and the Taliban government of Afghanistan, which had harboured bin Laden and his followers. In October a U.S.-led international coalition launched air attacks against Afghanistan; by the end of the year the Taliban and bin Laden's forces were routed or forced into hiding, and the Bush administration was negotiating with Afghanistan's many political groups in an attempt to establish a stable government there.

In 2002 the U.S. economy worsened, as consumer confidence and the stock market continued to fall and corporate scandals dominated the headlines. Nevertheless, Bush remained popular, and he led the Republican Party to majorities in both the House and Senate in the midterm elections of 2002.

Despite the economic difficulties, foreign affairs continued to dominate the Bush administration's agenda. In 2002 Bush focused world attention on Iraq, accusing Saddām Hussein's government of having ties to al-Qaeda and of continuing to possess and develop weapons of mass destruction, contrary to UN mandates. In March 2003, the United States and allied forces launched an attack on Iraq.

The United States launched a brief air bombing campaign in Iraq followed by a massive ground invasion, beginning from Kuwait in the south. The resistance was not as strong as expected, and the major cities fell under U.S. or British

织是沙特阿拉伯流亡者本·拉登领导的一个激进的伊斯兰集团，全力以赴对美国展开圣战。

针对9月11日的袭击，布什号召开展全球的反恐战争。他建立了一个国际联盟，反对本·拉登及其基地组织和窝藏本·拉登及其追随者的阿富汗塔利班政府。10月，美国领导的国际联盟对阿富汗发动空中打击，当年末，塔利班和本·拉登的军队被击溃或被迫隐蔽起来，布什政府已开始与阿富汗的各政治集团进行谈判，试图在阿富汗建立一个稳定的政府。

本·拉登

2002年，美国经济开始恶化，消费者的信心和股市持续下滑，公司丑闻成为头条新闻。然而，布什的声望仍然不减，他领导的共和党在2002年的中期选举中在众参两院获得多数。

control by the end of April; on May 1 President Bush declared an end to major combat.

Armed resistance, however, continued throughout the following year, mainly in guerrilla attacks on U.S. soldiers and on Iraqis assuming positions of leadership. The American goal of building a democratic state in Iraq proved difficult to achieve. Iraq's former leader, Saddām Hussein was eventually captured in December, but hard evidence of weapons of mass destruction had not been found. The lack of such evidence and continuing American casualties aroused criticism of the administration. Many people questioned the prewar intelligence gathered to support the invasion.

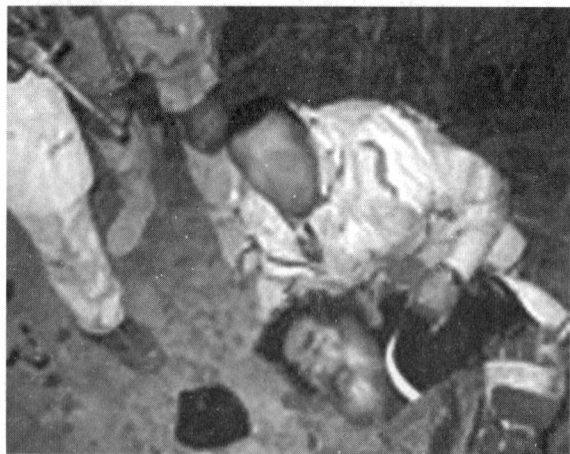

萨达姆·侯赛因被俘

尽管经济上遭遇困难，外交事务仍是布什政府日程表上的主要事项。2002 年，布什使全世界的注意力转向伊拉克，他指控萨达姆·侯赛因的政府与基地组织有联系，并违反联合国的决议，继续拥有和研发大规模杀伤武器。2003 年 3 月，美国与联合部队发动了对伊拉克的进攻。

美国先对伊拉克发动一场短暂的空袭，然后从南方的科威特发起地面进攻。抵抗不如预料的那么强大，4 月底主要城市就已落入美国或英国的控制之下。5 月 1 日，布什总统宣布主要战斗结束。

然而，武装抵抗在第二年持续了一整年，主要以游击战的方式袭击美军士兵和担任领导职务的伊拉克人。美国在伊拉克建立一个民主政权的目标证明难于实现。伊拉克的前领导人萨达姆·侯赛因最终在 12 月被俘，但大规模杀伤武器的明显证据并没有找到。证据的缺乏以及美军士兵伤亡人数的持续增加引起了对布什政府的批评。许多人对战前搜集的支持入侵的情报提出质疑。

题外话

颇具讽刺意味的是，基地组织本是美国中央情报局支持的反苏势力。

APPENDIX

Presidents of the United States

No.	Title	Term In Office	Name	Political Party	Life Dates
1.	President	1789-1797	George Washington	None	1732-1799
	Vice President	1789-1797	John Adams		1735-1826
2.	President	1797-1801	John Adams	Federalist	1735-1826
	Vice President	1797-1801	Thomas Jefferson	Democratic-Republican	1743-1826
3.	President	1801-1809	Thomas Jefferson	Democratic-Republican	1743-1826
	Vice President	1801-1805	Aaron Burr		1756-1836
	Vice President	1805-1809	George Clinton		1739-1812
4.	President	1809-1817	James Madison	Democratic-Republican	1751-1836
	Vice President	1809-1812	George Clinton		1739-1812
	Vice President	1813-1814	Elbridge Gerry		1744-1814
5.	President	1817-1825	James Monroe	Democratic-Republican	1758-1831
	Vice President	1817-1825	Daniel D. Tompkins		1774-1825
6.	President	1825-1829	John Quincy Adams	Democratic-Republican	1767-1848
	Vice President	1825-1829	John C. Calhoun		1782-1850
7.	President	1829-1837	Andrew Jackson	Democrat	1767-1845
	Vice President	1829-1832	John C. Calhoun		1782-1850
	Vice President	1833-1837	Martin Van Buren		1782-1862
8.	President	1837-1841	Martin Van Buren	Democrat	1782-1862
	Vice President	1837-1841	Richard M. Johnson		1780-1850
9.	President	1841	William Henry Harrison	Whig	1773-1841
	Vice President	1841	John Tyler		1790-1862
10.	President	1841-1845	John Tyler	Whig	1790-1862
	(no vice president)				
11.	President	1845-1849	James Knox Polk	Democrat	1795-1849
	Vice President	1845-1849	George M. Dallas		1792-1864

12.	President	1849-1850	Zachary Taylor	Whig	1784-1850
	Vice President	1849-1850	Millard Fillmore		1800-1874
13.	President	1850-1853	Millard Fillmore	Whig	1800-1874
	(no vice president)				
14.	President	1853-1857	Franklin Pierce	Democrat	1804-1869
	Vice President	1853	William R.King		1786-1853
15.	President	1857-1861	James Buchanan	Democrat	1791-1868
	Vice President	1857-1861	John C.Breckinridge		1821-1875
16.	President	1861-1865	Abraham Lincoln	Republican	1809-1865
	Vice President	1861-1865	Hannibal Hamlin		1809-1891
	Vice President	1865	Andrew Johnson	Democrat	1808-1875
			(nominated vice president by Republicans)		
17.	President	1865-1869	Andrew Johnson	Democrat	1808-1875
	(no vice president)				
18.	President	1869-1877	Ulysses Simpson Grant	Republican	1822-1885
	Vice President	1869-1873	Schuyler Colfax		1823-1885
	Vice President	1873-1875	Henry Wilson		1812-1875
19.	President	1877-1881	Rutherford Birchard Hayes	Republican	1822-1893
	Vice President	1877-1881	William A. Wheeler		1819-1887
20.	President	1881	James Abram Garfield	Republican	1831-1881
	Vice President	1881	Chester A. Arthur		1829?-1886
21.	President	1881-1885	Chester Alan Arthur	Republican	1829?-1886
	(no vice president)				
22.	President	1885-1889	Grover Cleveland	Democrat	1837-1908
	Vice President	1885	Thomas A. Hendricks		1819-1885
23.	President	1889-1893	Benjamin Harrison	Republican	1833-1901
	Vice President	1889-1893	Levi P. Morton		1824-1920
24.	President	1893-1897	Grover Cleveland	Democrat	1837-1908
	Vice President	1893-1897	Adlai E. Stevenson		1835-1914
25.	President	1897-1901	William McKinley	Republican	1843-1901
	Vice President	1897-1899	Garret A. Hobart		1844-1899
	Vice President	1901	Theodore Roosevelt		1858-1919
26.	President	1901-1909	Theodore Roosevelt	Republican	1858-1919
	Vice President	1905-1909	Charles W. Fairbanks		1852-1918
27.	President	1909-1913	William Howard Taft	Republican	1857-1930

	Vice President	1909-1912	James S. Sherman		1855-1912
28.	President	1913-1921	Woodrow Wilson	Democrat	1856-1924
	Vice President	1913-1921	Thomas R. Marshall		1854-1925
29.	President	1921-1923	Warren Gamaliel Harding	Republican	1865-1923
	Vice President	1921-1923	Calvin Coolidge		1872-1933
30.	President	1923-1929	Calvin Coolidge	Republican	1872-1933
	Vice President	1925-1929	Charles G. Dawes		1865-1951
31.	President	1929-1933	Herbert Clark Hoover	Republican	1874-1964
	Vice President	1929-1933	Charles Curtis		1860-1936
32.	President	1933-1945	Franklin Delano Roosevelt	Democrat	1882-1945
	Vice President	1933-1941	John N. Garner		1868-1967
	Vice President	1941-1945	Henry A. Wallace		1888-1965
	Vice President	1945	Harry S. Truman		1884-1972
33.	President	1945-1953	Harry S. Truman	Democrat	1884-1972
	Vice President	1949-1953	Alben W. Barkley		1877-1956
34.	President	1953-1961	Dwight David Eisenhower	Republican	1890-1969
	Vice President	1953-1961	Richard M. Nixon		1913-1994
35.	President	1961-1963	John Fitzgerald Kennedy	Democrat	1917-1963
	Vice President	1961-1963	Lyndon B. Johnson		1908-1973
36.	President	1963-1969	Lyndon Baines Johnson	Democrat	1908-1973
	Vice President	1965-1969	Hubert H. Humphrey		1911-1978
37.	President	1969-1974	Richard Milhous Nixon	Republican	1913-1994
	Vice President	1969-1973	Spiro T. Agnew		1918-1996
	Vice President	1973-1974	Gerald R. Ford		1913-
38.	President	1974-1977	Gerald Rudolph Ford	Republican	1913-
	Vice President	1974-1977	Nelson A. Rockefeller		1908-1979
39.	President	1977-1981	James Earl Carter	Democrat	1924-
	Vice President	1977-1981	Walter F. Mondale		1928-
40.	President	1981-1989	Ronald Reagan	Republican	1911-2004
	Vice President	1981-1989	George H. W. Bush		1924-
41.	President	1989-1993	George H. W. Bush	Republican	1924-
	Vice President	1989-1993	Dan Quayle		1947-
42.	President	1993-2001	William Jefferson Clinton	Democrat	1946-
	Vice President	1993-2001	Albert Gore, Jr.		1948-
43.	President	2001-	George W. Bush	Republican	1946-
	Vice President	2001-	Dick Cheney		1941-

附　　　录

美国历届总统

序号	职务	任职时间	姓名	政党	生卒年份
1.	总　统	1789-1797	乔治·华盛顿	无	1732-1799
	副总统	1789-1797	约翰·亚当斯	无	1735-1826
2.	总　统	1797-1801	约翰·亚当斯	联邦党	1735-1826
	副总统	1797-1801	托马斯·杰斐逊	民主共和党	1743-1826
3.	总　统	1801-1809	托马斯·杰斐逊	民主共和党	1743-1826
	副总统	1801-1805	艾伦·伯尔[1]		1756-1836
	副总统	1805-1809	乔治·克林顿		1739-1812
4.	总　统	1809-1817	詹姆斯·麦迪逊	民主共和党	1751-1836
	副总统	1809-1812	乔治·克林顿		1739-1812
	副总统	1813-1814	埃尔布里奇·格里		1744-1814
5.	总　统	1817-1825	詹姆斯·门罗	民主共和党	1758-1831
	副总统	1817-1825	丹尼尔·D.汤普金斯		1774-1825
6.	总　统	1825-1829	约翰·昆西·亚当斯	民主共和党	1767-1848
	副总统	1825-1829	约翰·C.卡尔霍恩		1782-1850
7.	总　统	1829-1837	安德鲁·杰克逊	民主党	1767-1845
	副总统	1829-1832	约翰·C.卡尔霍恩		1782-1850
	副总统	1833-1837	马丁·范布伦		1782-1862
8.	总　统	1837-1841	马丁·范布伦	民主党	1782-1862
	副总统	1837-1841	理查德·M.约翰逊		1780-1850
9.	总　统	1841	威廉·亨利·哈里逊[2]	辉格党	1773-1841
	副总统	1841	约翰·泰勒		1790-1862
10.	总　统	1841-1845	约翰·泰勒	辉格党	1790-1862
	副总统职位空缺[3]				
11.	总　统	1845-1849	詹姆斯·诺克斯·波尔克	民主党	1795-1849
	副总统	1845-1849	乔治·M.达拉斯		1792-1864

12.	总　统	1849-1850	扎卡里·泰勒 [4]	辉格党	1784-1850
	副总统	1849-1850	米勒德·菲尔莫尔		1800-1874
13.	总　统	1850-1853	米勒德·菲尔莫尔	辉格党	1800-1874
	副总统职位空缺				
14.	总　统	1853-1857	富兰克林·皮尔斯	民主党	1804-1869
	副总统	1853	威廉·R.金		1786-1853
15.	总　统	1857-1861	詹姆斯·布坎南	民主党	1791-1868
	副总统	1857-1861	约翰·C.布雷肯里奇		1821-1875
16.	总　统	1861-1865	亚伯拉罕·林肯 [5]	共和党	1809-1865
	副总统	1861-1865	汉尼巴尔·哈姆林		1809-1891
	副总统	1865	安德鲁·约翰逊 [6]	民主党	1808-1875
17.	总　统	1865-1869	安德鲁·约翰逊	民主党	1808-1875
	副总统职位空缺				
18.	总　统	1869-1877	尤利塞斯·辛普森·格兰特	共和党	1822-1885
	副总统	1869-1873	斯凯勒·科尔法克斯		1823-1885
	副总统	1873-1875	亨利·威尔逊		1812-1875
19.	总　统	1877-1881	拉瑟福德·伯查德·海斯	共和党	1822-1893
	副总统	1877-1881	威廉·A.惠勒		1819-1887
20.	总　统	1881	詹姆斯·艾布拉姆·加菲尔德 [7]	共和党	1831-1881
	副总统	1881	切斯特·A.阿瑟		1829?-1886
21.	总　统	1881-1885	切斯特·艾伦·阿瑟	共和党	1829?-1886
	副总统职位空缺				
22.	总　统	1885-1889	格罗弗·克利夫兰	民主党	1837-1908
	副总统	1885	托马斯·A.亨德里克斯		1819-1885
23.	总　统	1889-1893	本杰明·哈里逊	共和党	1833-1901
	副总统	1889-1893	利瓦伊·P.莫顿		1824-1920
24.	总　统	1893-1897	格罗弗·克利夫兰	民主党	1837-1908
	副总统	1893-1897	艾德莱·E.史蒂文森		1835-1914
25.	总　统	1897-1901	威廉·麦金利 [8]	共和党	1843-1901
	副总统	1897-1899	加勒特·A.霍巴特		1844-1899
	副总统	1901	西奥多·罗斯福		1858-1919
26.	总　统	1901-1909	西奥多·罗斯福	共和党	1858-1919
	副总统	1905-1909	查尔斯·W.费尔班克斯		1852-1918
27.	总　统	1909-1913	威廉·霍华德·塔夫脱	共和党	1857-1930
	副总统	1909-1912	詹姆斯·S.谢尔曼		1855-1912
28.	总　统	1913-1921	伍德罗·威尔逊	民主党	1856-1924

	副总统	1913-1921	托马斯·R.马歇尔		1854-1925
29.	总　统	1921-1923	沃伦·甘梅利尔·哈定[9]	共和党	1865-1923
	副总统	1921-1923	卡尔文·柯立芝		1872-1933
30.	总　统	1923-1929	卡尔文·柯立芝	共和党	1872-1933
	副总统	1925-1929	查尔斯·G.道斯		1865-1951
31.	总　统	1929-1933	赫伯特·克拉克·胡佛	共和党	1874-1964
	副总统	1929-1933	查尔斯·柯蒂斯		1860-1936
32.	总　统	1933-1945	富兰克林·德拉诺·罗斯福	民主党	1882-1945
	副总统	1933-1941	约翰·N.加纳		1868-1967
	副总统	1941-1945	亨利·A.华莱士		1888-1965
	副总统	1945	哈里·S.杜鲁门		1884-1972
33.	总　统	1945-1953	哈里·S.杜鲁门[10]	民主党	1884-1972
	副总统	1949-1953	艾尔本·W.巴克利		1877-1956
34.	总　统	1953-1961	德怀特·戴维·艾森豪威尔	共和党	1890-1969
	副总统	1953-1961	理查德·M.尼克松		1913-1994
35.	总　统	1961-1963	约翰·菲茨杰拉德·肯尼迪[11]	民主党	1917-1963
	副总统	1961-1963	林登·B.约翰逊		1908-1973
36.	总　统	1963-1969	林登·贝恩斯·约翰逊	民主党	1908-1973
	副总统	1965-1969	哈伯特·H.汉弗莱		1911-1978
37.	总　统	1969-1974	理查德·米尔豪斯·尼克松	共和党	1913-1994
	副总统	1969-1973	斯皮罗·T.阿格纽[12]		1918-1996
	副总统	1973-1974	杰拉尔德·R.福特		1913-
38.	总　统	1974-1977	杰拉尔德·鲁道夫·福特[13]	共和党	1913-
	副总统	1974-1977	纳尔逊·A.洛克菲勒		1908-1979
39.	总　统	1977-1981	詹姆斯·厄尔·卡特	民主党	1924-
	副总统	1977-1981	沃尔特·F.蒙代尔		1928-
40.	总　统	1981-1989	罗纳德·里根	共和党	1911-2004
	副总统	1981-1989	乔治·H.W.布什		1924-
41.	总　统	1989-1993	乔治·H.W.布什	共和党	1924-
	副总统	1989-1993	丹·奎尔		1947-
42.	总　统	1993-2001	威廉·杰斐逊·克林顿	民主党	1946-
	副总统	1993-2001	艾伯特·戈尔（小）		1948-
43.	总　统	2001-	乔治·W.布什	共和党	1946-
	副总统	2001-	迪克·切尼		1941-

注：

1. 艾伦·伯尔为第一任副总统，乔治·克林顿为第二任副总统。下同。

2. 哈里逊于 1841 年 4 月逝世，由副总统约翰·泰勒继任。

3. 1967 年前美国制订的总统继任法未规定副总统职位空缺的递补条款，故副总统继任总统后就出现副总统职位空缺。下同。

4. 泰勒于 1850 年 7 月病故，由副总统菲尔莫尔继任。

5. 林肯于 1865 年 4 月遇刺身亡，由副总统约翰逊继任。

6. 安德鲁·约翰逊被共和党提名为副总统候选人。

7. 加菲尔德于 1881 年逝世，由副总统切斯特·阿瑟继任。

8. 麦金利于 1901 年遇刺身亡，由副总统罗斯福继任。

9. 哈定于 1923 年 8 月病故，由副总统柯立芝继任。

10. 罗斯福于 1945 年 4 月病故，由副总统杜鲁门继任。

11. 肯尼迪于 1963 年 11 月遇刺身亡，由副总统约翰逊继任。

12. 阿格纽于 1973 年 10 月因经济丑闻辞职，由福特继任。

13. 尼克松于 1974 年因水门丑闻辞职，由副总统福特继任。福特成为美国历史上唯一的一个未经选举而当上总统的人。

邮购目录

书　　　名	开本	定价
风情英语①——看欧美风情学英语	32K	20.00
风情英语②——看世界名胜学英语	32K	20.00
童话英文①——看童话故事学英语	32K	18.00
童话英文②——看格林童话学英语	32K	20.00
智慧英文①——看寓言故事学英语	32K	20.00
智慧英文②——看趣味故事学英语	32K	20.00
智慧英文③——看励志故事学英语	32K	17.00
智慧英文④——看伊索寓言学英语	32K	19.00
笑爆英语①	32K	22.00
笑爆英语②	32K	17.00
笑爆英语③	32K	18.00
趣味故事乐园03——看幽默故事学英语	32K	16.00
趣味故事乐园09——看脑筋急转弯学英语	32K	17.00
趣味故事乐园10——看动物故事学英语	32K	16.00
趣味故事乐园11——唱　歌　学　英语	32K	22.00
趣味故事乐园12——看名人名言学英语	32K	19.00
趣味故事乐园13——看哲理故事学英语	32K	18.00
趣味故事乐园14——看爱情故事学英语	32K	18.00
趣味故事乐园16——看成功故事学英语	32K	19.00
趣味故事乐园17——看名人故事学英语	32K	19.00
英语成语源来如此	32K	25.00
英语词汇源来如此	32K	20.00
你不可不知道的英语学习背景知识——古希腊罗马神话与西方民间传说	16K	20.00
你不可不知道的英语学习背景知识——英美民间故事与民俗	16K	25.00
你不可不知道的英语学习背景知识——基督教与圣经	16K	33.00
你不可不知道的英语学习背景知识——美国历史重大事件及著名人物	16K	36.00
你不可不知道的英语学习背景知识——英国历史重大事件及著名人物	16K	33.00
教宝宝正确学英语	32K	15.00
英语幽默与笑话	32K	16.00
英语幽默与口语表达训练	32K	18.00
怎样起英文名字	32K	15.00
贺卡英语	32K	16.00
经典英文歌曲	16K	24.00
流行英文金曲	32K	19.80
有问必答——与中学英语语法对话(初中版)	32K	14.00
有问必答——与中学英语语法对话(高中版)	32K	17.00
有问必答——中考英语阅读高分技巧	32K	15.00
有问必答——高考英语阅读高分技巧	32K	15.00
有问必答——中考英语完形填空高分技巧	32K	14.00
有问必答——高考英语完形填空高分技巧	32K	15.00
中考英语作文高分技巧	32K	15.00
高考英语作文高分技巧	32K	16.00
中学英语常用词语辨析	32K	20.00

欢迎大家选购以上图书，邮资免付。　邮编：100097
地址：北京市海淀区世纪城远大园 4-12-1806 室　左小玉